Contents

'Living is easy with eyes closed, misunderstanding all you see,
It's getting hard to be someone but it all works out,
It doesn't matter much to me.
Let me take you down . . .'
                    – 'Strawberry Fields Forever', The Beatles

Foreword

I have lived with the Moors Murders since I was ten years old. Although I was almost nine when my brother Keith disappeared on 16 June 1964, it was not until October 1965 that the people responsible for his death were arrested and the Moors Murders first hit the headlines around the world.

I was an average kid but could read and write from an early age, and liked to believe I could think for myself, and always asked questions if I wanted answers. Those questions would usually be put to the two people in whom I had complete faith and trust, and whom I loved dearly: my grandmother and Aunt Jean.

It wasn't long after Brady and Hindley had been charged with murder that I became aware that the adults in the family, and the police, strongly suspected that these two knew what had happened to my brother. *Why?* was my first question. It turned out that Brady's home on Westmoreland Street was not far from where we lived when Keith disappeared. I also learned that the body of a teenage boy had been found in the house Brady had more recently shared with Hindley and that the bodies of two children had been found in a place called Saddleworth Moor. Another question: how did the police know that Brady and Hindley had definitely murdered those children? Because, I was told, someone had gone to the police after witnessing the murder of the teenage boy, which then led to the other children being found. Who went to the police? I asked.

A man called David Smith.

But even *before* I'd asked these questions, I'd 'seen' Brady and Hindley when the police called at Gran's home. I was sitting on a chair arm next to the door that led into the 'back room' when the knock came. Two men walked in – plainclothes detectives, I realised later – and as the second man entered, I noticed he was carrying a clipboard that protruded above his forearm and rested against his side. As he passed me, the clipboard came level with my eyes and I saw, in extreme close-up, the now infamous mugshots of Brady and Hindley. Their faces seemed to leap out at me and I dropped heavily back into the chair. This was no fall or slip; I actually felt as if I had been physically pushed away from the stark images, even though there was no one near me, apart from the detective holding the clipboard. I'd felt an invisible shove on the right side of my body, which had sent me backwards into the chair. I glanced at Gran, who wore a look of genuine surprise, and then I heard one of the detectives asking, 'Are you all right, son?' I let my gaze travel to the two men, who were watching me, mystified, then looked towards the door, expecting to see who it was that had pushed me. Nobody was there.

I felt an intensely strange feeling and was gripped by a fear that I didn't understand; I had to leave the room and get away from the two men and the photographs they carried.

From then on, Brady and Hindley haunted my childhood, and whenever I thought of them or saw or heard anything about them, I felt deeply frightened. Some time after the detectives visited Gran, I came to believe that it was Keith who had been responsible for pushing me away that day; he was trying to protect me in some way from the people whose faces were on the clipboard. Later, this belief grew stronger. It wasn't something I invented – it was how it was and has been with me ever since.

As the months wore on, 'David Smith' became an increasingly familiar name too, but by then there were other words attached whenever someone mentioned him: he was 'a bad 'un' who 'knows more than he's saying', who had acted 'to save his own neck' and was 'as bad as those two'. Young as I was, I remember wondering how the man who had informed the police about a murder was spoken of as if he, too, was a murderer. If that was the case, then why had he not been sent to jail with the other two? I tried to work it out, asking more questions and reading everything I could find about him. After much thinking, I could only come up with another question: Who's right? Were the police wrong for letting him get away with murder or were the people who believed he was guilty at fault?

I knew enough to try and make some sense of it all, but I found it hard to talk to anyone. Gone was the chattering, carefree, playful child; in his place was a young boy with only questions, endless questions, and so much confusion and sadness. But eventually I came to the conclusion that the people in the wrong were those whom I had no choice but to listen to, day after day. I believed that David Smith had put a stop to the murders and prevented others from taking place. Even at such a young age the things I saw and heard about David Smith made no sense to me.

By then, countless people had been to our house, asking probing questions of their own. They seemed to waft in from the street and out again in a jumbled mass of notebooks, cameras, lights, cables, fancy cars, large vans, motorbikes, bicycles, walkers, polite people, rude people, quiet people, loud people, foreign people and some very strange people. A curious thing happened: the more questions our visitors asked, the more the answers began to fit in with whatever they wanted to hear. Things changed suddenly and unmistakeably from the pain and distress that needed to be overcome somehow in order to answer the questions to the standard answers and furious outbursts that made for good headlines.

I began to stand back, watching with as much distance as I could, and that's where I stayed and remain to this day. I was never alone, but the person standing by me couldn't be seen, although he was there, always there. I talked to him at night when I was alone in the room we used to share, and he came back to life for me, both then and whenever I talked to Gran and Aunt Jean. He was unseen but ever-present.

The years passed. Argument followed argument about who did what, who was to blame, and what could and should be done. I refused to have any part in what was happening all around me. I saw rage and frustration becoming the norm, but

I found my voice and formed my own opinions based on fact, rather than headlines and what people wanted to believe or use as a vent for useless anger – and even more useless 'exclusive' publicity.

I've spent many years searching Saddleworth Moor in the hope of bringing Keith home. I've met and spoken to countless people whom I hoped might be able to help me and have written hundreds of letters for the same reason.

The one person whom I have never tried to contact is David Smith. I thought about it often. I've even written to him, but the letters remained unposted. Whenever I gave the matter serious consideration, as I often did, I was stilled by recalling the stories of violence and abuse he and his family had suffered ever since he did the right thing and reported the murder of Edward Evans to the police. He sparked off the Moors Murders investigation, brought the horror of it all to an end, and very probably saved the lives of other children who might have gone on to become victims of Brady and Hindley. I knew that he had been to the moor with the two killers, had spent many hours in their company and was married to Hindley's sister, Maureen. Surely, he might know of something that could be of use to me, so why *not* contact him? But I still couldn't get the belief that he'd suffered enough out of my head. The beatings he had taken over the years, and which were of great amusement to others around me, were undeserved in my eyes, as was the constant hounding I knew he and his wife endured. I was also aware that he'd spent weeks being questioned by police, who had taken him to the moor to see if he could recall any landmarks that might have aided their search for the bodies Brady had boasted to him about burying there. Admittedly, I was troubled by the knowledge that he'd 'sold out' to a newspaper during the trial, and had had a financial interest in the end result, but I'd seen so many others doing deals of one kind or another with the press that it began to bother me less and less. And the people who used that particular stick with which to beat him had sticks of their own stored safely and quietly in the offices of certain newspapers.

It seemed obvious to me that the lies Brady and Hindley told about him, and which people were so quick to believe, were designed to cast doubt on him in revenge for his 'betraying' them to the police. It worked very well; they spent many years in the happy knowledge that their whistleblower was never free from public hatred. Other thoughts disturbed me and prevented me from posting my letters to him; foremost of these was that I could never begin to imagine the horror brought before his eyes when Brady and Hindley finally decided to show him what they truly were. A lad of his own age, brutally axed to death before him, the terrible sights and sounds that accompanied the killing, were all part of a 'test' to find out if he was capable of the same monstrosities. Thankfully, he was not. He did go to the police to 'save his own neck' but not in the manner that so many came to believe; he feared for his own life, and in doing the right thing he brought horrors he knew nothing about to a disbelieving and sickened world.

So, as the years went by, the possibility of having any form of contact with David Smith grew smaller and smaller. Then, whilst working on her book *One of Your Own: The Life and Death of Myra Hindley*, Carol Ann Lee wrote to ask if I would be willing to speak to her, mainly about my role in the search for Keith. She assured me that she'd done extensive research and that it was of the utmost importance to her to get the facts about the Moors Murders correct at last. At that time, I was trying to overcome my disillusionment about a previous publication on the case, whose author I had spoken to only on the understanding that his book would be mainly about the search for Keith. I had been deeply disappointed by the outcome and cast aside Carol Ann's request as coming from just another author whose work would turn out in the same way as all the rest – feelings I now know I shared with David Smith when she approached him.

Nonetheless, I read *One of Your Own* when it was published and to my utter surprise discovered that it was completely different from anything else I had read about the case, or about Brady and Hindley individually. Although it was then too late to be part of something that had greatly impressed me, I contacted Carol Ann to congratulate her on the book. She invited me to her home to discuss what she had learned during her research and to look at the notes she had made, which she believed – correctly – might be of interest to me.

I was even more impressed after our initial meeting and now looked on her as a major authority on the case. We became very close friends and I found myself talking to her openly, even searching deep within myself and dragging out thoughts and feelings I thought would remain locked away for ever. I had never expected to share those memories and emotions with anyone again after the deaths of Gran and Aunt Jean, not outside the family. After Carol Ann and I got to know each other better, she told me that she had spoken at great length to David Smith and his wife Mary. Then she mentioned the possibility of writing a book with David about his life. She saw it as a story that needed to be told but was acutely aware of how David Smith was regarded by certain members of the victims' families.

She asked me what I thought. I had no such reservations and advised her to go ahead because it was time – in fact, long overdue – that David Smith had his say. We talked about the reactions such a book might provoke. I felt that it would, hopefully, enlighten many people and even help erase certain long-held fears for many others. It would be wrong to let such an invaluable opportunity slip away.

Carol Ann told David Smith what I thought. I was deeply moved by his response, especially that he wanted to thank me for my positive reaction to his wish to tell his story . . . me, a member of one of the victims' families. Was I supposed to detest the man who brought the murders to an end? Or bury my head in the sand and have no opinion about the events that have been an abiding dark cloud in my life? I could only give my support and encouragement to Carol Ann and, through her, to David Smith and his wife.

I am glad this book has been written, for several reasons. Foremost for me personally is that through David Smith's dogged recall of painful memories certain areas and landmarks of potential interest in the search for Keith have come to light. I have to add, with great sorrow in my heart, that this information was never allowed to come to the fore at the time of the original investigation in the 1960s, and the subsequent search in the 1980s, because of the hard-headedness and mishandling of David Smith by some senior detectives. Of course, there were exceptions, Joe Mounsey in particular, but the damage was done and the man who was the chief prosecution witness in 'the Trial of the Century' was reduced to a suspect too many times, and a bruised and battered man for decades.

My hope now is that this book and the truths within it will enable the public to understand that Brady and Hindley's lies brought intense pain and distress not only to the victims and their families, but also to many others. Years into her imprisonment, Hindley admitted that she had lied about David Smith and that she was sorry for it. She repeated the same thing to me personally when I visited her in Durham and then Highpoint prison to talk about the search for Keith and what she might do to help. Brady, however, will never admit the truth. Indeed, he invents new lies to replace the old ones when they lose their 'exclusive' media status.

A number of officers from the original investigation admitted they could and should have listened more closely to David Smith and treated him as a witness rather than a suspect. I suppose the errors can be explained to some extent by old-style policing methods, but it still doesn't alter the fact that chances were lost, that the chief witness was never able to tell the truth without fear and duress, and that he was forced to withdraw into himself in the belief that no one was listening.

We can only hope that those people whose lack of thought and darkness of soul caused David Smith and his family such suffering over the years never have to endure the same in order to make them finally realise the damage they can do.

Alan Bennett
Manchester, 2011

Preface

'What is your opinion about David Smith?'

The question comes from a quiet-looking man in his mid-20s, sitting in the back row. Immediately, there is a frisson in the room, as the audience turn first to peer at the enquirer, then at the woman seated directly to my right, who made a small noise of disgust in her throat at the mention of the name, and finally at me.

I hesitate before replying, aware that I need to choose my words carefully. This is the first talk I've given about my book, *One of Your Own: The Life and Death of Myra Hindley*, and it's being held in a room on the upper floor of the Deansgate branch of Waterstone's in Manchester. For the past 45 minutes, people have expressed their views with an intensity that few other murder cases can provoke. Whether it's Hindley's avowed remorse or how to persuade Ian Brady to reveal the location of Keith Bennett's grave, those who speak are resolute in their judgements. Feelings run feverishly high; someone suggests slowly stabbing Brady with knives until he confesses and the idea is met with clamorous approval and applause by three-quarters of the crowd. 'They should have let *us* deal with the murdering bastards before they put them away,' someone else calls above the noise, and the clapping breaks out afresh.

David Smith has already been mentioned, and a murmur of deep-rooted disgust passed then among the audience. Now they wait for my response to the question raised by the young man on the back row. The woman seated to my right is Keith Bennett's mother, Winnie Johnson, and I'm aware from my previous meetings with her that she regards David Smith with much the same loathing as she does her son's killers.

My reply is cautiously phrased but unequivocal: 'Well, I've no wish to upset Winnie or anyone else, but David Smith *is* the man who put an end to the Moors Murders. Not only that, but he also enabled those children who were missing to be found – apart from Keith – and his actions prevented more children from becoming victims of Brady and Hindley.'

There is an intense silence in the room. I realise that the majority of the audience are appalled at my response, including Winnie Johnson. Two people start to mutter angrily, until the young man from the back row asks in a loud voice, 'What do *you* think, Winnie?'

Instantly, the room falls silent again. We all look at Winnie, who after a moment of contemplation declares: 'I think David Smith is as rotten and guilty as them two swines. He did what he did to save his own neck. And I know that I'm not the only one to think that. Ask anyone and they'll tell you the same thing.'

'He *did* go to the police, though,' a smartly dressed man on the end of one row ventures.

'Yes, to save his own neck,' Mrs Johnson repeats. She looks out at the audience: 'I'm right, aren't I?'

The crowd nod in almost perfect unison; and David Smith's reputation remains unchanged from 45 years earlier, when his position as chief prosecution witness at the Moors trial brought him nothing but hatred and public vilification.

Months before the Waterstone's event, I'd written to David Smith asking if he would be willing to be interviewed for the book I was working on about Myra Hindley. I knew that he had never spoken in depth about the past and although my primary aim for contacting him was to discuss Hindley (and, to a lesser extent, Brady), I was also very interested in his life before, during and after his marriage to Myra Hindley's sister, Maureen.

His reaction was swift but disappointing, and clearly meant to dissuade me. But I wrote again, this time ending with a quote from one of his two great heroes, Bob Dylan (the other is John

Lennon). His second email arrived a few days later, slightly less abrasive, but still intended as a rebuff. I doubted then that he would respond to further communication.

To my surprise, however, I got a call from his second wife, Mary, to whom he has been married for 35 years. We talked at length, both on that occasion and during other phone calls. She told me of her hope that one day her husband would finally have the chance to tell his story in full. 'Not to try and alter anyone's perceptions of him necessarily,' she explained. 'But I think it's time to tell the truth in as much detail as possible. For our grandchildren, if nothing else.'

Although I was only really familiar with those aspects of David's life that were relevant to a study of Myra Hindley, I understood why Mary was so firm in her belief that his story was worthy of a book of its own. The idea hovered between us as we made arrangements for me to visit them in Ireland, ostensibly for an informal exchange about David's memories of Hindley and Brady, although he made it clear that he did not want to be directly quoted in the book I was writing. 'It always ends up as the same old garbage,' he said bluntly on the telephone. 'No matter how honest your intentions might be, you'll turn out like the rest of them. That's just how it goes.'

My first visit to them lasted three days. I went with my son, River, who was then nine years old. Mary was welcoming from the start; David was belligerent, guarded and, at times, rude. Within a few hours of our arrival, we were in his local pub, where he had called on his 'mafia' (his sons, their families, and friends) as support against what he thought would be another intrusive and pointless encounter with a journalist. I told him I wasn't a journalist and never had been; he gave a snort of derision. 'Well, no. You don't even look old enough to hold a pen, to me.' I didn't let him put me off for several reasons: I trusted Mary; I knew that his attitude was a test to find out whether I would give in and leave, perhaps following up my visit with an unpleasant article in the press; I wanted to hear what he would say, once his guard was down; and because he was so good with River, as he is with his own grandchildren.

By the afternoon of the following day, everything was

different. David was calm, relaxed and ready to talk. Together with Mary, we spoke at length about his memories of that particular time in the '60s. It was more obvious than it had ever been that his story deserved to be told on its own merits, rather than as an adjunct to a book about the Moors case. When I left Ireland, the three of us knew that we had work to do.

While I was writing *One of Your Own*, I met Ian Fairley, who attended the arrest of Ian Brady on the morning after the last murder. He was very keen to talk about David Smith: 'He was a bit of a rum customer, but if it hadn't been for Smith, more children would have been killed. People were so vicious about that poor lad after it all came out, but he saved lives *and* he enabled us to bring home those children who had already been murdered so that their parents could give them proper funerals. Without him, we would never have known where to start. Smith was the one man more than anyone who brought the whole thing to justice. Albeit unknowingly in parts, but he did it and it wasn't an easy thing to do. Because if he hadn't come to us, Evans [*Brady and Hindley's last victim, 17-year-old Edward Evans*] would have ended up on the moor and we would never have been any the wiser. The men who mattered on that inquiry – Jock Carr and Joe Mounsey – they believed in David Smith completely. Unfortunately, mud sticks and he ended up an outcast. But it's about time people started realising he's a hero, not a villain.'

Ian Fairley's view, and that of Joe Mounsey and Jock Carr, quickly became lost in the media furore that surrounded the Moors case. It's a curious and unhappy fact that despite their hatred of Brady and Hindley, a large section of the public chose to believe the two killers' insinuations against David Smith. The stories that abounded during the original investigation and trial had their source in the statements Brady and Hindley made about him, though it is also true that the revelations about David's juvenile convictions and his 1966 deal with the *News of the World* did him no favours. By the mid-1980s, when Hindley finally exonerated him of any part in their crimes, it was already too late. The old untruths are still doing the rounds, supplemented by new and often bizarre fictions. *Witness* tells the facts. It is not, as someone has already claimed, an 'apology' for David Smith, or even an attempt to 'rehabilitate' him in the eyes of the public. It is simply his story.

In 2003, Granada Television approached David with a view to producing a dramatisation of his life during his marriage to Maureen Hindley. When David and Mary agreed to the idea on the understanding that it wouldn't focus on Brady and Hindley, work began on *The Ballad of David Smith*. Following a meeting with Granada bosses, the script was shelved in favour of a dramatisation of the Moors case, which aired in May 2006 as *See No Evil: The Story of the Moors Murders*. During the many months of work on *The Ballad*, David had begun to write down his memories in lengthy but isolated fragments; these became the foundation stone of the present book. He started writing again after our initial meeting, and these reminiscences, together with our interviews and my research, form what is hopefully a coherent narrative of his life.

On that very first day in Ireland, Mary drove us through the village where she and David have lived for the past 15 years. He asked her to make a slight detour; although wary, he was determined that I should visit a particular place with him.

We drove past a modern housing estate to an overgrown field surrounded by rough limestone walls. At one end were the ruins of a long, low building with a collapsed orange roof. Near the wall was a wooden notice, beautifully rendered and inscribed. It told the history of the place: the ruin was all that remained of the local workhouse built in 1852 to accommodate 600 inmates and razed to the ground in the 1920s. The field in front of us, with its long grass and wild flowers, was the site of the graveyard, where many workhouse children had been buried anonymously, without coffins.

David became agitated as he explained that the sign was his creation, carved in his workshop. 'No one should lie in an unmarked grave,' he told us. 'Do you understand what I'm saying . . . no child should be without a headstone when they die, the very least you can give them is that – somewhere for their family to visit. A stretch of bleak field with no one knowing they're there . . . it isn't right.' He shook his head and bit his lip.

'I think you understand. I *hope* you do.' He gave Mary a nod and we drove slowly away.

All Brady and Hindley's victims have been found except Keith Bennett, who disappeared on 16 June 1964. His body lies somewhere on Saddleworth Moor, despite more recent efforts by Greater Manchester Police to locate his grave. Last year, I began corresponding with Alan Bennett, Keith's younger brother. As our friendship developed, I worried about how he might react to the book I was writing with David Smith. When I confided in him, his reaction was overwhelmingly positive and he has continued to be staunchly supportive of the book ever since. He has provided the Foreword here, and I owe him a huge debt of thanks not only for that, but also for his encouragement, courage and strength. I hope that others might share his clear-sightedness in reading this book.

*

Only a handful of people knew that this book was in progress. I must first of all thank my mother, as always, for taking care of River whenever I needed to work outside school hours. I'm grateful to my brother John and his wife Sally for their support, and to my friend Tricia, who accompanied River and me on our first visit to Ireland.

I must also thank all David and Mary's family, but especially their sons David and Paul. David provided the initial contact and Paul, together with his partner Gwen, often looked after River while I was working in Ireland. I have to thank Gwen's son, Mikey, too, for being such a good friend to River while we were there. And sincere thanks to Dave Lucey and his partner, Kath, for all their help; also to Ralf Beyerle, for providing the photographs of Dave and Mary by Hans-Jürgen Büsch.

Mary's belief in this project from the very beginning has ensured its completion. It's entirely due to her that David was able to set aside his reservations and dedicate himself to writing, talking and thinking more in depth about the past than ever before. Over the many months we've worked on the book I've come to value their friendship deeply. I want to thank them for that, and for their good humour, hospitality and many generosities. But most of all, I want to thank them for putting their trust in me.

Prologue

'If anyone were making a journey from Underwood Court to Wardle Brook Avenue after 11.30 p.m., the road on which they would travel would, generally speaking, be in darkness.'
– Leslie Wright, assistant street lighting superintendent for Hyde Corporation, evidence read at the Moors trial, April 1966

When the door clicks shut, he has to force himself not to run, moving steadily down the path and past the window where the light burns behind drawn floral curtains. Walking away from the house is the most terrifying thing he's ever done; the impulse to keep looking over his shoulder is almost unbearable. One foot slowly in front of the other, again and again, until he reaches the cut-through. The street lights are out, plunging the housing estate into blackness as he breaks into the fastest sprint of his life, accompanied by the eternal static hum of the pylons towering over Hattersley.

The cut-through brings him out on the road where he lives. Underwood Court is one of seven blocks of high-rise flats in the neighbourhood; tonight the thirteen floors of its starkly lit stairwell are as welcome as a lighthouse beam. Gasping from the 300-yard run, he holds his index finger on the intercom button, listening acutely for the buzzer. The snap of the door release seems deafening in the still night air.

Inside the entrance hall, his breathing begins to regulate as he glances at Flat Number 1, occupied by Mr Page, the jobsworth caretaker. He waits for a moment, half-expecting the middle-aged man to haul open the door with another threat of eviction, but silence echoes about the building.

The lift is to his right. Ignoring the stink of urine and takeaways that plagues the steel cubicle around the clock, he steps in, pressing his back to the wall, and drags trembling hands through his hair. A cold sweat begins to permeate his skin. On the third floor he gets out, glancing down the corridor. There are four flats, and the door to his, with its tarnished '18' above the spyhole, is slightly ajar.

The normality of the living room, where the collie stands wagging its tail, and the homely sound of his wife filling the kettle with water in the kitchen, confuses him. The reality of what he's witnessed and escaped from suddenly hits home. Calling, 'I'll be with you in a minute,' he dives into the bathroom and vomits until there is nothing left.

His wife appears at his side, kneeling in her nightdress, putting a concerned hand on his shoulders as he hunches over the toilet, spitting out long trails of bitter saliva. He hears her ask if he is all right, if he's been drinking.

'I haven't had *any* drink.'

He turns his head and in the stark light of the bathroom the look in her eyes agitates him afresh; it's as if she doesn't recognise him. He staggers to his feet and turns on the blue-spotted tap, letting the water run ice-cold through his fingers before splashing it up into his face. His wife stands apprehensively behind him. When he paces through to the sitting room, she follows.

'Sit down,' he tells her and they sit, knee to knee, on the settee. He puts out a chilled hand to the dog, who hunkers down at his feet. The cold sweat that began in the lift returns, but this time it pours from him like water.

Shivering uncontrollably, he blurts out in fits and starts what he's seen.

Afterwards, he looks at his wife and realises that she hasn't grasped any of it as he'd intended. She only keeps asking about her sister, wanting to know if she's all right.

'She's all right, but *she*'s part of it. Didn't you hear me, girl? Myra's *part of it.*'

But it's clear that she still doesn't understand. Frustrated, he gets up to splash more water on his face, then sits heavily in the chair by the electric fire. When the heating is on, the fire smells of burning wool and gives off a sound like a muted version of the pylons over Hattersley. Now it's lifeless, the bars grey. Without its glow and drone, the flat feels barren.

His wife is crying very softly, feeling for the tissue tucked inside one of the short sleeves of her nightdress. He looks down at his T-shirt, at the dark, rust-coloured specks and smears, and his mouth thickens with bile.

Swallowing, he states quietly, 'As soon as it's light, we'll call the police.' When she doesn't answer, he cracks his knuckles, one after the other, in a vain attempt to relieve the tension inside himself. 'All right, girl? We'll wait until there are other people moving about and then we'll go to the phone box.'

'And take Bob.' Her reply, spoken in a small voice, is that of a girl even younger than her 19 years. The dog, hearing his name, half-opens a bleary eye.

'Yeah, him too.'

He turns his head towards the glass door that leads to the balcony. Stiffly, he rises and crosses the carpet, then opens the door carefully so as not to make a noise. The air strikes his skin like a fist; the temperature seems to have dropped beyond reason. The sky over Hattersley is starless and unremittingly dark, but down there among the myriad houses, it's somehow possible to make out which row is Wardle Brook Avenue.

Minutes pass with painful sluggishness. He divides his time crouching in the chair beside the lifeless fire and leaning over the balcony screen to reassure himself that there's no one watching the flat – not from Wardle Brook Avenue nor from the car park below.

Because that's his deepest fear, in these last hours before daybreak. He feels safe as long as he and Maureen remain in the flat, but in his mind he pictures the two of them leaving Underwood Court and a car cruising up alongside, then a soft voice asking, 'And where do you think you're off to?' In the flat, he can just about cope with the knowledge of what's gone before, but if they leave and the nightmare scenario becomes reality, he will go to pieces, without a shadow of doubt; he will absolutely go to pieces. So he keeps guard instead, and waits for the right moment to present itself.

And it does, a little after six o'clock, when a shard of light breaks over the estate. He's left the balcony door open and hears the familiar sound of the milkman arriving on his rounds: first the trundle of the float on the road, then the faint chink of dozens of bottles. He gets up from the fireside chair to watch the white-coated figure carrying a red crate along the nearest terrace. Lights are going on as people rise for the new day; no more than a handful dotted about the estate, but enough to convince him that the time has come.

He turns to Maureen and she stares back at him, wide-eyed.

Taking a deep breath, he keeps his voice as even as he can: 'Get dressed and fetch your coat.'

He waits until she's walked through to the bedroom before entering the kitchen and pulling open a drawer. He tucks the bread knife prudently inside the waistband of his jeans, then pulls open another drawer filled with useless things gathering dust – small keys to unknown locks, old bus ticket stubs, a broken plastic spoon – and rummages until his fingers light on an object at the back. He takes out the heavy screwdriver and pushes it into his waistband next to the knife.

His wife stands in the sitting room, awkward in her coat and impractical shoes.

With the dog at their heels, they head for the fetid lift. The clunking mechanism shudders into life, jerking them down to the ground floor. They step out in unison, all three, and cross the hall with its prickly mat skew-whiff to the front door.

Maureen gazes at him. He opens the door slowly and takes a step outside, glancing in every direction. The roads are empty and the car park uninhabited. He looks back at his wife. Her black beehive is unkempt and her eyes, without their usual spit-slicked mascara and thick, pencilled contours, seem sunken and huge at the same time.

'Ready?'

She nods, clutching the dog's collar for comfort.

'Let's go for it, then.'

They refrain from running, but walk with adrenalin-induced speed to the long road bordering the estate. Fluorescent light spills from the newsagents' shop, and outside the chippy crumpled paper bags flutter while discarded pop cans clatter in a gust of wind.

The public telephone stands on the corner of Hare Hill Road. All three of them squeeze inside the peeling scarlet box with its tart iron-filings smell. He lifts the receiver and dials 999, the burr and clicks of the connection reverberating in the cramped space.

His call is logged at 6.07 a.m. by Police Constable Edwards, the duty policeman at Hyde station.

*

'I asked for a car,' David recalls quietly, 45 years later. He's sitting on a pine chair he made himself, in the kitchen of his home in a remote and beautiful corner of Ireland. 'I couldn't think of anything to say. There wasn't a story that I could give them over the phone. How could I sum up in a couple of sentences what had taken place that night? I definitely did *not* mention that there had been a murder. I just asked for a car. The bobby on the phone said, "Well, what's it for?" I told him, "Look, we *need* a car. It's an emergency. You've got to get a car to us. I'll explain at the station." He promised us a car was on its way, so we ducked out of the phone box and hid behind a privet hedge. I don't know if it was somebody's garden, I just remember kneeling down behind this hedge. Full daylight came, but still no car. I went back to the phone box and called the police again. I think I rang them twice or more because I wanted to be sure that the car was on its way. And it arrived while I was actually on the phone. I've never been so glad to see a copper in my life.'

* * *

From David Smith's memoir:
The police car driver says nothing, on the dash a knife and large screwdriver, in the back a young wife and large dog, me sitting silent next to him, looking out of the window. I notice he jumps all the red lights, the streets pass quickly and with a weird noise, woosh-*woosh*-woosh. I stare ahead, pressing my back hard against the seat, feet against the floor, breathing rapid and shallow but starting to relax, getting closer to where I want to be.

Are you all right, girl? I ask Maureen. She answers softly that she is.

Every ten seconds I feel the driver's eyes on me for an instant, but he says nothing and looks ancient to me, double my seventeen. I look away from him.

We approach the old Town Hall: Hyde police station and the magistrate's court are wedged under the same roof, inside the same blank red walls. Two or three traffic lights come up in quick succession, we jump every one. Early risers on the suburban streets, heading for work, just another day in the life for them.

I've entered a corridor that has only one exit, I know this and it comforts me, even though I don't know where the exit is and I don't know or even care where the corridor will take me. I only feel, inside myself, the madness of it all: Ian sitting composed and calmly nodding my dismissal, without seeing the Fall of the King. Myra smiling, eyes warm and friendly, without seeing the Capture of the Queen.

What was it that you think you saw in me, Ian? You felt confident enough to kill in front of me, but what happened in your head? You say I passed the test – what fucking test? You don't issue diplomas for this kind of thing. So we got drunk together and talked a load of shit together; it meant *nothing*, some bank robbers us. But to kill someone the way you did in front of me . . . Why you decided to do it only you know. Did you really believe your game, were you so fucking mad as to believe you were above everything? Didn't you see your mistake: *I* am your mistake. But why?

I need to know *why*.

I sit in front of a small desk, next to me Maureen holds Bob the dog, on the desk are my knife and screwdriver. A windowless room with a coal fire blazing away like something normal, the smell of detectives' pipe tobacco clogging the air from past interviews.

The same policeman who picked us up asks me what it's all about.

I don't answer straight away. I'm trying to remain calm, but whatever was with me a few hours before is beginning to fall apart.

Minutes pass. I look at the police officer, he says nothing and patiently waits. My eyes are beginning to feel hot and wet, fucking hell. I stare at the wall, refusing to blink in case the feeling pours out of me. I look at Maureen. She's crying quietly and very pale. I keep looking at her. We're in that corridor, her and me, the two of us, alone.

One dragged-up breath: I take the air in until my lungs and chest are bursting, I let it go in one long rushing gush.

'It's murder,' I say, and Maureen lets out a loud sob.

What was the plan that night, Ian? Not the 'rolling a queer' story, or the 'there was a fight' excuse. Myra must have known by then that if

25

you hadn't lost the plot already you were well on the way. A quick decision not up for discussion, just *do it*. There was no fight, no raised voices; just screaming after you'd hit him. He was as relaxed as he could be, smoking, talking to Myra.

You rehearsed every second of that killing.

The axe didn't live in the fireplace; there was never a domestic use for it. Before leaving the house to pick him up, did you put it under the settee? When he was talking to Myra, did you casually walk round the back of the settee and pick the axe up? Only seconds to go now, one strong blow and it's over. Except it wasn't: he moves, maybe cigarette to ashtray, the axe doesn't drop him.

'You could see the blow register in his eyes,' Myra said.

You figured one good belt to the head and he'd hit the floor. You had to have total control, but it was all going wrong: *hit him again, shut him up, neighbours could be out in the street, what's going on, hit him again.* You were meant to be watching me, noting my reaction: *where the fuck's Smith, what's going on?*

Then finally, fourteen long blows later, it's over. 'That's it, the messiest one yet,' you said.

Clean up time: at last you have control back and don't I know it. But why didn't you kill him before I got there, why wasn't there a body just lying there when I walked in, you watching my eyes and thinking, 'Now, you'll believe me.'

This time you got it wrong.

I'm willing to bet that, somewhere deep inside, Myra knew it too. She would've been thinking: *just let this go away, just let this be all right. Please let it be like it was, just the two of us. Fuck you, David Smith.*

Because this was to be a double killing; part two was me, in the middle of nowhere. 'Eddie' deep in the hole on the moors and you just blow my head off. How else was it all going to end – happy nights forever more, talking shite and getting pissed, growing old with our 'little secret'?

No way.

In the room that stinks of spent smoke, the policeman struggles with my story. He asks, 'Is it still there?'

'Yes,' I answer. 'It's upstairs.'

He looks at me, eyebrows vanishing into his hair. 'Upstairs?'

I nod.

'You took the body *upstairs*?'

I say slowly, 'Yes, me and him took it upstairs.'

And he gives me another look and goes out.

When he comes back, he's with a sergeant, who asks me to repeat my story. They go looking for notepads and take a short statement from me, Maureen still crying quietly at my side, me smoking every cigarette I can lay my hands on, eating the things.

Then the big boss comes in. Talbot, all buttons and braid. Scowling as I tell him the same things I've been telling his men all morning. Straight away he doesn't like me and I can't stand the sight of him.

The room seems to be filling up with people, all looking at me. Someone mentions going to the house. Talbot's shiny buttons catch my eye again and I know I have to warn him.

'Wait a minute' – I hear my voice as if it's from another room – 'he's got guns.'

Talbot swivels on his heel. 'You didn't mention guns before. What kind of guns? Shotguns? Airguns?'

'No, proper guns. A .45 and a .38 and a rifle.'

Talbot and his men stare.

'Has he got ammunition?'

'Yeah, he's got ammunition, lots of it.'

A flicker of apprehension passes from face to face as they realise: this is different.

I don't want to go back. When they say we need you up at the house, I feel myself go rigid. But while Maureen is left at the station with the dog, I'm driven to Hattersley by two detectives (they're wearing suits, so they must be detectives). The car smells strongly of their soap and aftershave.

Just before we reach the estate, by the Wall's factory, one of the men turns to me and says, 'They haven't found anything.'

I start to panic, wondering if they've managed to get rid of the body, but that wasn't the plan. I can't figure it out; my mind races with possibilities and outcomes, but we're already there, parking just below the house, the high wall of the New Inn to our left, the white fence that surrounds their garden to our right.

I sit mute in the back of the car, watching everything happening in slow motion. On this clean, fresh October morning both ends of Wardle Brook Avenue are blocked off by police cars. Neighbours are gathering, the usual routine forgotten, and I'm thinking: *why do the men group with the men and the women group with the women and the children stand close to their mothers?* I follow mouths moving like television with the sound turned down.

One of the detectives makes a noise in his throat and I look up at the house. Ian and Myra – he is handcuffed – walk along the path.

'This them?' I'm asked.

Ian is the first to pass. His eyes meet mine through the car window and I get a quick, sly smile and a brief nod. Myra follows a few yards behind, her white-blonde hair an immaculate cloud, make-up perfect. The look she gives me is seconds long but will stay with me a lifetime: her face is pure stone, black-rimmed eyes unblinking, locking onto me. An animal feet away from its prey.

I shrink back against the cold leather. 'That's them.'

The detective in the passenger seat climbs out of the car, speaks shortly to a colleague on the street, then gets back in again, his eyes finding mine in the driver's mirror.

'You were spot-on there, lad. It was upstairs.'

He looks at the other detective, who starts the ignition.

How did the metal feel as it snapped around your wrist, Ian? Did the curtain fall slowly or did the entire stage disintegrate beneath you? The uniformed men who watched as you dressed were uninvited strangers that you couldn't control. Could you feel it inside, both of you? Was it like dying on your feet? Listening to the sound of footsteps going upstairs. To the room.

Hessy, Hessy, can you hear it, it's over. Secrets, keep the fucking secrets, they belong to us, remember the lessons, tell them fuck all, no memory after ten days, you and me forever, you and me, don't show panic, tell them nothing, act normal. Fuck Smith, we'll have him, he's fucked. Maggots, they're all fucking maggots. Believe in me and I will save you.

You're finished, both of you.

But not quite, not yet. Because although I don't know it, you've still got the centre stage to take, and with your last bullet you'll get me.

You'll nail me, accusing me of every filth you've ever done and more. You'll feed the media the headlines they crave. You'll hurl so much shit I'll drown in it.

I will never, with every breath I am left to take on this earth, regret my actions concerning you two; whatever world you were living in was never my world and you know it, Ian.

But you'll do a good job on my name. You'll put it right up there with your own.

Hyde station is in chaos when we get back, uniformed police and detectives in suits and trilbies materialising from the walls as I go in through the side door, where every second person I see seems to own a pipe.

Myra stands with two officers in the corridor. There's no sign of Ian. I'm rushed past her and there's a lot of angry swearing behind me from the uniforms: 'For fuck's sake, find a fucking room, get her fucking out of here, it's like a fucking bus queue in this place.'

I'm put in the same room as before, where Maureen is still waiting with the dog. She sits lonely and scared in front of the desk, eyes red from non-stop crying, my empty chair next to her. Four or five people are already in the room, but she is alone.

I sit down and hold her hand. 'They've got them,' I tell her, but she doesn't hear me.

'How's Myra?' she asks, her fingers closing around mine.

'I think she's been arrested. I think they've both been arrested.'

She's bemused. 'But it was Ian, wasn't it? Didn't you say it was Ian?'

'No, girl, it was both of them, don't you remember? In our flat I told you it was both of them. Remember?'

'Oh . . .' She looks lost. 'Yes, I think so . . .' Her eyes are huge again. 'Is everything all right, Dave, is everything all right?'

The officers watch and listen.

'Yes,' I tell her, feeling self-conscious. 'Everything's all right.' I hesitate, then say again: 'They've definitely arrested Ian.'

She nods her head. That much she understands, but no more.

Our first statements are taken. Hours later we're still sitting together in that same room, surrounded by coppers, with Bob the dog sprawled and sleeping on the floor. A frustrated detective enters, fuming: 'Who the hell are Auntie Ann and Nellie? That girl is up to her neck in it and all she wants is a bloody family reunion with Auntie Ann and Nellie!'

Maureen smiles weakly. She explains that Nellie is her and Myra's mother, and that their Auntie Ann lives not far from them in Gorton. Hearing that the two women are being brought to the station makes things seem a bit more normal for Maureen; her shoulders slacken and a glimmer of light returns to her watery eyes. We're given tea again

29

and as many cigarettes as we can smoke while we go over our initial statements. The bedlam of the morning is sinking into something else, something I can't name, but everything is fading, falling fast, leaving nothing behind.

We're told that Ian has been charged with murder but Myra is free to go and we have to come back tomorrow. A tight knot of unease clenches my gut. While I try to make sense of the policeman's words, someone mentions that Nellie and Auntie Ann have arrived.

We leave the room and the two women are standing there in the corridor, faces stiff with hostility. Maureen calls to her mother but is met with rigid silence, and a policewoman puts out a hand to hold her back.

'No, love, just wait a few minutes, they're here for your sister. Myra's going home with them. You'll have to wait till they're clear of the station.'

We hang around at the other end of the corridor for a while. Then Myra appears, and is given the nod by a sergeant to leave the station with her mother and Auntie Ann. She throws a sharp, contemptuous glance at us and then she's gone, off to spend her last days of freedom in Gorton with her parents.

And us, we return to Ardwick for the night, to my childhood home, where six months ago the tiny white coffin of Angela Dawn, our daughter, rested in the parlour before we buried her. I call my dad and tell him to come home from London, where he's been working, then sit like a mute again with Maureen and the dog in that same parlour, thinking: *what the fuck happens now?*

* * *

A fortnight later, on 28 October 1965, the *North Cheshire Herald* reported on committal proceedings against Ian Brady and Myra Hindley, now known jointly as the Moors Murderers: 'A young couple who had been spectators in the public gallery were later chased across Hyde market by a group of shouting women. As cameramen's flashbulbs popped, the couple dodged in and out of the stalls. The girl, in high heels and a grey suit, had difficulty keeping up with the man accompanying her.'

The public hounding of David Smith, chief prosecution witness in the Moors trial, had begun.

I
Ghost Riders in the Sky
1948–61

Chapter 1

'The early years were good . . .'
– Fred Harrison, *Brady and Hindley* (Grafton, 1987)

From David Smith's memoir:

It's 2.30 on a hot Thursday afternoon in Ireland and I'm looking at a blank page. My fingers are cracked and crooked with arthritis and I find it difficult – and far too much trouble – to contemplate filling the page. But then, as always, a wisp of smoke appears in my mind, a thought, a feeling, somewhere to go, another corridor with no answers.

I allow the smoke to drift and dance away from me, not too far ahead and not too fast. I'm beginning to think and follow . . . in a moment the page will fill with words and today will be gone, leaving me locked in another time. I look out at my colour-drenched Irish world, then bend my head and follow the wisp of smoke again, back to the black-and-white streets of a Manchester suburb. It carries me quickly now down the long corridor, picking up speed . . .

39 Aked Street, Ardwick. I'm here to meet myself, nothing more than an old man thinking back the years, but my heart is in this house. It contains and stands for *everything* that is me, period. Once it was a place of happiness but confusion and sadness floods me as I drift back into it on that wisp of smoke, picking up the special smell of Sunday dinner and the background drone of the wireless.

On the top floor is the attic bedroom; it belongs to me but is filled with sepia-tinted photographs, mainly of a brown-eyed young man in uniform. Steep stairs lead down to the second-floor landing and to Mum's room, which smells of talcum powder and is softly feminine, where little trinket boxes gleam in the sunlight. Further along the landing is Grandad's room, a world away from its neighbour – all pot-under-the-bed smells and spittoon boxes thick with phlegm from the old man's endless throat-clearing. Next to Grandad's room is a rarity in Aked Street: a new fitted bathroom. We don't use it as often as we should; like everyone else, we have an old tin bath in the backyard which is brought in on Saturday night to wash the weekly grime from my skin.

The wisp of smoke carries me down another flight of stairs to the ground floor and the scullery at the back. All the cooking and washing are done in here, but I'm looking for something else, and behind the stove I find them: Mum's pint bottles of Guinness. I used to fetch these for her, racing down Exeter Street to the illegal off-licence, where they'd hand me the bottles in a paper bag. Then I'd head home again, down the back entries into our yard and straight into the scullery, fast as my skinny legs would take me. Next to the scullery is a simple kitchen with a table and chair, cold meat safe and ceiling clothes maiden. Beyond it is the dining room – the most used and busiest room of all, dominated by a huge wall cupboard stacked to bursting every Christmas with home-made mince pies, cakes, biscuits and other mouth-watering goodies.

The wisp of smoke evaporates, leaving me where I want to be most: the room at the front of the house, facing the street. My heart is in this room. The door is always bolted (children are not supposed to enter the parlour, after all) but nothing can keep me out. A chair, a stretch on tiptoes, a small hand feeling for the latch and . . .

The door to the parlour opens and welcomes me in.

* * *

Withington Hospital was originally Charlton Barlow Moor Workhouse, serving most of south Manchester's poverty-ridden inhabitants. It was converted to a hospital in 1864 and Florence Nightingale declared it 'one of the best, if not *the* best, in the country'. David Smith was born within its red-brick walls on 9 January 1948 to a woman he can't remember. Joyce Hull was in her late teens when she fell pregnant to John James (Jack) Smith, a 28-year-old engineer; they never married. Joyce vanished from her son's life when he was one year old, leaving his paternal grandparents to adopt him on Valentine's Day 1949. It was another 20 years before the opportunity arose for David to meet his mother.

'I don't know anything about Joyce,' he shrugs now. 'Not a

thing. Only that none of the family seem to have liked her, and in those days if you weren't liked, it was a serious business. I don't have a single memory of her.'

All she left behind were a few photographs of the two of them together. One, included here, shows them sitting with a department store Santa, while another, taken on a shingle beach somewhere in the north of England, hangs on the wall just outside the kitchen in David's home in Ireland. On both, dark-haired Joyce holds her warmly swaddled baby close, a wide smile on her strikingly pretty face. But within months, or even weeks, of the photographs being taken, she was gone and David Hull became David Smith, the adoptive son of John Richard Smith, a 'commission agent', and his wife Annie.

David grew up believing that Joyce was dead: 'She was just a name somewhere belonging to someone far away in the past. I knew I was adopted, but Annie was *always* Mum to me. She wrapped me up in cotton wool so thoroughly that there was no reason for me to ever question how things had turned out. Being illegitimate wasn't a problem in my early years – I wasn't some abandoned poor little bastard running loose in the squalid city streets. Besides, there were loads of illegitimate kids after the war; every family had a skeleton in their cupboard. The only Mum I ever knew showered me with love and spoiled me rotten. Anything I ever needed or wanted was mine, I didn't even have to ask.'

Annie was a tall and dignified woman. Slim as a cigarette, she wore her clothes – mostly print dresses and fashionable shoes, with a fur coat on occasion – as well as any professional model despite a slight hunchback. She was regarded as the matriarch of the family, yet there was a loneliness to her existence that David struggled to understand: 'I worshipped her, and we were unimaginably close, but I still felt there was a sadness to her. She and Grandad got on well, but there was never any intimacy between them – not a shared joke or a kiss, and she always ate alone in the back kitchen. That was her way, whether it was Christmas or Sunday dinner. She'd cook for the whole family but then disappear into the kitchen by herself. I don't know why. Her one indulgence, if you can call it that, was the Guinness. She enjoyed a tipple, but it was no more than that.

Mum never drank to excess – she was a proper lady.'

He pauses, fiddling with the cigarette he's about to light. 'I trusted her completely. If ever I had a tooth that needed pulling, she'd tie a bit of string to it and the other end to the door handle, then tell me to shut my eyes while she slammed the door. Out the tooth would fly.' He grins. 'You really have to trust someone to let them do that to you.'

Annie's secret melancholia probably stemmed from the loss of her son Frank, whose photographs adorned the walls and surfaces of David's attic room. He remembers being 'fed stories about how Uncle Frank had been part of the Normandy invasion or something similarly heroic. Any male relatives who'd died in the service of their country were regarded as saints. So it came as a bit of a shock when I found out later that Uncle Frank had died from pneumonia on the platform of Crewe railway station. He had been invalided out of the army and was on his way home. His photographs were everywhere I looked, this handsome boy in uniform with huge brown eyes, and I hated it. Mum talked about him constantly and I sometimes felt that she was shoehorning me into the Frank-shaped hole in her life.'

Annie's other children, including David's father, Jack, were scattered across the country. 'Three of my aunties moved up the social ladder by marrying southerners,' he recalls. Then he adds, with an amused curl of his lip, 'They gave their kids names like *Nigel* and *Virginia*. Only Auntie Dorothy married a local chap, from Reddish. When I was older, I'd visit her with Dad on a Sunday – there was always Carnation Cream involved in the tea we ate – and afterwards we'd have a stroll on Reddish golf course. I saw a lot more of my Uncle Bert – everyone else called him Alf, but I knew him as Bert, for some reason – and Auntie Bet, who lived next door but one to us, at 35 Aked Street, with their kids Frank, John and Graham. John was like a brother to me, and Auntie Bet . . . well, she and Mum were peas in a pod. Everyone called her the Duchess. She had airs and graces, and liked to pretend she was posh, telling people she'd come up from Kent when in reality she was born in Woolwich dockyard of all places. The Duchess and Mum were a combined force to be reckoned with – cronies, conspirators and joint matriarchs, in charge of everything remotely "family". Male role models? There weren't any: Dad was hardly ever around and Grandad was just an old man, not even a husband to Mum, in my eyes.'

David's grandfather was a bookmaker who liked to gamble himself; often he'd head off in a furniture van to Blackpool's gaming houses with anything he could lay his hands on to use as stake money. His winnings were usually spent on dapper suits and hats. 'Grandad was "Mr Cravat",' David remembers. 'People regarded him as a gentleman because he was always immaculately dressed, mostly in a spotless Crombie with a silk handkerchief poking out of his breast pocket. Every Saturday morning he'd iron his clothes and set them out while the house filled with the smell of his breakfast kippers. His hair gleamed with brilliantine and he always carried a smart walking cane, which he would use to point at people and things. Footballer George Best was a friend of his – Grandad addressed him as "Georgie Boy". He'd go into pubs, but he wouldn't drink alcohol. Only once in many blue moons would he allow himself a rum and black.'

Growing up with a bookmaker who liked a flutter made David keenly opposed to gambling: 'Underneath the staircase at home, in the cubbyhole where our dog used to sleep, was a pile of shoeboxes. On some days they'd be stuffed so full of money the notes would scatter across the floor, but on other days they'd be completely empty. Then Mum would have to traipse down to the pawn shop with her fur coat and whatever she thought might be worth something. A fortnight later, everything would come out of the pawn again. My dad was just the same, either rolling in it or without a penny to his name. That's gamblers in a nutshell: they shout it from the rooftops when they've had a win, but never own up to how much they've lost to get there.'

Until 1961, betting shops were illegal and usually located on a back street. 'Grandad would slip me sixpence to put each way on a horse and I'd leg it down Exeter Street – the street of a thousand vices,' David explains with a laugh. 'At the end of a couple of back entries was a terraced house where a woman used to stand at an open half-door running a book. If she wasn't there, I'd push open the door myself and go inside. There'd be a group of old men huddled round a table, smoking like chimneys and listening to the radio. I'd lay my bet while the woman wrote it down in her book – there weren't any ticket stubs then, mind.

That wasn't how Grandad pursued his own business; he was legit, a bookie on track, attending all the horse and dog races. My job as a boy was to run up and down the line to see who was laying what odds and report back. Then Grandad would alter his odds to suit. I'd watch him chalking the board and doing all the crazy arm-waving. Dad and Uncle Bert would sometimes be there too, putting bets on. I used to call them the "Crombie Boys" – all in their long coats and trilbies.'

The complexities of the family relationships were lost on David as a child: 'I never gave it a second thought. Grandad was just the old man with the smart suits and the spittoon boxes, and Mum was the centre of my world. As for Dad . . . we didn't see a lot of each other in those days, not for any length of time anyway. He would be away for months on end, working as an engineer. Those things were never an issue. My life revolved around Aked Street and I was a happy little fellow back then.'

One mile south-east of Manchester city centre, Ardwick was a small village in open countryside until the Industrial Revolution. Grand terraces of regency houses sprang up around Ardwick Green, a private park with an ornamental pond, but by the end of the nineteenth century Ardwick had altered beyond recognition: mills abounded in Union Street, limeworks lined the River Medlock and everywhere were factories – brickworks, chemical works, sawmills and ironworks. Waste was emptied straight into the River Cornbrook, renamed the Black Brook by disgusted locals. The wide terraces largely vanished, replaced by workers' homes: long, narrow streets of cramped housing and small backyards. Nonetheless, it was a thriving community, and by the early 1950s Ardwick was famous for its scores of shops, picture houses, pubs, dance halls and the vast market with two entrances: one on Stockport Road, the other on Aked Street.

* * *

From David Smith's memoir:
At the far end of my cobbled, gas-lit street stands Ross Place Primary, the school I attend from the age of five. At the other is the open-air market that heaves on Saturdays with the neighbourhood's many characters and con men: Bible-pushers, Jack the Lads and hawkers shouting out their 'never to be repeated' bargains.

Every day the housewives can be seen scrubbing the windowsills and yards of pavement outside their front doors with donkey stone. Any occasion is an excuse for a street party; out come the trestle tables on Guy Fawkes', with bed-sheets serving as tablecloths. Four or five tables are shuffled together in a long row and the women bustle in and out of the houses, carrying food they've cooked themselves. The air is thick with smells: parkin, toffee apples and crackling bonfires.

I'm an only child and I love it. Every day is a reason to jump out of bed with a smile, but Saturdays are best of all – Christmas and birthdays rolled into one. On Saturdays I become a miniature cowboy, learning my craft at one of the many picture houses showing morning and afternoon matinees: the Apollo, the Kings, the Queens, and the Shaftesbury. I can be the Cisco Kid at the Apollo in the morning and then at the Kings in the afternoon I'm the Range Rider or his trusty sidekick Dick West. I sit soaking up every gunfight and stagecoach hold-up, booing the Red Indians while sucking solemnly on an orange-flavoured ice-stick. I run home feeling like a real cowboy in my Davy Crockett raccoon-fur hat, shooting up the traffic with a two-fingered pistol and slapping my backside to spur on my imaginary horse, Lightning.

My weekly bath on a Saturday means more treats. Mum scrubs and dries me and then, whether it's needed or not, she delouses me, lovingly combing my head raw and squashing 'the bad little buggers' under her thumb. After that she doles out syrup of figs followed by the dark, sweet laxative chocolate that guarantees I'll be a 'good, clean little boy'. Topped and tailed, clean-headed and cleaned out, I'm ushered into the parlour and presented with almost every comic from the week's stands.

Those last two hours before bedtime are ours. It's just Mum and me, wrapped in the secretive comfort of the parlour. I love the soothing smell of the room, its cosiness and privacy. I curl up with my comics on the bulky, floral-patterned settee while Mum fetches her newspaper. Before sitting down she turns to the mahogany gramophone player and inserts a new brass needle from a little cup full of them, then winds up the gramophone and chooses a record to play. There are stacks of 78 rpm singles in brown paper covers and I know the words to them all. A rustling sound precedes every song; I read my comic, mouthing along to Woody Guthrie, Frankie Laine and Hank Williams. After a while, Mum chooses a record for herself, and the voice of Dean

Martin, usually followed by Doris Day, floats from the speaker. I peep from behind my comic at Mum's far-away expression until she notices me and smiles. I wonder if she's thinking about the photographs in our attic room, remembering her brown-eyed soldier boy.

There are photographs in this room, too. Unsmiling, sepia-tinted faces I don't know gaze down on us, dressed in their Sunday best, stiff and uncomfortable. My eyelids start to droop. With a mug of milky Horlicks in my hand, I'm gently guided up the two flights of stairs to my bedroom where, tucked up safe and snug as a bug in a rug, I drift off to ride like the wind with the cowboys in my dreams.

And in the morning, when I awake, I'm wrapped in Mum's arms. I love sharing a bed with her; I love the scent of her skin and hutch up as close as I can to feel her breath on my face. I want that breath to last until the end of time. Her room is on the floor below, perfect and feminine, meticulously clean, but she never sleeps in it, not once. The door is always shut, as is the door to Grandfather's room; I can hear his snoring and coughing, if I listen hard. But Mum always sleeps with me.

The summers were hot and long in Ardwick when I was a little boy and the streets were safe. I thought it would last for ever.

* * *

David's school, Ross Place Primary, was typically Victorian in structure, with soaring chimneys and a high brick wall around the playground.

'I was a good boy for most of my years there,' he recalls, 'though the only lesson that really interested me was English. All I ever wanted to do was read and write. My compositions were so long that I used to take home my exercise book to finish them. I had a strange obsession with filling the page – if I came to the end of a chapter, I'd make sure I could think of enough to write to fill every line, right down to the last inch of paper, cramming in as many words as possible. I loved to read as well, not just comics but any books that happened to be within reach. Mum encouraged me in that, even though she wasn't a particularly keen reader herself – the racing page was her favourite. And like every other house in the country, we had a full set of Dickens and the *Encyclopedia Britannica*, paid off at sixpence a week. I never glanced at the encyclopedia, but I read every line of Dickens. *Oliver Twist* stayed with me and not in a good way – the story of Nancy and murderous Bill Sykes scared me to death. Then I moved on to *Tom Sawyer* and realised that was who I wanted to be.'

The headmaster of Ross Place Primary was Mr Thorpe, a stern man with a booming voice. Together with Annie and the Duchess, he provided behavioural boundaries. 'Rights and wrongs are learned in childhood,' David states firmly. 'Later on, as I was growing up, I did things I'm not proud of and would rather forget. But I always admitted any wrongdoing – that was one rule that stuck, along with what you might call "normal morality", which was virtually ingrained from birth. Normal morality meant the basics: respect and manners. "Show some respect," you were told, and you did. "Mind your manners," you were warned, and you corrected yourself. If I *did* get into trouble at school, running home to Mum was never the answer. I'd be instantly marched back to Mr Thorpe and the corporal punishment he freely dished out – either six-of-the-best from the size-ten gym slipper, or the same from the fearsome, four-tongued thick leather strap. It was tough, but it worked for me. Between those three – Mum, the Duchess and Mr Thorpe – I learned that if you faced up to things and accepted the punishment that came with misbehaving, you'd come out all right. I was never a true rebel or anti-authority; I didn't kick against it, not really. The biggest crime was to lie, to cover up either for yourself or someone else who'd done wrong.'

Jack Smith, David's father, was never part of the equation in those early years. When the tall, rangy man in spectacles did put in an appearance, David was unable to summon any emotional response: 'I didn't feel as if he was my dad, even though I called him that. Mum would say, "Your dad's coming home soon," but I didn't associate that special heartbeat with him. He was more like a kind uncle coming to take me out. I didn't know anything about him, only that he'd been in the RAF during the war – that hero thing again – and of course I presumed he'd been a pilot and took some pride in that. In reality, he was a trained engineer and never left the ground.'

Returning from work at Fylingdales in Yorkshire, or further afield in London or Belgium, Jack spent much of his time in

Ardwick reacquainting himself with the neighbourhood bars. 'He'd get *steaming* drunk,' David remembers. 'I once woke up to a hell of a racket and ran downstairs to find Grandad in the parlour beating Dad with a poker. It was horrible, yet at the same time it was just a "domestic". A fight between father and son – there were plenty of those about. Dad wasn't a fighting drunk otherwise – he never laid a finger on me when I was small, and he didn't go looking for trouble, though he could handle himself if necessary. But I always associated the smell of stale beer with Dad.'

Gradually, Jack's visits became more regular and he made an effort to establish a relationship with his son, although his attempts often fell short of expectations. 'He'd roll up with a pocket full of money and presents for me,' David recalls. 'But they were daft things, like the time he'd been to Belgium and brought me a great stack of comics back. The problem was that the comics were foreign, *Asterix* and *Tintin*, and I couldn't read the words in the bubbles over the characters' heads. That was typical Dad: his intentions were always spot-on, and he was never anything less than generous, but he never got it *quite* right. There was a time when I desperately wanted a guitar and, sure enough, he arrived home with one for me . . . but it was plastic. A lovely little toy guitar, but I'd set my heart on a real one. On another occasion, I went for a walk down Stockport Road and in the hardware shop I saw a toolbox full of planes, saws, gauges and markers – all these fantastic hand tools in a smashing box. I was about eight then, and had started taking an interest in woodwork at school. I told Dad about the toolbox and kept on at him about it. I wanted it more than life itself – a typical kid with his heart set on something. Anyway, Christmas came: I woke up early and realised that Santa had been. I scrabbled about for my toolbox and, sure enough, there was a gleaming new toolbox full of plastic planes, bendy plastic saws . . . oh, the disappointment! But it was as much my fault as his, because I'd been so spoiled by Mum. She got me exactly what I wanted every time, but poor Dad always fell at the last hurdle.'

At a loss for how to please his son, Jack frequently suggested a trip to Gorton's Belle Vue, the vast entertainment complex that drew crowds from every corner of Manchester. Between its gates opening in 1836 and closing permanently in the 1970s, Belle Vue offered a variety of cheap, unrivalled attractions. Among its most popular draws were an amusement park and zoo, a circus, bars, dance halls, and a legendary speedway.

David recalls: 'Dad would pick me up – reeking of last night's booze – and off we'd go on the bus to Belle Vue. I can see us both now, heading through the gates on Hyde Road and pottering about the zoo with its different animal houses, each with their own strong smell. Mum would give me a bag of bread for the elephants and I'd join all the other kids walking around the moat, waiting for a great long trunk to come over the water to snaffle the crusts. There were two animals I *always* visited because I felt so sorry for them: the polar bear who was stuck in a concrete pit with a pool of dirty green water at the bottom, and the tigon, which was a cross between a tiger and a lion. He had predominant stripes and was massive, much larger than either of his parents, and lived alone without a mate. I used to stand for a long time watching those two – the polar bear endlessly circling the pool on a concrete ledge and the tigon pacing up and down a cage that was barely as big as an outside toilet. I didn't know what repetitive syndrome was back then, of course, but I felt such sorrow for them – kids and animals do have a natural affinity. That part of Belle Vue was terrible, but otherwise it was an amazing place to have on your doorstep. I loved the rides, especially the Bobs roller-coaster. I remember having to stand next to a measuring stick to get on that and being delighted when I could go on for the first time. Dad took me to the speedway as well, and the dog racing. They were good days, really.'

He pauses and gazes outside, where the two dogs he and his second wife Mary rescued are stretched out in a patch of winter sunlight. 'But everything was about to change and my world would never be the same again.'

Chapter 2

'From about 1954 until about April last year, 1965, I lived with my father at 13, Wiles Street, Gorton . . .'
– David Smith, Moors trial at Chester Assizes,
April 1966

From David Smith's memoir:
I trust my mother. I trust everything about her: the stories she tells, the falsehoods that cover my birth and illegitimacy, the tale about her being a nurse at Manchester Royal Infirmary. We lie together in the attic, surrounded by photographs of her dead son, but I trust her love for me even when she buys me the biggest scarlet piano-accordion in the world, hoping I'll learn to play it as well as Uncle Frank had done. It's the real thing, that red-and-cream contraption, not a plastic imitation. I give it a cursory squeeze once or twice in front of her in the parlour, but it makes me feel something unnameable that I don't want to feel so I smash it up, shouting, 'I'm *not* Frank, remember!' I trust her to understand, even then.

I still trust her after I find out she's lied to me. One afternoon I take it into my head to visit her at work. I'm about eight years old and get hopelessly lost in the labyrinth of corridors inside Manchester Royal Infirmary. I ask someone where I can find Annie Smith and they point me down another corridor. Off I go, expecting to find her in a crisp white uniform, leaning over some patient's bed, and instead I turn a corner and there she is with mop and bucket, washing the floor. It embarrasses her, but doesn't alter my feelings. It's only a little white lie, that one.

I go on loving her, untruths and all: I trust my mother.

* * *

At Ross Place Primary, David was entitled to free school dinners but couldn't understand why he was singled out: 'I don't know why it bothered me so much – it wasn't as if I was given smaller portions. But it niggled away at me and I asked Mum about it. She wouldn't answer, so I kept on . . . and on. Until all of a sudden this hulking great skeleton came clattering out of the cupboard.'

He shakes his head at the memory: 'I nagged and nagged. In the end she just snapped and shouted: "Your mum's not dead." The authorities knew that Joyce had walked out, leaving me the child of a one-parent family. It took the wind from my sails, I can tell you. Until then, I'd always thought that Joyce *was* dead – because that's what I'd been told. As soon as Mum uttered that line, I went berserk. I lashed out with my fists and feet and wouldn't stop thrashing and kicking . . . I was really hurting her, and I meant to do it. In the end, she had to defend herself, so she pulled out a thin tyre from an old pram that had a couple of metal strands running through the rubber. And she dealt me a good dose. In every which way, it hurt. But she didn't do it to be brutal – she did it to quieten me down. Mum had never struck me before, not even a slap on the legs when I was being naughty, and she wouldn't have done it then had I not completely lost it. I bloody well deserved that hiding.'

He regrets asking about the free dinner ticket even now: 'I wish to hell I'd kept my mouth shut. Because once it came out, I felt cheated, especially by Mum. The unconditional trust I'd had in her crumbled a fair bit. I was in a terrible mardy for about a week afterwards and wouldn't speak to her at all. Then I began calling her "Mrs Smith" instead of Mum. It took a while until things got back to normal. But if I'm truthful, I think that finding out about Joyce probably put that sizeable chip on my shoulder.'

In the aftermath of the row, David refused to eat school dinners and Annie resorted to giving him the money for fish and chips. His behaviour became deliberately disruptive and there were angry fights with the form prefects. Even then, chances are that he would have settled down again eventually. Instead, what happened next changed the course of his life for ever.

* * *

From David Smith's memoir:

Events occur with bewildering speed. My cousin John, together with his brothers and the Duchess and Uncle Bert, move into a pub in the city centre. I miss them. John is the closest thing to a sibling I have and the Duchess is a second mum to me. She'll appear again, many years from now, at times when I need a mother most. She'll be at my side when Mum passes away and after the death of my daughter, Angela. The Duchess alone will understand and keep the secret of my soul when I'm charged with the murder of my father.

But the other change, the great upheaval, happens not overnight but during it.

I'm snuggled up and cosy in my attic bed when I hear distant noises, doors banging, and raised voices from two floors below. I think I'm dreaming until footsteps sound on the stairs, growing louder, and then the bedroom door hits the wall. I hear the thud of a hand on the light switch and my sleepy eyelids burn as the overhead lamp goes on.

'Quickly now.' Mum reaches for me, lifting me out of the warm bed. I blink and squirm, swamped with confusion. She stands me to attention, spits on her hand a couple of times and wipes her palm across my hair to flatten its pillow-chafed untidiness. 'Quickly now,' she says again in an unsteady voice. 'No fuss.' Her eyes glisten with tears.

She drags a blanket from the bed and wraps it around me so tightly that my arms are pinned to my sides. Fright stills my voice as I lift one foot and then the other to let her pull on my socks, followed by slippers. 'Got to keep those feet warm,' she mumbles, picking me up and carrying me down the two flights of stairs to the hallway. She leaves me there and disappears into the living room, swiftly closing the door behind her.

Bewildered, I blink at the parlour door, where the gramophone sits gathering dust and the settee still bears the imprint of the last time I nestled into its flowery bulk. I stand wrapped tautly in my blanket, listening not to cowboy songs but to a hysterical crescendo of shouting from the shuttered living room. My eyes are drawn down the long hallway to the frosted-glass panels of the front door. A huge, dark shape lurches into view, rattling the letterbox.

All at once, the shouting stops, the living room door opens, and I'm gazing up at my father. He has the knack all adults have of being able to alter his mood in an instant. He smiles at me and is immediately calm. I feel his large hand on my shoulder, as he guides me towards the stranger waiting behind the front door. Mum appears in the hallway, face drawn and eyes glittering with unwept tears. Grandad is nowhere to be seen.

The stranger is a taxi driver, and in the thick darkness of the street he climbs behind the steering wheel of his cab while Dad pushes me towards the back seat, then turns to Mum. His voice is unemotional as he tells her, 'I'll call for his stuff sometime tomorrow.' I peer out fretfully at her: she holds herself very still, silent and more serious than I've ever seen her.

The taxi carries me away from her, towards a new life. Our moments in the parlour and the attic are finished; young as I am, I realise this as the hot stink of stale beer fills the air inside the car.

Sometimes the big people really fuck things up for the little ones they're supposed to love.

* * *

The taxi drove through the quiet, unlit streets for what seemed like an eternity to David. After a couple of left turns it pulled into a cul-de-sac and stopped outside the last house on the stunted street. Although David didn't know it then, this was to be his home until he was 17.

Number 13 Wiles Street was only two miles from the house he had just left in Ardwick, but it felt like another country; Gorton's streets were tightly huddled, a red warren zigzagging off the main thoroughfare of Hyde Road, punctuated every few spaces by weedy crofts, small corner shops whose windows were grey with industrial dirt, and four-square pubs almost never known by their given names. Wiles Street was a dog-leg from Gorton Lane, where the reedy Gothic spire of the monastery pierced the skyline towards the city, and the rumbling brick-and-iron sprawl of the foundry lay to the right, with the shabby Steelworks Tavern between. Nearby was the Plaza cinema, known by local kids as 'the Bug Hut', for obvious reasons.

David's father bundled him out of the taxi. If another skeleton was rattling against the cupboard door, causing the family to panic, it was never allowed to break free: 'No one ever came clean about why I was taken away that night,' David affirms. 'I was kept off school for a couple of weeks and wasn't allowed to see Mum during that time. The older family members closed ranks on what happened and I never asked about it, either fearing the answer or expecting to be fobbed off. To this very day, I hate that house in Gorton; I hate every rotten brick in it with a passion.' He shakes his head slowly, remembering: 'I can still picture myself walking into it for the very first time . . .'

* * *

From David Smith's memoir:

The front door opens straight into the sitting room. No welcoming hallway, no cosy parlour, just a cramped room that remains dark even with the bare fly-bulb switched on. We go through to the kitchen – a rotten, dirty room with a pot sink, short drainage board and an old table and chair near a cast-iron fire that doesn't look as if it's been cleared since the war.

The stairs in the kitchen lead up to two doors, two bedrooms. Dad flicks the light on in one and I gaze round fearfully at a small table covered in matchboxes and crumpled cigarette packets, and an unmade, sagging double bed. An old overcoat has been thrown on top of the coarse woollen blankets for extra warmth. Dad shows me the upstairs toilet: a foul-smelling, brown-stained bucket beneath the bed. I climb under the blankets as he gestures for me to do, trying to find a spot on the pillow that isn't greasy with Brylcreem. He leaves the light on but goes out of the room and, to my surprise, I hear the door next to mine open, then two voices talking quietly. I can't make out whether the second voice is male or female. When they fall silent, I listen to two sets of footsteps going down the wooden stairs, accompanied by the unmistakeable clipping patter of a dog.

I can't sleep. I pass the hours looking straight upwards, where a low-voltage bulb dangles at the end of its cord alongside a curling brown fly-catcher encrusted with dozens of tiny black corpses. The ceiling is a sheet of peeling whitewash whose damp patches form shapes I don't like: a bearded man, an old lady with a crooked back, a menacing elephant I wouldn't want to meet in Belle Vue.

And when a pale glimmer of daylight unfurls across the rooftops I hear, for the first time, the sound of the monster.

Quietly at first, clattering in the distance, its noise getting closer by the second. Then it roars beneath a bridge and thunders past the house, rattling windows like bones, billowing thick, acrid smoke from its metal bowels. The locomotive passes less than 50 feet from the house, leaving its clinging breath behind, clouding the windows, fighting to enter and fill every room with the strong smell of burning coke.

The locomotive, I soon discover, is born out of the huge steel belly of the Beyer Peacock factory, 500 yards from Wiles Street. The building and its offspring form the thudding, filthy heart of Gorton.

I fall asleep just after daybreak. When I awake, I look for Mum and realise with a slow, creeping dread that she's not there. For the first time, I'm sharing a bed with somebody else and there's a wide chasm between us. I know this man, I belong to him, but Dad is a prickly stranger compared to the love I associate with Mum. I want to feel safe and comforted; I want not only Mum but the Duchess too – I want to go *home*. I'm so frightened I can't speak. I don't know where I am. Where has my world gone? I can't get out what's building up inside me like the steam that screams from the passing locomotives: *I want Mum*.

I keep the scream inside and let the locomotives rend the air instead.

I sit at the table in the kitchen, hands away from the sticky plastic oilcloth. I'm still wearing my pyjamas and slippers, as I will for the next few days – Dad doesn't bother to pick up my clothes for a while. I'm not on my own; an old lady is making me tea and toast. She owns the house and the first time I catch a glimpse of her outside my bedroom, I'm terrified. On the side of her head is a huge purple cyst. It isn't her fault, of course, and I'm used to deformities in my small world – Mum's hump that comes to a point between her shoulders and her wedding-ring finger that's no more than half a stump – but Elizabeth Jones has a cyst the size of a cricket ball on her forehead. Even apart from that, she's small and ugly, and in my young eyes she's the Wicked Witch of the West. It was her voice I'd heard at the top of the stairs and her dog, Minnie, scrabbling on the wooden steps. I like animals but not Minnie, who sits by the fire on her fat haunches, baring her teeth every time I move. Miss Jones tries to be kind, but I'm too repelled by her appearance to respond. I don't see much of her, though: she has a cleaning job through the day and in the evenings she drinks herself to oblivion at the Steelie.

Dad keeps me under a sort of benevolent 'house arrest' for a fortnight, hoping I'll acclimatise to the place, and him. We while away the hours playing noughts and crosses and snakes and ladders; he saves his clean shirts for the pub in the evening and sits opposite me in his vest and trousers, fingers mottled with nicotine. I feel slightly better when he collects my clothes from Mum: they're at the bottom of my bed one morning, bagged up, neatly folded and freshly ironed. Among them is Geoffrey, a white plastic giraffe. In Aked Street, he used to listen to all my woes without saying anything in return. I'm ridiculously pleased to find my oddball friend tucked among the tops, trousers, underpants and socks.

When Dad and Miss Jones are out, I stand on the doorstep gazing up and down the street, wondering which direction might carry me home. At one end of the cul-de-sac is a wall of railway sleepers and at the other, a corner shop. Sometimes, two children come out of the house next door but one to mine. The boy is fairly thick-set and wears National Health glasses with lenses like milk bottle bottoms. The girl is slightly older than me, but only by a couple of years; she has dark hair and a very sweet face. She smiles shyly at me. Her mother appears at the door to watch them leave for school. I hang back, embarrassed but curious.

Slowly, I get into a routine, helped by returning to school. For a couple of weeks, Dad travels with me on the 109 bus to Ross Place and at the end of the school day he's there again, waiting for me among the cluster of mothers. I'm still not allowed to see Mum, but he's making supreme efforts to create something real for us. Wiles Street is a tiny house with tiny, dirty rooms; sunshine never enters it, but Dad proudly produces a television, a few new chairs and a clean single bed for me. I'm especially pleased with the bed because now I can sleep alone without his chronic flatulence and beery breath as a nightcap. He gets the place fumigated, too. Until then, I sleep on a pillow streaked with red squish marks and slithers from the infestation, and at night I crush bugs beneath my fingernails against the wall. Then the fumigator arrives, sealing up the house and bringing in a cumbersome contraption to smoke 'em out. The insects return later, though.

A few days after the fumigator's visit, I sit in the living room surrounded by rolls of wallpaper and tins of paint. Dad grins at me, rolls up his sleeves and gets stuck in, and over the weekend a major transformation is achieved. He works into the night, stripping walls and mixing paint, a cigarette hanging permanently from his lip as he toils. His vest turns grey with sweat and is splattered with paint. Miss

Jones cleans up in his wake, bagging and binning the debris. Every now and then Dad rests for a while in his new chair, a well-earned bottle of beer in his hand, satisfaction etched in the gritty furrows of his forehead. Together, we watch our new television and the house breathes again, becoming lighter and smelling fresher. Dad is happy and rejuvenated, the hideous but kindly Miss Jones becomes house proud at last and we all feel different about ourselves. Only bad-tempered Minnie seems not to notice the phenomenal change that one person has achieved.

The stink of the locomotives returns gradually, together with the rolling smoke. There's no plumbed-in hot water either, just a cold tap drizzling into the pot sink. Bath night means boiling water in a pan on the stove and having a scrub-down at the sink. But it's still better than when I first arrived.

Dad trusts me now to travel to and from school on my own. In the mornings I leave early with Miss Jones and we walk to a house in nearby Benster Street. I push my hands deep into my pockets, clutching my bus fare and a few extra pennies for spends. I'm happy to make this short journey every weekday morning. Miss Jones opens a door into a backyard and my heart lifts as she leaves me to walk past the outside loo and in through the kitchen door, where a voice is calling me to 'Come right in.'

I enter a world of noisy, happy-go-lucky family bedlam. I come here every day to be 'minded' before catching the bus to school and it's always the same. Mrs Cummings stands in her apron, swathed in steam that makes her hair stick to her forehead, busily ironing the creases out of a mountain of newly laundered school clothes. Around her, children of all sizes and ages – proper ragamuffins – dart about in vests, knickers, underpants and socks, reaching for clothes to dress themselves, grooming each other like monkeys, arguing, laughing and teasing. One of the older kids holds a long toasting fork in front of the open coal fire, burning a slice of bread, then passes it to a sibling who splatters it with margarine before pushing it towards the waiting hungry mouth of a toddler.

I'm mesmerised by this family; I feel like Oliver Twist in Fagin's chaotic lair and I love it. There are twelve kids – seven boys and five girls – under the roof of a house exactly like the one I've just left in Wiles Street, but *this* hovel teems with happiness, even though Mr Cummings has tuberculosis and doesn't work. His wife has an occasional job at a local pie factory. The couple, together with their yelling, laughing brood, offer me safety and care – and morning toast that's never tasted better.

After school each day I exit the gates, turn left and stand for a while on the corner of Aked Street, daring myself to go 'home'. But when I eventually find the courage to run down the street and hammer on the door, no one answers. I change my tactics: gulping down my dinner, I sneak past the 'gate lady' in the schoolyard and rattle the letterbox of number 39, then stand to one side so that I can't be seen through the glass door panels. Mum receives me sternly and we go through to the kitchen. She sits opposite me and the firm facade softens as she struggles to explain the situation: I can't come 'home', I'm not a naughty boy but there are new rules to follow. Nonetheless I manage to extract a promise from her that she'll talk to Dad and 'sort something out'.

We return to school, where she speaks quietly to the lady on gate duty. I'm never able to sneak out again, but a few days later I emerge to find Mum standing in her usual spot, alone and apart from the other much younger mums. She's kept her promise as I knew she would, and I'm allowed to go home to Aked Street every day after school for an hour or two, provided Mum puts me on the bus to Gorton at teatime. I travel back with a bag of goodies and my usual comic books; the order for them is never cancelled. My daily existence has become a lot less dark – I've won visiting rights.

But I don't know why I've got to be back at Wiles Street for teatime. The house is always locked and empty until late. I sink down on the doorstep, day after day, whatever the weather, reading my comics and munching the last of my treats, to await the inebriated Miss Jones.

Often, the pretty girl from next door but one joins me, keeping me company even in the rain. Her mother sends her out to me with cups of tea and jam butties. We sit shoulder to shoulder, talking quietly. In time, we graduate to holding hands and dare a sweet, secret kiss. She is pure innocence and her name is Pauline Reade.

* * *

David's last year at Ross Place Primary was his most troubled. At home in Wiles Street, he and his father argued regularly, and the fights quickly became physical. 'Dad had never laid a finger on me before,' David explains with a frown, 'but it was a different story once we were living together. There were many, many fights and I always came off worst – I was only eight when he took me away from Mum, remember. But as I got older and learned how to handle myself, the fights started to be less weighed in his favour. When I was about ten or eleven, I got up one morning and couldn't find a clean shirt to put on, and moaned at Dad. He grabbed a dog-chain and hit me with it, right across my back. I retaliated and punched him in the face. I regret it now because he was my dad, when all's said and done, but I never lost another fight with him after that.'

There were other battles, more evenly balanced, at Ross Place. 'I was rebelling by then and saw myself as the cock of the school,' David laughs. 'Us illegitimates were *always* cock of the school. I suppose we felt we had something to prove. I stopped concentrating in class and started smoking when I was nine. Mum would give me a bag of sweets to take to school and often she'd hand me a two-shilling piece, which was a lot of money in those days. I'd spend it on fags in the school tuck shop, where they used to split packets of cigarettes – you'd buy only what you needed or could afford. It sounds shocking now, smoking from such a young age, but kids then were brought up in a smoker's world. *Everybody* smoked.'

He pauses, remembering. 'When I wasn't smoking, I was scrapping. One fight stands out from that last year: me and a boy called Tony Jackson were caught knocking lumps out of each other on the cricket field. The teachers broke it up on the understanding that we'd take part in an "organised" fight against each other, after school. Word went round – anyone who wanted to watch could do. All the kids turned up, of course, and stood around this makeshift ring in the middle of the playground, chanting, "Fight, fight, fight." One of the teachers stepped forward to act as referee and I was completely dumbfounded when he strapped a pair of boxing gloves on me. *Boxing gloves*! I'd never worn them before in my life. It was like putting clown shoes on a long-distance runner – a real handicap. Tony Jackson was twice my size anyway, and I wanted to gouge my nails into him, pull his hair and stick my fingers in his eyes. That, to me, was fighting. But Jackson was used to boxing, so he threw me all over the place that afternoon and was declared the winner in front of the whole school. I was gutted, but it didn't take me long to bounce back.'

Sticking with his seditious mood, David set his mind resolutely against preparing for his 11-plus exam. Aware that he was expected to pass English with flying colours, he ignored the set questions and scribbled down the lyrics of a Ray Charles song instead, then turned over the paper and waited impatiently for the bell to ring. 'I didn't want to push myself or yield to anybody's expectations of me,' he admits with a shrug. 'I couldn't be bothered with all that. Obviously I realise now just how stupid my attitude was, but aged 11 I saw things from another angle entirely. I upset my English teacher by deliberately fouling up my exams. He knew what I was capable of because he'd read the compositions in my exercise books. But the bottom line was I didn't give a damn.'

There was a particularly harrowing element in his home life that he couldn't articulate to anyone. Miss Jones' nephew occasionally stayed overnight, sharing David's bed. He abused David while the 11-year-old boy lay there terrified and silent, eyes tightly shut, pretending to be asleep. David told no one about the abuse and pushed it to the darkest recesses of his mind. He found unexpected solace in a place far beyond Gorton: 'I had some good friends back then – Roy and Dennis Cummings, and an older boy called Walter King who I got to know through our mutual love of comics. One afternoon, Roy and Dennis suggested that we should all go camping at Alderley Edge. I'd never been there before, but it soon became a favourite spot for all of us. We had to go by train, but we never paid – we'd sneak on and then jump off before the conductor caught up with us. At Alderley Edge there were woods and water, we'd climb trees, swing on ropes and build fires. I broke my collarbone after falling off a rope-swing and had to travel back on the train in agony. But I also used to go to Alderley Edge by myself and that's when I found the cave . . . it was my secret hideaway. I'd swim and paddle on my own there. It was somewhere to feel happy, far away from the misery of Gorton.'

Despite finding an escape route, David's behaviour spiralled out of control and he ended up in serious trouble, harming someone to whom he'd been close. He and one of the Cummings boys had come to blows and when Dennis Cummings pitched in to defend his younger brother, David retaliated with a knife.

'It was a terrible thing to do,' David admits, swallowing hard. 'Dennis recovered fully, but it was an unforgiveable thing that I did. These people had looked after me ever since I moved to Gorton out of sheer kindness and compassion, and that's how I repaid them.' He swallows again. 'Not good. Not good at all.'

At the age of 11, David was brought before magistrates on an assault and wounding charge. He was put on probation. Ironically, it was his aptitude for fighting that sparked the interest of the headmaster at Stanley Grove, the secondary school he began attending in autumn 1959. Sidney Silver ran a boxing club – and saw David as a potential champion.

Chapter 3

'Now there are three steps to heaven
Just listen and you will plainly see
And as life travels on
And things do go wrong,
Just follow steps one, two, and three.'
                    – 'Three Steps to Heaven', Eddie Cochran

School uniform was compulsory at Stanley Grove, but on the number 53 bus up Kirkmanshulme Lane into Longsight, David got out a needle and thread to narrow the regulation brown trousers, and only put on his school blazer when it was time to disembark. He was medium height for his age, of slim build, and out of school he favoured skinny jeans, black or white T-shirts, and winkle-pickers. Occasionally, he was sent home for infringing uniform rules, but Sidney Silver was eager to harness David's rebellious streak into something that would benefit rather than blight the school's reputation.

'You didn't get on at Stanley Grove unless you were able to bring in medals and trophies,' David recalls with a slight grimace. 'It was that sort of place. The headmaster was obsessed with accolades, which suited me down to the ground for a while.' Encouraged by Silver, David took up boxing and acquitted himself extremely well in a number of inter-school matches: 'I liked it, though the Queensberry Rules weren't my cup of tea. I just used to keep punching with my right fist until I brought my opponent down. But together with another boy called Willatt, I trained at Stretford Boys Police Club, in a room within the police station itself. We both got drawn in the Manchester Schoolboys Boxing Championships. I didn't own a pair of proper lace-up boxing boots like everybody else – I wore galoshes. But Dad promised me some boots if I won.'

The finals were held at Kings Hall in Belle Vue, home of countless amateur boxing matches. Jack Smith yelled himself hoarse among the roaring ringside crowds. 'Dad wept like a baby with pride when I won,' David recalls. 'He grabbed my certificate and was straight down to the pub with it, bursting with pleasure that his boy had come out on top. When I saw him later that night, the certificate was full of beer stains from being passed around his mates. He kept to his word, though, and bought me some proper boxing boots.'

Questioned about the relationship with his father as he was growing up, David struggles to find the appropriate words. Sensing the difficulty, Mary interjects. 'Let me answer that. They loved each other to bits, without a shadow of a doubt, but they fought like cat and dog all their lives. Even then, after an *explosive* row, Dave would chase after his dad as soon as it was over, to apologise and make sure it got sorted quickly.'

David nods, 'That's exactly it. We were all right, weren't we, when it really came down to it?'

'Very much so,' Mary replies. 'Very close, unbelievably close despite everything. Jack was always there for Dave when he needed him. Jack worshipped him.'

Keen to clarify the relationship, David explains, 'In all the books that have been written about the case, and in *See No Evil: The Story of the Moors Murders*, my relationship with Dad was only ever shown as abusive, but there was so much more to us than that. It wasn't only physical fights and shouting. Did we love each other? Yes, of course. Did we cause each other a lot of pain? Without a doubt. Women caused the biggest ructions between us as I got older because Dad was an out-and-out misogynist and I couldn't handle that. But that came later. He was beside himself when I won the fight at Kings Hall.'

Despite being selected to represent Manchester against Oldham in the 11–12 years bracket, David decided to abandon boxing after Annie told him he'd ruin his looks if he continued. 'She told me I'd end up with a broken nose and cauliflower ears. I was her baby – a substitute for the handsome boy who'd died in Crewe station – but still her baby. I was discovering girls at this point, too, and the combination of not wanting to put them off and my habit of always following Mum's advice put an end to my boxing career. Funnily enough, Dad wasn't all that concerned – he wouldn't push me into something I didn't want to do. But Sidney Silver was very displeased indeed.'

The headmaster asked to see David and Jack. It was a broiling hot afternoon as he indicated that Jack should sit opposite him, while David was made to stand. Listening to the headmaster's barely disguised irritation and watching the beads of sweat gather on the man's thin moustache, David felt his temper beginning to fray.

'Sidney Silver was well known for his handiness with the strap and slipper,' he recalls. 'If you were sent to his office, you knew something wicked was about to happen. But he was in pompous mode that day, harping on about how I was more capable than Dad realised and that he had great expectations of me in the ring. Dad didn't say a word in his own defence, but I was fuming. Being forced to stand in the hot sunlight in the study while the headmaster prattled on didn't help. All at once my temper snapped: I lunged across the desk and punched Sidney Silver square on the nose. And that was it. I was expelled on the spot.'

He gives a lopsided grin: 'I suppose there's a certain irony in my boxing career coming to an end after I floored the headmaster who didn't want me to give it up.'

Departing Stanley Grove in disgrace, David was taken on as a pupil at All Saints' School, opposite Gorton Monastery. He hated it there: 'I couldn't settle. I still only had one interest at school and that was writing. At home I'd even write short stories and poetry, just for myself. But the rest of the school day meant nothing to me.' Within a year of enrolling at All Saints, David was again in serious trouble: 'There was a fight in the playground. A boy called Percy Waddington – whose name always reminds me of a deck of cards – called me a bastard. Now, I never used illegitimacy as an excuse for my behaviour, but this *was* a period when the word "bastard" would fire me up. I was immature and still smarting at being taken from Mum. In my own eyes, I was never a bastard, but if someone else called me that . . . I couldn't just turn the other cheek.' In retaliation, David picked up a cricket bat and broke Percy's fingers. His strict probation officer, Mr Wright, was appalled when informed about the incident. With one assault and wounding charge already to his name, David was hauled before the courts again.

'Was I scared?' He nods. 'Yes. Not scared of the court itself, but really frightened about what the outcome might be.'

A short, sharp shock was proposed by the magistrates in an effort to bring David into line. Outside the courtroom a police car waited to ferry him to a substantial building set in vast grounds, from which there was to be no unsupervised leave for several weeks: Rose Hill Remand Home.

* * *

From David Smith's memoir:

I'm Tom Sawyer and the biggest confederate there ever was, Jesse James, rolled into one. Saturday is my day and I have so much to do that it gives me a headache just thinking about it. I'm a ranch-hand on his wild white steed, weaving through the traffic on Stockport Road; I'm a gunslinger holding up stagecoaches on the corner of Aked Street, and run into the hallway singing, 'Mothers, don't let your babies grow up to be cowboys.' At night, after I've had my bath and been topped and tailed, I spend an hour in the parlour behind the settee with my wooden rifle and handkerchief mask going *pom-pom* at the bad guys stalking the alleys outside . . .

. . . but then the whistle shrieks and I wake to a house I loathe, the dingy back entries of Gorton replacing the lovely cobbled streets of Ardwick. I tell myself I'm still Tom Sawyer, I am *not* David Smith, I am *not* David Hull either. Leave me alone and let me find my adventures. Gorton is not my world, it's full of thick locomotive smoke that fills my bedroom and the sun never crawls properly over the rooftops. Sleep is always ruptured by the foundry horn and late in the afternoon labourers are released from work to that same awful sound. It just goes on and on. I lie in bed trying to convince myself that these dark streets where rain falls like stair-rods aren't my streets. My street has a happy market and it has colour. Wiles Street is empty and lifeless; it's black and white, a monochrome nightmare.

I turn bad and want to be free. I am an outlaw and I want to run away, as far from Gorton as I can. And I find a place – my place – miles away at Alderley Edge: this is a secret world with a river, wonderful woods, and a cave that I call my own. I go there whenever I can, taking my sleeping bag with me. I build a raft and hide it away until I can come back again, eat beans and bread that are tastier than ever before, and wash them down with a stolen bottle of milk. David Smith has gone; I'm Tom Sawyer again and nobody knows me.

It doesn't last. They find me and take me back. They steal my world, my adventures and dreams, and put me back in their world, in Gorton, with the bedbugs and the choking, black locomotive smoke. They put the boot in and force me to grow up.

Then they send me to remand home.

* * *

Rose Hill was in the Northenden district of the Greater Manchester sprawl. Originally the ostentatious seat of the Watkin family (Sir Edward Watkin was known as 'the second railway king') throughout the Victorian era, it was acquired by the Manchester Poor Law Guardians during the outbreak of the Great War. The building served as an ophthalmia school, a convalescent home for children, and then as a residential nursery until its re-branding as a remand home in August 1955. After several incarnations, it eventually closed in May 1990. Seventeen years later, amid a large-scale investigation into children's homes in Greater Manchester, one hundred and sixty-eight former residents of Rose Hill were awarded £2.26 million as compensation for the sexual and physical abuse they suffered there. Since then, Rose Hill has been converted into luxury apartments and the enormous grounds have been divided into plots for further development.

David was not a victim of sexual abuse during his weeks at Rose Hill, but as the police car turned in at the lodge on Longley Lane, he braced himself for the harsh drill system in place at all remand homes: 'I knew it wasn't a holiday camp and I was really upset at being sent there – I wasn't nearly as hard as I made out. Like all newcomers, I went through reception upon arrival: registration, followed by a bath and the doling out of uniform. *That* came as a shock, I can tell you. They took away my leather jacket and skinny jeans and handed me a white T-shirt, green shirt, short beige trousers, knee-socks and clumpy shoes. I'd been a hip young dude until I walked through the doors of Rose

Hill, then all of a sudden there I was dressed as one of the Famous Five. I can't begin to describe how mortified I felt. If the authorities wanted to bring me down a peg or two, they were definitely going the right way about it.'

Rose Hill could accommodate up to 120 boys at a time. Most were classified 'juvenile delinquents'. Many had run away from home or institutions, had a history of truancy or disruptive behaviour at school, or criminal convictions. Most had a background comprised of several such elements. The approach among staff was to focus on 'character building' as a means of encouraging the young residents back onto the straight and narrow, through a strict timetable of work, recreation and gym.

'Rose Hill was a correctional facility where every hour of the day had to be accounted for,' David recalls. 'There weren't any high fences or tall gates but the front door was always locked and no one was permitted to go outside without adult supervision. The house itself was actually very picturesque, with enormous rooms and high, ornate ceilings. We slept in a long dormitory in neat rows of beds covered with the stiffest starched sheets imaginable. The dorm smelled super-clean because the sheets were washed with something called "lanery", which gave them their cardboard-like feel. We had daily lessons in a huge schoolroom and a certain number of boys were given tasks to do: each morning we'd line up in the big association room, where we were allowed to play pool, darts or cards in our "leisure time" and the gardener would troop in wearing his wellies and flat cap to pick his work detail for the day. The chosen few went off to a couple of greenhouses at the back of the grounds or tended the vegetables. Meals were dished out in an enormous dining room and only after dinner in the evening were we allowed into the association room to relax a bit. Everything was regimented and all activities seemed to begin and end with standing in line. It was tough, and we behaved ourselves because of that. Even gym, where you could usually let off a bit of steam, was bloody hard. We were made to play British Bulldog and goaded into really charging about and going hell for leather at each other.'

He pauses. 'You've got to remember that in those days, physical violence in places like Rose Hill was just the norm. You took your punishment whether you deserved it or not because it was all part of the correction process. At Rose Hill, a chap called Butterworth was the "dish it out" man. He'd literally punch you to the ground and you couldn't complain to the governor about it because everyone got slapped around. Funnily enough, I took to Mr Butterworth because there was something about him – not just the violence – that commanded respect. Like I said, I wasn't as anti-authority as I seemed.'

Visits from family and friends were permitted once a week and usually took place in the grounds if the weather was fine. David's dad turned up regularly with gifts of fruit, biscuits and cigarettes; the latter were a privilege at Rose Hill and any misdemeanour resulted in their immediate confiscation. Annie never visited, which came as a relief to David, since he had no wish for her to see him in there. He had other female visitors, however: his girlfriend, Maureen Siddall, and her cousin.

'Maureen was known as the Bomber,' he recalls with a smile. 'She used to wear these leather jackets and boots and was a hard case. Her cousin was known as Basher Bradshaw. What a pair, eh? Bomber and Basher. Maureen was four years older than me, but I didn't give a thought to the age difference, strange though it might seem, and neither did she, as far as I know. Having said that, those short trousers I was forced to wear at Rose Hill didn't do me any favours. And every Sunday all the residents had to take a long walk, in a well-behaved line, wearing our Rose Hill uniform. We went to Ringway Airport, of all places, and one of the streets on our journey was Brownley Road. Who should live at number 223 but my girlfriend, Maureen Siddall. Thank God she never saw me marching past in my short trousers and sensible little haircut. But she came to visit and I don't think she was impressed because she turned up on a later date with a neck full of love bites. That was the end of our relationship.'

David's release from Rose Hill found him in 'educational limbo', as he terms it: 'The authorities didn't want to know. I was still only 13, but no school was willing to take me in for ages. Then all at once I was accepted into St James's in Gorton.'

A 1968 letter from Canon Cecil Lewis, who taught at the school, reveals the staff view of David: 'He was found to be a difficult boy and it was thought that our headmaster might be able to cope better with him. This in fact proved to be true so far as school time was concerned, when at least he conformed, even if he did not really cooperate . . . I always regretted that he did not come to us earlier. I always found him on the defensive, if ever I tried to speak to him – always thinking you were against him . . . I sometimes wish I had pushed a little harder to try to win his confidence.'

For his part, David viewed St James's as 'the last chance saloon. But I didn't care, even then. I had no interest in lessons, other than English. The teacher for that subject was a big bloke called Mr Drummond. I respected him, and enjoyed his classes, but even then I was often disruptive. During one lesson, he got so fed up with me that he bawled me out on a threat. He followed me into the corridor and closed the classroom door. I braced myself, expecting to be punished, but instead he said very quietly, "Right, David, I'm going to pretend to hit you and I want you to make the relevant noises. Then you're going to return to your desk and get on with your work." I was flabbergasted and from then on I worked like hell in his lessons. The best thing about St James's was that I knew all my fellow pupils already. And it was there that I met Gloria Molyneaux.'

There had already been other girls, besides the Bomber. Barbara, who taught David how to kiss; Valerie, the greengrocer's daughter, who noisily ate an orange throughout intercourse; Pat, who let him go 'all the way' whenever they were together; posh Maureen Verity, whose increasing obsession with Cliff Richard sounded the death knell on their romance, and several clandestine 'encounters' with sisters of close friends. He also remained on friendly but chaste terms with Pauline Reade, whose sensitive brother he used to wind up mercilessly, pretending to be a vampire on one occasion and on another convincing him that the devil could be summoned from the fireplace with a few taps of a poker on the hearth.

But Gloria was 'something else'. She was different from the girls with whom David had grown up; her naturally blonde hair was long and chic, and she spoke nicely. The daughter of the church caretaker, she lived with her family on Hyde Road, out towards Reddish way. Her arrival at school caused a stir among the girls *and* the boys, with the latter immediately vying for her attention. 'Gloria had real style,' David recalls. 'She really was *posh*. Nothing like the Gorton girls. All the boys fancied her, but there were only two real contenders for her affections: me, and Tony Latham, who had been cock of the walk at St James's until I turned up. We decided to fight it out, but in a very civilised fashion – Tony knocked on my door to call for me beforehand and off we went to the back entry near the croft at the end of Bannock Street. Tony won the fight, but I got the girl, so it was a bit pointless really. But that's boys for you.'

The relationship quickly developed between David and Gloria: 'At first it was just a case of her popping round to Wiles Street to spend an evening with me. But then we started sleeping together and worried about Gloria getting pregnant because we were "at it" constantly. I knew about condoms, but we just wanted to be sure and felt that we needed some adult advice. So we visited a teacher from St James's: Mr Fitzgerald. He was only a little fella, but I got on very well with him and so, one night after school, I knocked on his door with Gloria at my side. His wife let us in and made up a tea tray while we went into his parlour to talk. I suppose we were very forward, and I realise now what an awkward position we put him in because we were clearly underage. But he was very sensible, and gave us plenty of sound advice about condoms and so on, adding that if we had any more problems we were to speak to him and could rest assured that he wouldn't betray our confidence. We trotted off feeling very pleased indeed, as if we'd got the stamp of authority on what we were doing.'

He pauses and reaches again for his cigarettes. 'But it wasn't long before another girl came on the scene. I was still seeing Gloria, but there were a handful of nights every month when she was "washing her hair", so to speak, and I was at a loose end. This other girl . . . I got to know her just hanging around the street corners and waiting in the queue at the chippy – that sort of thing. Very casual.'

He taps a cigarette on the broad kitchen table and takes a deep breath before exhaling slowly: 'At first, it was just necking – me and this other girl would be at it up the back entries and in Wiles Street on the nights when Gloria was "washing her hair".' He gives a short laugh. 'I wasn't about to sit in on my own in them days. But then the necking became a proper relationship. It was difficult because I was still courting Gloria, although things went downhill rapidly after the headmaster hauled us both into his office following a complaint about me from Gloria's dad. He read us the riot act, big time.'

He smiles, remembering: 'Gloria was very similar to the Sandra character from *Grease* and I was . . . well, from another movie altogether! Gloria left school anyway, soon after the meeting in the headmaster's study. She moved out of the area and found work in a nursery. I kept seeing her for a while – Sammy Jepson used to give me a lift on his motorbike to the nursery, but our time had been and gone, really.' He shakes his head and laughs again, '*And* little did I know, but after Sammy dropped me home he would roar off back to the nursery alone to spend a bit of quality time with Gloria himself. But that didn't last either, because he got someone else pregnant. In the meantime, my relationship with the other girl became serious. More serious than I realised . . .'

* * *

From David Smith's memoir:
I picture you on the street corner, Maureen Hindley. Hair in rollers and wearing a headscarf, cigarette hanging from the side of your lipstick-slicked mouth.

Someone's brought a transistor outside and we're all stood round listening to Jimmy Savile on Radio Luxembourg.

You grab a girlfriend – your best mate, Basher Bradshaw – and start to jive madly, skirts flying high, with one hand holding down the front for decency, every wild twirl exposing thighs and a flash of knickers. You can dance, girl, and you look the part, too: heavily lacquered, bleached blonde backcombed hair and eyes made-up like Dusty's – huge and ringed with thick pencil and heavy mascara.

We boys watch you while we slouch against the wall (no one *leans* against the walls in our gang; we slouch, an art form that takes hours of serious practice). When Elvis starts to sing 'It's Now or Never', we unpeel ourselves from the bricks and move in for the smooch. I make my play, throwing away my half-smoked cigarette before claiming you. My arms go around your waist, your arms go around my neck, and we move in close. You make for my neck like a vampire and I expose it like a peacock, allowing you to suck until it hurts, letting you cover last week's love bites without asking where they come from. We rock and we roll, we laugh together, and we don't care about anything because we're young.

Later in the day I sit in Sivori's cafe, drinking coffee with the boys. We all wear the Belt: a leather buckled thing, crammed with as many chrome studs as it can hold, worn for style but often used for fighting. Knuckledusters and flick knives are brought out to be admired. Most of the boys – Sammy, Pete and the O'Gorman brothers – wear cocky Andy Capp hats pushed back just enough to show off the quiffs below. The caps come in two different shiny shades: blue and black stripes, or red and black. But I never wear one because I don't want to hide the hair I've spent so long getting just right. I look down at my shoes: full-pointed winkle-pickers with cowboy-style buckles – no blue suede shoes or beetle-crushers for me – worn with black jeans and the chrome-studded belt. Twelve-inch zips run down the outside of each leg of my jeans, enabling only the thinnest of shocking pink or baby blue fluorescent socks to be pulled on beneath. I always wear a T-shirt, either black or white. I prefer black, worn with a crucifix, which these days is more of a fashion statement than evidence of the Catholicism of my childhood.

And you, Maureen, you have your style. A good blouse, often teamed with a very long cardigan, and a skirt so tight above the knees that you can only hobble – or else a full skirt with a wire in the hem (mostly for dancing). The full skirt is dangerous if you sit down without thinking: the front might pop up around your face, revealing the stockings and suspenders we all love.

Today, as usual, you sit with the girls, pretending not to notice me. I wait for the record on the jukebox to finish. Then I get up, amble towards the boys, share a laugh with them and stand by the neon machine, biding my time. I know you're waiting and listening. I feel the jukebox with both hands and press the money into the slot.

Bill Fury's languid voice fills the room. I glance across, unsmiling, and hold your gaze. You don't look away and so I allow the smile.

Halfway to Paradise is about right . . .

Sitting around, watching the girls, or cruising on the back of Sammy's motorbike . . . summer lasts for ever around Sivori's. And those early long summers with the boys and the girls will one day fade away, but I know I'll always remember the kisses and the moves. Years later, hearing 'Hey Paula', 'Ebony Eyes' and 'Leader of the Pack', I smile secretly and feel good inside.

On this sunny afternoon in Sivori's, you're there for me, just as you will be in the weeks, months and years ahead. We don't court in the conventional sense, but when my mother dies, you'll comfort me; when I break with a girlfriend, you'll listen to me; and when I fight my father, it's you I'll turn to afterwards. We love each other against the damp walls of the back alleys, and on the bumpy Saturday night couch in your parents' home on Eaton Street, with Elvis crooning from the Dansette. Sometimes you wear a skirt so tight we have to fumble our way to each other, but we don't give up until we get there.

Without knowing it, you'll own my teenage years. You'll become part of me without agreeing to anything. You'll be my confidante before I understand what that means – and it's the same for me, getting to know you, and your family.

You loathe your father, Bob, and worship your mother, Nellie, whose mannerisms you've inherited. You get on fine with your gran and aunties and cousins, especially Auntie Ann's daughter Glenys.

And you have a sister.

Myra.

II

When It's Dark the Music Stops

1961–65

Chapter 4

'I fell into a burning ring of fire
I went down, down, down,
And the flames went higher, and it burns, burns,
burns,
The ring of fire
The ring of fire.'

– 'Ring of Fire', Johnny Cash

The Hindleys lived at 20 Eaton Street, Gorton. Bob Hindley, Maureen's father, was in his late 40s when his younger daughter began hanging around with David Smith. Having served as an aircraft fitter attached to the Parachute Regiment during the war, he found it hard to adjust to civilian life after being demobbed. For a time, he was employed as a labourer at Beyer Peacock and earned extra money fighting in the local 'blood tubs' until an accident at work left him a semi-invalid. He became a morose drunk, spending his days shuffling between an unhappy home and the vault of the Steelworks Tavern. His marriage to Nellie Maybury was a tempestuous one, fraught with blistering rows and physical violence on both sides, while neither of his two daughters were inclined to spend much time with him, taking their mother's part instead.

Maureen was the less academic of the two girls, with a lackadaisical attitude to life. Born on 21 August 1946, she was timid as a child and relied on her elder sister, the tomboyish Myra, to protect her from neighbourhood bullies. As a practical arrangement, Myra had lived since the age of four with her widowed gran, Ellen Maybury, a frail, diffident lady in her 70s who doted on her firstborn granddaughter. Despite living apart

(Maureen with her parents in Eaton Street, Myra with Gran in nearby Bannock Street), the sisters remained exceptionally close. Myra usually addressed Maureen by the childhood nickname 'Mobee'. She was still as protective towards her younger sister throughout their teenage years, even though Maureen had learned to stick up for herself by then; she was one of the Taylor Street gang, tough-talking and hard to beat in a fight. Physically, the two were very different, though they both wore their hair in permanent stiff clouds of candyfloss blonde and favoured heavy eye make-up, but Maureen was slim with birdlike features while Myra was sturdily built and sporty. They differed in their ambitions, too: Maureen was happy in her surroundings and looked forward to marriage and motherhood, while her sister dreamed of a life beyond Manchester and wanted to share it with someone more sophisticated than the boys she knew. Maureen worked in a succession of low-paid factory and retail jobs, but by 1961 Myra had a position 'with prospects' as a secretary at Millwards Merchandising, a chemical wholesalers off Levenshulme Road.

Ruminating on his early relationship with Maureen, David explains: 'She was just always there. Saturday night in the chip shop: Maureen. Friday in Sivori's: Maureen. Every single day on the street corners: Maureen, again. She was part of my clique. That was the thing about Gorton: I hated the place, but I loved my mates and the girls. I loved Taylor Street chippy, Maureen Hindley, Basher Bradshaw, Sammy Jepson and his roaring 750cc Vincent motorbike, and the Cummings lot. In a way, it was like being part of an extended family. Everyone knew each other and life revolved around those streets – hell, my life *was* those streets. Loitering in cafes and necking up the back entries, with girls actually *asking* for love bites – I was only too delighted to oblige. But I always went back to Maureen.'

He was aware of Myra but had little to do with her then: 'She didn't hang around the streets like the rest of us. The only time I ever saw her out and about was when she was "in transit" between Eaton Street and Bannock Street. She'd either be walking very fast and purposefully with her arms folded, or clicking in her high heels down the street carrying two plates balanced on top of each other. Nellie cooked tea for her daughter and Granny Maybury every night.'

Then he grimaces: 'The only other time I'd see Myra was when she was in a temper, heading home to sort out her drunken father. Husbands in those days were real Jekyll and Hyde characters. Street angels and house devils, we used to say.'

* * *

From David Smith's memoir:

I'm lazing in Sivori's, bored, playing the jukebox for myself: Duane Eddy's 'Rebel Rouser' and The Everley Brothers' 'Ebony Eyes'. Smoking nineteen to the dozen and enjoying feeling moody, as teenagers do.

Maureen's sister Myra pushes open the door and approaches me with a smile: 'Hiya, have you seen our Mobee? I need to speak to her.' I tell her I'm waiting for Maureen myself and ask what's the message, though I can probably guess. It's Saturday, which means 'girly night' for the sisters, who have a routine of doing one another's hair every weekend. Tonight Myra wants Maureen to do the honours; Bob and Nellie will be going out separately as is their ritual, so Eaton Street will be free to serve as this week's salon.

I slyly note their plans. I'm happy: it gives me a place to go on a Saturday night, plus I might get lucky on the settee instead of making do with a knee-trembler up against the wall of a back entry. These days are good days, hot and long, played out to the music of America, hormones ready to offload by the bucketful.

Myra leaves with a smile – 'See ya, Dave' – and Maureen arrives about an hour later: a much slimmer version of Myra, with panda eyes and the trademark cigarette in hand. She always enters with a flourish, full of life, posing, pretending not to notice me, giggling with a few friends while I sit faking a mood. Eventually she comes across and we spend the afternoon together in Siv's, drinking espresso and feeding the jukebox until it's time to go.

We walk down Taylor Street, my right arm slung around Maureen's shoulder and her left arm about my waist, gripping my studded leather belt. When we arrive at Eaton Street, her parents are out. The house is a carbon copy of every other in the neighbourhood: a poky back-to-back with a loo in the yard. I go for a piss in the damp little brick outhouse. Yesterday's *Daily Mirror* has been ripped into squares and pinned to a nail on the wooden door. The only luxuries are a well-used toilet brush and a rubber plunger.

Back indoors, Myra still hasn't turned up, so I busy myself choosing records from Maureen's music collection. There's a good coal fire going, but the chimney needs sweeping – smoke burps throatily into the living room. Old dinner smells filter through the house: Maureen's meal of boiled cabbage, meat and gravy sits on a pan of simmering water, kept warm with a lid that rattles every so often. I get up and open the front door to draw the fire. Smoke wafts out onto the street as I sit down to listen to Elvis warbling from the red-and-cream Dansette.

Suddenly Myra appears in the doorway, flustered. 'Sorry I'm late, got behind with my job, you're not going out tonight are you, Mobee?' She pulls a face and wheedles, 'Say you're not going out, oh please, please, my hair is a mess, be a little angel and do it for me . . .'

She sets down two large bottles of Bulmers cider and throws Maureen a packet of Park Drives. Sound, I think to myself: a drop of cider, ciggies, the chance of a promise – this is what I call a Saturday night. Maureen brings in three coffee mugs. No posh glasses in this house, just mugs and a pint pot belonging to Bob. The set-up among the Hindleys is much the same as any other family in these streets: Bob's a fighter, Nellie's a bawler, and the two girls accept that being female is a hardship.

That's just how it goes.

The Hindleys are no better or worse than the rest of us; we've all got our problems and most of them are pretty similar. Take the girls' parents: Bob and Nellie both drink in the same pub, the Steelworks Tavern, but Bob drinks in the men-only vault and Nellie sits in the lounge with the women. Every Sunday night, Bob joins his wife in the lounge bar. Those nights are 'safe', but Fridays and Saturdays, when they drink in the same pub but in separate rooms, are unpredictable and often deadly.

But, like I said, that's just how it goes.

We sit with our cider and ciggies, listening to Brenda Lee and the Big Bopper. The girls are as close as sisters can be and both share the same priority: Nellie. Myra is the big sister not only to Mobee, but to her mother as well; she's the mannish female with nice legs, great tits and the punch of a heavyweight boxer. She can flash a smile one minute and cut you to ribbons with a glare the next. That's the Myra I know.

The girls natter about Granny Maybury and gossip about the neighbours – who's going with whom and who's finished with whom

– but Maureen's evading Myra's most pressing question. In the end, out it comes: 'So, how's Mam then, Mobee?'

Maureen's answer is quick, practised and level: 'She's fine, Myra, she's fine. She's gone out with Brenda Johnson from number six. Yes, she's fine. She's OK.'

'And how was *he* last night?' Myra never refers to Bob as anything other than 'he'. 'Pissed as usual?'

'Oh, he wasn't bad. Mum got herself off to bed the minute he came in. She gave him his supper and left him in his chair. Everything was all right, Myra. I swear it.'

Myra frowns, her pencilled eyebrows meeting beneath the blonde cloud. 'Well, if he steps out of line, you come and get me. Do you hear me, Mobee? Even if it's the middle of the night, you come and get me. No matter what, if he fucking kicks off, you leg it round to our gran's and you get me. Promise me you will, Mobee. *Promise*.'

Maureen agrees, but Myra isn't quite finished. 'Never let anybody hurt you either, and if they do you come and see *me*, understand?' She flashes me one of her special hard looks to emphasise that she's in the 'all men are bastards' mood. I stare back, then shrug my shoulders, thinking, 'Screw you, Myra, you're some bit of stuff.'

The girls go into the kitchen. Maureen washes Myra's hair at the Belfast sink. I listen to them laughing together and re-stack the Dansette: time for a bit of Eddie Cochran to liven the joint up. I picture Bob and Nellie drinking in their separate rooms at the Steelie. Poor lonely sods. After all these years they've finally lost each other, nothing to show for their lives but two daughters, nothing else in common any more.

The girls enter the living room. Much preening of Myra's hair follows, a lot of backcombing and lacquer fizzing overhead. It smells like a proper salon, all wet and then slightly scorched. They chat about the latest mascara brands and whisper about their monthlies. A real rock 'n' roll Saturday night out for me.

Myra takes a turn at the Dansette and Mobee greets her choice with a scream of approval. The girls grab each other and dash to the middle of the room. I quickly push the Formica coffee table out of the way and the girls begin to jive. Mobee spins like a whirlwind, out of control. Myra catches her, mirroring every move as they sing 'Da Do Ron Ron' at the tops of their voices, laughing hysterically – just happy girls together.

*

Two or three weeks later, the Saturday after Good Friday. Why *do* we Catholics call it Good Friday? In Gorton, there's nothing good about Fridays. Pay day and getting double-pissed, the wife's housekeeping to one side and the undeclared leftovers down your sodding throat, screw them all, the long, the short and the tall. That's Friday in Gorton.

Late afternoon finds me in Siv's again, preening myself and messing about with the jukebox. Maureen comes in without her usual giggle and tease; she's white-faced and drawn, smoking like one of the filthy locomotives that pass my window day and night.

'Dave, it's Mam. There's been a bit of trouble – *he* kicked off again last night . . .'

Good Friday.

'. . . and he's at it again today. Come to the house and talk to him. He'll listen to you.'

Will he *fuck*, I think, knowing Bob is long past listening to anyone, stuck as he is in a two-up, two-down shit hole, surrounded by angry females and nursing his memories. He used to be a muscled paratrooper, now he's an unemployable cripple; why the hell should he listen to anyone, least of all me?

'He's not himself, Dave. If Myra finds out, she'll go off her head. *Please* come to the house with me – have a cup of tea or something.'

I know Bob's safety isn't paramount to Maureen; she's frightened about what might happen if Myra and he come to blows.

I slide reluctantly off my chair and follow Maureen's clacking heels down Taylor Street, insisting there is no *way* I'm arguing with Bob. His reputation at the back of the Steelie is enough for me.

We arrive at Eaton Street. The front door opens straight into the living room, just like my home in Wiles Street. A well-oiled Bob sits hunched and morose in his chair by the fireplace. Maureen goes through to her mother in the kitchen.

I take a seat opposite Bob, lowering myself into Nellie's chair. 'How's it going then, Bob?'

He lifts a half-filled glass of whisky above his head in acknowledgement. 'Sound, you fucker, fucking sound.'

Bob is still fighting the war – this time out of a bottle.

Insistent female voices reach us from the kitchen, raised not in temper but pleading. Nellie appears carrying two covered plates for Myra and Granny Maybury, as is her daily ritual. I'm familiar with the routine, but the sight of her face startles me. She makes no effort to hide the battered mess: one eye is completely closed and swollen, bulging blackly from its socket, and her top lip is engorged, the bloated flesh almost touching the tip of her nose.

She struggles to speak as she stands there, determined to show that she's still a proud woman despite everything. The words come out in an injured lisp: 'Fuck you, Bob Hindley, fuck you to hell and back!'

I sense real misery behind the anger, even though she obviously means every muffled syllable.

Bob erupts, shouting at his wife and to the rest of the world: 'Fuck off!' I flinch as he hurls his glass across the room. It doesn't break, but rolls noisily across the floorboards into a corner. 'Just *fuck off*!'

Nellie goes out, still carrying the covered plates, and I sit silently, tapping my fingertips on the chair arm, bracing myself for more trouble.

It's not long in coming.

The front door flies open with a resounding bang and Myra strides into the room, cursing Bob to the heavens. She stands quivering with fury before him as he struggles up from the chair.

'Come on, you bastard!' she screams. 'Get up, fucking stand up, you fucking useless piece of shit!'

But Bob can't. He's too drunk, and unsteady on his feet at the best of times. His fists are clenched, though, waiting for the fight, but he's no longer any match for Myra; she hammers into him, punching fast and full in the face. Bob is too slow to protect himself from the onslaught. Blood spurts from his nose and mouth, scattering down his shirt.

'Fucking bastard, fucking *big man*!' she screams. 'Come on, fucking come *on*!'

With both hands, she grabs Bob by the hair, lifting him clean out of the chair. He makes a clumsy attempt to grab her throat, but Myra is quick and strong; she throws him to the floor like a rag, smashing the coffee table.

Then she snatches up his walking stick from the side of his chair.

I turn my face away, having learned a long time ago that no one thanks you for intervening in a Hindley brawl. Head averted, I listen unwillingly as Myra brings the walking stick down on her father's spine, again and again, whack after sickening whack.

Then Nellie arrives home. She doesn't interfere either, but stands by the door with her arms folded, watching.

When it's over, Bob makes no effort to lift himself up. His damaged mouth moves against the floorboards: 'Fuck off, all of you, just fuck off.'

Myra throws the walking stick down and crosses the room, enveloping her mother in a bear hug. 'Mam, you tell me if this piece of shit even *looks* at you the wrong way again.'

Maureen stares big-eyed at the scene from the kitchen, her arms tightly folded. Myra then dispenses a hug to her, adding firmly, 'Mobee, we have to look after our mam, she doesn't have to put up with this. How can we look out for each other if you don't come to me?'

Maureen clings to her sister.

I lean forward, elbows on knees, and turn sideways to peer at Bob heaving himself back into his chair. His long face is blotchy with blood and rage.

Myra disentangles herself from Maureen's hold to point a rigid finger at him: 'And you, not one word. If there's a next time, you end up in hospital or the fucking cemetery.'

He glares at her and spits, 'Fuck off.'

She's across the room in an instant. The flat of her hand lands on his face in a stinging wallop. 'I *said*, not one word. That was *two*. Now keep your fucking mouth *shut*.'

I get up and go outside.

Maureen, Myra and Nellie aren't far behind me, but I leave them at the door and walk to the end of Eaton Street. I can hear Myra telling Nellie and Maureen not to be scared, that she isn't going out tonight and will be at Granny Maybury's if they need her. I loiter on the corner, nudging a small stone out of a crack in the pavement. Myra kisses her mother and sister, then Maureen links arms with her mum and the two of them go indoors. Nellie disappears, Myra marches back to Granny Maybury, and Maureen emerges from number 20 to shuffle in her tight skirt up the street to me.

Situation sorted.

* * *

In 1963, David's world altered irrevocably when Annie died from cancer. Following treatment for her illness, Annie spent six months convalescing at the hotel owned by the Duchess and Bert. David was on his way to visit her one afternoon when an old man sitting on a wall hailed him at the bus stop.

'You know your mum's dead?' the man called.

David froze. Then he began running, and arrived at the hotel to find the whole family already gathered, talking quietly about Annie's passing. The Duchess took his arm and led him into the bedroom where Annie lay, the colour blanched from her skin. He looked down at her for a moment then walked out, roaming a nearby park in stunned silence. He told himself she had no right to die on him: 'She should have fought for me. And it shouldn't have been up to some bloke on the street to tell me she's gone.'

After a while he boarded the bus back to Gorton: 'I was 15 and broken within. I felt like nothing was left for me but the streets where I lived, and Maureen. She'd always been there. I went to her house and we disappeared into the darkness of a back entry on Eaton Street. Then I let everything out, ripping my shirt to shreds, punching both fists into a door until my knuckles bled. The pain left me empty and crying like a baby. Maureen kissed and comforted me, giving me that special feminine sympathy that makes all hurt little boys feel better.'

'I was growing up quick,' he reflects. 'I'd worked out long ago what the real family relationships were and had more or less got used to it. Mum was ill for a long time, so it didn't come as a shock as such – it was how I found out that got to me. That – and not being allowed to go to Mum's funeral. The family felt that was best for some reason. And, boy, did that hurt – physically and mentally, it really bloody hurt. They were firm I wasn't to go and never explained why. I needed to say goodbye to Mum properly, but that was denied to me and I never got over it . . .'

* * *

From David Smith's memoir:

On the day of Mum's funeral, Maureen is the only one I can share my tears with – she allows the thunder to roar out of me again and keeps the secret of my grief between the two of us. I still don't know if it's love or just the moment that brings us fully together and sets the time bomb ticking.

I go back to Aked Street for a while after Mum's death, but it's not the happy house I remember. Standing on the doorstep, cold but calm, I watch the empty street for the family's return, cursing the aunt or uncle who decided I should look after Grandad. My duties go no further than cleaning his stinking room and removing the overflowing phlegm boxes. At night, I telephone Maureen – red Ardwick telephone box to red Gorton telephone box – and she listens patiently to me. I don't need anyone but her.

There's no sign of the black cars, so I leave the front door open and wander through the house. In the scullery, I stand beside the small mountain of booze that usually only appears at Christmas: several crates of beer and numerous bottles of whisky, brandy, port and Harveys Bristol Cream. On impulse I peer into the old hiding place behind the unused stove. Reaching in, I pull out exactly what I expected to find: three dust-covered pint bottles of Mum's precious Guinness. I give a small laugh, remembering all the times I sprinted to the off-licence back in my cowboy days.

Replacing the bottles, I return again to the front step, but the street is still empty. I lean against the door. Mum is dead and I can accept it in my own way, with the memory of kissing her cold, pale skin so recent in my mind. But I shouldn't be here alone in Aked Street while she's lowered into the earth. I want to be at the graveside, saying goodbye as it should be done; she raised me to do the right thing. I squeeze my eyes shut and imagine myself standing with the rest of the family as she goes down to rest beside her brown-eyed soldier boy. Just to be there, to let fall a handful of earth among the flowers, to do what is right before walking away for the last time – that's what *should* be happening. Not this pain that will stay with me for ever, the one that rips through me like the knife I always used to carry.

A low rumble reaches me from the end of the street. The cars turn in slowly and I flick my half-smoked cigarette into the gutter. A moment ago everywhere was deserted, but as the two black Princess limousines (courtesy of 'Stiles the Undertaker') pull up slowly outside the house, people appear all along the street until there isn't a doorstep without a housewife or married couple silently paying their respects.

It isn't a big family gathering, just the 'immediates' and me. I watch them emerging from the cars, middle-aged men and women in their sombre best, looking almost regal for once. I stick out like a sore thumb in my drainpipe jeans, winkle-pickers, white shirt and bootlace tie. Dad and Grandad appear, followed by the Duchess and Uncle Bert, and finally all the posh aunties who haven't set foot in Mum's house for years: Ida, Barbara, Dorothy and Debora. I watch as two sisters help their seemingly distraught father indoors; Grandad knows how to play to an audience, even when it's only the locals. I step aside and mutter a polite hello to the women who, despite my adoption, have always remained aunties to me, never siblings.

The Duchess comes in last and I know she's hung back purposely to have a word with me.

'Have you remembered to light a fire in the parlour, David?'

I nod my head.

She touches my arm. 'Good lad.' She gives me a searching look. 'Are you all right?'

I open my mouth for a glib reply, then admit, 'No, not really.'

She pats my arm gently, 'I know . . . I understand.' And I believe her.

I leave the rest of the family to settle themselves down. In the backyard I smoke a couple of cigarettes and tell myself, 'This is Mum's day. This is *my* mum's day.' When I return to the kitchen, our neighbours Mrs Barnes and Mrs Yates are busily arranging sandwiches, cakes and a fresh pot of tea on the table. Both ladies ask sympathetically how I'm bearing up and I tell them fine, thanks. I like Mrs Barnes a lot; she has a son just a few years older than me – a 100 per cent, straight-up, dyed-in-the-wool Ted. Not a thug, just a good old boy who knows how to dress to impress and loves his mum and the music. Decent people.

My nerves are starting to splinter, so I head upstairs for a leak before facing the gathering. Coming out of the bathroom, my feet move on instinct towards Mum's room. I turn the white doorknob, but the door seems to open of its own accord anyway.

A deep silence fills the room like a presence. Throughout the house all the curtains have been drawn to mark our mourning, but in here I can still make out the furniture, pictures and ornaments as if sunlight floods the room. Everything is just as Mum left it, perfectly in place. Her double bed is neatly made with the ironed creases visible on the turned-down sheet. It feels as if she hasn't rested her head on the pillows here for years, as if she's passed this room eternally by to climb the second flight of stairs to where her beloved dead son waits. I stand before her dressing table and gaze at my reflection unseeingly. I feel very young and very small. My hands hover over the surface of the dressing table. It's crowded with fancy containers of every shape and size, all positioned very precisely; the essential female accoutrements that are forever a mystery to men.

I lift a small but surprisingly heavy box. A very noble swan has been hand-painted on the ice-blue porcelain lid. Inside is a fine, pale brown powder. When I hold it to my nose, the gentle smell stirs forgotten memories, and I rub a fingernail of dust over my cheekbones, near my nose. I rub so hard that my skin burns as the powder sinks into my complexion, leaving only its scent. I breathe in deeply and sense that Mum is near, very near.

The rising murmur of conversation from the floor below disturbs me. I put the box back among its companions and go swiftly downstairs. Outside the parlour, I pause: that door has never been left open as long as I can remember. Today it's slightly ajar and I glimpse relations through a haze of cigarette smoke. The latch that I used to lift while standing tiptoe on a chair is well within my reach now; I push the door and close it behind me again.

All the chairs are taken, so I lean against a wall, fumbling for my cigarettes, and stand quietly alone, thinking, 'This isn't right, it's all *wrong*, everyone shut up and stop ruining my memories. This is *my* world, mine and Mum's, our special room, this is where I come from, so shut the fuck *up*.'

I force the tension to pass, holding the smoke in my mouth and putting a finger against my cheekbone to bring the fragrance of Mum's powder out. Across the room, above the fireplace, hangs another of the many sepia photographs dotted about the house. I gaze at Mum and Grandad standing youthfully within the glass oval, sharing a loving look and surrounded by small, uncomfortable children in smart outfits. One little boy returns my stare more piercingly than the others. Frank is the only one missing from this gathering in the parlour. Or is he here? Unseen by any of us, but leaning against the wall in his khaki uniform, brown eyes watchful and knowing.

I shouldn't be here, I tell myself, lowering my eyes from his. I don't want to be here. I notice Mum's lovely gramophone being used as a drinks trolley, half-empty bottles of port and Harveys Bristol Cream forming sticky rings on its gleaming mahogany top.

The Duchess catches my eye from the opposite corner, where she sits with an empty glass. I mimic taking a drink myself while pointing at her, and she nods with a smile. So I leave the parlour, shutting the door quietly, and walk to the scullery, where several empty bottles have appeared on the table.

'Fuck it,' I tell myself, reaching behind the stove to grab a bottle of Guinness. I flick off the dust and the cobwebs, open the top, and take a half-pint glass from the table before returning to the parlour, where my aunties are clustered on the settee. I have to pass them at close quarters to reach the Duchess and decide on the spur of the moment to let the devil in me loose. Faking clumsiness, I stumble, grab the stockinged knee of the lady closest to me, giving it a bit of a squeeze and causing the women to fuss like hens.

Ignoring them, I hand the Duchess her Guinness and say loudly, 'Mum left you a drink.'

The Duchess beams at me, then replies equally loudly, 'Tell her thank you from me.'

Auntie Ida's voice freezes the smile on my face: 'David, love, be an angel and open that door for a bit of air. I can hardly get my breath in here.'

Open the parlour door and *leave* it open? Get some air into a room that's never been sullied by fag ash and smoke, booze drunk and booze spilled? *No fucking way*, I think, but instead I nod, 'Not a problem, Auntie Ida.'

I walk over to the door, open it and leave it ajar. I go into the hall and move towards the front door. It crosses my mind to turn back and shut the parlour door, fastening the latch to lock the lot of them in, but I place one foot determinedly in front of the other until I'm out into the street.

Somewhere deep within me I know that this will be the last time I ever see my family en masse, but the thought doesn't slow me. It's time to draw the curtain on my memories of that house and this street; I go on walking until home is out of sight and I'm on the traffic-congested thoroughfare of Stockport Road, its bland, busy pavements giving me the anonymity I crave.

I think I've said goodbye to Aked Street. But in a few short months I'll return twice to seek refuge in the parlour again: first to pass an endless night grieving for my baby daughter and the second to find sanctuary following the savage murder of a boy my own age, from these same streets.

I wait for the bus, feeling as though I've finally left my childhood behind. On the top deck of the 109, I light a cigarette, rub my cheek again, and think of Maureen. She isn't expecting me today, but I can't wait to be with her. When I jump down from the bus, I have to fight the urge to run through the red warren of terraces, crowded corner shops, pubs and empty churches. The houses are so small you can almost hear what's happening behind each front door.

I reach Eaton Street and knock loudly, excited and breathless, happy to be back in the shit hole where I now belong.

Nellie appears, unable to hide her surprise at seeing me.

I'm painfully aware of the daft grin plastered across my face as I ask, 'Hello, Mrs Hindley, is Maureen home?'

Nellie knows it's Mum's funeral today and can tell from my expression that I'm not myself. 'Is everything all right, David?' she questions, then corrects herself: 'Are *you* all right?'

I shuffle impatiently. 'I'm fine, thanks, everything's fine. I just need to see Maureen.'

Nellie frowns. 'Well, she's gone out somewhere. A couple of the girls called for her about an hour ago and they've gone for a walk.'

'Right, thanks, Mrs Hindley. I'll catch up with her. Bye.'

I know she's watching me, arms folded Hindley-style, as I stroll down the street and turn the corner. Out of sight on Taylor Street I break into a desperate run.

It's too early for the chip-shop meet, so I run along the main roads to Sivori's. I know that's where Maureen will be – she's got to be, I tell myself. Stopping short of the cafe, I stand before a shop window to get my breath back, straightening the bootlace tie and taking the metal comb from the back pocket of my jeans to marshal my hair into an immaculate quiff. I give myself the once-over and like what I see, then pause deliberately before pushing open the door.

The pulsating rhythms of rock 'n' roll and the reek of strong espresso hit me as I walk in, posing as usual, cool and moody: *the Image is Back*. Maureen sits with her gang of girls, eyes panda-black, cigarette dangling limply from her fingers in a way only she can make sexy. Before her is a small white cup with a lipstick smear, and below the table she taps her court shoes to Del Shannon's latest hit.

Then she sees me and her smile lights up the cafe better than any jukebox neons.

She waves and I slouch over to sit among the girls. Leaning across, I kiss her softly on the cheek – something I've never done before. She reacts with obvious shock and her eyes spill concern. I listen with total lack of interest to the bubbly chatter of her friends while Buddy Holly raves on from the spinning black vinyl. I realise that Maureen has fallen silent and is watching me, her face serious and still. Something new is happening between us; I can feel it and know that she does, too.

I get up, needing to occupy myself, and feed coins into the jukebox, pressing the buttons before walking to an empty table and sitting with my back against the wall. I stare at Maureen and she returns my gaze, paying no attention to her giggling girlfriends. She's listening to every line of the record I've chosen and after a minute excuses herself from the gang and walks towards me. The girls look across the tables knowingly, as she slides in next to me on the bench.

Her shoulder touches mine. I kiss her on the cheek again, while her friends turn tactfully away. She asks how my day has gone and I tell her it went all right for *them*, but I feel nothing now. The sadness has gone; I'm right where I want to be, close to the only person I want to be with, and we sit together talking about nothing in particular, drinking espresso until we're wired, filling up the ashtray. We take it in turns to own the jukebox, letting Elvis speak for us. I feel Maureen's leg against mine and her hand squeezing my hand, slipping her fingers through mine to lock us together. The girls glance over their shoulders, giggling again, but I don't care and neither does Maureen. This is different from teenage passion in the back entries, where zips go down and skirts go up; we're only holding hands, yet it feels more intimate and erotic than any knee-trembler we've ever shared.

Later when it's dark the music stops, the coffee machines die with a splutter and the cafe empties. I leave Sivori's with my arm around Maureen's shoulder and her arm around my waist, gripping my studded belt.

We walk the full length of Taylor Street entwined together, rounding the corner into Eaton Street and ignoring the temptation of those shadowy back entries. Standing outside the Hindley house, with such lonely people existing miserably within, I kiss Maureen goodnight, softly, lingeringly. We don't make a 'date' for tomorrow; we'll be together every day from now on.

I return to the dim, silent house on Wiles Street, feeling more content than ever before about crossing the threshold. I wash in the usual biting cold water and go upstairs. Passing Dad's empty bedroom, I open his door and turn on the light to give him something to aim for when he returns home smashed out of his mind. I'm glad to get to my own room, and drop with deliberate heaviness into bed, making the mattress springs groan. Crossing my ankles, I draw deeply on a cigarette and stare up at the ceiling, thinking back over the day.

This morning I lost someone for ever, but by the end of the afternoon I had someone else to love and I'm confident that she loves me, too. I shut my eyes calmly, picturing Maureen and ignoring the mountain of unhappy baggage that surrounds her in the form of her family.

June 1963, I say out loud, letting the words drift on the dark, smoky air. I'm 15 and the summer is already hotter than any I can remember. It feels like a storm is building on these streets, pressing down on the huddled houses and approaching slowly from somewhere beyond the railway line. People, I think, people will be the problem. Not my dad – I can handle him, his moping and drinking – but someone from the Hindley side. Not Bob; he doesn't give a fuck about anything. Nellie's a handful at times, but if Maureen stands her ground we can wear her mother down.

Myra, then.

Myra is the threat, the ominous funnel of black air in an otherwise unclouded sky. I've seen how she conducts herself on the street and how she batters her dad; Myra will screw this thing up for us, one way or another. Everyone is aware that me and Maureen are a couple – Bob and Nellie tolerate me around their home, but once it's clear that there's more to us than just a bit of teenage misbehaving there are bound to be comments from the adults. That doesn't bother me. What makes my stomach tighten with anxiety is the deeper shadow that falls across Maureen: her sister.

For no reason I can name, Myra's new boyfriend comes into my head. I've only seen him two or three times, but it's enough to sense that we won't get on: he's a smartly dressed, nerdy, snooty-looking Scot who's arrived on our streets from nowhere. In my ignorance, I imagine Myra priming him for a mortgage and a couple of kids. I haven't got a clue what's inside that storm gathering over the city of Manchester this summer of '63.

And so I lie there, on the lumpy tick-mattress, unsettled about Myra's influence over Maureen. Tiredness overwhelms me and at last I shrug: so what, let the storm come. Against the odds, today has been a good day, so screw you, Myra Hindley. *Que Sera, Sera . . .* whatever will be, will be.

I finish my fag, flick out the light and fall asleep with a smile on my face.

Chapter 5

'She used to go dancing often. I was not worried at first,
but I became alarmed when she failed to return . . .'
– Joan Reade, quoted in the *Gorton & Openshaw*
Reporter, 2 August 1963

After Annie's death, there was speculation among the family
about where David should live. His grandfather wasn't involved
in the discussions. David recalls: 'I hated the man. He couldn't
have cared less about Mum: when the chap from the Cooperative came to sort out the life insurance, Grandad put on a
gala performance, weeping and wailing, pretending to turn his
head away. "Oh, it's blood money," he cried, then snapped his
neck round to make sure a wad of notes was in the offing. "Just
leave it there . . . I won't touch a penny of it, it's blood money
– just leave it there, on the table, that's right, in a neat pile . . ."'
David grits his teeth in disgust. 'As soon as the insurance man
left, *whoosh*, out shot Grandad's hand and the money disappeared
into his pocket.'

The possibility of a new home with Bert and the Duchess
was mooted, but in the end David remained in Wiles Street
with Jack. 'Miss Jones, the landlady, moved out,' he recalls.
'She went to live in Chapel-en-le-Frith with her sister Martha.
Dad took over the tenancy of number 13 and we carried on as
before, just the two of us. I was never at home, though. I spent
all my time with the Taylor Street Boys – Ferguson "Fergie"
Lester, Paul and Tony O'Gorman, and a few other lads. We
were a proper gang, though not as violent and territorial as
gangs are today. But we got up to mischief all right, and there
was a lot of rivalry with the Openshaw Boys, whose "manor"

was on the north side of Ashton Old Road. We'd sneak into their pubs and hide razor blades in the soap in the Gents, and some of the boys wore Andy Capp hats with blades in the peaks, ready for a fight.'

One of the most notorious street battles occurred when the Openshaw Boys strayed onto forbidden turf to beat up Paul Cornwell (part of the Taylor Street gang) in front of his girlfriend at the Essoldo cinema. David gives a rueful grin: 'Paul was a mate of mine. We all met up in Siv's and decided to call in the "heavies" – the Deaf and Dumb Boys, who lived in Brooke House flats opposite Gorton library. It turned into a massive ruckus in Ashton Old Road. But there were lots of scraps like that. The police would escort us down the street in an attempt to stop aggro breaking out but as soon as their backs were turned we'd run up to the parked cars and rock 'em like hell to turn 'em over. I had an airgun as well, and once shot my mate Chris Hamnett in the leg when we were messing about on the croft. His mum used to complain about me to Granny Maybury.'

He's quiet for a moment, remembering. 'I was wild, but no more so than the rest of our crowd. And there was another side to me that only Maureen saw back then.'

* * *

From David Smith's memoir:
This thing between us will never be love. That's a word we'll never share. Only years later with someone very different will the true meaning of that word become real to me. But the feeling between Maureen and me is genuine enough, in its own way.

For a while after Mum's funeral everything is quiet. But the shift in my relationship with Maureen soon becomes clear to everyone. That's when the trouble starts.

When I call for her, it's a battle to get past the habitual folded arms and stony eyes of Nellie Hindley, but it's even worse when Maureen calls for me. Dad hates virtually all women and can't stand to see me happy with Maureen. When she turns up on the doorstep, he greets her with contempt and a wicked-sounding, 'And what the fuck do *you* want?' I shout at him for talking to her like that and he bawls back at me; she and I leave the house to a barrage of 'fucking little bitch' and 'stupid cow'. Sometimes he flips his ace out after us: 'You came out of a cunt and you've taken up with one.' Maureen has to grab my collar then with all the strength she can muster, pulling me down the street as I spit venom over my shoulder.

This is the storm that worried me, but it's not the one that's about to break.

We spend our time strolling together through nearby Sunnybrow Park, with its neat paths and ponds. In Sivori's, we're no longer part of the gang but a young couple who need to be alone. There's no frantic action up the back entries before saying goodnight any more; instead we cling and kiss until the clock calls us in.

One late June evening, I'm sat at home in Wiles Street waiting for Maureen. Dad slumps, sullen and seething, in his chair. The empty teatime plates are still on the table, food eaten in silence. When the knock comes at the door, we look at each other in united bafflement because that's not Maureen; it's a sharp, loud blow against the door that isn't meant to be ignored.

I answer it and there she is: Myra Hindley, in fierce older sister mode, arms folded and make-up pristine, dressed for a night out but with a face you could weld iron on. A blonde anvil.

I prepare myself for a row as in a cold, quiet voice she tells me, 'Get inside, this is private.'

I stand aside and she steps into the living room. Temper has drained the colour from her face even underneath the make-up, but she's still perfectly in control. I purposely keep at least four feet between us, not wanting to feel her claws on my skin, and knowing that if it happens I'll land out at her and we'll end up punching the crap out of each other like two blokes.

When she speaks, it's in a hard, deliberate monotone: 'Maureen's waiting for you on the corner. I'm here to lay down some fucking ground rules and, for your own good, you'd better mind yourself and listen for once.' Seeing me start to protest, she jabs a finger towards my face: 'Keep your mouth fucking shut.'

I don't need telling again, but listen tight-lipped as she outlines the rules.

'I've tried to explain to our Mobee what an arsehole you are. But for some reason she still wants to be with you, so I'm telling you now' – the finger jabs again – 'if you ever, *ever*, hurt her in any way you're a dead man. Do you get me? A dead man. This *thing* between you both will be tolerated but you better mind your back because every step of the way I'll be watching you, David Smith. Right? Every fucking step you take. Got it?'

I nod, livid, but realising it's in my best interests to keep quiet.

Myra gives me one final glare before spinning on her heel and wrenching open the door. She lets it bang shut and I stand there for a moment, then turn.

Dad looks at me. He raises an eyebrow and goes slowly through to the kitchen. I take a deep breath, wait until Myra has had time to round the corner of Wiles Street, then go outside and into Maureen's arms.

* * *

David's schooldays were coming to an end. Music was still the greatest love of his life to date and in his leather jacket, T-shirt, drainpipe jeans and winkle-pickers, hair greased with Loxene, he bore more than a passing resemblance to Stuart Sutcliffe, the bass guitarist in the newly popular Beatles; Sutcliffe died from a brain haemorrhage that year, aged 22. David was already a huge fan of the band: 'The Beatles blew rock 'n' roll out of the water. They were *thunderous*. They were singing stuff that only black people sang. Suddenly Elvis became an old fogey and Cliff Richard was . . . well, he was never cool, in my eyes. The Beatles changed everything for us kids. We started dressing differently, walking differently, talking differently, even thinking differently. Lennon was my favourite – I loved his sarcastic twang.'

The 'in' place to listen to music was at Belle Vue: 'The jukeboxes there were terrific, and all the teenagers would gather in front of them. The boys danced together outside the arcades, right in front of the jukeboxes, while the girls watched. There were dance-offs in Openshaw as well, on the top floor of a working men's club. You could win ten bob if you were good. And again all the lads danced together at first, while the girls were with the girls. Then after a while you'd approach the girl you thought was the best mover and ask her to dance. The two of you would go crazy, surrounded by all these other couples on the floor, about twenty altogether, twisting like mad as the music got faster. The judges walked around, tapping shoulders until only two couples were left for the dance-off. My legs would feel like elastic bands, but I'd give it one more push, just to get that ten bob and be crowned the winner. I never bothered with the lass afterwards and she didn't bother with me – it was just about winning, splitting the ten bob and then a friendly goodbye.'

He laughs at the memory. 'I was a good dancer, you know. I taught Sammy Jepson, Wally King and the Cummings brothers how to do the twist in my bedroom. And in the living room I plastered one wall from ceiling to floor with magazine and newspaper photos of my musical heroes: Eddie Cochran, Elvis Presley, Susan Maughan, Chubby Checker.' He gives his characteristic wry grin: 'It was the only way I could afford to decorate the place.'

Then he remembers something else: 'The other great thing was the fairground. When that hit town – wow. Once a year it came, in those long summer holidays, pitching up on the recreation ground (the "red rec") opposite the Cummings' home. That was rock 'n' roll as it was *meant* to be heard – music blaring from the waltzer, with the smell of hot dogs and onions, and the sound of rifles going off on the shoot-'em-up stalls. It was *fantastic*. Us local boys would stand at the rail, jealous as hell about the fairground boy who walked easily between the spinning waltzers, whacking the tubs to make them go faster while the girls screamed and laughed. On the speedway they used to shout, "The louder you scream, the faster you go." I'd stand with my mates, glaring at the fairground boy all night, thinking, "I hate him." Music never sounded so good as it did then."

David left school that summer, 1963. By then, his involvement with the Taylor Street gang had led to petty crime. 'It was wicked stuff,' he recalls quietly, the laughter fading from his face. 'We'd break into people's houses and take whatever we could carry. I'm acutely ashamed of it now – just thinking about it makes me physically cringe. Why did we do it? God only knows. Me and Tony were the most adept at breaking and entering, but it was me and Sammy Jepson who were caught. We'd stolen a quantity of electrical goods for Sammy to pass on to his contact, who just happened to be his sister's boyfriend. When we appeared in court, Sammy was sent down, but I was treated more leniently. I had a probation officer, of course, having been in trouble before, and in my pre-sentence report the illegitimacy "issue" was highlighted – I think that was used as a bit of an excuse for my actions, in all honesty. That, and being an only child.'

David appeared in court on 8 July 1963. He was placed on probation for three years on charges of house-breaking and larceny, and store-breaking and larceny. His most recent brush with the law was the talk of Gorton only for a short while. Less than a week later something happened which reverberated around the streets like a thunderclap in the clear summer skies.

On 12 July 1963, David's 16-year-old neighbour, Pauline Reade, vanished.

* * *

From David Smith's memoir:

Ian Brady is a lanky oddball of a fella, quiet and aloof. He appears seemingly out of nowhere as Myra's boyfriend. I spot him occasionally in front of Granny Maybury's house on Bannock Street, getting on or off his 200cc Triumph Tiger Cub, wearing his crash helmet and long coat. Beneath his outer clothing is the waistcoat and suit he's had tailor-made from a 'club man', paying for it on the weekly. He wears turn-ups on his trousers, which is odd for someone his age, and stands out a mile from the rest of us. I can't help but shake my head when I see him, this gangly, long-legged weirdo in his old-fashioned suit riding a bike that's no bigger than a scooter. He ties a couple of cans to the back of the Tiger Cub if he's sleeping at Myra's house to stop kids taking it for a spin.

Often he and Myra pass me on the street, the two of them astride the bike, heading into the countryside, where no one else ever bothers to go. Some nights Myra tells Maureen not to call at their gran's because Ian is busy recording on his eight-track machine or developing rolls of film. These instructions become commonplace, an accepted part of the routine. Occasionally, I see Ian arriving at Myra's house on a Friday evening, carrying the cheap red wine he gets from the off-licence shop on Stockport Road (close to his home in Longsight's Westmoreland Street); the shop has large wooden barrels on the counter where customers can fill their own bottles. And on weekday mornings I usually see Ian and Myra leaving together for work at Millwards, where Maureen also has a job as a filing clerk.

A life of routine, week in, week out, so normal that the streets soon stop noticing them.

* * *

By midday on 13 July 1963, virtually every household in Gorton was talking about the disappearance of Pauline Reade. Her family scoured the streets frantically, asking people if they had seen Pauline, who set out from home the night before to attend a dance at the British Railways Social Club in Cornwall Street. She hadn't been able to find a friend to accompany her because most mothers objected to the alcohol on sale at the club, but two girls who knew Pauline well had tailed her for part of the journey, incredulous at the thought of their reserved friend daring to go to the dance alone. They watched her pass by in her pale blue 'duster' coat, pink Twister dress, new white shoes and gloves, and waited to catch up with her not far from the club. When she didn't appear around the next corner, they simply assumed she had returned home.

The police drew a blank in their investigation, which led to far-fetched rumours that Pauline had eloped with a fairground worker or run off to Australia. No one who knew her believed such tales, but the idea of Pauline getting into a car with a stranger was equally unthinkable. On 19 July, the *Gorton & Openshaw Reporter* highlighted her disappearance under the headline: 'Gorton Girl Went to Dance: Missing'. A few days later the newspaper tried again, featuring a photograph of dark-haired Pauline on their front page; she looked strikingly pretty, giggling with her best friend while her brother Paul pretended to play a guitar. Canals were dragged, crofts searched, coffee bars – including Sivori's – visited, fairgrounds torn apart and scores of people were questioned, but there was still no trace of Pauline.

'The police knocked on our door a couple of times,' David remembers quietly. 'They wanted to speak to us as part of their routine inquiries – we weren't suspects; no one was, in fact. Dad and me sat at the table, answering the coppers' questions. They asked about the sort of girl Pauline was, whether I had noticed anyone suspicious in the neighbourhood and when I last saw her. None of us paid any attention to the rumours. Pauline wouldn't have gone off with someone she didn't know and she wasn't the sort to do a flit with a boy, especially not one of those cocky fairground types. It was a strange, unsettling time. Her disappearance became the Great Unspoken Event, quietly simmering under the surface of normal life. There was a big wave of sympathy for the Reade family, even if no one knew what to say to them. I saw Mrs Reade very often, walking up and down Wiles Street, looking left and right, so lost, so alone. A mother in deep, deep distress.'

Three months after Pauline vanished, David had his first real encounter with Ian Brady. 'It was October,' David recalls, 'and Maureen told me that one of her co-workers at Millwards had pinned her against a wall and tried it on. That didn't go down too well with me, though I did wonder if she was making it up. If that really *had* happened, then Maureen would have been more likely to run crying to her sister. Believe me, Myra was well able to sort out *any* bloke. But Maureen told me this tale and the next day I went down to Millwards, spoiling for a fight.'

It was mid-afternoon when David arrived at the offices. He settled down to wait his opportunity in the tin-roofed cut-through area in the yard, hiding behind some chemical containers. It was dark by the time the offices began emptying: 'Myra and Ian passed without noticing me and Maureen went by as well. I stayed quiet and, sure enough, out came this chap in his 20s. For a split-second, his eyes met mine. Then he bolted. I ran after him in hot pursuit, itching for that fight. He scudded past Myra and Ian, who were by their car with Maureen. I was gaining on him, but Myra yelled, "Hey! Pack it in! Get back here, you!" I skidded to a stop. Myra hissed at me, "Get in the bloody car. We don't want any trouble. *Get* in the car."'

David got in the car. Maureen said nothing but wore a smug little smile, quietly pleased that he'd rushed to her defence. 'We sat in the back together,' David recalls. 'Ian hadn't said a single word. He looked completely deadpan, sitting in the passenger seat next to Myra. She drove us home; it was only a few streets. On the way she asked, "What the bloody hell was all that about?" I sat there in a filthy temper and Maureen said in a timid little voice, "Oh, I'll explain to you later, our Myra." As for Ian, he said nothing again. Not a word. Just that expressionless face, staring straight ahead.'

One month later, in Ashton-under-Lyne, a twelve-year-old boy named John Kilbride went missing. His distraught family knew, as the Reades before them had done about Pauline, that John had no reason to run away from home. He was the eldest of seven, particularly close to his eleven months younger brother Danny, and a familiar figure about the streets where he lived for his habit of whistling or singing while he walked. John's disappearance from Ashton market during the early evening of 23 November 1963 – one day after the assassination of President Kennedy – left police baffled again.

On Monday 25 November, the *Manchester Evening News* devoted their front page to John: 'Dogs Join in Massive Comb-Out for Boy'. Ashton Market was torn apart in the search, while attics, sheds, rivers and areas of waste ground were painstakingly probed by police and volunteers. Three weeks later the local press reported on the 'Mass Hunt for a Boy', which had turned into the 'biggest search ever mounted for a missing person'. By mid-December, the situation was desperate, as the press began interviewing clairvoyants in the hope of turning up something useful. But despite every conceivable lead being followed, and the indefatigable efforts of the Kilbrides themselves to find John, the trail went swiftly and irretrievably cold.

* * *

From David Smith's memoir:
The Union, the Rembrandt, Liston's Bar . . . every public toilet in the city, every night of every week. Train station piss-stones, viaducts and alleys, it's always there. We've got *Last Exit to Brooklyn* before it's even written.

There are evenings, many evenings, when Myra turns up at Wiles Street alone and throws herself into a chair, sighing to Maureen, 'Put the kettle on, our Mobee, I've just dropped Neddie off in Manchester. He's gone people-watching as usual, at Central Station.' Neddie is Myra's nickname for Ian. Then her lips curl into a smile: 'Neddie likes to watch the maggots crawling about.'

She spends the evening with us, relaxed and girly, laughing and sisterly. I put another record on the Dansette and the two sisters jive together to 'Red River Rock', and then launch themselves at me, tickling until I shout for mercy. When they go back to jiving in the middle of the sitting room, I sit smoking a cigarette and think of Ian, trying to imagine what it involves – 'maggot-watching' at Central Station.

I find out later.

Whether it's Central Station or the Rembrandt, the Union or Liston's, they're all the same to him: full of maggots, businessmen and stock-clerks. They dress the same, looking for the rush, the high, the heat, eye contact, running their hands through their hair, posing, waiting, giving the smile. Scored, they think, unaware of the truth.

Because for one man, this isn't 'people-watching'. This is a hunting ground.

* * *

Immediately after leaving school, David was taken on by Albert Sudlow & Sons as an apprentice electrician. His father secured him the job. 'A cousin of mine – another Frank – was doing "very well" as a trainee in the same line of work,' David explains. 'The family went on about how he was earning "bloody good money for a lad his age". But I didn't want to be a Frank-type worker. I didn't want to be a Frank-type anything – I'd had more than my fill of that with Mum. So my career earning bloody good money lasted no more than six or seven months. Afterwards, I worked as a labourer for a fella called Jim Miller who lived on Gorton's Railway Street. He was a one-man-band property repair business. But I was bored, restless. I didn't last long there either.'

Years later, Myra Hindley claimed in her unpublished writings that she had intervened to win David his job back following his dismissal by Miller for poor time-keeping. He snorts derisively, 'Rubbish. Can you see Myra doing that for me? Not true. I was unemployed for quite a while after working for him.'

In March 1964, David was idling away an afternoon in Sivori's when Maureen appeared, less animated than usual. 'She sat down next to me,' he recalls, 'and she was very quiet. I didn't think much of it at first, just another "bad hair day" probably. Then all at once she blurted out that she was pregnant. For a moment, the wind was taken out of my sails, but neither of us was upset. After Mum died, there was no attempt at stopping nature's course from my side or hers. There was a mutual, unspoken *allowing* it to happen. I was 15, and wanted something to replace what I'd just lost. Getting Maureen pregnant seemed to be the answer.'

He sips at a fresh mug of tea. 'I was delighted, absolutely over the moon. Maureen had never mentioned missing her monthlies – she just came out with it, there and then. I felt on top of the world. She wasn't quite as thrilled because of having to tell her family. She didn't cry or get upset, but she was concerned. I held her hand tightly and told her that she had *nothing* to be scared of because I was with her every step of the way. Besides, she'd stood her ground against Myra over seeing me and that showed that she could be tough if she needed to be, not the meek younger daughter or timid little sister. We talked, and after a while she was as excited as me over the baby. We couldn't have been happier. We both believed we would make it as a couple, and as a family.'

Jack Smith reacted better to the news than they expected; he acknowledged that they wanted to plan a future together. Bob Hindley had nothing to say about the impending birth of his first grandchild, but Nellie was furious when David and Maureen broke the news, and made David leave the house. To the young couple's surprise, Myra appeared to accept her sister's pregnancy, only expressing mild concern for Maureen's well-being.

Jack, Bert and the Duchess urged David to make his relationship with Maureen 'respectable'. 'I wasn't bothered about a band of gold on my finger,' David recalls. 'The getting married bit didn't come from me or Maureen. All we cared about was becoming parents. Nothing else mattered from then on – not our mates, hanging around the streets or in Sivori's, nothing. But illegitimacy was still a big stigma back then and "the adults" didn't want Maureen or the baby to suffer that. The wedding was sorted out within a couple of months and we were happy to go along with it. Maureen moved in with me and Dad while arrangements were made for us to get married.'

But before Maureen Hindley became Mrs Smith, another child in Manchester vanished. Keith Bennett was the same age as John Kilbride when he went missing; he'd turned twelve just four days before. On 16 June 1964, he set off from home with his mother to spend the night at his gran's house, where his brothers Alan and Ian and sister Maggie were waiting for him. Earlier that week, after swimming a length of the old Victorian baths near home for the first time, he'd broken a lens in his glasses. His mother saw him across bustling Stockport Road safely, but Keith never arrived at his gran's; his path there in the evening sunlight took him past Westmoreland Street, where Ian Brady lived.

Again the police mounted an all-out search and local newspapers highlighted the case, but there were no leads: Keith had vanished without trace.

Chapter 6

'[David] is good when he wants to be.'
      – Nellie Hindley, Moors trial at Chester Assizes,
                              April 1966

On Saturday, 15 August 1964, 16-year-old David and 18-year-old Maureen married at All Saints Registry Office in Manchester. The only surviving photograph from that day shows the two of them grinning artlessly, Maureen's hair dyed jet-black for the occasion. 'She was as blonde as her sister when I first got to know her,' David recalls, 'but from that day on she kept her hair dark. It went well with the turquoise maternity suit she'd bought for the wedding. I wore a light-coloured jacket with a black velvet collar and new tie. It was a good day and neither of us was particularly nervous. Our guests were Dad, Uncle Bert, the Duchess and my cousin John. No Hindleys. Were they invited? Nobody was *invited* as such – it was more a case of me and Maureen just being taken to get wed. Afterwards, we went into a greasy spoon Greek cafe for a proper fry-up and Dad and Uncle Bert insisted we celebrate at the Hyde Road Hotel. We stayed there for a few hours, and then Maureen and me slipped away on the 109 bus back to Wiles Street, leaving Dad, Uncle Bert and the Duchess in the pub. John beetled off on his little motorbike. And that was that: we couldn't afford a proper reception or a honeymoon – most people couldn't in those days. I wasn't working and Maureen had given up her job at Millwards because she was seven months pregnant. But tradition wasn't really our thing anyway – Maureen didn't stay away from me the night before the wedding, for instance. Our home life was very happy then, and Dad was fine with the two of us – he bought our wedding rings. We even had a couple of dogs, Peggy and Rusty, to make the house cosy. Life was good.'

Later that evening there was a knock at the door. Maureen opened it to find her smartly dressed and perfectly coiffed sister standing there. 'Ian would like a drink with you,' Myra told the newly-weds, who immediately spruced themselves up and went round to Bannock Street, where Granny Maybury was already in bed. The Dansette was playing in the background and a bottle of red wine stood by the fire; Ian had a habit of putting bottles there to watch the heat pop the corks out. There were plenty of other bottles – white wine, whisky and a further jug of red wine – on the table. Myra was slightly giddy with drink as she chatted away to Maureen, and Ian seemed very different from the mutinous, unfriendly bore David had always judged him to be.

'That was the first time I'd socialised with them as a couple,' he remembers. 'When we arrived, Ian was nothing like the person I'd seen on the street, all gangling limbs in his long coat with a snooty expression. He chilled out that night. The waistcoat and trousers with a stiff crease down the centre of each leg were still there, but his shirt collar was undone and he was welcoming. He looked like a cross between a nerd and a gangster, if you can imagine that. A lot of drink flowed. Ian had a taste for Liebfraumilch, which I've never liked, and he'd brought whisky and jugged red wine from the offy near Westmoreland Street. We downed the whisky and warm red wine and the girls sipped the Liebfraumilch. Beer wasn't really Ian's thing – I think he thought it was a bit common. The only time I ever saw him nursing a beer was when we popped into the Wagon and Horses on Hyde Road for a pint. It was a very handsome old pub, all oak beams and gleaming brass, where the beer is served in those "bobbly" pint glasses. He held his with both hands, as if he couldn't manage to lift it otherwise. I've never seen anyone do that – it was awful wimpish.'

Much to his surprise, David was able to relax at Bannock Street. Granny Maybury's collie, Lassie, and the eight-month-old puppy from her litter that Myra had kept and named Puppet stretched out at his feet. He felt himself grow warm with the fire and the wine. 'It was the girls who really created the atmosphere,' he remembers. 'My friendship with Ian developed because of them. Myra stood near the record player, a drink in one hand

and a cigarette in the other, bopping about and choosing the vinyl for us. She liked Alma Cogan and any sort of pop. The girls danced and sang together, and I got up and had a jive as well. It felt like a small party, just the four of us, celebrating the wedding – a regular happy occasion. They made a fuss of us that night – Ian was *Mein Host*, hovering with his bottle so that no one's glass was ever empty. He'd squeeze past Myra with a fag hanging from the corner of his lip and give her an affectionate hug. Just an ordinary bloke having a good time, in full flight. He'd never have got up to jive with the rest of us, but he was thoroughly enjoying himself and there was nothing sinister to it, as far as I could tell. We went home in the early hours. I was three sheets to the wind and singing, and Maureen was laughing like a drain as we stumbled back to Wiles Street in the dark.'

The following morning, as the sun clambered high above the foundry and the sooty streets surrounding it, David and Maureen were woken by Myra's unmistakeable rap on the front door. David fumbled into his jeans and lurched downstairs to answer it. His sister-in-law glanced him up and down, arching a thickly pencilled eyebrow before instructing, 'Get ready and we'll pick you up in an hour. We've got a surprise for you.'

Despite his hangover, David was soon washed and dressed, and was waiting with Maureen in the sitting room when Myra's white Morris Mini-Traveller purred up. Maureen slid into the front seat next to her sister; Ian folded the rear bench seat flat so that he and David could sprawl out with the obligatory red wine and cigarettes.

They headed north out of the city to the Lake District. The plan was to visit Lake Windermere, but it was heaving with day-trippers. Myra turned the car towards Bowness, where they found somewhere to park eventually. Ian was generous in his spending, paying for a boat trip on the glittering lake, lunch in a cosy restaurant and more supplies of alcohol for the journey home that evening. 'The day in the Lakes was their wedding present to us,' David explains. 'We didn't have the money for such things. I climbed into the back with Ian again and stretched out to carry on drinking, while the girls nattered in the front. Ian began philosophising but nothing too heavy – no more than any opinionated drunk. He talked about the distribution of wealth but never mentioned robbery then, as some journalists claim. He waffled on a bit about class and society in general, but again nothing ominous.' They arrived back in Gorton around midnight and, as David later told an attentive courtroom: 'We had a meal and most of it was drink.' At 4 a.m., the Smiths left Bannock Street and headed home.

The two couples met up every fortnight, either at Bannock Street or Wiles Street, following the trip to the Lakes. 'We'd get fish and chips, play cards, drink and listen to music,' David recalls. 'Ian had terrible, old-fashioned tastes – Cole Porter and Glenn Miller. It was a very ordinary time, no heavy conversation or hints of what was to come. The relationship between Ian and Myra was normal, as far as I could see, too. There was no question of one dominating the other. She could give as good as she got, anyway. They rowed occasionally, but only over daft stuff. He loved his Heinz macaroni cheese straight from the tin and could have lived on it. She hated it and would shout at him that it was worse than dog food. And if he got very drunk and started rambling or raising his voice about something, she'd give him a withering look like women do and he'd belt up.'

David's own relationship with his sister-in-law had thawed considerably. 'We were OK with each other then,' he states with a shrug. 'If I saw her in the street, she'd stop for a chat, arms crossed as always, asking what I was up to and how was Maureen. She'd accepted that I was married to her sister – what else could she do, with a baby on the way as well? But she was fine with it. She'd had her moment, reading me the ground rules, telling me not to lay a finger on Maureen or mess her about, but after that everything was OK. I felt very comfortable around her then. Again, the relationship between the two of us was nothing like it's been portrayed in books and dramas – reduced to filthy looks and constant sniping. We were all right.'

While he and his new wife prepared for the birth of their first child, the landscape around them was in the process of an epic transformation. Seventy thousand homes in Manchester had been declared unfit for human habitation and a vast slum-clearance programme was under way. Suburbs were earmarked for demolition, including Gorton, where once-thriving industries had fallen into eerie disuse and businesses were collapsing. Satellite towns were proposed, where communities would be self-contained with every conceivable necessity to hand. Gone were the endless, crumbling brick terraces with their outside lavatories; residents moved family by family into larger council houses with plumbed-in baths and toilets, and high-rise flats with lifts and laundry chutes. An improvement, in theory; the reality was somewhat different, with many homes built before the essential facilities, and as extended families found themselves living in distant neighbourhoods, crime levels burgeoned to equal the dissatisfaction many felt with 'modern living' in Manchester's emergent metropolis.

One morning in September, Myra arrived at Wiles Street with the news that she and Granny Maybury had been allocated a home in Hattersley, the largest new town, with 14,000 inhabitants. Her delight at leaving Gorton was plain, but the elder Hindleys struggled with the prospect of relocating. Bob had suffered a stroke and Nellie was having an affair with a man named Bill Moulton; she was reluctant to move as far as Hattersley with her invalided husband and held out for another offer from the council.

One month after Myra and Granny Maybury left Gorton, Maureen gave birth to a daughter, Angela Dawn. She and David were ecstatic at becoming parents and life quickly settled into a new, fulfilling routine. 'I was working alongside Dad at Moseley Brothers, just behind Ardwick Green and close to Gary's Hotel, earning a regular wage,' David remembers. 'We were a very happy little unit. There was no longer any friction between Dad and Maureen, and straight after work, I'd play with Angela before sitting down at the table with Dad to eat the dinner Maureen had cooked. At weekends and in the evenings, we'd take Angela out in her pram and walk the dogs. I still looked like a rebel, but now the older people on the street smiled, chatted to Maureen and made baby-talk at Angela. I felt content, and didn't even make a fuss over visiting the in-laws on a Sunday afternoon. Maureen laughed a lot and Dad was a changed man – he would babysit while the two of us had a night out at Three Arrows on the corner of Hyde Road and Church Lane, near Belle Vue. We'd sort of graduated from Sivori's to there. Nellie had mellowed as well, and was just as you'd expect a grandma to be. When we used to call round with Angela in the pram, she'd pick her up straightaway for a cuddle. Bob was too wrapped up in his own misery to care.'

Although Myra was no longer living nearby, and Ian spent almost every day at the new house in Hattersley until he moved there permanently a short time later, the couple were regular visitors to Wiles Street. But neither displayed any interest in Angela. 'There was no doting Auntie Myra and Uncle Ian,' David remarks dryly. 'Myra's only concern was for Maureen. She'd just ask, "Does she sleep all right for you? Is she giving you some rest during the day?" She wasn't a touchy-feely auntie and *never* held Angela. What was shown on screen in *See No Evil: The Story of the Moors Murders* couldn't have been further from the truth. If she saw us out pushing the pram, she'd stop to talk to us, but there was no peering in and chucking the baby under the chin. As for him . . . I remember changing a nappy once in front of Ian. Maureen brought Angela down because she was wet and gave her to me. Brady stared at the fire, at the wall, fiddled with his glass, anything but look at the baby and me. He did *not* want to see the little legs kicking in the air, and the billing and cooing. I noticed his embarrassment and teased him about it, waving the talc in his face, but he kept his head firmly turned and ignored me.'

David pauses and drains his tea. 'Whenever the pair of them came to the house, I always hoped that Dad would be out until they'd left. Ian Brady and my dad did *not* get on.'

* * *

From David Smith's memoir:
The fag-end of 1964, and the Beatles and the Rolling Stones rule the world. The music I live for has been given a massive shot in the arm, ripped from America's stranglehold by four lads from Liverpool. Merseybeat and Detroit Motown take over as the new teenage religions and the summer seems to linger on and on.

I throw my legs out of bed. It's early morning but already unseasonably warm. I yawn and listen to the trains forever roaring past the window, making the glass rattle. I reach for my first cigarette of the day and have a good splutter. The pink-painted cot, wedged between bed and wall, is empty and the blankets dishevelled. I can hear homely noises from downstairs as I reach for 'the Image', which is strewn across the floor. On go the tight, black drainpipe jeans with six-inch zips at the bottom, black studded belt, white T-shirt, thin socks and winkle-pickers. I pull on my shirt and tuck it into my jeans, raising the collar at the back and leaving three buttons undone to show off the crucifix. Then I reach into my back pocket for my comb and run it through my hair, pushing my fingers into the front to pull it into a sultry quiff. Image complete.

The winkle-pickers clunk on the stairs; we never did get round to putting a carpet down. The kitchen hasn't changed much either apart from a lick of paint, but it feels a lot cosier with nappies and baby clothes drying on the wooden frame in front of the fire. I run the only tap – still no sodding hot water – and the arctic blast wakes me up. I comb my hair again and rearrange the quiff while another train thunders by, making the crockery clatter.

Maureen stands at the kitchen table making sandwiches for two pack-ups, the dogs at her feet. Dad is in the living room; he and I work at the same factory in Ardwick, where he's an engineer and I'm a labourer. At dinnertime he nips to the pub for an hour with the other engineers and I eat my pack-up on a bench in Ardwick Green opposite the hotel. I like it there.

The kettle whistles and Maureen makes a fresh pot of tea. I hear the factory hooter calling the workers in for their shift at the foundry. I realise we're running late, but Maureen calms me by explaining that Dad has had a word with a workmate who's going to clock us in on the sly. I relax and sup my tea, leaning against the sink and disguising boredom as she outlines her plans for the day. It sounds like every other day, to me: a visit three streets away to her mam, a visit two streets away to Auntie Ann and cousin Glenys, and a nice stroll with Angela Dawn in her pram in Sunnybrow Park. Lovely, I say.

Then she looks at me brightly, 'Oh, Dave, I nearly forgot. Myra and Ian want to come round tomorrow night. Is that all right?'

That *will* be all right because tomorrow is Friday (pay day), no work on Saturday, and I can get merrily pissed with Och-aye from Glasgow.

I finish my tea and muse on how things have changed between Dad and me. I look forward to going to work with him; it makes up for a lot of the bruising we've dished out to each other. He slumps in his chair, thumb and finger at his temples to squeeze away a hangover. The ashtray on the table overflows, but he keeps on puffing away. Maureen brings me toast and another pot of tea, knowing how much I love our mornings, especially sitting on the settee with Angela before leaving for the factory. I tickle and play with my daughter for a few minutes and then it's time to collect our pack-ups and head off. Maureen holds

Angela in her arms and sees us off from the door.

Dad's first stop is the corner shop on the end of Wiles Street to buy his fags and *Daily Mirror*. I choose a bottle of milk from the crates stacked outside. The shop itself is so poky it can only cater for five people at a time and often there's a queue down the street. Inside, crudely built shelves are crammed with no thought to order: baked beans next to firelighters, tights beside Spam. Potatoes bulge from the rolled-down hessian sacks in the corner and a monstrous brass till squats on the counter.

This morning there's only one customer in the shop: our neighbour from number 9, Mrs Reade. She stands close to the counter with her head bowed, having a whispered conversation with Mr Hodges, the shopkeeper. Dad picks up his paper from the pile near the till and automatically opens it at the racing page. We wait patiently for Mrs Reade to finish. Always a very slight lady, she seems to have shrunk further in the year that's gone by.

Dad asks her politely, 'Morning, Joan. How are you today?'

She replies in her quiet voice, 'Fine, Jack. Not too bad, thank you.' She gives us both an unconvincing smile and leaves the shop, clutching the bits she's just bought close to her. Mr Hodges shakes his head and rolls his eyes in a sad, hopeless gesture that's kinder than it looks. Then he reaches under the counter and hands Dad his daily two packets of Capstan Full Strength before opening the thick tick-book to log the transaction; the cost of a week's living comes out of a Friday night pay packet.

As we leave the shop, I glance quickly down the street. Mrs Reade is going into number 9, head bowed, while Maureen stands on our doorstep with Angela, waiting for us to turn the corner. She waves and shouts cheerily, 'See you both tonight.' I lift my hand, then turn away as both doors close.

Dad licks the end of his stubby pencil as we walk, marking off another nag to back. I bide my time before mentioning, as casually as I can, that Myra and Ian fancy a drink at ours tomorrow night. His reaction is exactly what I expect: face contorted with suppressed anger, he replies that he couldn't give a shit because he's going drinking in the Hyde Road Hotel straight from work and not to bother with his dinner – he'll bring something home from the chipper.

We walk towards the bus stop in silence.

*

I meet up with Dad after work, outside the factory gates; we're both grimy from a day's labour but who cares, it's Friday. Dad's in good form: he's had a 'treble up' on the horses and has a thirst coming on. Not bothering to open his wage packet, he takes a green bundle of notes from his pocket and peels off several pounds with the order to 'pay Maureen my board, settle up with the shop and get our Angie something nice'.

I walk the half-mile with him to the Hyde Road Hotel. As we near its Victorian bulk, we're greeted with the heaving noise of laughing men and the chink of glasses being collected for the next round. Dad pushes open the door. The thick smell of beer and a sudden draught of Woodbines escapes. As he disappears inside, I notice that he's got the *Daily Mirror* tucked in his back pocket, dirty and well-thumbed but still open at the racing page. I laugh to myself and catch the 109 to Gorton, sitting upstairs and enjoying a well-earned cigarette, glad to know I've got a pocket full of wages, Dad's happy and I can have a good scrub and nice bit of dinner before the evening kicks off.

Maureen's left the front door open and the smell of boiled ribs and cabbage hits me as I walk through the living room into the damp heat of the kitchen. I cast my unopened wage packet onto the table along with Dad's ill-gotten gains. Maureen calls a hello over her shoulder, as she busies herself with pots, pans and plates. She chatters away once she starts buttering slices of bread and I lie to her that it's been a gruelling day just to get a bit of the old feminine sympathy. In a corner of the kitchen, Angela sits upright in her pram, eyes bright as pennies, dressed in pink and smelling wonderfully of fresh baby powder. She grabs at the air with her chubby little fists, trying to catch something only she can see. I laugh, amused by her determination and the way she's sitting, lopsided but comfortable, kicking her blanket away as if it's a whole new game. I spend a few minutes trying to sit her up straight, but her arms and legs move faster at the attention and I give up, leaving her gurgling to herself.

At the sink I scrub, comb my hair and rearrange the quiff yet again before pulling up a chair to the table and tucking into a bloody good dinner. Life is sweet.

Myra and Ian arrive at seven o'clock. The Morris is parked up for the night, with its white bonnet almost touching the railway sleepers at the end of the street, and the two of them walk into the house without bothering to knock. They're always charitable visitors: Ian carries a couple of bottles of Bell's and two or three records under his arm; Myra follows with a box crammed with red wine in an assortment of corked bottles and several Babychams and Cherry B's. I perk up even further as we say hello, sensing a good night is on the cards.

Dad and Maureen have shaped the condemned house into a clean, cosy home. In front of the fire where the dogs lie, we now have a lightweight settee and on each side of the range are chairs, one for Dad and one for me. Our old table, scrubbed spotless, stands in the middle of the room and against the wall is a second-hand but sturdy sideboard. Maureen's precious Dansette sits on top of it, along with two tall stacks of records: my large collection of blues and rock 'n' roll and her smaller set of Elvis. *My* wall holds centre stage, plastered from floor to ceiling with images of teen-beat cool and defiance: Muddy Waters, Chuck Berry, Eddie Cochran, Gene Vincent, Little Richard, Sam Cooke, Jerry Lee, a very young Bob Dylan . . . Tucked away in the corner is a small group of Elvis photographs to appease Maureen.

The girls disappear into the kitchen to fetch glasses and have a sisterly natter. Ian stands before the wall for a moment, mockingly shaking his head at my creative efforts, then gives a friendly tut of disapproval as he takes a seat by the fire. I'm in mischievous mood and pile the Dansette with a selection of black singers, hoping to wind racist Ian up. But this time he ignores my deliberate attempt to annoy him and sits smoking his cigarette tranquilly.

Maureen and Myra return, sitting down shoulder to shoulder at the table to share a box of Maltesers and bottles of Cherry B. I look at Ian: he's dressed immaculately, as usual. Cuff-linked white shirt, tie fastened with a traditional single knot and his favourite grey three-piece suit, with its two-inch trouser turn-ups. Other than my wedding tie, the closest I ever got to that kind of neatness was a Texas bootlace affair with a sliding metal knot. He removes his jacket and pours two large slugs of jugged wine. When he hands me a glass, it's like being served by John Dillinger – he's got the look and the waistcoat, just not the gun-holster. We settle back with our drinks before the fire and unwind quietly for a while.

Maureen rises to prepare Angela for bed. Myra sits watching her without a word and doesn't ask to hold the baby, or kiss her forehead. Not even a 'Good night, God bless'; only a curious silence. Maureen passes Angela over to me for the last ten minutes of her day and I reach for her eagerly, loving to hold her as she nestles against me, snuggled up all pinkly tired and tidy, smelling sweetly of Johnson's baby powder. Ian prods and pokes at the fire. His and Myra's lack of attention towards our daughter doesn't bother me; they just have different ways to us. Angela is teaching me new feelings all the time and I'm greedy to learn with her. I hold her a little too tightly, contemplating how life has altered in a year: I'm 16 now, wear a wedding ring and have a beautiful daughter. Being married suits me. The Image is beginning to feel outdated and unimportant; even the reason for the wall is fading fast.

I kiss Angela goodnight, pass her back to Maureen and give Ian a quick grin of sheer pleasure at the joy of being a parent. He frowns at me before turning back to gaze at the fire again, lost in thought.

Hours later, the bottles of Cherry B and Babycham stand empty on the table and cigarette smoke floats thick as a dream around the light bulb. Longsight's cheap red wine has kicked in and I act as DJ while the girls jive together, both laughing and shrieking as they twirl and catch each other at high speed. I spin Del Shannon's 'Runaway' and 'Hats Off to Larry', Eddie Cochran's 'Twenty Flight Rock' and 'Summertime Blues', and just for Maureen, I even let rip with Elvis: 'It's Now or Never' and 'Are You Lonesome Tonight?' Ian sits with his tie loosened, heavy-eyed and glass in hand, not listening to the music or the girls singing. He's no rock 'n' roller and he's no Fred Astaire; he doesn't even tap his feet to the beat. I leave the Dansette and jive with the girls until the whisky makes the floor uneven, then stagger out into the street for some air.

I leave the door open to let out the coiling smoke and the sound of Gene Vincent giving it the old 'Be-Bop-A-Lula'. Ian follows me out into the dark, carrying the sort of whisky measure you can never buy in a pub. He puts his cigarette to his lips and his glass on the roof of the Morris, then jumps backwards onto the bonnet, long legs dangling. I lean against the wall of the house, looking up at the inky, star-scattered sky and listening to a train hurtle by, waiting for the smoke to vanish from the street. I know that train; it's a cargo wagon full of coal. When I was a kid, I'd hide in wait with the Cummings boys for a train like that to pass, fancying ourselves as Jesse James and the Younger Brothers. Miniature desperados, we'd walk the tracks with sacks to scour the line for treasure: black gold nuggets. If a bag was too full or heavy, we'd stash it on the embankment and continue the search. Often we were chased by the dreaded railway 'Pinkerton Men' and would make our escape only to return later to retrieve the loot, dragging the bags up the embankment to our outlaws' hideout – Mrs Cummings' kitchen. I shake my head and give a half-laugh: Jesse and the James Gang in short trousers and rolled-down woolly socks. Well, it makes for a happy memory.

Ian sits sipping his whisky on the car bonnet, watching the street corner. I notice the forlorn shapes of Joan and Amos Reade – Pauline's parents – coming towards us on their way home from the Steelworks Tavern. I stand away from the wall, a little unsteady, not wanting to appear yobbish.

'Evening, Mrs Reade.' I speak as clearly as I can, hating the embarrassment of being wobbly-drunk.

'Hello, David.' She gives me the faintest of smiles. Mr Reade nods in greeting.

Even through the fuddled haze of red wine and whisky, I feel uncomfortable with the raucous music pouring from the open door, but Mrs Reade is not the kind of lady to complain about anything. Her husband gives me another silent nod in goodnight and they disappear into their private silence behind the door.

I lean back against the wall again with a sigh.

Ian sips his whisky thoughtfully. 'Them the parents of that missing girl?'

'Yeah.'

He gazes at the railway sleepers and takes a long drag on his cigarette. 'So, what's the story behind that? What do you think happened to her?'

I tell him about the rumours Pauline fell for a lad from the fairground and ran off with him to a new life, perhaps abroad. Ian pulls down the corners of his mouth and draws on his cigarette again. I add that the police came to our house, asking questions.

A flicker of interest passes across his face. 'What kind of questions?'

I shrug. 'Just what you'd expect: what sort of girl was she and was she the sort to up and leave.' I pause. 'She wasn't.'

'No?'

I think of Pauline, bringing me tea and jam sandwiches on the doorstep in the rain when we were both kids. 'No. She was quiet. Nice. Not that sort of girl at all.' I scrape one heel down the bricks. 'Fuck knows what happened to her.'

Ian sits swinging his legs to and fro on the bonnet of the white Morris, downing the rest of his drink in one.

I go back indoors to join the girls. After a while, Ian returns and fills up his empty glass. He wears a scowl and moves slowly across to the stack of discs that I've fanned out on the floor to play. He fumbles on the table for one of the records he's brought and removes the song playing on the Dansette, replacing it with his own before clumsily dropping the needle. I sit on the floor, gloomy in the knowledge of what's coming: the bloody Goons and that nutter Spike Milligan. The whisky aggravates my mood and I wish I had the sense to avoid it because it never fails to screw with my head. I sit closer to Maureen for comfort, pushing away my glass, talking to her in an effort to clear the fog from my brain. Ian and Myra join in with the Goons, hysterical with laughter and mimicking the voices on the record. It's not my sort of humour; I just don't get it.

Finally, the pantomime put on by our guests ends. I clamber into my chair as Ian tops up my glass with more whisky, ignoring my slurred protests. He stumbles back to the Dansette and puts on his other record. When he turns the volume dial, the small, inadequate speaker vibrates with the pounding rhythm of thousands of stomping jackboots. A crescendo of 'Sieg Heil, Sieg Heil, Sieg Heil' fills the sitting room. Hitler's voice opens out into the space left behind by the chanting and Ian's face is animated at last.

I've lost the ability to move: the drink has gone to my legs, so I sit pinned to my chair, listening to a language I don't understand and wonder glumly what happened to 'C'mon Everybody'. The night has lost its way. Everything is getting loud, distorted and too hot. Maureen's gone into the kitchen for something and I wish she'd hurry up and come back. The room shrinks to Myra and Ian talking in short bursts of German. Ian frequently stabs at his knee with a bony finger to emphasise parts of the Führer's rhetoric. Sometimes he speaks to me as if he's a paid interpreter: 'He's saying this now, Dave' . . . 'He means that now, Dave.' He asks me if I get it. Do I? No, I flaming well do *not* – it takes me all my time to decipher Ian's own glutinous Glaswegian, never mind Hitler in full rant.

I stare at Ian's mouth, trying to focus on his narrow lips, but they move like a puppet's useless maw. I listen hard but can't hear anything he's telling me and close one eye in a vain attempt to control my swirling double-vision. Maureen is in the room again at least and I'm glad of that, even though she's sitting next to Myra on the floor and talking to her while Ian carries on excitedly picking out bits of Hitler's speech for me.

Despite being almost catatonic with booze, I'm the only one who hears the sound of a key scrabbling at the door.

Dad crashes in blind drunk, arse over heels, hanging onto the key in the lock. I feel myself tense up; Dad's crossed swords with Ian before and despises him. His entrance on this particular evening will live with me for ever: he hits the floor on all fours, dropping his precious soggy parcel from the chipper. Struggling to his feet, he gathers up the wrapped fare and stands unsteadily with a crooked smile that vanishes as he takes in the situation. Hitler's voice seems to roar from every wall as Dad slams his parcel down on the table and glares furiously at Ian.

I think to myself, 'Fuck, Ian's sat in Dad's chair.'

Then, to make matters worse, Ian announces in a drawling *Dixon of Dock Green* voice that drips sarcasm, 'Evening, all.'

I edge forward on my seat, waiting for the explosion.

Dad spits at Ian, 'What the *fuck* are you doing in *my* fucking house?'

Ian answers slowly and deliberately, gleefully aware that he only has to breathe to inflame the older man: 'Well, I do believe, *Mr Smith*, we have been invited.'

I watch Dad intently. I know his moods inside out and feel it when his rage breaks over us like a colossal, fiery wave.

'I'm not having that fucking *shit* played in my house! Get it off and get your fucking self out after it.'

Ian leans back in Dad's chair, taps the tailing ash from his cigarette onto the hearth and casually crosses his legs. 'It's a free country, Mr Smith, it's a free country.' He blows a chain of perfect smoke rings into the air. In the background, Hitler's screams seem to implode within the speaker, spilling out into every corner of the room.

Dad stands and sways, his hands on the table as if to support himself, but I know he's inching closer to get a good run at Ian. 'Fucking free country!' he bellows. 'Fucking free country! What do *you* know about it, you fucking shit-stirring, German-loving *bastard*! You know fuck all about anything!'

A smile spreads across Ian's face. He goes for the jugular. 'Don't forget Dresden . . . You call your laddies heroes, Mr Smith, but what about the massacre of innocents at Dresden? Answer me that.'

From her position on the floor, legs tucked sideways beneath her, Myra slyly glances at her boyfriend, cranking up Dad's mood. 'Come on, Ian, leave it, love. Can't you see the man's drunk? He doesn't know what he's saying, does he?'

I see the volcano erupt in Dad's eyes and leap up out of my chair to grab him as he flies at Ian. I hate this. I know only too well what it takes to control Dad, especially when he's got the drink on him; he has to be injured to put a stop to it all. I stand my ground with some difficulty, shoving him to a standstill with my hands planted flat against his chest.

'Get the *fuck* out of my house!' he screams at Ian, and Myra. I feel the spray of his temper splatter on my face. Locking eyes with him, I tell him through gritted teeth to get himself off to bed, that this thing isn't between me and him but if I have to stop him, I will, even though it's the last thing I want. He sweats with anger and pushes against my hands, but when I shove back and ask him to please just sod off to bed, he relents.

Glowering across my shoulder at Ian, he mutters, 'Just get that bastard out of my chair.' Relief trickles through me as he suddenly turns, slamming and banging his way into the kitchen and upstairs.

I sink into my own chair, letting out my breath slowly. Ian hasn't moved an inch; he sits cross-legged, smiling calmly and nipping the end of his cigarette. I realise Hitler has stopped ranting and let my head droop. But then comes the clatter of heavy boots on the stairs and Dad storms back in. I rise in apprehension, but he's only there to grab his parcel from the table. At the kitchen door, he twists round awkwardly, his eyes burning: 'I told you to get *him* out of my fucking chair.' Then he swivels his gaze round to Myra, who's laughing quietly. 'Fucking bitch,' Dad spits.

Maureen lowers her head, upset and embarrassed. I wait to see what's going to happen, but Dad isn't in the mood for a fight any more and exits loudly. Ian calls cheerfully after his retreating back, 'Goodnight, Mr Smith. Sleep well, now.'

Silence falls on us for a while. Ian and Myra exchange triumphant glances, then Ian lights up another cigarette and launches into a diatribe, addressing no one in particular: 'So-called fucking Tommy war heroes can't handle the *facts* . . . it's all *propaganda*, that's what it is, fucking propaganda . . . the truth has been suppressed for too fucking long, this is *reality*, the whole planet is in the grip of stinking Jews, that's what's behind everything . . . fucking Kennedy clan are nothing but a tribe of *cunts* . . .'

Eventually the drink overwhelms him. In a sullen hush, he rests back in the chair with his eyes closed, cigarette spent. Myra begins gathering their belongings to leave. She folds Ian's coat neatly and drapes it over one arm, waiting until he's hauled himself out of the chair. I get to my feet. Ian throws an arm around my shoulder, squeezing me tightly before brushing a clenched fist playfully across my chin: 'Good party, eh?'

I sink into the chair again, leaving Maureen to see them out. I'm angry with Ian, Dad and myself, too – what a waste of time and effort everything is. I slug back the last of the whisky, clenching my empty fist. A clammy head-sweat swamps me. The heat of the roaring fire, the whisky, the jugged wine, and boiled ribs and cabbage knot my innards before springing open like a burst valve.

I dive through the kitchen and hit the fresh air of the backyard, bumping and scraping against the wall to the outhouse. Brutally ramming two fingers down my throat, I bring up a waterfall of hot, evil-smelling liquid. Gasping, I stand in the yard for a while and everything helicopters in front of my face. I stumble indoors, seeing double as I follow a trail of yellow chips up the stairs, using my hands as an extra pair of feet. I stand outside Dad's bedroom door and listen to him snoring for England, then stumble into the other room.

On the bed I share with Maureen, I sit gazing at Angela's cot, ashamed of how the evening disintegrated. Hearing her snuffles, I feel a semblance of normality return and undress with quivering fingers. The Image lies on the floor in an untidy jumble as I fall back onto the mattress, thinking dizzily 'Where the fuck is Dresden anyway?' before slipping into blessed unconsciousness.

I rise late the next day, feeling dog-rough, poisoned and rotten. I'm half-dressed as I clamber down the stairs, thinking *I can't be arsed with the Image today*. Maureen silently hands me the pot of tea, nodding towards the living room. I take the pot from her, clutching my cigarettes, and join Dad in our chairs by the fire. We sit quietly for a few minutes, and I eye the sad figure as he begins sorting out what's left of his pay packet.

'Bad night at the cards, was it?' I ask softly, hoping to break the tension.

Dad takes a deep breath. 'Got fuck all to do with cards. It was a bad night all round.'

I read his mood less by his words and more by his calm, empty speech. He's not angry, but I know it's wiser to leave him alone and return to the kitchen. While I'm talking to Maureen, the front door opens, then slams shut.

I spend the weekend sobering up, happy to stroll with Maureen through Sunnybrow Park pushing the pram, throwing sticks for the dogs and talking about nothing in particular. Dad has hit the Hyde Road Hotel and is drinking heavily again, but it's his way of sorting things out in his head. At night I lie in bed listening to him fumbling his way up the stairs and trying to be as quiet as he can. In the morning, his chair is empty.

On Monday, everything is back to normal.

* * *

'Have You Seen 10 Year Old Lesley? Big Search for Lost Girl', asked the *Gorton & Openshaw Reporter* on New Year's Day, 1965. The article highlighted the vanishing of Lesley Ann Downey, who had not been seen since visiting Silcock's Wonder Fair near her home in Ancoats on Boxing Day evening. Mention was also made of Pauline Reade, John Kilbride and Keith Bennett. Lesley's mother and stepfather appealed for information, stressing how much her three brothers were missing their shy sister, and her best friend appeared on the Granada kids' television programme *The Headliners* to discuss in a halting voice how Lesley had suddenly left their small group to run back alone to the alluring lights of the fair. Six thousand posters bearing Lesley's image were printed, five thousand flyers distributed and more than six thousand people interviewed, but despite alleged sightings of the little girl in Blackpool, Belgium and any number of places in between, Lesley remained missing.

Ten months later, however, Maureen Smith would tell a hushed courtroom of an incident that occurred in February that year, when she and her sister were retiring for the night after an evening's socialising: 'Mrs Downey [*had*] offer[*ed*] a reward of £100 to anybody who could give any information as to where her daughter, Lesley, was. I said to Myra: "Her mother must think a lot of the child."'

Prompted by the barrister as to her sister's response, Maureen said quietly, 'She laughed.'

Chapter 7

'Let me take you down
Cause I'm going to
Strawberry fields
Nothing is real . . .'
    – 'Strawberry Fields Forever', The Beatles

From David Smith's memoir:
Saddleworth Moor. What is it about this place and the dark?

We've been up here before, the four of us, during the daytime, and it held no more interest for me then. There are few trees and no birdsong. It's always cold – the wind cuts through everything – and difficult to walk any distance. I trudge about in my Cuban-heeled cowboy boots, feeling the ground give as we follow wherever Ian decides we should go. He strides 20, 30, 40 yards in front of Myra, Maureen and me. He walks with a sense of purpose, smiling, hands in pockets, as he negotiates the land without a care. I glance at him, wondering if you need to be a bloody Scotsman to enjoy this kind of bleak, barren landscape. But Myra loves it here, too; it's *their* place. And, as far as I'm concerned, they're welcome to it.

In daylight, Ian follows the many deep-sided streams and we traipse behind until he finds a spot he likes. We drink the wine and whisky we've brought with us, and the wind blows our cigarettes out. Occasionally we have a radio with us, but not often. There are rocks nearby, along the roadside, great lumps of black stone. If we come here at night, that's where we go, clambering over those rocks in the solid darkness to a flatter spot. He wears his stock-clerk shoes; she's in her heels. We look down across the vast, dusky valley to the reservoir far below, a pale sliver of water. We wrap ourselves in blankets, cold at first, then whisky-warm.

I live for this place, he tells me. It owns my soul.

At times, he's a mad man, walking off very quickly, hands in pockets again, alone, searching. When we catch up with him, he's breathless and smiling: a junkie who has taken his fix. His expression alters if he catches sight of someone else on the moor – hikers send him into a rage. But that only happens during the day. By night, no one comes here but us.

One afternoon in April 1965 we head to the moor and don't return home until nine. We drink ourselves close to oblivion and play cards carelessly, moods slipping. Ian suggests going back to the moor. We crawl into Myra's car and speed away from the lamp-lit streets to roads that are blacker than the wagons shunting past my window.

It's very late now. We squeeze out of the car near the rocks, where the moon glimmers on the reservoir far below. We're very drunk, especially Ian and me, stumbling about in the dark. Myra is carrying the blanket. I can't see my hand in front of my face, but Ian strides off in a direction he knows well. His voice is thick with drink and whisky sloshes in the bottle pushed inside his coat pocket. We lurch from one bog hole to the next and my socks grow wet, Cuban heels sinking into the long grass. Every time one of us loses our footing, Ian swears, a habit he slips into when drunk. Often he stops, glancing across at the reservoir as if to get his bearings. Finally, he finds the place.

It all looks the same to me, but Ian is happy. We wait for the girls to catch up with us. He's friendly, affectionate even, as we stand looking across at the gleaming water. His arm is around my shoulder, hand gently squeezing, soothing.

Myra unfolds the blanket and we sit down. I'm comfortable apart from my wet shoes and socks; all of us are warmly dressed. The girls share a flask of tea and talk about their mother and Angela and things of the past. I neck the whisky with Ian, listening to the drone of the girls' voices, enjoying the sensation of the alcohol warming my insides, burning my throat and spreading to my head. Ian is on a roll, spouting again about the peace that this place brings him and cursing the maggots down in the city. I realise he still has his arm around my shoulder and I'm thinking: *this must be true friendship*.

The night just got darker and I didn't see it.

* * *

Before that particular visit to the moor, in early 1965 David and his old friend Sammy Jepson almost came to blows when Sammy started a rumour that he and Maureen had slept together. Meeting him by chance soon afterwards, David landed a punch before Sammy ran off; he called at his friend's flat in Longsight to settle the score once and for all, but Sammy managed to duck away from him and raced off down the street. At the same time, David's old adversary Tony Latham was putting about a similar story about himself and Maureen. David had no doubt that both Sammy and Tony were lying over their involvement with his wife, but he was infuriated nonetheless.

Almost every weekend, Ian and Myra would drive over to see David and Maureen, bringing a generous supply of alcohol to drink late into the night. The girls usually fell asleep just as Ian was getting into his stride, expounding on his philosophies and talking about his time in Borstal. He was interested in David's past misdemeanours, prompting him one evening with the words, 'I believe you've got a record.' Often in the early hours of the morning the two of them would go outside to urinate behind the lock-up garages opposite; Ian brought along David's starter pistol ('All lads had starter pistols back then,' David recalls) to shatter the night air with a single shot.

Occasionally, David and Maureen stayed overnight in Hattersley. The neat, half-timbered house at 16 Wardle Brook Avenue had 'all mod cons' and was surrounded by a white picket fence with a front and rear garden. The road through the estate ran in front, sloping ten feet as it passed the house behind a brick wall. Directly opposite was the New Inn pub on Mottram Road, which Myra would sometimes nip across to for cigarettes. On the horizon and clearly visible from the upstairs rooms of number 16 were the dark contours of the moor.

While David and Maureen were waiting to hear about their own move from Gorton, on 25 April 1965 the life they had built together was obliterated by the sudden death of their daughter, Angela Dawn.

* * *

From David Smith's memoir:
Something is about to happen; something unstoppable.

I'm getting ready for work. Maureen is in the kitchen, making my pack-up, and I spend the last ten minutes of my morning at home sitting on the settee with little Angela tucked beside me. Then all at once those minutes are gone – there's no time left, Dad and me have a bus to catch. On the upper deck he reads his *Daily Mirror* and we talk about nothing. I work all morning without much thought and wait for tea break. Half the day is done and I'll soon be home.

Then I get called to the office. I'm told to go to Ancoats Hospital; Maureen is there, but nothing to worry about, *she's not hurt, just get yourself off.* I slope out of the factory and stroll to the hospital, puzzled but unconcerned, enjoying the warmth of the afternoon. At the enquiry desk, I ask for Maureen.

Somewhere there's a clock ticking, but it's about to stop.

A nurse approaches me quickly, guiding me by the elbow into an empty room. She tells me she'll only be a moment. A moment. How long is a moment when it lasts for ever?

I stand, glancing about at the room, which seems to be for examinations of some sort. There is a couch with a roll of white paper at one end, and not much else, just a few leaflets in a rack on the wall and a trolley of medical odds and ends. I think I can still hear the clock ticking.

The door opens and the same nurse comes in with a doctor.

I'm asked my name and address and told to sit down. I refuse, not seeing the need to rest my legs. The nurse is holding a great wad of tissues for some reason. The doctor speaks quick and soft: *your daughter is dead. I'm very, very sorry.*

Angela Dawn Smith, aged six months. Gone.

The clock stops.

I think someone makes me sit down, but I don't remember moving, and my hands are full of tissues but I'm not crying. *We'll fetch your wife,* they say and go out, closing the door quietly, leaving me alone.

My world detonates.

I smash the room to bits, destroying every last thing within it. Nobody comes in to stop me, even though they can hear it all. I'm spent and more broken than I've ever been. I can't feel anything but a pain so acute that it makes me vomit.

Maureen appears, hysterical, a mess. Someone calls a taxi for us and not a word is said about what I've done to the room. In the cab, Maureen splutters through her tears: *morning feed, bath, changed nappies, afternoon nap in the cot, she didn't wake up, I went in and I couldn't wake her, she didn't wake up, Dave, she didn't wake up, she didn't wake up.*

At home, I don't speak for hours. Maureen won't leave my side: I move, she moves, I stand up, she stands up. It's strange, what you do together in grief.

I remember my beautiful little girl, my baby on the settee, round-eyed and laughing. Ten minutes, hours ago. Poor Maureen has had the full horror to face and I wasn't there. I feel a rage so deep it makes my head burst. I gather all of Angela's clothes, iron them and pack them away into a suitcase. No one must touch anything of hers. When Maureen's Auntie Ann turns up out of genuine kindness, offering to sort out my baby's belongings, I shout at her to leave. Then I take the suitcase to a railway embankment and throw it over the fence with all the might I can muster.

John Lennon says only women bleed. He's so fucking wrong.

They bring Angela home one night in the smallest of white boxes. We're at Mum's house, 39 Aked Street, unable to face living at Wiles Street once I've got rid of the suitcase.

I take Angela from the undertaker's men at the door; she's ours and we don't need anyone else's help. I carry her to the parlour, my special place, where Dad has prepared a table. For such a little box it's very heavy . . . or perhaps I have lost all feeling in my limbs.

Maureen and I spend the longest and loneliest night of our lives in the parlour with Angela in her coffin. The next day Maureen is a girl no longer. The difference can be seen in her eyes: they've become dull and empty, and the light will never quite come back into them. Her normally husky voice is nothing more than a whisper. We both recognise that our first attempt at growing up and sharing love with each other and with a child of our own has been razed to the ground.

We don't recover.

Relations and in-laws arrive to say goodbye to Angela. I find myself heading for the front door. Opening it, I stop and glance back. Maureen is standing at the end of the hall. She nods at me without a word and I step outside.

Hours later I'm flat on my face outside the house in the dark, pissed up like I've never been before. The lights are on behind the tightly drawn curtains. I press my skin to the cold concrete and listen to the voice of madness in my head: *well, Be-Bop-A-Fucking-Lula, this is the day the fucking music died, no more street jiving, no more giving a shit about the hair and the clothes, no more Jimmy fucking Savile, screw being a Catholic, who gives a fuck about Dylan and Lennon anyway?*

I close my eyes tightly, knowing what's behind the closed curtains. I blink and twist slightly on the ground, my cheekbone scraping against the concrete. There at the end of the street is my old school. Why can't the clock start ticking again, but this time send the hands spinning backwards until I'm there in my short trousers, comics and sweets in hand, running happily around the schoolyard at playtime? I want to be small again, I want to stop this day from happening. Why me, why fucking me again? I want the pain to leave me, I want to beat myself to a bloody pulp. I want . . .

The front door opens and a shaft of yellow light spills out. I don't look at the feet of the person standing there; I want it to be my mother, reaching down for my arms and taking me in for a steaming mug of drinking chocolate. Anger flares inside my stomach and erupts in my throat: fuck her too, for leaving me when I needed her most, fuck her for letting me grow up, for not stopping all the bad things, for not living long enough for us to grow old together. Fuck life and fuck death.

I close my eyes and think of that little coffin. Please take this pain away, someone.

Two days ago I held my daughter in my arms; she looked up at me through her long eyelashes and laughed as I squeezed her gently to me. I said goodbye to her that morning, but I didn't mean it to be for ever. Give me those moments back, give them all back. Or just a week, a day, an hour . . . ten minutes in the morning. I hate God, there is no God.

I feel gentle hands on me, lifting me to my feet. I sob against her shoulder, *I'm sorry, I'll be a good boy tomorrow, I promise*. She guides me upstairs, her arms around me as she pushes open the bedroom door and lays me down. I close my eyes as the world whirls into oblivion and Maureen tucks the blanket in around me, kissing me softly.

She waited up for me, alone with the box.

The white Morris pulls up slowly outside the front door. I answer Myra's unmistakeable knock; she stands there silently, holding a huge bunch of flowers with a card: *Another little flower for God's garden*. I let her in and wait for Ian. He sits like an effigy of himself in the passenger seat of the car, staring straight ahead, unmoving. I can't work out what's going on and turn around, heading back down the hall to join Maureen and Myra in the parlour.

Angela lies in deathly perfection in the open coffin. There is a moment, just a moment, when tears fill Myra's eyes. She wipes them quickly away, muttering that we mustn't tell Ian. Maureen helps her blot the smudges and applies a black pencil close to her lashes. I leave them to it, feeling for my fags as I pull open the front door again.

I light a cigarette and look across at the car, waiting for Ian to acknowledge me, but I might as well wait for hell to freeze over. I stand there, not even six feet from him, with my daughter lying in her coffin and he can't even look at me. Instead he sits there motionless, an elbow carelessly resting on the open window, smoking too, his eyes fixed straight ahead. No 'sorry for your troubles'; not even a nod. Nothing. Fuck all. The bastard just sits there, sucking it all in. He's in *my* street, near my people, my blood, wallowing in my grief less than a dozen streets away from his own mother.

I smoke my cigarette down to the filter, then flick it into the street.

Myra emerges behind me, with Maureen. She is more composed now, hugging Maureen and nodding at me before climbing into the car and starting the ignition. Not a glance between her and him; they drive away facing the windscreen like a pair of crash-test dummies.

You knew I was watching you that day, Ian. You knew. And that's when you decided what it was that you wanted, and how to make it happen. We stood there, two heartbreaks waving you off, and I know you were smiling as Myra turned the car into Stockport Road.

Another little flower for God's garden.

* * *

'The turning point was Angela's death.' David reaches for the mug of tea Mary has just made for him and clutches it with both hands. 'That's when Brady decided which way he was going to go with me. I've got no reason to believe that, other than a gut feeling, but I'm sure of it. That day, when he was sat outside the house . . . not even a nod of acknowledgement. I was looking right at the car, parked towards Ross Place, and he was drawing on his cigarette, blowing the smoke into the air as if I didn't even exist. Did I mention it to him later? No. It wasn't that I wanted to talk to him especially – I'd gone out to get some air that day, more than anything. It was just that complete lack of respect for Angela's death and what we, as parents, were experiencing. As for Myra's tears, that wasn't anything in the grand scheme of things. Again, it was shown differently in *See No Evil*: she wasn't weeping, it was just a couple of seconds of wet-eye, then "Don't tell Ian" and she was gone. The card that came with the flowers was the most emotional she ever got over the death of her niece. They drove off, and that was it. Except it wasn't, because Ian had already decided, there and then, to involve me in their little secret.'

Following the death of their daughter, Maureen returned to her former job as a part-time machinist with her mother at a factory in Gorton. David abandoned his position at Moseleys, 'bailing out', as he puts it, from routine. Neither of them could bear to return to Wiles Street; they remained at 39 Aked Street, with David feeling acutely that he was back where he'd started. But Ian and Myra were there for them when they needed to get away from the small web of condemned streets that seemed to trap them in their misery.

'They'd call for us and we'd go off for the day or just the evening,' David remembers. 'We went up to the moor very often, taking wine and the pistols that he and Myra had bought after she'd joined a gun club. Sometimes we went to another spot in Derbyshire – we'd take the rifle with us then instead, using it for target practice on trees. He taught me how to play chess when we stayed in, but more often than not we all went out together. On one occasion we were heading to Blackpool for the day, the girls in front, me and him sprawled out in the back as usual, when another car came past and overtook us a bit sharpish. It was full of lads, larking about. I didn't think anything of it until Ian started banging on the partition, his face contorted with anger. He yelled at Myra to go after them, burn them off.'

He pauses to cough, lighting another roll-up from his tin. 'We shot off, the car juddering as it picked up speed. Ian started moving towards the back, feeling for one of the empty bottles of wine we'd drunk. He picked it up as Myra swerved the Morris in front of the car that had overtaken us. Then she hit the brakes: the driver of the other car slammed on his brakes, too, and at that moment Ian hurled the empty bottle straight at their windscreen. Myra put her foot down and the other car shrank into the distance. Ian's mood altered immediately – he realised then that he'd lost control, even though it was only for a moment, and told Myra to turn around and head for home. So that's what she did. We never got to Blackpool.'

David smokes his cigarette in silence for a while, then speaks quietly: 'The moor was their sacred spot. That's where we went most of all.'

* * *

From David Smith's memoir:

Saddleworth Moor again: hell's garden, an abyss where devils play and souls can never rest. I hate the place with a passion, even though I don't particularly know why.

I am on my back, the plaid blanket itchy against the nape of my neck. Myra sits straddling me, pinning me down, holding my hands above my head. Bottles and sandwich wrappings lie scattered about, and out of the corner of my eye I can see Maureen nearby, laughing as she hasn't done since we buried our daughter. The sun burns brilliantly behind Myra, stinging my eyes and turning her blonde hair into a white cloud. We're having a play-fight, teasing, having fun. Myra wears a simple white blouse with too many buttons undone. I can feel the warmth of her legs across me, below the billowing floral skirt she wears. I'd have no trouble in wrestling her off, but I don't even try. Hair lacquer tingles my nostrils and I can feel her breath as she pins me down tighter.

Hold him down, Ian is saying, *keep him down*. He's lying on the blanket beside us, holding one of the long grasses that grow so thickly on the moor. He prods at my ear with the blade of grass, irritating me. I flick it away and he laughs: *who's a little baby, then?* The red wine has got to us all; he digs his fingers into my waist, tickling me until I scream with laughter and Myra pushes me down ever further into the ground.

God, why do I like this day? I hate this place, it does nothing for me, but for the first time since I lost my baby I'm able to laugh and Maureen is laughing too, her head thrown back against the sun. I take in another lungful of hair lacquer, trying to wriggle away from Ian's bony fingers on my skin, and give in to the laughter.

Now it's early evening on the moor; everything is bathed in the glow of the sun sinking behind the hills. The wine is finished and the picnic blanket lies rumpled among the long grass. Maureen is running in front of me, laughing, her black hair catching in her mouth as she turns to look at me following behind her, my feet sinking into the warm earth. I hear Ian's voice carried on the warm breeze: *grab him, Hessy, bring him down, hold him there.* My limbs are feeble with alcohol and sun – I tumble over the uneven ground and roll in the cotton-grass. Myra is on top of me again, hands on my shoulders, legs around mine, forcing me back. I'm shouting through my laughter: *get off, leave it out, just get off me* . . .

I can't move as she bears down on me, knees pressing into my waist, hair lacquer choking me again. I catch a glimpse of Maureen sitting in silhouette against the dying sun, her mouth lifted in a gentle smile.

When the sun slides behind the hill and the reservoir is nothing but a black inky stain in the valley, we gather the empty bottles and the blanket and leave the moor, heading home to the sleeping city.

Chapter 8

'Now I want to come to the subject of the books.'
– William Mars-Jones, QC, Moors trial
at Chester Assizes, April 1966

On 23 July 1965, David and Maureen moved into their new home at 18 Underwood Court, Hattersley. It was Myra's 23rd birthday. A month earlier David had helped Ian decorate the house on Wardle Brook Avenue. Gone was the distempered cream interior of all the new homes on the estate; Myra had chosen a pink emulsion for the walls and imitation brick wallpaper for the fireplace. Underwood Court was 300 yards away and despite the abundance of stark rules in the communal lobby ('When the buzzer goes, please push front door'; 'No dogs permitted'; 'Will persons please keep this door closed for their own interests', etc.), both David and Maureen were pleased with their new flat and keen to make a fresh start.

'We'd been living with Grandad in Aked Street since Angela died,' David recalls, 'and asked to be re-housed on compassionate grounds. Our old home in Gorton was still privately owned by Miss Jones and Dad paid rent to her. But that house, like all the others in the neighbourhood, was put under a compulsory purchase order. People were given a choice of three areas for the move. Some turned places down – you'd find streets where almost every house was boarded up but for those families holding out for the area they wanted. Hattersley wasn't popular with people from Hyde because it was too full of "Mancs". Dad would eventually move in with us towards the end of the year, but he was working away a lot at the time and carried on living in Wiles Street with my dog Peggy – we couldn't bring her to

Underwood Court because of the rule on not keeping dogs. Rusty had died of distemper. We got a couple of cats instead – Maureen loved her cats.'

There were seven tower blocks in Hattersley. Most new occupants found it difficult to adjust to living several storeys above the ground, surrounded by building plots and with no amenities. 'There *were* things about the flat that I really liked,' David admits. 'It was modern and light, with under-floor heating and a proper bathroom. And the balcony was a real novelty, of course – Ian envied us that because of the views. He'd be straight out onto the balcony whenever he came to see us. But the biggest drawback was Mr Page, the caretaker. He was a proper jobsworth and had it in for me from the very beginning. I tried to stay out of his way, but not a single bloody day went by when we didn't bump into each other and he would give me the old gimlet eye or have a go. The neighbourhood around Underwood Court was like a moonscape back then – barren and undeveloped. Mobile vans came round selling groceries because there were no shops, and everyone had cigarette machines at home for the same reason. It was a world away from Gorton.'

Living in close proximity to each other, David and Maureen socialised with Ian and Myra more than ever, but it was still the older couple who decided when the four of them would meet and how their time together would be spent. They could be curiously awkward: on several occasions David strolled round to Wardle Brook Avenue only to be told by Myra that Ian didn't want to be disturbed. Sometimes in the evening she would ask David to wait by the wall of the New Inn while she checked with Ian; if it was all right for him to come in, the landing light would flash on and off, on and off. During one visit, Ian and Myra rose from their chairs in silence and remained upstairs until David and Maureen took the hint and left.

Sometimes the pair were even less welcoming, as Maureen later told a crowded courtroom: '[If] we called unexpectedly . . . Myra would do a lot of moaning and shouting and Brady would go upstairs.' She then recalled another incident: 'I had been working on some cushion covers for my sister [*and*] took them round to Wardle Brook Avenue. It was about 9 p.m. I knocked and could get no answer. As I began to walk away, Brady opened the door. I told him about the cushion covers and he barred the way. He put his arms around the door and said they had company. I gave the cushion covers to him and went home.' There was no question that Myra could be every bit as sullen and disagreeable as Ian; her temper often had the edge on his, and sometimes her wrath was directed explicitly at David.

* * *

From David Smith's memoir:

Summer 1965: the Beatles have just taken the top spot in the hit parade with 'Help!', knocking off the Byrds' 'Mr Tambourine Man'; girls' skirts are getting shorter as men's hair gets longer; the war in Vietnam is raging; Great Train Robber Ronnie Biggs has escaped from prison. England is swinging, but me and Maureen are stuck on Planet Hattersley, an overspill estate full of overspill people, a vision of the future that's standing still.

In Manchester, there's a polio scare and mass inoculation is being doled out to the population on sugar cubes. I haven't bothered to have mine and don't give it another thought until I pay a visit to Wardle Brook Avenue with Maureen. It's the weekend and Ian greets us in fine form, relaxed and friendly. Myra, on the other hand, is agitated and in one of her dark, serious moods. She has them from time to time and is prone to slipping into them at odd moments. She goes through to the kitchen to make tea with a mardy look on her face. Unwisely, I call out to remind her that I take two sugars. A harmless enough request, it nonetheless triggers something in her head; she returns with the hot teapot a minute later and launches into a fanatical rant about the polio scare. Then her gaze falls on me.

'Have *you* had your sugar cube at the doctor's?'

Picking up bad vibrations, I shrug and admit cautiously, 'No, not yet.'

She goes berserk: 'You fucking moron! You stupid bastard! You could be carrying it, killing us all, and what happens then, eh? *Eh?* Go on, get out, get the fuck out of my house right now, you fucking moron!'

My own temper snaps: 'Shut your fucking mouth. It's up to me whether I have the vaccination or not. You don't fucking tell me what to do.'

Maureen is sitting next to me. She bursts into tears and covers her face with her hands. Ian looks up in mild amusement from the chair where he's sat, one ankle crossed over the other knee.

Myra screams: 'I said get the *fuck* out of my house!'

She comes at me psychotically, the scalding teapot in her grip: 'Out, out, get the fuck OUT!' I duck just in time; the teapot flies across the room, spilling its contents in a brown arc before shattering in the corner near the television.

Maureen runs for the door, arms clutching her head. I rise to my feet, fists clenched.

Myra stares at me, frozen with unadulterated rage, and I stare right back.

A soft voice comes from behind us: 'Myra, cut it out.'

But she persists with the blazing, spiteful glare until he speaks again, his words sterner but his tone equally serene: 'Myra, fucking stop now. Just leave it.'

Her shoulders drop and the flame in her eyes is quenched by the sound of his voice at last; it's over.

I turn and leave. Maureen waits for me at the end of the short path, sobbing as we walk past the new houses with their bald little gardens. A small group of children stop kicking a football against the wall of the terrace to stare at us. I hurry Maureen home, my anger still smarting from the memory of my sister-in-law lobbing a red-hot teapot straight at my face.

It's hours before I'm able to relax, but just as we're getting ready for bed the entry phone rings. Maureen buzzes our caller upstairs. I stand behind her in the small hallway as she opens the door to Myra.

It's obvious from her smart clothes and perfectly teased hair that she and Ian have been out for the evening, but when she speaks her manner is subdued and remorseful: 'Ian's told me to come and say that I'm sorry.'

Noticing Maureen's relieved smile and sideways glance at me, I mumble, 'All right,' but I'm lying. All is forgiven because Ian commands it? No way.

Failing to recognise my mood, both sisters lean quickly forward to give each other a hug.

Myra untangles herself from Maureen's arms and jerks her head towards the lift. 'Ian's got plenty of drink in. Why don't the two of you come over for a bit?'

Unable to bite my tongue, I murmur, 'Well, only if you're sure I'm not contagious . . .'

The eyes flash again, but Maureen says eagerly, 'That'd be great. Give us a minute to get our things . . .'

Jackets and footwear on, we head out from Underwood Court. The girls are very chatty and hold hands as we follow the now-familiar route in the light of the muted streetlamps: Underwood Road, cut through Pudding Lane and into Wardle Brook Avenue. I push my hands deep into my pockets, dragging my heels and thinking, *screw you, Myra, if it wasn't for Ian you'd be nursing a busted face.*

Ian opens the door with a beam on his face like the Cheshire cat's Scottish cousin. In the cosy little sitting room it looks like bloody Christmas: on the Formica coffee table are three bottles of red wine, white wine and whisky next to two plates piled high with the shortbreads Ian loves, and the dark chocolates that are my favourite. I feel suddenly silly for nursing a grudge when they've gone to so much trouble. Ian, sensing my embarrassment, wraps an arm firmly around my shoulder and guides me to a chair, pointing out the chocolates and telling me to help myself as he uncorks the wine, cigarette dangling from his lip.

There's no time for empty glasses; memories flow and the laughter is easy. The girls talk loudly about their childhood in Gorton over the blaring trumpets of Ian's beloved Glenn Miller. 'In the Mood' gets us all going and I picture Mr Braithwaite, the Jamaican man from next door, walking on the path outside, hearing the brass getting into its swing, glasses chinking, and the sound of our laughter. Ian is raucous as the whisky slides down his throat with practised ease: *fuck them niggers and monkeys next door and fuck the Jews as well.* I laugh and join in: *yeah, dead right, fuck them, robbing Jew bastards*, even though I've never met a Jewish person in my life and don't know anything about them or their religion. But so what, fuck everyone and, whilst we're at it, let's get some good old ranting Hitler speeches on, even though we don't understand a word. Baby, this is the way to spend a Saturday night, we're so fucking great, screw my hero Bob Dylan too, he's Jewish . . .

The whisky and wine explode together. Myra's skirt rises a little too much as she wriggles herself into a more comfortable position on the settee, maybe she hasn't noticed. Ian obviously hasn't, and I'm not going to mention it, why ruin the day now that Myra is laughing again? She and Ian roll about in hysterics on the rug as the Goons yap like mad dogs on tape, *Ying Yang* this and *Neddy* that, what the fuck are they on about? My head is throbbing, but go on, fill my glass again, cause life just got a whole lot better.

* * *

One of the dogs scrabbles at the kitchen door: David gets up to let it out into the yard area and it dashes, an auburn blur, past the fine greenhouse he built for Mary and across the lawn.

He returns slowly to his chair at the table and sits deep in thought for a moment before explaining: 'Until Angela's death, Brady couldn't "get" to me. Before she died, everything was good in my life, as far as I was concerned, and he knew it. All the Hitler stuff . . . he had those speeches put onto vinyl by a company specialising in that sort of thing. He'd bring round his latest record of Hitler and Goebbels addressing rallies, and some German marching songs. He'd get right into it, banging his fist on his knee, pointing with a bony finger to insist that this bit or that bit was important, translating it for me. I wasn't interested back then and couldn't understand a word – it was *his* thing, him talking *at* me while I was drunk. I'd nod away, but I wasn't really listening. He used to watch a programme called *All Our Yesterdays* as well – it showed wartime newsreels and he'd set up his camera to take photos off the telly of Hitler, waiting for a good shot. Myra was just as obsessed. But it was the *sound* they loved more than anything because, let's face it, their German wasn't that good. So although he tried his best to get me into it all, it didn't work because there wasn't a great deal Hitler and Goebbels said that he actually understood.'

He pauses, frowning. 'And you've got to take into account the massive part alcohol played in all this. I'm not using that as an excuse for one minute, but just bear in mind that whenever we met up, drink was always involved. Even when we still had Angela with us . . . I needed the drink because I wasn't interested in what he was saying otherwise. I was into my rock 'n' roll – Nuremberg rallies weren't my idea of a party. It pissed me off when Brady slung aside my Gene Vincent records in favour of Hitler ranting away about Jews.'

David gives a mocking laugh. 'He was a funny sort of DJ – Herman Saville. And of course, none of it made sense. He'd say he hated Jews, but a Jewish tailor made his clothes and he was dead pernickety about those threads. Yet he'd launch into a spiel: "Do you know America is run by Jews? What do you think Marks & Spencers is all about? The Jews are in charge of everything . . ." When he was on a rant, the records would be turned down low and he'd talk with that bloody finger of his in the air. Where were the girls? They were there for some of it. At Wardle Brook Avenue, me and him had a chair each and the girls would perch on a drop-leaf table – that was the table where Edward Evans fell and Brady dragged him out from under it . . .'

He breaks off and is silent for a moment, then returns to the subject of those nights: 'So, the girls would sit on the table and chat away, not paying us any attention. When they went to bed, the atmosphere would change. More drink would flow and he'd become more intense. We'd leave the chairs. I'd be on one side of the Formica coffee table and he'd be on the other, ashtray filling up between us, booze on the floor, music or speeches playing in the background. I found it very hard to understand him then because I never really got to grips with that accent of his, but when he was drunk . . . he'd really go for it, spittle gathering at the corners of his mouth, beady eyes – a mad man intent on having his say.'

The seismic shift in their friendship came immediately after Angela's death; that changed everything. 'Brady saw an opening then,' David repeats. 'That's when he decided which way things were going to go. He knew that I was totally vulnerable. Nothing seemed to mean anything to me any more. I bailed out of life – my own, and everybody else's too . . .'

Ian Brady had a tried-and-tested means for drawing someone deeper into his world. In the early stages of his relationship with Myra Hindley, he encouraged her to think not only about politics and culture as she had never done before, but also recommended certain literature for her to read. He pushed her towards the classics – Blake, Wordsworth and Shakespeare feature in their post-arrest writings to each other – but also urged her to read philosophy and erotica, beginning with Henry Miller and Harold Robbins and progressing to the then largely forgotten Marquis de Sade, whose books are filled with sexual cruelty and murder. 'If crime is seasoned by enjoyment, crime can become a pleasure' ran a line from de Sade's novel *Justine or The Misfortunes of Virtue*. Superficially, this subversive 'education' was intended to expand her knowledge, but in truth it became a means of exploring their own increasingly brutal desires – and acted as the stimulus towards making them a reality.

David recalls his initiation: 'I didn't know what Brady was leading up to – only he, and possibly Myra, knew that. He gave me Harold Robbins' *The Carpetbaggers* to read first. Robbins was a very popular author at that time anyway. Brady recommended his books and others with mildly sexy stuff in them. Then he gave me *Fanny Hill*, which was banned, and *The Adventures of Molly Brown*, which was a variation on *Fanny Hill*. I was a 16-year-old lad, so I was happy to skim the dull passages to get to the raunchy bits. You've got to remember the era itself as well – censorship was still firmly in place and would be for a while. There was only one cinema in Manchester that showed what were known as "continental" films – Cinephone on Market Street, where the Arndale Centre is now.' He grins suddenly: 'The audience was all blokes sitting far from each other, with their overcoats folded across their laps, waiting to see a bit of Swedish boob. It wasn't any ruder than that because of the British censor. The films themselves were utter rubbish, but no one went for the storylines.'

His smile subsides as he picks up the thread of the conversation: 'So, I read *The Carpetbaggers*, *Fanny Hill* and *Molly Brown*. Then all of a sudden Brady handed me *Sexus* by Henry Miller. Now, to a 16-year-old lad in 1965, that stuff was really naughty. Miller was regarded as an intellectual and Brady viewed his work as classy erotica. I read the sequels to *Sexus* as well – *Nexus* and *Plexus*. Brady would say to me, "Try reading that one, Dave," and he'd hand me the novels with pages thumbed over to indicate the pertinent bits. It was just plain daft, all of that; two blokes sniggering over mucky books. Then Brady switched gear again.'

Tib Street, in the centre of Manchester, had an eclectic mix of shops and a seedy reputation: pet shops sold puppies with distemper and the bookstores were those where the majority of sales were 'under the counter' paperbacks and magazines. It was 'literature' from a Tib Street shop that Ian now suggested David should study in depth, books with titles such as *The Kiss of the Whip* and the ubiquitous de Sade.

'Brady wanted me to compile some notes on those books to find out what I thought about them in more depth,' David recalls. 'I did as he asked and took my little notepad round to

Wardle Brook Avenue so that he could have a look at it. With hindsight, I can see what he was doing, but at the time I just accepted it. Brady was ten years older than me – I was fifteen when we met and he was twenty-five. Two years down the line, that gap hadn't narrowed as it would have done had we been middle-aged men. I was intellectually naive – streetwise, but uneducated. I thought I was learning something useful from him, even though I didn't have a clue what it might be. But I'd read the latest book he had for me and try to write some sort of dissertation on it. I couldn't write it out word for word, obviously, but I'd interpret what I'd read into my version of the original, in order to demonstrate that I'd understood it. He would then read my notes and go through the "set text" with me, discussing what he felt the author was trying to express.'

David stops abruptly, rubbing his chin and grimacing. 'Later, in court, they failed to get to the bottom of that. In the '60s, no one knew about grooming – grooming was combing your bloody hair. But looking back, that's what was happening, although I wasn't aware of it. The defence tried very hard to imply that the notes I'd made were my own ideas, but they were wrong. It was simply me proving to Brady that I'd understood the books – the philosophies behind them weren't my own. I did it for him. And one of the passages that interested Brady was de Sade's rumination on murder. It begins: "Should murder be punished by murder? Undoubtedly not . . ."'

The passage is from *The Life and Ideals of the Marquis de Sade*. It continues: 'The only punishment that a murderer should be condemned to is that which he risks from his friends or the family of the man he has killed. "I pardon him," said Louis XV to Charolais, "but I also pardon him who will kill you." All the bases of the law against murderers is contained in that sublime sentence . . . In a word, murder is a horror, but a horror often necessary, never criminal, and essential to tolerate in a republic. Above all it should never be punished by murder.'

In an address to the Medico-Legal Society in 1967, one year after the trial, William Mars-Jones, QC, quoted from David's notes about de Sade: 'You are your own master. You live for one thing, supreme pleasure in everything you do. Sadism is the supreme pleasure!!! Look around, watch the fools doing exactly what their fathers did before them. The book, they live by the book!!' Mars-Jones added: 'That is a quite remarkable composition for a lad of this background and this education. It is clear that this was a lad of above average intelligence. He had the misfortune to be born illegitimate, as was Brady. It may well be that the fact that they were brought up by relatives gave them cause to have some grievance against society. Brady was above average intelligence. In the light of the evidence, I hope that you will be satisfied that in this case the power of the written word was clearly demonstrated.'

* * *

From David Smith's memoir:

I'm stoned on red wine, my mood dark, listening to Ian: *niggers, black bastards, monkeys, filth, kill them all, black tide, send the bastards back to the jungle, right?* Yeah, dead fucking right. *Think about going with one, seen the kids, like apes they are, that's where it should be stopped, stop the bastards breeding. Hitler was right with the Jew bastards, inter-breeds the lot, drag them out, kick the shit out of them, get fucking rid . . .*

Maureen and Myra went to bed a long time ago, sleeping hutched up together like they used to as kids, in the single bed in Myra's room. The full-blooded conversations between Ian and me only happen when the girls aren't there. Myra knows what's going on, what Ian is building up to, long before I do. But she isn't part of it. His ideas are hers, though; they share the same views on everything and he's doing a good job on me now that Angela is dead. Religion means nothing to me any more. My daughter's death is everybody's fault and I haven't found a way of coping with it. I don't care about anything, least of all myself. So let Ian spout his philosophy into the night as long as he shares his whisky and wine.

Between us on the coffee table, surrounded by empty bottles and a full ashtray, is a chessboard. Three pawns lie on their side where Ian knocked them over during a fevered rant about how the Nazis got it right and Churchill was a stupid bastard. I try to focus on the black, upright King and Queen. But the alcohol gurgles inside my brain, making the small sitting room spin. I'm seeing double dogs and inside its cage the budgie is making a racket that goes right through my skull. The drinking has been hard and fast, conversations manic, and now Ian's eyes are kaleidoscoping, as he spits out another load of spleen.

I struggle off the floor into a chair and put my head in my hands. I want to vomit, but if I get up I'll keel over. I don't know why Ian's put the electric fire on – it feels like the roasting belly of a ship's engine room and the whisky is heating my insides to boiling point. I raise my head as he says my name. He grins and lifts his glass: 'Prost.' More fucking German . . . why can't he just say 'cheers' like everyone else?

His raised glass is the last thing I see.

Hours later, I wake up on the fold-down settee with a blanket over me. The room is dark, the fire out, even the ever-chirping budgie has gone to sleep. I'm in the middle of the worst hangover of my life as I struggle to semi-consciousness, mouth rotten, head screaming pain. In the pale light filtering in through the curtains, I look across at the table. Glasses are overturned, the ashtray is piled high, and chess pieces lie like strange figures on a battlefield.

Then I feel his breath against my neck.

Slowly, I turn my head, letting my eyes slide to where Ian lies behind me on the settee, shirtless but in his vest and trousers. I know he sleeps here every night, and Myra with him. But how did I get here? From the chair to the settee? A towering wave of nausea crashes over me, as I check myself quickly, making sure everything is in order, and almost pass out with relief when I realise it is.

But I feel like hell. I'm terrified of standing up because my head's going to roll – hammers bang inside my temples. Carefully, I slide my legs off the settee and, by a miracle, make it up the stairs to the loo, vomit, douse myself with cold water and head back downstairs again.

Ian is sitting up on the bed, looking as if nothing has happened. And it hasn't, but I still feel odd. Taking off his shirt and getting in next to me . . . I can't get my sorry head around it and don't want to, either. Usually the pair of us sleep wherever we conk out, and that's fine by me.

'Cup of tea?' he asks softly, pinching the bridge of his nose with a long finger and thumb.

I nod and cough, and when he goes through to the kitchen I ease myself into a chair by the dead fire, cracking my knuckles and thinking: *I'll be so fucking glad when it's daylight.*

Chapter 9

'He asked if I was capable of using a gun, or of murder.'
       – David Smith, Moors trial at Chester Assizes,
       April 1966

Money was tight while David was out of work; for a time, only Maureen was bringing in a regular wage. Ian had a suggestion to solve their financial problems and his own: robbery. But what appeared on the surface to be an extreme solution to their difficulties was also Ian's means of testing David, to see how far the 17 year old was able to enter into his and Myra's secret world, without baulking at the tasks they set for him.

'We discussed robbing the Williams & Glyn's bank on Ashton Old Road,' David recalls. 'The idea was that I would stake it out – and this plan involved Myra. One morning the pair of them drove me down to the bank, opposite Grey Mare Lane market, and dropped me on the corner. I had a notepad and pen to jot down comings and goings – a bit like the tutorship thing again. Brady reckoned that the security van pulled up at a side entrance, and he told me to keep an eye out for when it appeared and left. He loaned me a watch because I didn't own one. The difficulty was that I only had a clear view of the doors from the street corner, but I didn't want to draw attention to myself, so every couple of hours I would walk to the other end of the road. I was there from half past eight until closing time, and had nothing on me but my bus fare home. I jotted down page after page of nonsense, really, just to get something on paper. But I thought I'd done a good job and was meticulous about noting everything down. Afterwards I caught the bus back to Hattersley and went straight to Wardle Brook Avenue. I took it seriously, thinking we were in the early stages of something big, which is why what happened next really annoyed me.'

He pauses briefly, frowning. 'When I handed my notebook to Ian, he lit a cigarette and asked, "How did it go?" Very casual, like. I told him, "Not too bad. Didn't see any security vans or anything like that, but I think we did all right. I don't know if there's anything handy in there . . ." I pointed towards the notepad and Brady glanced down at it, then without so much as opening the first page he tossed it onto the coffee table and went through to the kitchen.' David shakes his head: 'Dismissive wasn't in it – he didn't even *pretend* to show any interest. I was fuming; but now, of course, I realise it was just an exercise to him. He was "putting me through my paces", seeing how far I would go.'

He pauses again and then explains slowly, 'It was through the *idea* of the robbery that he was able to raise the subject of murder . . . would I be prepared to kill, if necessary? It went like this: a few nights prior to my hanging about outside the bank, he outlined a scenario: "Imagine you've gone into the bank with the gun, Dave. What if you're confronted by a security guard? What if he comes at you – we're talking big money, remember. High stakes." My reply was to use blanks, because the noise alone should do it – I had that starter pistol and if you put a blank cartridge in it, the thing made a hell of a racket. Brady used to fire it in Wiles Street when he was drunk. It was harmless enough, but the deafening crack it made was horrible. Your ears would ring for a long time afterwards. But Brady waved away my suggestion, insisting, "No way. We're talking *live* ammunition. The guard is there in front of you. You've got to drop him, you've got to be ready to kill. Are you up for that – we're talking murder. Myra will be in the car, waiting to get us out of there afterwards . . ."'

David lets the words tail off and hunches forward in his chair. 'He had no intention of robbing a bank. The "stakeout" was a ruse of his, to give the idea a whiff of authenticity, but after I handed in my notebook he never mentioned it again. It was a test. Brady had his guns, the Webley .45 and Smith & Wesson .38, which we'd used for target practice on the moor, shooting at an oil drum on an old railway sleeper down in the valley. That was just larking about, as far as I knew, but he tied it in with the imaginary bank job to find out how far I would go – if I *could* kill someone. Then one night he turned the gun on me . . .'

* * *

From David Smith's memoir:

Ian's lost it. Why didn't I see this coming?

We're in the middle of our heaviest drinking session yet at Wardle Brook Avenue. Reason has flown out of the window and ego fills the room like brutal helium. The girls are asleep in Myra's room upstairs, leaving us to our madness.

Ian wears his customary white shirt, tie, waistcoat and fancy cufflinks. At first glance he looks exactly what he is, a minor company stock-clerk . . . apart from a single detail: the Webley sitting snug in the heavy leather gun-holster under his left arm. That little accessory transforms him from an office worker to a city gangster, a 1920s throwback.

He's got it into his wine-and-whisky-pickled head that I never believed his talk about robbing banks and shooting the moronic hero who's prepared to die for the business. He doesn't realise that I couldn't give a fuck about anything any more. Life is running in slow motion or on pause, depending on my mood when I wake up. This dreary little house at the end of a dreary little terrace is just somewhere else to go, a place to get stoned on booze and talk about nothing. If I have to listen to shit to get pissed for free, then I will, and if I agree with what he's saying, it's just because I can't be arsed to argue, but tonight Ian's taken it personally and is spoiling for a verbal brawl.

The Formica coffee table displays the usual still life: empty bottles, overflowing ashtrays and an abandoned chessboard. There's just one difference: the bullets Ian's emptied from his gun. I half-close my right eye to focus, stumbling through the numbers . . . one short.

I hear a sudden whir across the table and jerk my head up as Ian spins the gun chamber. His narrow mouth is drawn back in a grin and his eyes are unusually bright.

'This is how easy it is to kill,' he murmurs. 'Look at me and then look at the gun. Look at the fucking gun . . .'

I stare past his outstretched arm and straight into his face. The smile doesn't reach his eyes. I'm thinking: *he means it, he's gonna do it.*

Ian raises his voice: 'Into the gun, look into the hole of the gun, you're not going to see it coming, blink and you won't even know I've shot you, look at the fucking gun . . . You're about to die . . .'

He squeezes the trigger and I close my eyes tightly, a tremor passing from my skull to my feet.

Then silence.

I open my eyes slowly. He disengages the chamber and I watch one bullet fall to the floor. I sit with my head still on my shoulders, no screaming agony and no warm blood oozing from the centre of my forehead – just a cold finger of fear scraping down my spine.

'That's how easy it is, Dave.' His voice is back to its normal low level. 'You just have to press the fucking trigger . . .'

I feel numb. The tremor is a memory; I am still and quiet, as cool as Ian himself.

He watches me and I smile at him, the numbness growing stronger with each passing second. 'You fucker,' I say, and realise he's no longer drunk but completely sober.

When I was a child, my mother would pull out my teeth herself when they were loose. I trusted her and hid my panic, but inside I was scared stiff. Now, looking at Ian's pitiless face, I feel the cold, clean rush of absolute fear but somehow I am still able to subdue it and smile . . .

Writing this more than 40 years after that night, I wonder why I couldn't see things more clearly then. But reflecting back on life is difficult. All the pieces that once seemed murky and blunt as glass washed up by the sea are suddenly transparent and sharp again. But at the time it's very different – the intensity and speed carry you forward on a wave, thunder in your ears and salt in your eyes. Or maybe that's just crap and life itself is meaningless in the end.

That night I felt death approaching, accelerating with unstoppable velocity.

I thought it was my own.

* * *

During another drinking session at Wardle Brook Avenue, Ian posed a question: *Was there anyone David hated enough to not want around any more?* Eventually, David told him about the rows with Sammy Jepson and Tony Latham. Ian asked for a few details and homed in on Tony rather than Sammy, for no other reason than that Sammy lived in Gorton. He told David that he would need a photograph of Tony; David replied that he could easily get a snap of him on his new Polaroid camera and the best place to do it was in Tony's favourite pub.

A couple of nights later, Myra and Ian drove into Manchester and dropped David at the back of a cinema known by locals as the Flea Pit. Clutching the Polaroid, David climbed out of the car and walked down Hyde Road to the Dolphin pub, where Tony was chatting with a group of mates. David joined in their conversation, using the camera itself as a ruse and passed it round the gathering to give them all a closer look. When they handed it back, he pressed the shutter quickly in Tony's direction, then nipped into the toilets before the photograph popped out. Examining the camera, he discovered he'd forgotten to load it with film. Mortified, he returned to Hattersley on the bus, convinced that Ian would be furious. Yet when he called round the following evening to explain, Ian merely shrugged. The subject was ditched as swiftly as the idea of the bank robbery.

'Did we seriously intend to kill Tony Latham?' David shakes his head slowly. 'It was all part of the same nonsense, said in drink and about as real as anything else we discussed together . . . so no, it was just more crap. An element of intention was there, but what kind of assassin sets out to snap his victim without putting film in the camera? It was never followed up because, at the end of the day, it was just "big talk" again. I thought that's all everything was . . . but I was wrong.'

David's suspicion that his own life hung in the balance wasn't without foundation: in September 1965, Ian Brady and Myra Hindley discussed whether or not they should kill him. Over a bottle of wine on the hills above Buxton, the couple debated his murder. Ian declared himself profoundly irritated with David's 'domestic' problems; Maureen had recently discovered she was pregnant again and David, still reeling from the loss of Angela Dawn, reacted angrily. The couple had a serious row, and Maureen left to stay at her mother's house in Gorton. But she was only there for one night; David turned up full of apologies and they began looking forward to the birth of their child, due the following May. Ian was scathing about their relationship and uneasy about what he termed 'a flaw' in David's character, which made him a potential liability to their future plans.

More than 20 years later, Ian Brady told journalist Fred

Harrison how he had intended to get rid of David, but Myra convinced him otherwise: 'Head out of Manchester. Take the .38 Smith & Wesson. Blow his head off. Mo [*Maureen*] some days or weeks later would have enquired if we had heard anything from him. Nothing. [*But*] it was always Mo this, and Mo that. [*Myra*] didn't want to hurt Mo. Mo baby – you know, she was the younger sister.'

At the end of the month, David found out that his much-loved dog, Peggy, whom he had been forced to leave behind in Wiles Street, had been put to sleep. Jack Smith was then working several days away from home in London and had taken the decision to have Peggy destroyed without consulting his son. David responded by downing copious amounts of alcohol, and when Ian and Myra arrived at Underwood Court from a short holiday in Scotland they found him in bed, distraught and inebriated.

'Ian walked into the bedroom and asked me if I was all right,' David recalled for the benefit of the courtroom in Chester several months later. 'Then he turned round and he said: "It's that bleeder who should have got the needle and not the dog." . . . I wasn't angry with [*Dad*]. I was upset about the dog . . . He had had it humanely destroyed . . . Myra went out of her way to try and save the dog. She drove all the way down to the dog's home . . . she was just too late.' Despite the ban on dogs at Underwood Court, within days he and Maureen had acquired a handsome collie whom they named Bob. Taking Bob for walks was problematic; David had to sneak him down the stairwell, directly past the door of caretaker Mr Page, who was rapidly getting to the end of his tether with the young couple in Flat 18.

Earlier that month, Ian had considered killing David. For reasons known only to himself and Myra, he now set aside his unease completely about the 'flaw' in his younger friend. Having bided his time while he weighed up whether David could be trusted or not, he took the final plunge one night after the girls had gone to bed. Following vast quantities of wine and whisky, Ian Brady at last split open the secret he and Myra Hindley had so carefully concealed for the past two years.

* * *

From David Smith's memoir:
2 October 1965, Wardle Brook Avenue, long after midnight.

Away from Myra, Ian is changing. He's becoming intense, and conversations are always long and involved. Something is eating away inside him, compelling him to talk. Gone are the half-baked plans for robbery; now, he's opening up his world to me: a world where people are worthless, maggots and morons, where human life is less important than swatting a fly. He's obsessed with the idea that I doubt him and it makes him excited, overwrought.

Away from Myra, he's heading for an experience unlike any other, searching for the ultimate kick, and is keyed up by the need to take us all with him, to the floor of his abyss.

He thinks he has me. In *his* mind, when I agreed to stake out the bank and talked about wanting an old acquaintance wiped out, that was a commitment to him. He might have had his reservations about me, but they're gone now. He trusts me.

In a voice whisky-thick and wired with energy, he talks about religion as lobotomy, and the genius of de Sade. Then he asks, banging his fist down on his knee, 'What's wrong with killing somebody if you're prepared to accept responsibility for your actions?'

The whisky makes his accent stronger, the r's rolling, like the mist across the moor, and he emphasises certain words, clenching and unclenching that fist. 'The victim's *family* has the *right* to kill you. An eye for an eye, a tooth for a tooth. Let the murderer face the family of the one that he's killed. That's de Sade's philosophy for you in a *nutshell*. He was right . . .'

I don't answer, but I nod, almost involuntarily, aware of the stink from the ashtray, where red wine has been spilled into the pile of spent cigarettes.

After a pause, he starts again, leaning forward across the table, his eyes unnaturally bright as always during a tirade.

'Think about it. No, no, think about *God*. Where was *he* when Angela died? If there is a God, he had no *right* to let that happen, did he? *Bastard*. What life did she have? Six months is *fuck all*. God murdered your child. But there *is* no God, God is *nothing*. God killed your fucking daughter, who the *fuck* is God?'

I don't say a word. I keep the whisky in my mouth and listen, head bowed, stoned out of my brain on booze.

His fist is on the coffee table as he rages at me: 'Your *dad* had no right to kill Peggy. It should have been your fucking *dad* who got the jab. You get fuck all from people, dogs are better, they give you devotion, they give their *lives* for you. You see them two dogs there, Lassie and Puppet, stretched out by the telly? They mean and *give* more to you than any two-legged arsehole. Fuck parents, lovers and kids. They all do what *they* want in the end . . .'

The whisky shoots through my skull, filling every corner of my brain with its blistering fog. My forehead is almost resting against the edge of the coffee table. I feel something building in the room, a moment that's been a long time in coming.

His voice is calm when he says it. One short, sharp breath and out it comes: '*Listen* to me. *I've killed*. I've done it. I know what it's like.'

I don't believe him.

'You think I'm lying, don't you? You think I'm a lying cunt, but it's been done, *I've killed*, more than once. Ach, but you don't believe me. Maggots, they're all fucking maggots . . .'

I don't believe him. Through the fever in my head, I'm thinking: *like fuck, you haven't killed anyone*. I raise an eyebrow sceptically and it ignites something in him, bringing his words down on my head: 'I've got photographic *proof*, and you've sat on one of the *graves*. Get the bastards over 16, that's the easiest way, they're nothing to the police then, just some sad missing kid, runaways who've fucked off to *London* and the bright lights, file and forget. Jews, winos, queers – who gives a shit about *them*? They're fucking *germs* and worth fuck all, even the police see them as numbers and know the world's well rid. Who's gonna give a *fuck* about some dirty little shirt-lifter? Hitler had the right idea, that's just my point, he had the right fucking *idea* . . .'

Shut up, I'm thinking. *Let me lie down and sleep. Talking a load of drunken shite again. Bank job, here we come. Tony Latham, here we come. I am a murderer, here we fucking come. Shut your fucking mouth and let me rest.*

But the momentum spins; Ian's pale eyes start out of his head: 'Listen, there are two ways to do it, I'm fucking telling you, *two ways*, not just one. First method: get the car and yourself ready, prepare the *lot*, clean the car, cover the inside with polythene, count *all* the buttons on what you're wearing and note *everything*, mustn't leave anything behind – do you fucking *understand*, are you *listening*? Right, so you get out of the car, find the maggots – Central Station, Union Hotel, Rembrandt bar, queers – just *get* them, splatter them away. But that's not the best way to do it, there's too many *risks*, you have to clean your clothes and everything else afterwards. Not enough *control* in the situation. Second method, this one is *better*: get them and do them in a place where you have *full* control, even over the fucking *body*, you can't get caught then, 'cause the police are thick fuckers, give them fuck all and they *do* fuck all. Plan ahead, and if you're questioned, give them the old spiel about not remembering anything more than ten days ago, that's *normal* . . .'

He sits back suddenly, spent, breathless.

I look at him and his eyes narrow.

'It will be done again.' He nods slowly. 'But this one won't count. I'm not due another yet, but it *will* be done.' His lips curl in a sly smile and I feel unnaturally tired.

He's speaking again, but my brain scarcely registers his soft, insistent voice: 'You know what I get from it? *Control*. You're in control and that's the biggest fucking high you'll ever have, you're in *control*. You can even control death, do you fucking understand me, it's all a matter of *control* . . .'

* * *

'He'd been building up to that moment for some time,' David explains, running his thumbnail along a deeply scored groove in the kitchen table. 'It went back to the day of Angela's funeral, when he'd sat in the car without acknowledging my grief. His attitude that day had a purpose – he was already thinking ahead to how he would use it, twisting it into his philosophy about there being no God and life worth so little. He waited until he felt he had me in his grasp. The books, the note-taking, the soft porn and the stronger stuff, the bank robbery and Tony Latham – all of that was "grooming". Then he sprang the trap: "I've killed."'

After a long silence, David clarifies Myra's perception of how things stood between them: 'She definitely wasn't pleased about his desire to bring me into their little secret. She would have been aware of what he was after long before it ever occurred to me, because she was able to recognise the pattern and what it had led to between the two of them. When we were discussing the bank job, she knew about it and wasn't tidy with it at all. *She* didn't want me on board – that came from him. I'm sure they would have talked about what was happening with me and agreed on a strategy – kill me if anything went wrong. She could tell that he was overstretching their boundaries and there was no need for it. And I'm positive – because I could see it in her whole attitude – that she wasn't happy with any of it, especially given that he was on this insane, downward spiral where he was *losing* control.'

He frowns. 'I can't emphasise this enough – how Brady changed within the space of the year that we became friends. It was a colossal transformation from the Mr Nice Guy who invited me and Maureen round on our wedding night to his confession at Wardle Brook Avenue. But the fact is that he *wasn't* the man who took us on that freebie trip to the Lakes – that was the pretence. He didn't turn *into* something – he reverted *back* to what he really was. My first glimpse of the real Ian Brady was on the day of my daughter's funeral. Six months later, he'd gone into freefall. But Myra hadn't. She had far more control than him, and it must have given her a few sleepless nights knowing he was preparing for the final spilling of the secret, all that build-up to driving the nail in. Everything that came before that night was his way of introducing the hammer to the nail. But that "I've killed" – that was the impact happening.'

Spurious plans were in place for another robbery, this time an Electricity Board showroom. A date had been mooted to carry out the crime: 8 October. 'I didn't really believe in that, to be honest,' David states firmly, shaking his head. 'It was just stupid. What could we have nicked? People only went in there to pay their bills, it wasn't big money. But I went along with it. Beforehand, Brady asked me to bring round what he called "incriminating material". I didn't know what he was going to do with it, or why it would have any bearing on the robbery if we were caught. Because these things I had to bring, they had nothing to do with any theft, as far as I could see. What did I take round? Books mainly, and my starter pistol, I think. It was early evening when I called at their place.'

Myra answered the door. Ian was upstairs; Granny Maybury was at a neighbour's house. Myra took the brown paper parcel David handed over and placed it on the coffee table in the sitting room. Inside the package were books that included *Mein Kampf, Tropic of Cancer, The Kiss of the Whip, The Life and Ideals of the*

Marquis de Sade, Justine, Orgies of Torture and Brutality, and *The Perfumed Garden*. Ian appeared, said a quick hello and took the parcel back upstairs. He returned a short while later carrying two large suitcases, one brown, one blue. Their contents strained the fabric of the cases.

Ian and Myra went out to the front garden, with David following in the last of the evening sunlight. The Morris Traveller was in its usual parking spot, directly below the wall that ran the length of the short terrace. David vaulted the white picket fence and stood below the wall, ready to pass the suitcases from Ian to Myra, who was standing beside the car. As Ian angled the second suitcase over the fence to David, he said unsmilingly, 'Don't drop it or it'll blow us all up.'

Five minutes later, with both suitcases safely placed away, Ian joined Myra in the car. They drove off, leaving David to head back to Underwood Court alone, wondering where they'd gone, and why.

Wednesday, 6 October 1965 was a beautiful, crisp autumn day. David mooched about the flat all morning and managed to sneak Bob out for a walk. At some point, the rent man called at Underwood Court and pushed a note under the door of Flat 18. It read:

> Mr Smith, I want £14 12s 6d at the Town Hall on Saturday or I shall take legal proceedings. Mr Page is doing his job and if that dog is not out of the building by tonight I shall have you evicted. If there are any more complaints of Teddy boys and noise I shall take further action.

When David showed the note to Maureen, she scribbled on the back of it:

> Dear Sir,
> My husband and I are at work, and because we are not on the best of terms with Mr Page, I shall personally deliver the rent to the Town Hall on Saturday.
>   Mrs Smith.

143

The two of them decided to ask David's dad for a loan, although the matter of what to do with Bob the dog was unresolved.

Gloomy about the way his day had gone, that evening David called round at Wardle Brook Avenue. Myra was in the process of shooing Granny Maybury up to bed with strong sleeping pills and a cup of tea. David was struck by Myra's and Ian's appearance. She wore an animal print tight-fitting frock and high heels, hair coiffed to perfection and make-up dramatic. Ian had on his grey suit, waistcoat, white shirt and tie. David told him about the note from the rent man; Ian adjusted his cufflinks and shrugged, 'There's nothing you can do about it.' He suggested getting rid of the dog, if David and Maureen didn't want to lose their tenancy at Underwood Court, then told David that he would have to leave, as he and Myra were ready to go out.

David walked down to the Morris Traveller with them, still talking to Ian as Myra started the ignition. When she put her foot down on the accelerator, David watched the small white car as it sped away, in the rapidly dwindling light, towards the city. He loped home and spent the rest of the evening watching telly with Maureen, moodily dwelling on the note and Mr Page's part in it. The young couple decided to have an early night and were already asleep when the entry phone to their flat buzzed.

It was not quite 11.30 p.m. Maureen slipped out of bed and picked up the receiver from its cradle on the wall.

'It's Myra,' said the caller.

Chapter 10

'Edward went out between 6.15 and 6.30 p.m. I didn't see him alive again.'
— Edith Evans, mother of murdered Edward Evans, quoted in *The Reporter*, 17 December 1965

David pulled on his jeans and padded out into the hallway. When Maureen opened the door to Myra, he was immediately struck by his sister-in-law's unkempt appearance.

'Earlier that evening, at Wardle Brook Avenue, she was ultra dressed up,' he recalls. 'Full war paint, tight dress, hair sprayed into a stiff beehive – far beyond the smart secretary look she normally wore. But when she turned up at our flat she had on an old skirt with the hem hanging down, a cardigan and scruffy pumps. The lacquer had gone from her hair and her make-up was smudged. Something had happened before she came to us. She looked a proper mess. It wasn't even that she'd got changed out of her evening gear into something more comfy – she looked a right state. Were they her killing clothes? I don't know. But the expression on her face was . . . well, she wasn't smiling, put it like that. She was edgy, very edgy.'

Maureen said nothing to her sister about her appearance, but she was puzzled by her sudden arrival at their door. She explained in court: '[*Myra*] said she wanted to give me a message for my mother. To tell her she would see her at the weekend, and she could not get up there before . . . I asked her why she'd come round so late and she said it was because she'd forgotten earlier on and she had just remembered. I asked her why she had not got the car, and she said because she had locked it up . . . She asked David would he walk her round to 16 Wardle Brook

Avenue because all the lights were out . . . David said he would, and he got ready. Then he said he would not be two minutes, and then they both left.'

David carried his 'dog-stick': a walking stick he had made for himself, which had string tightly wound around one end to form a grip. Myra asked him what he was bringing it for, and when he said that he always took it out with him at night, she eyed him and said, 'You're in the frame, you are.'

In his official statement to the police, David described what happened next:

> As we approached the front door, Myra stopped walking and she said: 'Wait over the road, watch for the landing light to flick twice.' I didn't think this was unusual because I've had to do this before whilst she, Myra, went in to see if Ian would have me in. He's a very temperamental sort of fellow. I waited across the road as Myra told me to, and then the landing light flicked twice, so I walked up and knocked on the front door. Ian opened the front door and he said in a very loud voice for him, he normally speaks soft: 'Do you want those miniatures?' I nodded my head to show 'yes' and he led me into the kitchen, which is directly opposite the front door, and he gave me three miniature bottles of wine and said: 'Do you want the rest?'
>
> When I first walked into the house, the door to the living room – which was on my right, standing at the front door – was closed. After he put the three bottles down in the kitchen, Ian went into the living room and I waited in the kitchen. I waited about a minute or two, then suddenly I heard a hell of a scream; it sounded like a woman, really high-pitched. Then the screams carried on, one after another, really loud. Then I heard Myra shout, 'Dave, help him.'

*

At half-past ten that night, Ian Brady and Myra Hindley had picked up 17-year-old Edward Evans from Manchester's Central Station. Tall and slim, with light-brown hair and an engaging smile, Edward lived with his parents, Edith and John, and brother and sister at 55 Addison Street in Ardwick. Born the same month and year as David Smith, Edward had grown up almost around the corner from David's childhood home. His father worked as a lift attendant. Edward had found himself a job with prospects and better pay as a junior machine operator at Associated Electrical Industries Limited on Trafford Park industrial estate. He worked hard and liked to relax at night in the city bars with friends or at football – he supported Manchester United and was a regular face in the stands at Old Trafford. That night Edward had gone to meet a friend at a pub in town, expecting to watch the match between his team and Helsinki. But because Edward hadn't confirmed a time, the bar was empty when he arrived and his friend remained at home.

After spending the night hanging about town, some time between ten and half-past, Edward made his way to the buffet bar in Central Station. Finding it closed, he walked across to a milk-vending machine. It was there that he encountered Ian Brady, who invited him back to the house in Hattersley, which he shared with his 'sister' Myra, for a drink.

* * *

From David Smith's memoir:
Forgive me, Father (and that eternal fucking mother thing). It's been too many years since my last confession.

I am forever a Catholic, an illegitimate stink off the cobbled streets of Manchester, brought up correctly by a deformed old woman whom I adored. As a child, I was happy with my religion, saying my prayers just like good boys do, thanking You for everything – good and bad – and I really did believe that life itself was governed by Your will.

And then You turned away.

Years ago, I found this story: *'One night a man had a dream. He was walking along the beach with the Lord while scenes from his life flashed across the sky. In the sand, for every scene, there were two sets of footprints: one belonging to him and the other to the Lord. When the last scene had taken place, he looked back at the sand again and noticed that occasionally there was only one set of footprints, and that this occurred during the lowest and saddest times in his life. He questioned the Lord about it, asking: "Lord, you said that once I decided to follow you, you'd walk with me all the way. But I've noticed that in my darkest hours there is only one set of footprints. Why did you leave me when I needed you most?" And the Lord answered, "My child, my precious child, I love you and I would never leave you. During those times of trial and suffering, when you could see only one set of footprints, it was then that I carried you."'*

It's a nice little story, isn't it, Father? But where were Your footsteps when *I* needed them? Instead of walking next to me, or carrying me, You turned away. Couldn't You face my questions? Couldn't You face Your answers? All the crap I was brought up on – when I needed my faith, You took it away and disappeared. You left me with nothing. I was surrounded by blood, shit and spilt brains, and what did You do?

You left me to choke on it.

Inside I was screaming. Why couldn't You hear my silence? Why couldn't You see that I was falling apart? You left me hanging off the end of a fucking rosary instead.

Fucking cunt, dirty bastard . . . In a nice, normal overspill living room Ian is killing a lad with an axe, repeating those same words over and over again. The lad is lying with his head and shoulders on the settee, his legs sprawled on the floor, facing upwards. Ian stands over him, legs on either side of the screaming lad. The television is the only light in the room.

The lad falls onto the floor, onto his stomach, still screaming. Ian keeps hitting him; even when the lad falls beneath the table, Ian goes after him, drags him out and hits him again. He swings the axe and it grazes the top of Myra's head. There is blood everywhere. Then he stops and shouts: *get the fucking dogs away from the blood, get the fucking things out of it . . .*

The lad is lying on his face, feet near the door. Ian kneels down and strangles him, pulling something tight around his throat. The lad's head is destroyed already; he rattles and gurgles, a thick, wet sound, a low sound. Then lower: more effort from Ian, and lower, and lower, then nothing but silence, everlasting silence.

Ian stands, breathing heavily, but casually looking at his hands, drenched in blood. His voice is blunt as he speaks to Myra: *that's it, the messiest one yet . . .*

Oh Mother of Jesus, Christ Almighty, I'm out of here, through the door, through the window, through the fucking ceiling, if need be.

But I'm rooted to the spot.

Ian passes me the axe. *Feel the fucking weight of that – how did he take it?*

Fuck me, I answer and smile at him. *I don't know.*

He smiles back.

Jesus Christ, the axe is covered in blood. It's all over my hands now, where I held it. This isn't real: the lad's brains are on the floor and we're standing face to face, smiling at each other. I'm thinking: *he's not doing that to me, I'm not fighting my way out of this house and being smashed to bits like that lad.* At the same time, I know that this *is* real: Ian is looking at me with a crazed light in his eyes and his clothes are saturated with the lad's blood, yet he's as friendly and normal as if we're out in the street.

A shout from upstairs: Granny Maybury wants to know what's happened.

Myra coolly moves into the hallway to reassure her: *it's all right, Gran, I dropped something on my foot, just go back to sleep.* She comes back into the room, stepping over the lad as if he's not even there, concerned for Ian, who's hurt his ankle: *are you all right, love?*

Yes, it's fine, I must have caught it, but I'm OK. Can you bring in the cleaning stuff?

Then he turns to me, his eyes still demented: *there's a hole in the wall next to the fireplace, put your finger in that. I felt the fucking thing bounce off his fucking head, that's when it swung back into the wall . . .*

This is a Godless house and always has been. God is not on my side either – I am alone and all He does is watch as I feel the survival instinct seeping through me. I'm calmer than Ian, calmer than Myra – calmer than the two of them together. I will not die here, not tonight, not like that lad there, on the floor with his brains bashed in. I'm getting out of this Godless house alive.

Ian bends to his knees, rooting through the lad's clothes. I notice with that same appalling sense of calm that the lad's top button and zip on his jeans are undone. The smell coming away from him is pure filth, something rotten.

Are You listening, Father? Can You hear me after all these years have passed? It's a smell you can talk about but never imagine, a smell from this world that belongs to another, a smell that comes back to me even now in a field of bright flowers. Father, I can look straight into Your eyes and that smell will be pouring out of my brain and nostrils. Why am I telling You this when You turned away from me and hid behind Your all-forgiving cross?

Ian slides his fingers through the lad's wallet. He pulls out a green identity card. *Edward Evans. Apprentice at Associated Electrical Industries Limited, Trafford Park. The fucker's name was Edward Evans. Eddie. Did you know him, Dave? He's the same age as you and from Ardwick as well, did you know him?*

I look down at the oozing mess on the floor. The lad has gone, but now he has a name and suddenly he's real to me again. Fifteen minutes ago, he was alive and still warm. Edward Evans. I didn't know him, but I was here when he took his last breath, screaming for his mother. They say death is a long sleep, but this wasn't a peaceful closing of the eyes. God didn't care about Edward Evans, either.

I don't know him. Who is he?

Forget it, it's nothing. Small fucking world, though, eh?

Ian grins at me and I grin straight back, a rictus smile stretching my mouth ear to ear.

Myra comes in from the kitchen: *God, look at the mess. No wonder Joey is going mental in his cage. Look . . .*

Ian frowns: *cover the fucking budgie up, then.*

Things begin to slow down. An insane normality envelops me, as we stand in silence, all three of us, listening for any sounds from the Braithwaites next door, holding our breath. *Fucking niggers, always knew they had coconuts stuck in their ears*, Ian grins. We all nod and smile, and then Ian is on the floor next to the body of Edward Evans, covering his ruined head while Myra brings in polythene and a blanket for the next stage.

Outside, the world has stopped; the only living things are in this room – it's just me, and him, and her. I accept this matter-of-factly. It makes sense to me in this moment to know that no one else is alive, only we three.

Fucking rope, we haven't got any fucking rope.

Myra looks blankly at Ian as he repeats, *we've no fucking rope, how can we do him up without fucking rope?*

My hands reach for my dog-stick that's fallen on the floor; around one end is a tightly wound piece of string. I pass it to Ian: *Is this any good, will this do?*

The sheets are laid down.

Get the bastard's shoulders, Ian tells me. *Get him over here.*

I put my hands on Edward. His blood is very thick and slippy, and it's everywhere. Ian holds his feet and dumps him on the sheets on his back, head covered, trousers undone. Ian uses my string to tie him roughly, using a lot of force, pressing down on him with his knee and pulling the string as taut as possible: *get the bastard's legs and push them back.* I grab one leg and the other drops sideways out of my hands. Ian stands above me: *use your weight, I need them right back.* I hold Edward's knees together and bend his legs, pushing them against his chest. *Fucking hell.* I turn my head away; the smell is full in my face and putrid. But we go on. I keep the pressure on Edward's legs and Ian uses the string to truss him up until he's in the shape of a ball, head forward to meet his knees. We wrap him in the blanket and then it's time for a break.

We both sit on the settee, with the bundle that was Edward Evans to one side of us. Through the serving hatch, I can see Myra in the kitchen, organising bowls and cloths for the clean-up. I pass Ian a cigarette, casual and normal. He smiles broadly, his eyes glittering. He's relaxed. We sit there, smoking together, with our shoulders almost touching.

How are the dogs, Hessy?

Myra replies through the hatch: *fine, a bit quiet.*

The fuckers could smell the blood, couldn't they, eh? I was worried they would get too excited. He turns to me: *we'll finish up in here and then get a cup of tea down us. How does that sound?*

Fine, just the job, I answer.

He stands up and walks to the back of the settee, facing the serving hatch. *Myra, I was just saying to Dave, we'll get this thing out and finish up in here.*

Myra calls through to say that she's going upstairs to check on Gran.

All the time I'm thinking, *what the fuck is he doing behind me, he's gone behind the settee, I need to see him, I need to know where he is, don't turn around, don't look, he'll see it in your eyes, act normal, say something, any sort of shit to make it seem as if you're OK.*

Jesus, it'll take us all night to clean this lot up, I tell him. I pull hard on my cigarette and keep myself still. I blow the smoke up into the air, noisily.

Jesus has fuck all to do with this, he replies.

I laugh and tell him, *you can say that again, all right.*

Myra appears: *Gran's OK, she's settled down.*

Ian jerks his head towards the bundle. I get to my feet and together we drag it to the staircase in the hall. *It'll have to go in the bedroom, we'll shift it tomorrow*, Ian tells Myra. She watches us half-lift, half-drag the bundle up the first couple of steps.

Eddie's a dead weight, Ian grins. Myra starts to giggle uncontrollably.

The shape and heaviness of the bundle makes it difficult to handle. We're both out of breath, bumping it up each stair to reach the tiny landing. I have to edge past Myra, who holds Granny Maybury's door shut. We drag the bundle into the cramped second bedroom that contains nothing but a narrow bed and wardrobe; this is Myra's room, but she only uses it when Maureen stays the night.

We set the bundle down beneath a small window to the left, and for a minute or two Ian stands in the centre of the room, looking curiously at it. I watch him from the door. He grunts to himself and picks up a few books, tossing them on top of what is left of Edward Evans. Then he turns and smiles: *right, let's get on with it.*

Downstairs, Myra provides bowls of hot water and the cleaning begins. At some level that I can't explain, this is the very worst of everything. There is a strong sense of calm between the three of us, yet the smell of the killing is thick and heavy in the air – it is a wicked smell of blood, brains and defecation, more in common with a battleground than a suburban living room. Pieces of bone and black clots are picked up and dropped into a plastic bag. Cloths are used to soak up the blood and then wrung out, time after time, into the bowls. More fresh hot water, watching it turn from pale pink to dark red, moving on all fours about the floor, into corners, under the table, even the budgie's cage gets a going-over.

Ian straightens and picks up the axe. He holds it in his right hand, then passes it to his left and back again, feeling its weight. He smiles at me and I look up and smile at him. He pushes the axe into a carrier bag and somewhere in the core of my calmness I feel a jolt of relief. Myra playfully slaps me across the arse with one of the wet cloths.

That's it, we've finished, it's all done.

The room is back to normal, enough to receive the nosiest of visitors, but this is the most dangerous time for me. Everything has to unfold slowly – nothing must be rushed. The front door, the exit to civilisation, is within reach but still shut.

Myra plonks herself down in the chair by the fire. I sit next to Ian on the settee, sipping hot, sweet tea and smoking a cigarette. The clock is ticking, but I'm struggling to tell if it's still moving forwards or back in time.

Ian's excitement has returned: *Myra, how the fuck did he take that, what do you think?*

I don't know, love, but you could see the blow register in his eyes, he didn't know what hit him, I was looking right at him and he didn't know a thing . . .

They chat as easily as if they're old friends meeting in a doctor's waiting room. Myra prompts him: *do you remember that time we were burying a body on the moors and a policeman came up?*

Ian gives a short laugh.

She turns to look at me, a half-smile on her lips: *I was in the car with a body in the back. It was partitioned off with a plastic sheet. Ian was digging a hole when a policeman came and asked me what the trouble was. I told him I was drying my sparking plugs and he drove off. I was praying that Ian wouldn't come back over the hill . . .*

Ian breaks in with a more immediate concern: *how the hell do we get Eddie out of here, though? I went over on my ankle, it's pretty sore, we can't carry the bastard past the neighbours in broad daylight . . .*

I haven't said a word until now, but I realise if I can come up with an idea, it might just guarantee that the axe stays in the carrier bag.

Angela's pram, I tell them with great effort. *It's still at Mam's house in Ardwick. Myra can pick me up and we can bring it back here, get him into it and push him out to the car.*

My idea gets a laugh from them both, but they take it seriously.

Myra offers me more tea. *No thanks, better get back, don't want Maureen waking up and finding me gone.*

Myra sees the sense in this: *tell Mobee I'll be round to see her later on.*

The final minutes approach. I stand while Ian remains seated, looking up at me. *Right*, he agrees, *we'll sort it out tomorrow.* I nod. He gives me a last, broad smile.

Myra sees me to the front door. When she opens it, I want to leap out: there's the wall of the New Inn, the lights on the road and the cleanest, freshest night air I've ever felt against my skin.

I brush past her, slowly, until I'm on the path. For a moment, my feet are pinned to the ground. *OK, then*, I force myself to say, *I'll be off, but see you both later on.*

Yes, Dave, you will. She gives me a warm, genuine smile.

As I walk away, I hear the click of the door shutting behind me. I take a deep breath that seems to last for ever and suddenly I feel frightened to fucking death.

The only way out of the house that night was to do whatever ungodly thing there was to be done and slowly, calmly, walk away.

There are no footprints between Wardle Brook Avenue and Underwood Court, not even my own.

III
Blacken Smith at All Stages

1965–66

Chapter 11

'What Smith said sounded like a nightmare, but it was not the sort of nightmare that anyone in his right mind could possibly dream.'
 – Detective on the Moors Murders case, 1965

Ian Brady's statement, given to police within a couple of hours of his arrest on 7 October 1965, read:

> Last night I met Eddie in Manchester. We were drinking and then went home to Hattersley. We had an argument and we came to blows. After the first few blows, the situation was out of control. When the argument started, Dave Smith was at the front door and Myra called him in. Eddie was on the floor near the living-room door. Dave hit him with the stick and kicked him about three times. Eddie kicked me at the beginning on my ankle. There was a hatchet on the floor and I hit Eddie with it. After that the only noise Eddie made was gurgling. When Dave and I began cleaning up the floor, the gurgling stopped. Then we tied up the body, Dave and I. Nobody else helped. Dave and I carried it upstairs. Then we sat in the house until three or four in the morning. Then we decided to get rid of the body in the morning early next day or next night.

He chose his words carefully, with three clear objectives in mind: to convince police that the murder wasn't premeditated, to absolve Myra of any involvement, and to implicate David to the hilt. Not yet facing charges, Myra's approach when questioned was the same, culminating in a single line that she repeated like a mantra in the months – and, indeed, years – ahead: 'I didn't do it and Ian didn't do it, ask David Smith.' She maintained that David was 'a liar', and in response to hearing that her brother-in-law had claimed she helped remove evidence after the killing, snapped: 'Yes, and I suppose he told you he sat on the chair benevolently looking on while I cleaned up.'

The couple's insinuations fed into the immediate suspicions of several detectives. During that first day at Hyde police station, David was questioned almost continuously. Police Constable John Antrobus conducted the preliminary interview, followed by Detective Sergeant Roy 'Dixie' Dean of Stalybridge's more gruelling method of inquiry. Recently promoted Superintendent Robert Alexander Talbot, who had been due to depart for his 12 days' annual leave that morning, then interviewed David in the presence of Detective Sergeant Alex 'Jock' Carr, a young, stocky Scotsman.

While Talbot and Carr were talking to David, Ian Fairley arrived at the station. Twenty-one years old and with a Scots accent as strong as Jock Carr's own, Fairley was still on probation as a member of the CID. Now the sole surviving Hyde detective from the original Moors inquiry, he recalls seeing Roy Dean leave the interview room in disgust: 'I have no idea why, but Dixie Dean said the lad [*David*] was talking a load of shit. I suppose it did sound a bit far-fetched at first, but it turned out to be true.'

The bewildering flock of police flitting in and out of the interview room where David spent the entire day with Maureen and Bob the dog swelled further with the arrival of Cheshire's Detective Chief Superintendent. Six days into his promotion, portly Arthur Benfield booked himself into the Queen's Hotel in Hyde, expecting to wrap up the investigation within a couple of days. David's insistence that Ian Brady had boasted of killing others and burying them on the moor failed to register with Benfield, who regarded the case as a tidy one, with the murder victim's body already recovered and the killer in custody, having admitted to the crime. Benfield's greatest dilemma was whether or not to arrest David and Myra. While mulling it over, he and Talbot returned to Wardle Brook Avenue, where pathologist Dr

Charles St Hill was unravelling the bloody wrappings from Edward Evans. St Hill detailed his findings in court:

At about 1.15 p.m. on 7 October 1965, I was shown a large bundle beneath the window in an upstairs bedroom at 16 Wardle Brook Avenue. I opened the bundle . . . The body was bent up with the legs brought up to the chest and the arms folded across the body. The legs and arms were kept in position by two cords. It was further secured by two loops of cord, which kept the neck bent forwards to the knees; these cords passed round the neck and were attached to the other two cords, which bound the legs and arms. I found a blood-stained cloth wrapped round the head and neck, and a piece of electric light cable was around the neck but not tied. The body was enclosed in a white cotton blanket which had been knotted. A polythene sheet lay outside this, and was itself covered by a grey blanket . . .

The body was that of a fairly slim youth, 5 ft 6 in. tall and of about 9–10 stone. It was fully dressed but there were no shoes on the feet.

There were fourteen irregular lacerations distributed over the scalp, right cheek and ear, with surrounding bruising . . . There was widespread bruising of the back of the neck and over the back of the tops of the shoulders and upper back. There was a 1 in. bruise in the small of the back. There was extensive lacerating and bruising of the backs of both hands, the left forearm and the right upper arm; these wounds are accurately described as 'defence wounds' . . . The greater part of the right side of the skull was fragmented and a somewhat rounded depressed fracture was present on the right frontal region . . .

There was much blood on the surface of the brain, with extensive bruising on both sides . . . The lungs were congested with a few haemorrhages on their surface. The right side of the heart was dilated and there were numerous haemorrhages on this surface . . .

I came to the conclusion that the cause of death was

cerebral contusion and haemorrhage due to fractures of the skull due to blows to the head, accelerated by strangulation by ligature.

During his initial examination, St Hill removed the books David had watched Ian pile on top of the body the night before; these included *The Red Brain (Tales of Horror)*. Forensic experts combing the house found numerous samples of hair, blood and stained clothing despite the exhaustive clean-up operation of a few hours earlier. Two tape recorders and tapes, hundreds of photographs and negatives, a tartan photo album, photographic light bulb, two revolvers and bullets, and the carrier bag containing the murder weapon were also removed from the house.

Edward Evans's body was then transferred to the small mortuary at Hyde police station. His mother, a slight, stooping woman in horn-rimmed spectacles, arrived later that day to identify him. DS Alex Carr was with Myra Hindley when the sound of Mrs Evans's uncontrollable anguish pierced the interview room. Carr noted the younger woman's steady hand as she lifted a teacup, sipping at it without betraying a flicker of emotion.

As darkness fell, David and Maureen remained cloistered with police in the small, smoky inquiry room. Benfield left for Hattersley again and, having satisfied himself that there was nothing of significance left in the house, skittered down the slope to examine Myra's car. On the dashboard lay Ian's wallet; inside were three sheets of paper divided into columns. Obscure abbreviations had been scrawled within the columns, but there was enough detail for Benfield to realise at once that he was looking at a blueprint for murder.

When questioned that evening, Ian admitted that the writing was his but argued that he had drawn up the disposal plan *after* 'Eddie' was killed. Benfield disbelieved him and knew instinctively that some of the explanations Ian gave him for the coded words were false. David swore that he had never seen the disposal plan and couldn't assist the police in deciphering the riddles it contained. He baulked when told his name appeared prominently several times on the pages.

At 8.20 p.m. on 7 October 1965, Ian Brady was charged with the murder of Edward Evans. He responded, 'I stand on the statement I made this morning,' and wrote the same words on the charge sheet before being led away to a basement cell. Benfield then turned his attention to David, and Myra. Ian Fairley recalls: 'A decision was made not to charge Smith, the argument being if you're going to charge Hindley, you're going to charge Smith, because what you had at that time was Hindley helping clear up, no more than that. Who else helped to clear up? Smith. We took Smith's shoes off; there was blood on his shoes and Brady said Smith had kicked Evans. He had this stick, too, and the stick wasn't as thick as your finger, bit of string tied on it, that had blood on it . . . The dilemma is: Brady admits the murder, the other two are both accusing each other. In those days, you didn't lock people up easily, so Smith and Hindley left, and Brady was kept in custody.'

David couldn't face returning to Underwood Court. Instead, he and Maureen and Bob the dog pitched up on the doorstep of 39 Aked Street, where elderly John Smith was dumbfounded by his grandson's halting explanation for their visit. David slept fitfully that night, agonisingly aware that his sister-in-law and her boyfriend were bent on framing him for the murder he had witnessed – and potentially more besides.

Today David reflects: 'I think the two of them discussed turning it *all* on me. I'm sure they didn't expect me to go to the police, but they'd have had a back-up plan for that eventuality because that's how they operated. Their line of thinking would have been: "Cover all bases, and if he's in with us, we'll go further and do another couple before killing *him* and going on as we were before." If we'd buried Edward Evans that night . . . I'm not convinced I'd have got off the moor alive. Having said that, I'm not even satisfied that they'd banked on disposing of him on the *moor*. He was chosen at random and, as far as anyone knows, they hadn't been up there to dig a grave beforehand. No spade was found in Myra's car either, and the vehicle hadn't been prepared to receive a body as was their "custom".'

He shakes his head. 'I've always believed that if we'd buried the lad somewhere and I'd returned to Hattersley with the two of them . . . well, I wouldn't have lived to tell the tale much longer, put it like that. Because there would have been three musketeers on the loose then, and I know for a fact that one of them wasn't a happy musketeer. The whole thing would have got bigger, dirtier and more complex. It would never have worked – not for Myra, nor for me. My "career" in their little gang had no prospects because, let's face it, I was always going to be their next victim.'

* * *

From David Smith's memoir:

The police want to take me back to Wardle Brook Avenue. A few days have passed since I made the telephone call and in that time I've got into a routine: down to Hyde station for nine o'clock, remaining there for the rest of the day in front of an endless succession of coppers before being allowed to go home, wrung out like a dirty sheet.

But on this particular day their questions focus on the house. My head spins. They keep going on about the axe: *Have you ever seen it about the house?* No, I haven't. *So that would be unusual then, would it, for Brady to have it in the sitting room?* Yes, very unusual. *You're sure you never saw it next to the fireplace?* No, never. *Outside?* No. *In the car?* Definitely not. *Right then, we're going to take you back.* Back where? *To the house. We want you to walk us round from Underwood Court, show us the route you took, that kind of thing.* But I've already told you. *We know, but it's not the same. We need a proper reconstruction for our records. You OK with that?*

I want to tell them to fuck off, no way am I doing that again, but I tell them OK.

The police car pulls up directly below our flat in Underwood Court. I've left Grandad's and am living back here with Maureen and Dad, who moved in with us after I rang him at work in London to tell him everything. But being in the flat with Maureen and Dad is one thing; retracing my steps and setting foot in the murder house is another.

Here we go, though: me, Talbot – who I can't stand the sight of, and I know he feels the same about me – and two other detectives in suits and trilbies climb out of the car. They follow me down Pudding Lane on a dismally grey day, below the crackling pylons, into Sundial Close and left onto Wardle Brook Avenue. The house is 50 yards away at the end of the terrace. No one else is about, most people are either at work or school, only a spoon-faced housewife coming out into her back garden to tut at the likely rain, thinking that the washing will have to be hung up indoors instead of on the line.

I notice with surprise that Talbot and his men have gone ahead of me and are waiting outside number 16. I shake my head: 'We didn't do that. Me and her – Myra – came down by this wall. Then I waited while she checked to see if it was all right for me to go in.' They dutifully troop over to the tall wall of the New Inn and look up at the house, as if expecting the sky to darken and the landing lights to flicker. I feel my knees start to weaken, but the suits are already crossing the road again.

Talbot asks, 'What happened after the lights flashed?'

I stutter slightly, like I always do when I'm on edge. I hope he won't try to finish my sentences for me because I hate that. But I get it out: 'I knew it was all right. So I went up.'

'Here?' asks Talbot, jerking his head at the slope.

'Yeah.' I bite my lip.

'Was that normal? Or different that night?'

'Normal. We never used to walk down past the houses because she – Myra – always parked the car here. We'd go up the embankment and climb over the fence. And vice versa.'

'Right, let's do that, then.'

I lead three smartly dressed detectives on a swift scramble up the slope. We vault the fence in unison. I'm glad no one is about, but I feel the twitch of every net curtain on the estate.

We stand at the door in a small huddle.

Talbot asks, 'What happened next?'

'Well, then the door opened and —'

I almost pass out with fright as the front door is whipped open. Detective Chief Superintendent Benfield fills the gap into the hallway, startled to see us, too. My knees turn to jelly; I want to crouch down and give in to the fear but tell myself to get a grip, it's just silly old Benfield in his trilby and tweed. He always wears the same jacket, with leather elbows – a right country cop.

Talbot frowns and hurries me into the house. There's no room for us all in the narrow hall, with the staircase to our left, living room to our right and kitchen in front. The others go straight through to the kitchen, shoulder to shoulder in the cramped space. I'm in danger of falling apart – I can't get my head around how everything looks the same, *exactly* the same. If forensics have examined the house, then I can't tell – it's no different to how it was when I left it. Nothing has been tidied up, or put away. But then I realise there's a positive side to this: the miniature wine bottles are still there, lined up on top of the cabinet in the kitchen.

Relief courses through my veins: no one seems to believe me when I explain why I went into the house that night. *Miniature wine bottles? Pull the other one, son, it's got bells on.* But there they are and I'm absolutely delighted to see them, lined up neatly like toy soldiers.

Talbot turns to me. 'So then, after seeing these bottles, you walked into the living room, did you?'

'That's right.'

'In you go, then.'

I don't want to do this. I really, *really* don't want to do this. I'm almost as desperate to get out of the house now as I was that night, but Talbot gives me a sharp nudge and in we go.

This is terrifying. I clench and unclench my fists and hold my arms rigid at my sides. Every detail of that room is scored on my memory, the ridges and furrows of a warped battlefield I'll never leave: the mare and foal ornament on the mantelpiece, the binoculars on top of the telly, the magazine rack, the picture of the Alsatian dog on the wall, the settee where the lad fell screaming to the floor, the table where he tried to wriggle desperately away from Brady's unstoppable axe . . .

Jesus Christ, fucking get me out.

One of the detectives walks over to the settee and drops down on it. The other stands behind the settee. Both of them look back at me, expectantly.

Talbot nods at the men and swivels his gaze round to meet mine. 'Right, we've got to get a full picture of what you've told us, so we're going to go through it step by step. All right?'

A minute ago my limbs were as stiff as the wall of the New Inn. Now I feel the need to clutch something solid to stop me from sinking to the floor. I know this has to be done, I understand the need for it, but, fucking hell, I wish it wasn't me who has to be here with them.

I take a deep breath and stutter out a few instructions. The two detectives on the settee move according to what I say.

So Brady was in what position? Was he holding the axe like this? Grabbing the lad like that? More to the side there?

I watch as the detective who sat down first is picked up roughly by his colleague and trips forward a little, unsteady on his feet. Talbot's voice is in my ear again: *Was Evans more on the settee, was he pushed back on it, had he started to slide off it at this point, where was Hindley?*

The detective acting out Brady's role raises his arm suddenly and brings it down close to his colleague's head, again and again and again. *Was that how he did it?* asks Talbot, his breath on my ear, *like that, blade down, or more cutting sideways like that? How did he stand over Evans? Did he bring the axe straight down while the lad was facing upwards from the floor or . . .*

We get through it. I don't know how, but somehow we press on through the re-enactment until Talbot flicks his thumb for me to go back into the hallway.

I want to lean against the wall and feel something cool on my forehead, but the thought of touching anything repulses me. When my breathing slows, Talbot tells me to go upstairs and into the room where we left the body.

The four of us stand in Myra's bedroom. I point to a spot directly below the window: 'We put him over there.'

Talbot nods and grimaces. 'What about the books?'

'Books?'

'Yes, the books that were placed on top of the lad. Why was that done? Was there any significance in it? Or the titles?'

I shake my head, bemused. 'I don't know. I just don't know why Brady did that.' And I don't. Putting the books there made no sense to me. None of it did.

Talbot asks me to describe how we dragged the bundle into the room and exactly where we positioned it. I stumble over my words again. Then it's back downstairs and into the foul living room once more. I'm starting to switch off, only half aware of what's being said, concentrating instead on holding in a scream: *let me out.* I hear Talbot asking something about the signal with the lights again, and mumble that there was nothing unusual in that – it wasn't *new* – Brady had done that in Gorton, too.

'Why?'

I lift my shoulders and let them fall heavily. 'For . . . when he was recording stuff or . . . developing photos. It was just one of his quirks . . .'

'*Recording* stuff?' Talbot's blue eyes pierce my skull.

'Yeah, he had a tape recorder, an eight-track or something. It was usually in here . . .'

Benfield has come into the room, and a look passes between the two men that I don't understand.

'Tell us more about the tape recorder,' Benfield prompts.

I stutter again, 'I-I don't know what else to s-say. It was always' – my eyes scan the floor quickly, but there's no sign of the machine – 'in here.'

Benfield and Talbot nod slowly, silently. I don't know why they should be so interested in a tape recorder. Then Talbot speaks the words I'm desperate to hear.

'Right, I think we're done here, lads.'

And for the last time in my life I get out of that house, gulping in the morning air as if it were pure crystal.

* * *

The first public reference to the case appeared in the *Manchester Evening News* on 7 October 1965. Under the headline 'Body Found in House – Murder?' was a brief description of the discovery made by police in the rear bedroom of 16 Wardle Brook Avenue, where 'Mrs Ellen Maybury, aged 76 . . . has lived for 12 months with her granddaughter Myra Hindley, aged 23.' Talbot gave the standard quote: 'A man is helping us with our inquiries.' Brady remained unnamed, and no mention was made of David having witnessed the killing, nor of his informing the authorities.

The following day another column appeared in the *Manchester Evening News*, reporting on the morning's events at Hyde Magistrates' Court: 'At a three-minute hearing at 10 a.m., a man was charged with the murder of Edward Evans. As he left the dock, he nodded at a blonde woman friend.' For the next few days, there was a steady trickle of information in the local papers, including the news that Myra Hindley had been charged as an accessory to the murder.

Then, on Tuesday, 12 October, the *Manchester Evening News* splashed an exclusive across its front page: 'Police in Mystery Dig on Moors'. National press interest in the case erupted, as the public clamoured for details. Denied access to the two central figures, journalists converged instead outside Underwood Court, and within hours of Tuesday's headline the entry phone to Flat 18 was permanently jammed, as David and Maureen found themselves in the frenzied eye of a very public storm.

Chapter 12

'Mr Mounsey said, "Have you discussed killing people and burying their bodies on the moors with David Smith?" Brady said, "Yes, I talked about it in a vague sort of way. It was all part of the fiction to impress him."'
– Detective Superintendent John Tyrrell, Moors trial at Chester Assizes, April 1966

Initially, David was largely able to avoid the press, since his days were spent closeted in an interview room, often for ten hours or more. 'I'd be told to be down at Hyde station for nine,' he recalls. 'Maureen and Dad would come with me. They'd wait in the canteen and only left when I did. I ate in the interview room – someone would bring in a burger or chips for me and I'd be given half an hour to get that down before we were off again with the questions. I was always put in the same room at Hyde, but occasionally a bobby would appear and say, "Right, there's going to be a couple of Manchester lads coming to speak to you today." I was a bit bewildered the first time but soon got used to it. They'd take me down to Manchester regularly, where their coppers would ask me identical things from a slightly different angle. I hated that station. It was old and gloomy, and I was always interviewed by the same pair of "heavies": Mattin and Tyrrell. Their boss, Nimmo, conducted the first interview I had there, but that was just a superficial thing before he handed me over to them. Nimmo stayed in the background after that.'

He pauses and chooses his next words carefully. 'From the outset, Mattin and Tyrrell were always . . . very stern. It was another atmosphere altogether. The station itself was grim, with interview rooms that felt like prison cells and an ancient smell of misery about the place. Mattin and Tyrrell never gave me time to think about what they were asking – if I didn't reply immediately, one of them would bang down a fist and say, "Come on, you've got to give us an answer, we're waiting." Sometimes I needed to think it through, but they wouldn't make any allowances. Hyde wasn't much better. I hated having to sit with Benfield and Talbot to go over things. I couldn't stick Talbot – we wound each other up – and I found Benfield faintly ridiculous. He looked like a womble, chubby, with little spectacles, and puffing away on his pipe until the room was so thick with smoke I could hardly see. At the end of every day I felt whacked out, drained of every emotion and incapable of thought. Then the next morning it would start up all over again.'

He takes the cup of tea Mary has made for him and explains: 'No one listened to me. They all wanted to speak to me, but everything I said fell on deaf ears. The Hyde brigade were only interested in Edward Evans and ignored what I tried to tell them about other murders – the ones Ian had boasted to me of having committed. I think Jock Carr wanted to know more, but the big brass weren't interested. Talbot and his cronies saw me as someone out to save his own skin. They didn't believe what I had to say, that much was obvious. I couldn't understand it because all I wanted was someone to listen to me. But no one did – until Joe Mounsey came along.'

Among the items removed from Myra Hindley's bedroom at Wardle Brook Avenue was a notebook belonging to Ian Brady. When it turned up with the other exhibits at Hyde station, Ian Fairley flicked through the pages and in the midst of random doodles – roughly pencilled gangster caricatures and a list of film stars – one name stood out: John Kilbride. A call was put through immediately to Detective Chief Inspector Joe Mounsey at Ashton-under-Lyne; the case of the 12-year-old boy who had vanished from the town's market on 23 November 1963 fell under his jurisdiction. His appointment as CID chief at Ashton-under-Lyne came in 1964, several months after John's disappearance, but his determination to crack the riddle of the young boy's apparent vanishing into thin air led to John becoming known in police circles as 'Mounsey's lad'. Upon being told about the notebook, Mounsey drove out to Hyde to look at it for himself. Then he asked to speak to David.

'I had a great deal of respect for Joe Mounsey,' David states unequivocally. 'He was the first senior detective who took me seriously. He was like no one else. He didn't bark questions at me, he never raised his voice or came down heavy, and he listened acutely, to the point where I could actually *see* him taking it all on board. The relief I felt at knowing someone believed me at last was just incredible.'

With Mounsey's involvement, David's days were split between Hyde, Manchester and Ashton-under-Lyne. He gives a short laugh: 'I kind of looked forward to going to Ashton for questioning. The police station there was modern and clean, all sparkling glass, and I was only ever seen – as far as I can recall – by Mr Mounsey. He had a couple of sidekicks, but he was in charge. Being told I was going to Ashton meant a good day ahead because his technique was laid-back and calm. That was the impression he gave and it worked to his advantage – no one else got me to speak at length like he did. The interviews I had with him were more like straightforward conversations. He would open with: "OK, lad, how are you today? Got enough cigarettes? Right, then, in your own time. No rush. Just take it steady and we'll get there in the end." He'd send out for extra ciggies if necessary and give me a proper tea break instead of just having a pot brought in. We'd go to the canteen together and he'd chat to me about rugby or football to make sure I had a rest from everything. When we returned to the interview room, he'd let me ease into it again and if there was a difficult question to answer, he'd tell me, "Take as much time as you need, lad, on this next one. I have to ask it, but no panic. When you're ready." He'd wait five or ten minutes if he had to, which is a long time to sit in silence. That was the big difference between Ashton and everywhere else: I was treated as a suspect at Hyde and Manchester, but at Ashton I was seen as a witness.'

During the course of their interviews, Mounsey pushed forward a number of photographs found at Wardle Brook Avenue and asked David if he knew where they had been taken. Many were what the police termed 'scenic shots' or 'moorland views'. Some featured Ian and Myra and their dogs, but others were of the landscape alone and seemed eerily devoid of purpose. In one, Myra's car stood parked against a dark, jutting rock formation – the same rocks on which the couple posed individually in other shots. David was unable to identify the scene but agreed to visit likely spots with Mounsey in an attempt to narrow down the location.

In theory, it was an impossible task: hundreds of square miles of moorland lies between Manchester and Huddersfield and, other than the rocks, there were no immediately identifiable landmarks in Ian Brady's photographs. Nevertheless, one Sunday afternoon Mounsey and Talbot collected David and Maureen from Underwood Court in an unmarked police car and headed out of the city in a direction with which David felt reasonably familiar. Driving east along the A57 Snake Pass, the winding road that leads out of Glossop, both detectives noticed a sign to Woodhead; 'WH' was an unresolved abbreviation on the disposal plan.

David recalls the difficulties he faced in trying to match a place to the photographs: 'I was usually sat in the back of the Mini van whenever we'd gone out with Myra and Ian, completely blotto, and nodding along to Ian's ramblings. I wasn't even looking in the direction we travelled – my view was of the disappearing city and then lanes and fields. And we went out with them very often, to lots of different places. I never took any notice of names either, and it wasn't until the police were later able to identify the spot by the reservoir that I knew, for instance, that the place in question was Saddleworth Moor. None of what I could tell them before then was of any use. But they did their best and took me to quite a few areas that might have been significant, though some obviously weren't. But if a place had "special" meaning for Ian and Myra, they didn't share that with me. It was between the two of them.'

The accused continued to keep their silence, unwilling to cooperate with the police on the matter of the photographs. In desperation, Mounsey asked David if he had any ideas for encouraging them to be more amenable. David's reply was immediate: threaten to kill Puppet to rattle Myra, and release an insect into Ian's cell. He recounted how Ian had recoiled in terror when a spider scuttled across the living room floor at Wardle Brook Avenue and that he'd reacted much the same when a daddy-long-legs had fluttered in from the balcony at Underwood Court. On both occasions Ian had screamed for Myra, who dealt with the cause of his panic swiftly and calmly. Mounsey listened in some amusement, but there was no question of following through with his suggestions.

Ultimately, it fell to a child to lead the police to the graves of other children.

Twelve-year-old Patty Hodges lived next door but one to Ian and Myra on Wardle Brook Avenue. Together with her siblings and a couple of other children on the estate, she had been befriended by the couple, and often spent time at their house or accompanied them on picnics to the 'countryside'. Brought forward by her mother, Patty told surprised detectives that she was certain she could identify the spot she had visited with the couple but would have to be driven there because she didn't know the name; Ian and Myra had only ever referred to it as 'the moor'.

Patty led the police up to Saddleworth, and as the car followed the turn in the road, the jutting rock formation from the photographs loomed into view. Within the hour, the tentative search that had been taking place at Woodhead switched decisively to Hollin Brown Knoll.

The *Daily Mail* broke the story nationwide. When it was reported that police forces around the Greater Manchester area were checking their records for missing children, the news went global. Clive Entwistle, then a young journalist from Rochdale, recalls: 'The whole thing just exploded. We had the world's press coming to us. Not just Britain, but everywhere – New Zealand, America, Japan, France . . . It was a colossal story.' Every night journalists would gather in the bar of the Queen's Hotel in Hyde to trade information with the police. The case remained in the headlines for the next six months and sightseers' cars clogged the A635 during the ongoing search of the chill, rain-spattered Knoll.

On Wednesday, 13 October, Edward Evans was laid to rest in Southern Cemetery. Two days later, on Alex Carr's orders, Ian

Fairley collected David from Underwood Court and brought him into Hyde for further questioning. Carr decided to head back to Hattersley to conduct the interview; the station was under siege. But when the three of them returned to Underwood Court they found David's flat without electricity and none of them had a two-bob bit for the meter. Undeterred, Carr insisted on interviewing David in the car park below; the press had gathered in Hyde and on the moor. Ian Fairley sat in the driver's seat of the CID car next to 'Jock', with David in the back. They remained there throughout the afternoon; twilight had fallen across the vast housing estate by the time the interview was wrapped up.

Ian Fairley's contact with David had been minimal until then, but the young detective was quietly impressed with him: 'Smith was cooperative, he never hid anything, and he never changed his story. He was . . . not belligerent, but I think he was fed up. During the course of the interview, Jock asked him where they spent their time. Where did they go? David said he'd already gone through all this – the moors, drinking, at home, drinking. Did they use the guns? No, only for target practice. Then he talked about this robbery they'd plotted and at that point mentioned the fact that Brady had told him to bring anything he had that was incriminating back to him. Like what, we asked. He said books, and we knew what he meant, the sort of rubbish you could pick up from a dodgy place. He said he'd taken it all back to Brady and we asked him what had happened to it then. He said, 'Well, they put it in the suitcases.' Suitcases? *What suitcases?* Now, I don't know how many times this lad had been interviewed, and I don't know if he had mentioned the suitcases before or not, all I know is that it was the first time Jock Carr and I heard about the suitcases. We asked him again about these suitcases and he said, 'They were huge, packed with stuff, but I don't know what else, just the stuff I handed back.' We knew that no suitcases had been found because obviously there had been a search, and there was nothing. We started asking him again where they'd gone and he repeated what he'd said before. Then we asked where *they* went, Brady and Hindley, and he said sometimes they went into Manchester and Brady would go to the railway stations . . .'

David nods slowly when asked about the interview in the car park of Underwood Court. 'I remember that. We were there for a long time – hours. It was dark when I got back to the flat. I *had* already mentioned the suitcases, but no one paid it any attention. The old story – no one seemed interested. Jock Carr picked up on it, though. He must have twigged it was significant, especially the link between the suitcases and railway stations, and wasn't going to let it drop. He was a brilliant detective. It was through him that *the* major breakthrough was achieved.'

Alex Carr contacted the British Railway Police and asked them to search all their left luggage departments. By ten o'clock that evening, the suitcases had been found. A few days later, the receipt for their deposit at Central Station on 5 October was discovered in the house on Wardle Brook Avenue, tightly rolled in the spine of a prayer book given to Myra Hindley for her first Holy Communion in 1958. The finding of the receipt cleared up another enigma in the abbreviations on the disposal plan: 'P/B' (prayer book) and 'TICK' (ticket).

By mid-morning on Saturday, 16 October, news of the suitcases had spread to other constabularies and Hyde police station was inundated with senior officers arguing over access to them. Benfield had departed for Cheshire the day before, convinced that everything was cut and dried; he returned to Hyde quickly, together with Eric Cunningham, head of the Number One Regional Crime Squad, and Joe Mounsey. Benfield was firm that Hyde would remain in charge of the inquiry, since it was through his officers that the suitcases had been discovered.

With that settled, the objects in question were brought into his office and detectives from every neighbouring force looked on curiously as the buckles on the suitcases were unfastened and the lids thrown open.

* * *

From David Smith's memoir:
Saturday morning, and I'm hoping for a day off from the suits, thinking that I might take Bob for a walk, then mooch around the flat, for a change. Nothing out of the ordinary, just getting back to normal for a while – or pretending to, at least. I know there are a few gentlemen of the press lurking in the car park but not many, not yet. They don't

bother me if I keep away from the balcony doors and ignore the intercom.

It doesn't happen: today is when the whole thing erupts. After this, there's no more pretending and no going back to any sort of life we knew before.

I'm picked up in an unmarked police car and whizzed to Hyde station. Even as I get out of the car on a typically grey, wet day I can feel the invisible quiver of something different in the air. In silence, I follow the copper who collected me from Hattersley; since telling me I was wanted down at the station he's said not one word.

Inside the red-brick building there are so many detectives knocking about the place I begin to feel claustrophobic. The curtain of pipe smoke is dense enough to part, as well. I pass the desk sergeant, who glances up at me and then averts his gaze quickly, avoiding prolonged eye contact. I frown, thinking: *what the fuck is going on?*

I'm being led towards my usual interview room, the one I've spent so many hours in that I actually think of it as mine. But as I walk by the first office, for some reason I pause and look in.

The suitcases are on a table, the blue one and the brown. Both are open, their heaving contents spilling out like something wicked across the Formica surface. I'm rooted to the spot by what I see: a black wig, books with lurid covers – some of which I recognise – papers, photographs and several reels of tape. I remember the look that passed between Benfield and Talbot in the house when I mentioned Ian recording stuff on his eight-track and I feel a sudden chill without knowing why.

Someone ushers me along the corridor, towards my little room. I'm left there for ten minutes or more by myself and sit stiffly, cracking my knuckles and listening to the muted sounds in the rest of the building. There is a constant murmur of grim conversation, doors opening and closing, chairs being scraped back.

A copper I've never seen before enters my room and looks at me for a moment before saying, 'Well, lad, we've found plenty of stuff all right.'

I sit up straight in my chair and wait for the questions to begin, but instead he tells me I can go home. I'm dumbfounded but don't need telling twice. It's only as I leave the station that I realise the suitcases probably haven't been examined thoroughly yet and, until the coppers have got their heads around it all, they won't know what line to take with me. I get an easy ride that day, in the sense of being allowed to go early, but my stomach is in knots, wondering about the black wig, what those photographs show and what the hell might be on the spools of brown tape . . .

I spend my free afternoon in town with Dad. We do our best to avoid the newspaper stands, where every black-and-white placard reads: 'Moors Search Continues'. I try not to think of that dark landscape and the reservoir lying at the bottom, still and silent under a full moon.

My efforts to forget don't work, as the hours tick by: I can't get the moor out of my head. I've been there again recently with Joe Mounsey, who explained as we drove out through the old mill villages that they'd managed to identify the place in the photographs as Hollin Brown Knoll. The name meant nothing to me, but as we rounded a sharp, high bend and the boulders came into view on the horizon – great black ugly rocks, like rotten teeth – I felt a sudden jolt of recognition. We parked below the boulders and crossed the road together, just me and Mr Mounsey at first, then with an army of coppers following us, clipboards at the ready. We stopped at the place I thought must have been where I'd stood with Ian the night before Angela died. It looked different in the watery daylight – the reservoir seemed wider, less of a silver streak bordered by high banks of land. I tried to answer Mr Mounsey's questions, concentrating hard. *Was the reservoir far away when you stopped, David? Was it this far or a bit further? Did it seem bigger or smaller than this? Would it be this angle or slightly to the side? Was the ground spongy beneath your feet like this, sinking in, or was it firmer, more rocky?* I felt painfully inadequate, as I stumbled out the truth: *it was dark when I was up there with Brady, and I hadn't even realised it was a reservoir until he told me so – I thought it was a river. I was wearing cowboy boots that night and the heels sink into anything that isn't concrete* . . . Mr Mounsey, to his eternal credit, didn't mock or become impatient: he nodded thoughtfully and paced about, occasionally waving me across to him and asking if *this* was actually the place I'd stood with Brady that night, or this . . . I wanted to help more than ever, to be able to point at the exact spot, but I couldn't. As we walked back to his car, I felt as if the whole thing had been a waste of time, because without knowing for certain which was the precise area, nothing could come of it. Their search methods were medieval: push in a bamboo stick, sniff it for any hints of decomposition and then repeat. One pace in the wrong direction meant they could so easily miss something – or someone.

*

It's getting dark in the city. Dad and I wander aimlessly; it's as if the news-stands are being put out ahead of us because everywhere we look there they are, updated to announce that this is the last day of the search. Apparently the big brass have decided it's too expensive to carry on doing the needle-in-a-haystack thing. I turn my head away from the paper shop on Market Street and tell Dad we ought to think about getting back for Maureen. He nods but doesn't speak; he's got about as much conversation in him as I have, and together we turn up our coat collars against the damp, bitter mist and shuffle through the babbling crowds towards our bus stop.

We've spent too long in town. In the alleys and down side streets it's particularly dark – that deep, early dark peculiar to cities. The lights from the shops and offices turn the pavement rain into luminous patterns and when I step into a small pool of water, the light scatters at my feet.

We're heading past the wide square of Piccadilly Gardens, the smell of exhaust fumes, fish and chips and beer stinging the wet air, when Dad squeezes my arm, forcing me to stop.

There is a placard to our left, outside a small shop with a yellow *Manchester Evening News* hoarding. Four words in black and white loom out from behind the criss-cross wire: 'BODY FOUND ON MOOR'.

I close my eyes tightly shut. Ian's voice fills my brain: 'Maggots, they're all fucking maggots . . . you've sat on one of the *graves* . . .'

Dad's grip on my arm increases. I open my eyes and look at him. We stand there silently, letting the crowds surge round us, two small pebbles in a stream of people looking forward to tea and telly and Saturday night down the boozer. Dad moves first, hauling me on towards our bus stop further up, past the bright, busy shop fronts. The Hattersley bus is already there, and Dad pays our fare while I stagger upstairs like a man twice his age and slump into the front seat on the right. I lean forward and put my head in my hands.

This is real now. Everything is real. Ian wasn't bluffing. He's killed. Three or four, he said, you've sat on one of the graves. It wasn't the drink talking. BODY FOUND ON MOOR.

Dad drops heavily down into the seat, his leg and elbow against mine. I don't look at him and he doesn't speak to me. What is there to say?

The engine starts up and the bus pulls out, a rumble of normality in a world I'm not part of, on the long road to Hattersley.

David's first home: Aked Street in Ardwick. (Manchester Local Studies)

David with his birth mother,
Joyce Hull, in 1948.

David with his grandmother,
Annie Smith, who adopted him.

Wiles Street in Gorton, David's home from 1954 to 1965. He and his father lived at number 13; Pauline Reade, Brady and Hindley's first victim, lived at number 9.
(Manchester Local Studies)

David Smith and Maureen Hindley on their wedding day, 15 August 1964.
That evening, Myra Hindley and Ian Brady invited the couple to Myra's home in Bannock Street, Gorton. It was David's first real encounter with Brady.
Unbeknown to anyone else, Brady and Hindley had already committed three murders.

Brady and Hindley with Maureen, outside their home at
16 Wardle Brook Avenue, Hattersley. They moved there in late 1964.

David and Maureen in their flat at
18 Underwood Court, Hattersley.
They moved in on 23 July 1965.
(from David Marchbanks,
The Moor Murders, London;
Leslie Frewin Publishers, 1966)

16 Wardle Brook Avenue, where David
witnessed the brutal murder of 17-year-old
Edward Evans on 6 October 1965. (from
David Marchbanks, *The Moor Murders*, London; Leslie Frewin Publishers, 1966)

Detective Chief Inspector Joe Mounsey, holding an album of Brady and Hindley's 'moorland views', stands on the rocks of Hollin Brown Knoll in October 1965. To his right are Detective Chief Inspector John Tyrrell and Detective Inspector Norman Mattin.

Sightseers flock to the moor during the search of October/November 1965. (from David Marchbanks, *The Moor Murders*, London; Leslie Frewin Publishers, 1966)

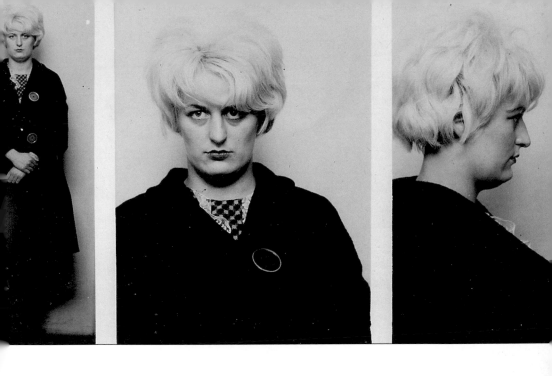

Hindley and Brady's mugshots, Hyde police station, October 1965. Their trial was held at Chester Assizes during April/May 1966. Both were jailed for life. David was the key witness for the prosecution. (Greater Manchester Police)

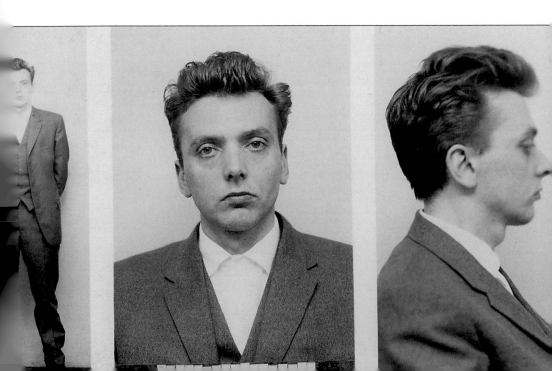

David and Maureen pictured after the trial in 1966. They divorced in April 1973.

On 15 February 1975, David married Mary Flaherty. Standing to David's right are Uncle Bert and Mary's mother, Hazel; the Duchess and Mary's father, Martin, are to Mary's left.

David and Mary with David, Paul, Jody and John.

David on Saddleworth Moor during the 1986–7 search for the bodies of Pauline Reade and Keith Bennett. Pauline's grave was discovered on 1 July 1987; Keith Bennett has not yet been found. (© Mirrorpix)

David and Mary in their home in Ireland, March 2011. (Hans-Jürgen Büsch)

Chapter 13

'I want to take some photographs, that's all.'
– Ian Brady, tape recording of Lesley Ann Downey,
Boxing Day 1964

The small body recovered from the moor was swiftly identified as ten-year-old Lesley Ann Downey. She was found by Police Constable Robert Spiers, who had moved away from the search party on Hollin Brown Knoll after feeling drawn to the higher ground behind the jutting rocks. He saw what he thought was a white, withered stick, but upon investigation it turned out to be part of the little girl's forearm poking out of the water-logged peat. In a statement later read to court, Dr Dave Gee described the state in which she was found: 'The body lay on its right side; the skeletal remains of the left arm were extended above the head, and the hand was missing. The right arm was beneath the body, the hand being near the right knee. Both legs were doubled up towards the abdomen, flexed at hips and knees. The head was in normal position. The body was naked.' Lesley's clothes and shoes lay piled at her feet, together with the string of white beads her elder brother had won for her at the fair the day before Lesley disappeared from there on Boxing Day 1964.

On Monday, following the discovery on the moor, David and Maureen were taken up to Hollin Brown Knoll again by Joe Mounsey. A green tent concealed Lesley's grave and a long line of police fanned out in a circle from that spot, probing the ground with the now ubiquitous bamboo sticks. Mounsey had several maps with him, but although David and Maureen walked around the area with him at length, neither could be of further assistance. David was taken back to Hyde, where the police station was in organised uproar, having been transformed into the headquarters of a momentous murder inquiry; the canteen was serving as the press room and a vast press conference – the first in Britain to be filmed – had been planned for that week.

David was ushered into 'his' interview room for the toughest day of questioning yet. He was asked about the books found inside the suitcases (among them *Sexual Anomalies and Perversions*, *Cradle of Erotica*, *Sexus*, *The Kiss of the Whip*, *Tropic of Cancer*, *The Life and Ideals of the Marquis de Sade* wrapped in the *Daily Mirror* and *Mein Kampf* wrapped in the *News of the World*), the pornographic magazines, two library tickets belonging to his father, a bandolier and ammunition, a cutlery box containing a cosh and a black mask, and another cosh with 'EUREKA' on it.

'The police didn't show me everything,' he recalls, 'but they asked me what I'd taken round to Ian's the night before Edward Evans was killed and I told them: a notepad, books, a cosh, my starter pistol and the blank shells that went with it. That was it. Then they brought everything I'd listed as mine into the room and asked me if I could positively identify it all. I did – though I have no idea how those library tickets belonging to my dad came to be in there. That's a complete mystery to me. I didn't like admitting that the home-made cosh marked Eureka was mine, but I wasn't going to lie about anything.'

He pauses. 'The notepad proved to be the biggest sticking point. It contained my interpretation of the books Ian had given me to read and the police pounced on it straight away. It was a major interrogation issue.' Inside the notepad David had compiled a list of the novels recommended to him by Ian Brady, with some extracts from the texts and his own understanding of the authors' intentions added alongside.

'I thought it was clear enough that the notepad was a sort of diary of what I'd read,' he reflects, 'but it became a real battle to try and prove that these were not necessarily my views, as such. I understood why the police needed to get to the bottom of what I'd written, but I really struggled to convince them that the notebook wasn't what it seemed. And I ended up becoming very defensive, which was the last thing I wanted. I'd never asked for a solicitor, not once, because I didn't want the obstruction and constant interjections of some legal bloke telling me I didn't have to answer this and that. Being upfront about the things that belonged to me in the suitcases might not have been the path a solicitor would have advised me to take, for example – he might have said that it wasn't in my best interests. But as far as I was concerned it was the only option. I knew which way I wanted to go and I knew it was something I had to do on my own.'

Detectives moved away from the issue of the notepad and turned instead to other items found within the suitcases. These included a set of photographs, which were brought into the interview room and placed face down on the table. After waiting for a moment, one of the detectives flipped over the first photograph.

It showed a small, dark-haired child naked but for her shoes and socks and a gag pulled tight around the lower half of her face. The detective turned over another photograph, and another, and another – nine in all, each of the same little girl, standing, lying down, kneeling and bending, as she had been told.

'The photographs were . . .' David lifts his hands, helplessly. 'I couldn't take in what I was seeing. The detectives presented them in a certain way, and rightly so, to get an honest reaction from me. I freaked out and couldn't stand to look at them. The detectives started barking at me, as they turned the photographs over: "What do you think of that? How does it make you feel? You know who that is, don't you? It's Lesley Ann Downey, isn't it? That little girl is Lesley Ann Downey and her body was found where you used to go for picnics with your sister-in-law and her boyfriend. What do you think happened to her after this was taken? Come on, let's have it – *what the fucking hell happened to her*?" That was their attitude.'

He shakes his head repeatedly. 'I realised then what Brady had meant when he'd told me that he had "photographic proof". That burned itself into my mind. His words meant nothing until then. And it was obvious to anyone who saw those pictures that Lesley Ann Downey would never have been able to go home after they'd been taken.'

Leaving aside the matter of the photographs, detectives brought an eight-track tape recorder into the room and loaded it with a reel found in one of the suitcases. 'I was in a state at that point,' David remembers, 'but there was no gentle "Prepare yourself" or "We'd like you to listen to something." One of the suits said to me, "You're going to listen to this and you're not getting up or going anywhere until it's finished."'

The tape, recorded in Myra Hindley's bedroom at Wardle Brook Avenue, opened with Ian Brady announcing, 'This is track four.' He spoke angrily to the dogs, then the sound of footsteps could be heard, muffled voices, and a door banged before the silence was shattered by a child's scream. For several minutes, the tape went on revolving, relaying the last moments of Lesley Ann Downey's life, as she pleaded in desperation with Myra Hindley and Ian Brady to let her go home. The recording ended with the saccharine voices of the Ray Conniff singers – added to the track afterwards – singing 'Jolly Old St Nicholas' and 'The Little Drummer Boy', then footsteps fading into silence.

'The police acted fairly in how they played that tape,' David insists. 'They needed an honest reaction from me. And that was, in this case, to cry. I cried, I got very upset, but they played the whole thing from beginning to end, and by the time the music came on I had my head in my hands, sobbing uncontrollably. It was completely horrific, that tape. Afterwards, I couldn't find my voice. But they had their questions: "You know that was Lesley, don't you? What happened to her after the tape ran out? When it went quiet, what was going on then? Get it off your chest, lad. Admit to it – she wasn't going to bloody walk home, was she?"'

He takes a deep breath and rubs his jaw. 'I know that later on Myra Hindley claimed she never used that bedroom again after Lesley Ann Downey was killed. But I can say for a fact that she was lying. That's where she and Maureen would sleep when me and Ian were having one of our all-night drinking sessions. Time and again, she slept there. The murder committed in her bedroom didn't trouble her at all.'

Ian and Myra were also confronted with the photographs and tapes that day. Both attempted to pin Lesley Ann Downey's murder on David. Ian admitted taking the photographs but insisted the little girl had been brought to the house by two men, one of whom he knew well but wouldn't name, and that afterwards she had departed with the same men. Later he went further and not only named David as one of the men, but also claimed it had been his idea to take the pornographic photographs.

Myra was even less reticent in her interview with the police. After being shown the photographs, Benfield informed her that Lesley's body had been recovered from the moor; the child's clothing was placed on the desk. He then presented her with Ian's alibi: 'Brady has told us the girl was brought to your home by two men. One of them came into the house and remained downstairs while Brady took the photographs in your presence.' At first, Myra refused to comment, but after listening to the tape, she embellished the story that Benfield had handed to her: 'As far as Lesley Ann Downey is concerned, Ian didn't kill her, I didn't kill her. I suggest you see Smith.' Pressed again, she stated, 'You know Lesley Ann Downey was at the house. She was brought there by Smith and taken away by Smith.'

With hindsight, David muses, 'They could have pinned all that on me far more effectively than they did. I realised that pretty quickly after being shown the photographs of Lesley Ann Downey and being forced to listen to the tape. Because on the night that Brady came out about committing murder, those photographs and that tape must have been in the house. When he said, "I've got photographic evidence," it was because I'd looked at him disbelievingly. He could have decided then: "Fuck you, you bastard, I'll show you," staggered to his feet, got out the photos of Lesley and handed them over. And what would have been on those pictures then? My fingerprints. It was that easy. But I think he bottled it. I think he was itching to show me those photographs but lost his nerve at the last minute. He'd got to me that night by talking about Angela, my little girl, remember. So to then consider showing me the photos of someone else's young daughter, a child that *he* had murdered . . . He couldn't do it without ruining everything for himself. It would have been a step too far.'

David muses, 'There was another way, though. On the night that Edward Evans was killed, the eight-track tape recorder was in the sitting room. Why didn't Brady have it running, if that murder was something I was involved in as much as he and

Hindley claimed? They would have had absolute proof of my complicity then – evidence of an attack on one man by two. But they didn't want to risk it. And, to be honest, I don't think I was even supposed to witness the murder that night. I think Brady intended to kill his victim before I got there, and wanted me to walk in and find the body. But he was out of control, desperate to prove himself to me. So, instead he waited until I turned up, working himself into that murderous frenzy. If he'd killed Edward Evans ten minutes earlier, that heat would have cooled down – he might have lost his nerve again. He had to show me, physically, what he was capable of and he was waiting for the right moment. And in I walked, right on cue.'

* * *

From David Smith's memoir:

This is a seven-days-a-week circus, held in the Big Top of every police station in the Greater Manchester area. Ringmasters change on a daily basis: Talbot, Benfield, Nimmo, Mattin, Tyrrell, Mounsey, Carr, Cunningham. Different days in different stations with different detectives, all still asking the same fucking questions. Interview rooms filled with inter-force rivalry and testosterone-fuelled egos thicker than pipe smoke; it's the old good-cop, bad-cop routine, each suit hunting his piece of glory.

These men keep me awake at night. It brings me out in a cold sweat to realise that not only are my sister-in-law and her boyfriend trying to pin their crimes on me, but also that men like Talbot suspect me of things I don't even know about yet. At Hyde, I am a suspect. At Manchester, I am a murderer, no two ways about it. Stalybridge is the same. And no one makes their views clearer than Eric Cunningham, who, along with his anonymous smug-faced sidekick, interviews me for hours at a stretch as if he's speaking to shit on his shoe. He tucks into tea and chocolate biscuits and raises an eyebrow when I ask for a glass of water. I don't get anything to drink, or eat. In the end, his attitude makes me break my own rule: I refuse to answer any questions he puts to me. When I'm told that he's coming to interview me again, I tell the desk sergeant, 'I am not speaking to that man,' and I mean it.

The rest of the suits, at Manchester especially, have got a dirty tricks campaign up and running. Maureen's interviews with the police have been over for a while now, but she and Dad accompany me to every station. I feel sorry for the two of them, having to pass long hours in the canteen, smoking and drinking endless cups of tea. Lately, they've had a couple of visitors: Mattin and Tyrrell. The two suits stroll into the canteen and pitch up at Maureen and Dad's table, confiding, 'We're getting close now, we're almost there with your David. He's almost cracked. We're that close' – finger and thumb held together – 'to breaking him.' Dad struggles to contain himself, and Maureen bursts into tears, not understanding that she's being deliberately wound up.

When I join them at the end of the day, Maureen is still upset and shaking, and Dad wants to know what the hell is going on. I have to fight the urge to explode, and do my best to explain that Mattin and Tyrrell are playing a game. Often the two stooges nudge Dad and say, 'Your David has told us this . . . What do you reckon? And you, Maureen? You're his wife, you know him better than anyone. Is he capable of something as bad as that?' Within minutes, Tyrrell and Mattin are back in my room and one of them, usually Tyrrell, shakes his head regretfully: 'Poor Maureen . . . she's sitting out there, all upset. In tears, poor girl.' I'm baffled, then angry. That's when the two suits launch into a fresh barrage of questions, thinking that if they can rile me, I might just slip up and say something incriminating. Somehow, Dad and Maureen hold it together. Dad deals with it privately, on his own. Maureen just wants to know, 'Is everything all right, Dave? Is everything all right?'

It's down to Joe Mounsey that I don't cave in under the pressure. He rises head and shoulders above the other suits. He's a big bloke, though since I'm only 17, rake-thin and five foot nine in my winkle-pickers, all detectives look burly to me. But where the rest are prone to plumpness in their suits, ties and trilbies, with necks as fat as their arses, Mr Mounsey is something else. I know that one thump of his fist could reduce the heavy desk between us to smithereens, but his very presence, in the new, clean interview room at Ashton-under-Lyne, has a positive influence on me. He's a patient man and that helps. Sometimes I literally cannot speak, struck dumb by the cold realisation that the killing of children was part of Ian and Myra's life together. Mr Mounsey sits quietly waiting, letting me get my thoughts together. Occasionally I stammer badly and he calls a halt to proceedings, taking me into the canteen for a coffee. As we chat about sport, I silently give thanks for another day spent with Mr Mounsey, a very special man whom I like a lot.

After one long and tiring day for both of us, Mr Mounsey leans forward, resting his elbows on the desk, and sighs heavily, bringing the 'conversation' to an end. We sit together, allowing the emotional level between us to drop. He asks softly, not as a question, but more as a concerned statement: 'You couldn't get out of that room, could you? No matter what it was, you couldn't get out.'

He has an insight into something that only I can feel. The survival instinct that kicked in on the night of Edward Evans's death has shaken me to my core; it's a primitive feeling, so cold and deep that no words can describe it. I sit opposite the detective with my head bowed, staring at the floor between my pointed shoes. I am unable to voice the thoughts that fill my head. How can I explain to him or anyone that my mind tortures me every minute of the day with thoughts I can't control, taking me on a non-chemical trip that's relentless and unforgiving, filling me with nothing, leaving me frightened of myself? How do I explain to him or anyone that my mind leads me on a journey into the head of Myra Hindley, leaving me looking at the stranger that is me? Cold sober or crazy drunk, I can't stop it from happening. It's cruel and it hurts, but I have to go back there, to find the root of that hatred, of something I fear inside myself.

This is the start of the madness that will bring me close to suicide a few years from now.

In Ashton-under-Lyne police station, Joe Mounsey's words have set the whole thing in motion again; I close my eyes and give in to it . . .

*

I'm back in the living room of Wardle Brook Avenue. A few short hours ago a boy my age and height, who came from the same streets as me, was sitting exactly where I am now. Not enough time has passed to remove the brutality of his last seconds of life. But I'm not seeing the room or its history through my own eyes; I'm inside Myra Hindley's head, looking at myself on the settee next to Ian. It feels . . . how can I describe this? It's as if I'm peering through the cut-out sockets of a Ku Klux Klan hood.

Well, David Smith, look at you, sitting there as cool as you like. I never saw this coming. How did my Ian see this thing in you? How did he know that what's inside you is the same as it is in us? How could I have been so wrong about you? I thought Ian had lost the plot. I couldn't understand why he wanted you when he had me, but there you sit, bang to rights, just like Ian guessed. Still, there's one thing you ought to know, you little bastard.

You'll never come between us. Our world is ours alone.

I see the real me leaning forward, grinning with Ian. We're comparing our injuries, me and him. He's gone over on his ankle and I'm showing him a dent in my left shin where the axe grazed the skin. My blood has frozen in my veins. My heart doesn't beat. I have no emotion. I am an abomination of myself.

Ian and I share a cruel, quick humour and the laughter brings him down gently from his high. I draw on my cigarette, throw my head back and blow smoke rings into the stuffy air. Ian bends down to make a fuss of the dogs and I do the same. He's not manic now, but his speech is still fast and his eyes are full of light. The longer this goes on, the happier he is. I'm not sweating, stuttering or trembling. I am relaxed, letting time pass at its own speed. I don't care if I have to stay here all night. Ian has totally accepted me and if this was a test, then in his eyes I've passed with flying colours, all right. Myra sits on the edge of her chair, making small talk with me but thinking to herself: *What have you done, Ian? How did this happen? Why would you want it to be like this? Look at you both, laughing together as if this is the start of something. It's not. You've gone too far, Ian. I don't know this Dave Smith at all. Look at you both, shoulders touching, brothers-in-fucking-arms. It should be you and me, no one else. You wanted to blow this piece of shit away not so long ago. Now look at you. What have you found that I can't feel? Where will it end?*

Ian stands up and hobbles around the room, clutching chair backs for support. He curses loudly about his injured ankle. I'm aware of him behind me, fumbling. The fear I thought I could never feel again rises high and swift: a cord suddenly around my throat, being dragged up and backwards, eyes bulging, arms thrashing in mid-air, unable to get at him. I suppress it all. I show only concern for his pain when he finally sits down again next to me. I am desperate for a piss, but I hold it in. I have to be where they are, I can't risk leaving them alone together while I'm still in the house.

We talk about collecting Angela's pram and Ian nods, a wide smile spreading across his face. He's relaxed now, long legs stretched out, hands clasped tight behind his head, eyes half-closed and dreamy, looking up at the ceiling. I feel the pressure of the growing silence and realise I'm coming back to earth, where any small, normal emotion will betray me. One mistake, one wrong word, a bead of sweat . . . I have to get out.

I stand slowly, stub out my fag and try to ignore the walls suddenly sliding towards me, narrowing the room to the smallest of boxes. The doors and windows have been bricked up from the outside. There is nothing out there at all . . . *shut up*, I tell myself. I have to be rational, but not too rational – a clear head will put me in danger.

Ian sprawls on the settee. I tell him it's time for me to go. He looks up with a nod, and dismisses me. We part as friends.

Myra walks me to the door. I turn to look at her. I've faced her many times as the enemy, but now we're the same. Inside her head is a black, steel void and the only light is the cold clear light of control. Her eyes are not a woman's eyes – they're not even human. They are the eyes that engaged a young man's final seconds of life and watched as an axe crashed down on his skull.

She smiles, 'See you later.' As I walk away I feel her eyes drilling into me, embedding me with eternal fear.

Fuck you, David Smith.

*

Joe Mounsey's soft voice brings me back. It's late evening in his office and I'm very tired.

'No matter what it was, you couldn't get out,' he repeats again, then adds, 'but the way it happened is the only thing that brings us where we are today.' I realise he means this as a sort of validation, but I shake my head. I'm lost and frightened of myself; I'm hurting deep inside and I don't know why. I did what I had to do – I did the right thing, but it's how I got here that torments me.

Almost half a century later, it still does.

Chapter 14

'Brady, a bushy-haired man wearing a grey suit and a
white open-necked shirt, was brought into the dock
first . . . After a few moments Hindley was brought up,
between Detective Policewoman Margaret Campion
and Policewoman Hazel Simpson. Hindley, wearing a
cherry red coat, appeared to have had her blonde hair
freshly set.'

– Gorton & Openshaw Reporter, 1965

Public interest in the case intensified following the discovery of
Lesley Ann Downey's body, threatening to hinder the search for
further victims. On 20 October 1965, the *Manchester Evening
News* reported: 'Hundreds Flock to Watch Moor Hunt . . . in
small family cars and executive limousines . . . sensation-seekers
have rolled up in their hundreds . . . Some stayed for only a few
minutes. Others parked their cars by the roadside and settled
down with vacuum flasks and sandwiches.' A disgruntled police
spokesman called it 'morbid curiosity at its worst. All we needed
was a hot-dog vendor.'

Two hundred foreign journalists descended on Manchester,
shuttling between Saddleworth, Hyde and Hattersley. 'The press
were always there,' David recalls, 'but all at once the place
seemed to be teeming with them. Even then, until the committal
it was still possible, more or less, for Maureen and me to avoid
them. I was in turmoil, trying to come to terms with the full
story, as it began to unravel. I thought nothing could have been
worse than the murder of Edward Evans, but as the days rolled
on that night became just one element of something so vast and
terrifying that my part in it dwindled into insignificance. The

whole thing snowballed, horror upon horror. I felt like a tiny speck of a person in the shadow of an avalanche that just kept coming.'

On Thursday, 21 October 1965, the body of a second child was found on the moor. A photograph of Myra Hindley crouching on a dark patch of ground with Puppet, then only weeks old and tucked inside her coat, led to the discovery. Mounsey was convinced that the snapshot – in which Myra wore an eerie half-smile and stared down at the peat and stones beneath her feet – was grimly significant. Scene of Crime Officer Mike Massheder worked on the photograph, burning-in the background, which then revealed the rocks of Hollin Brown Knoll, seen from the other side of the A635.

With habitual patience, Mounsey traipsed the moor until he was certain he'd found the spot on which Myra was shown crouching. Inspector John Chaddock, present that morning, later told the court: 'I pushed my stick a short distance into the ground . . . Upon withdrawing my stick, there was a strong smell of putrefaction on the end of it. We removed the topsoil to a depth of about nine inches and uncovered a boy's left black shoe. Underneath the shoe I saw some socks and what appeared to be part of a heel . . .' Mounsey had found his 'lad', 12-year-old John Kilbride; the young boy's grave was where David had stood with Ian Brady to look at the moonlit reservoir. Buried face down, feet towards the road, John's body was fully clothed except for his trousers and underpants, which had been pulled down and knotted, indicating the sexual torture he, like Lesley, had suffered prior to death. Decomposition was so far advanced that his mother could only identify him by his clothes and a few strands of hair.

Police continued to search the moor until the second week in November, when the weather closed in. There were still two missing children, Pauline Reade and Keith Bennett, whom detectives strongly suspected had been murdered by Ian Brady and Myra Hindley. One photograph of Myra on Hollin Brown Knoll bore striking similarities to the shot of her posing on John Kilbride's grave; it was taken on the site of the trans-Pennine gas pipeline. Benfield enquired about digging in that area and was told that the gas supply would have to be diverted first – at a prohibitive cost of £10 million. The search was called off.

As police prepared to wrap up the inquiry, a concentrated effort was made to 'break' the two accused and to assess whether David had been involved in their crimes. 'I was brought before Mattin and Tyrrell in Manchester,' he remembers. 'They were waiting for me in the interview room with their jackets off, shirtsleeves rolled up and ties loosened. There was no mistaking what they wanted. I was told, "If you walk out of this room today, boy, you'll either walk out into fresh air or you'll find yourself banged up in a cell with the other two."'

He pauses. 'It was tough going. I was there from first thing in the morning until last thing at night with *nothing* to eat or drink. Every question was accompanied by controlled aggression – fists thumped down on desks and against doors, shouting, chairs kicked over, that sort of thing. At one point Mattin grabbed my shoulders and squeezed so hard I thought my collarbone would snap. Then he shook me like a rat and bellowed, "Come on, lad, come on! Let's have it, what have you done, eh? Get it out, you'll feel better for it. You can't live with what you've been part of, can you? Help the families now and you'll feel as if that weight you've been carrying around has been lifted." I shouted back that I hadn't done anything, and he shoved me off my chair. I wasn't having that, so I told him, "That's it, I'm off," but he grabbed me and bounced me back down in my seat with another bellow: "You're not fucking going anywhere until we've had the truth, you lying little piece of shit!"'

David shakes his head. 'This went on for hours, endless hours. It was awful, but I've got a great deal of respect for Mattin because he did his utmost to break me within the rules of conduct, though he sailed pretty close to the wind sometimes. He put the fear of God into me that day. If I'd been guilty of anything, he'd have got it out of me, no question. Right up until the last hour, I think both Mattin *and* Tyrrell were convinced I knew more than I was letting on. They were determined to get to the truth, whatever that turned out to be. The two of them were up to their old tricks again as well – during their breaks they'd go straight to the canteen where Dad and Maureen were waiting and wind them up. Then I'd get five minutes with Dad and he'd be frantic: "What the hell have you told them, Dave? What the fuck is going on in there?" They were telling Dad that I'd said all sorts and I'd panic: "I didn't say that, Dad, I didn't say it." I was a wreck.'

He shakes his head again. 'Mattin and Tyrrell were tough old-school coppers. Between them, they pressed every button I had and pushed me to the limits of what I could take. Both of them screamed at me repeatedly that I was a lying little cunt and a no-good bastard. By the end of the day, we were all exhausted and emotionally drained. Mattin, a great big lump of a lad, fell into a chair and sat with his arms behind his head, fingers locked together, staring up at the ceiling with his eyes watering. I felt a real sense of relief, though, because that was the end of it – they knew I had nothing left to give, no secrets to tell. When they said "All right, lad, you can go," it was obvious that their view of me had changed for good. And that was true of all the police. I was no longer a suspect. From then on, I was a witness for the prosecution.'

Public feeling, however, was running high. Thousands lined the routes for the funeral processions of Lesley Ann Downey and John Kilbride. The fear that it could have been anyone's child snatched from streets once regarded as safe was very much in evidence. The passing of Sydney Silverman's Murder (Abolition of the Death Penalty) Act on 8 November 1965 only served to inflame matters; that the two accused would now be spared the hangman's rope was seen by many as an affront to justice. Brady and Hindley's remand hearings in Hyde became opportunities to give vent to that outrage, with hundreds queuing outside the courthouse doors at first light, regardless of the weather. When David and Maureen were spotted leaving on foot through the market, a large group of seething people – mostly women – pursued them.

'Two storms broke,' David agrees. 'The case itself and the press and public interest in it. After Lesley Ann Downey and John Kilbride were found, everything went haywire. Reporters kept pushing their cards through our letterbox, wrapped up in fivers, with scribbled invitations: "If you fancy a drink and a chat, give us a ring." By evening, there would be a small pile of cards on the hallway floor. The car park at Underwood Court *swarmed* with reporters and photographers. Lenses were trained on our balcony and the main door downstairs.'

He grins suddenly. 'I found a way of dealing with the scrutiny, though. Because of the difficulty in getting Bob past old Mr Page's door, we often let the dog do his business on the balcony. When the press came, I'd let the muck pile up on purpose, fetch the big sweeping brush, throw some water down to make it all good and sloppy, then sweep the stinking mess off with gusto, straight onto the cars below. None of us residents could afford to drive, so I knew that any cars down there had to belong to reporters. It used to cheer me up no end, that little task. Apart from that, I didn't have anything to do with the press for a while.' He pauses and rubs his jaw thoughtfully. 'The problem was that by ignoring them, I didn't see the bigger picture. I had no idea what was coming – the attention set to engulf us. I lived within a bubble of Underwood Court and various police stations. To some extent, it was a self-imposed bubble – I needed to protect myself and Maureen, who was almost three months pregnant.'

The bubble burst on Monday, 6 December 1965. On that date, committal proceedings against Ian Brady and Myra Hindley opened at Hyde Magistrates' Court. The purpose of a committal is to establish whether there is a case for trial; in 1965, that meant presenting the full prosecution case before magistrates, with the press allowed to report on events unless instructed otherwise (both Brady's defence lawyer, David Lloyd-Jones, and Hindley's defence lawyer, Philip Curtis, failed in their plea to have the evidence heard in camera). Eighty witnesses were called to read their statements, a long and expensive process lasting eleven days.

David was the lynchpin of the prosecution's case. 'It wasn't something I looked forward to doing,' he admits. 'I dreaded having to face Ian and Myra again. I hadn't seen either of them since the day after Edward Evans was killed. There had been no contact between Maureen and her family either. Two camps sprang up straight away: "us" – me and Maureen and Dad – and "them" – the Hindleys. They'd made it clear Maureen was out of the fold. We were still in our bubble at that point, right up to the day when we had to give evidence. But in the run-up to the committal, I couldn't sleep or think straight at all. Knowing I'd have to take the stand while Ian and Myra sat only a few feet away brought me out in a cold sweat. And the press, too, became unbearable.'

Shortly before the committal opened, reporters set up unofficial 'headquarters' at the Queen's Hotel in Hyde, 500 yards from the courtroom. The ensuing publicity made minor celebrities of the magistrates themselves: former Mayoress Mrs Dorothy Adamson, a JP since 1938 (fond of wearing quirky little hats in court), Harry Taylor, retired secretary of Hyde Weavers' Association, and Sam Redfern, a retired master baker.

The prosecution outlined their case on Tuesday, 7 December 1965. David was due to step into the witness box the very next day.

* * *

From David Smith's memoir:
Condensation fogs the glass of the balcony doors; it's a bitterly cold morning in Hattersley. Maureen has switched on two bars of the electric fire, but I can't feel any warmth as I prowl about the flat. I haven't slept, and the cigarettes I've spent the night ingesting, one after the other, have left me with a banging headache and a throat you could use to grate cheese. I've thrown so much cold water over my face that I'm starting to worry I might sprout fins in place of ears. Vomit rises and then sinks again in my gut, my nerves feel as if they're wired up to the pylons over the estate, and on top of everything I'm so exhausted that my eyes burn; I keep having to squeeze them tightly shut to try and stop them smarting.

Two policemen stand in the living room, heads politely bowed, waiting for me to organise myself. They haven't spoken since Maureen let them into the flat and their silence agitates me. I head through to the bathroom, closing the door loudly, and hold on to the sink. It's icy cold under my fingers. A tremor passes through my knees and I grip the porcelain until my knuckles are white and protruding. My reflection doesn't look like me at all.

'Come on, lad, get yourself together – it's time to go.' The copper's voice on the other side of the door is stern but not unkind. It panics me nonetheless and I shout, 'Fuck off, leave me alone for a fucking minute!' I stare wildly at the mirror, wanting nothing more than to smash my skull into it with a scream.

Minutes pass. There is a gentle knock at the door and Maureen pleads softly, 'Come on, love, come out. Everybody's waiting.'

I grab a towel. The bobbly blue material darkens with the sweat from my face and armpits. I let it fall to the floor and unlock the door. Maureen stands there, eyes huge with concern, flanked by the policemen. She places a gentle kiss on my cheek. Then suddenly we're leaving the flat, the two of us tightly holding hands, heading towards the lift with the policemen following. One of their colleagues stands inside the narrow, stinky cubicle, holding the door open with a security key. We step inside and descend the three floors in silence.

Downstairs in the lobby, another policeman stands just inside the glass entrance door, while a second waits outside, his broad back obscuring our view of the car park and road beyond. The copper indoors moves towards us as we step out of the lift: 'There's a load of press outside and a fair-sized crowd. Go careful.'

Maureen's fingers tighten over mine. I squint at the glass and recognise a couple of faces at the front of the crowd as our neighbours from upstairs. They're only waiting to be allowed into their flat, but the police take no chances and hold them back with the rest. I reach into my pocket for two pairs of black sunglasses and hand one set to Maureen. With those pitiful pieces of protection in place, I give the police a nod.

As the door opens, a monumental wall of abuse, as ferocious as it is deafening, hits us. At the side of the kerb is a police car; we're herded towards it at a run. The crowd's screams reach fever pitch and the sound of their feet scuffling as the coppers push them away from us is startling music in itself. I know from experience that most of them are women, and many will have brought their kids along. They start spitting, and an animal-like howl of emotion goes up from their struggling number. Then it's the turn of the reporters, running alongside us and shouting ludicrous questions that make me want to break through the police cordon and start landing punches. I hear one yell: 'How are you today, Maureen? Any news from your sister?' I explode and start fighting my way through to the culprit: 'Shut your fucking mouth, you stupid fucking—'

The large hands of a copper seize my shoulders and swivel me back to where I was before. We're manhandled into the car; the doors slam shut and fists pound on the windows in another unforgettable symphony of hatred. The driver presses his boot down on the accelerator and the cacophony fades as Underwood Court disappears from view, leaving only a ringing silence.

The air inside the police car feels like cotton wool; it's stifling with the windows shut and the heater on full blast. I sit back in my seat, sick and claustrophobic, trying not to think of what lies ahead. Then I look at Maureen. 'All right, girl? How are you?'

'Scared.' She stares straight ahead. Her face, beneath the heavy make-up, is pale and drawn. I squeeze her hand and turn away.

When we stop at a red light, two carloads of press pull up right next to us, with more behind, their cameras trained on our windows. The policeman in the front passenger seat swears and the driver, equally irate, over-revs the engine, his eyes fixed on the traffic lights, waiting impatiently for red to turn to amber. He speeds away the instant it changes, leaving our pursuers far behind. Then the radio crackles, alerting our escorts to 'a substantial gathering' around Hyde Magistrates' Court. The policeman in the passenger seat glances at us in the mirror: 'Prepare yourselves for a bumpy ride.' Then he adds, 'There's a blanket back there if you want it for cover.'

My shoulders drop. I think to myself: why should we hide when we've done nothing wrong? What the hell is all that about? No way am I crawling under a blanket like a fucking criminal, no fucking way.

'Get ready for it,' the driver warns in a loud voice. The indicator blinks loudly, as he turns the car into a street heaving with people. A barrage of flashbulbs bursts like shellfire, turning the inside of the car into a photographic negative, making it impossible to see. The driver curses, as he attempts to nudge the car into the yard behind the police station and is forced to stop. The fists are back again, pounding and banging, and huge black lenses poke through the sea of hands like bruised eyes. Our driver and his colleague start to panic; the copper in the passenger seat urges, 'Drive, for Christ's sake, push them back, get to the yard, keep going or we've had it, keep going.'

Maureen clutches my arm and leans against me. She's terrified, and more so because of her pregnancy. From behind the sunglasses, I look out at the frenzy surrounding us and for a moment the sight is so surreal that I view it like an outsider. The strange fusion of anger and desperation contorts people's faces as they press up against the window. Further back, the crowd melts into one screaming mouth. We inch forwards towards the safety of the station yard and yet the swarm of bodies keeps closing in, almost lifting us from the concrete. Flashbulbs burst on all sides and the banging fists on the car form a hollow, painful rhythm, making the vehicle rock like a boat. The figures lurch back and forth and I think to myself: a plague of deranged zombies, that's what they are, just creatures from a B-movie, not real at all.

Suddenly the car jumps forward, into the yard of Hyde station, and the heavy metal doors close behind us with a resounding clang.

Although I'm not aware of it, across the street the person who will prove to be my salvation years from now is watching the madness, too.

Hyde Town Hall is a multi-purpose building: apart from the usual municipal business, it serves as a police station and Magistrates' Court. Directly opposite is Greenfield Street Primary, and on this particular cold December morning in 1965 a nine-year-old girl stands with her friends in the schoolyard. Long brown hair tightly plaited by her father that morning, she clings to the railings in excited curiosity, ignoring the teachers' instructions to go indoors.

All the commotion – what is it for? Strangers in dark glasses, cameras, journalists, noisy crowds . . . perhaps, she thinks, it's a film. She presses her face closer to the railings, feeling the cold iron against her skin. She's never seen anything like it but is disappointed when she doesn't recognise the couple in sunglasses. They're not even off the telly, so why all the fuss?

The teachers wade in, remonstrating crossly, finally managing to convince the children to come away. The sudden downpour of rain helps. Still chattering about the goings-on at the courthouse, the children file in through the main doors, parting like a sea to find their classrooms.

Mary Flaherty is the last to be prised away from the railings. She waits until the couple in dark glasses disappear and the flashbulbs stop popping. Then she walks across the schoolyard, thoughtfully chewing one of her too-tight plaits.

In the corridor, I sit with Maureen, holding her hand. I keep my head bowed and shoulders hunched. The corridor seems endless, a trench dug out of hell. The wooden bench is hard and cold as steel. Somewhere there is a clock ticking, yet the minutes take hours to pass. Occasionally, I hear a whisper from the policewoman sitting on Maureen's other side, kindly offering reassurance. I hope Maureen is comforted by her words; she might as well be talking Chinese, as far as I'm concerned. Between my feet is a steadily growing pile of cigarette butts. I clear my throat, but it's rank with nicotine and, like the ashtray it too often resembles, could do with a wipe with a damp cloth.

I look down the corridor. At the very end is a black-robed usher, waiting by the courtroom door, his face blank with boredom. I try to remember what the police said: committal proceedings aren't 'as bad' as trials, it's just a matter of the prosecution presenting their case, no cross-examining by defence lawyers. But still I don't feel comforted.

The policewoman leans forward and asks if I'm all right. I nod, knowing that I'm not. My eyes keep being drawn back to the courtroom door. It's what lies on the other side that disturbs me most. I light another cigarette and lean back against the wall.

I haven't been this close to Ian and Myra since we sat together after the killing of Edward Evans in Wardle Brook Avenue. Images from that night flitter through my head, a stream of bloodied tickertape. I try to fight the memories, but the effort causes cold sweat to trickle under my hairline and bead my top lip. I close my eyes and see another corridor from which there's no escape: the one in my mind. A thin foam of bile rises inside my mouth. Eight weeks have passed since that night, but it's nothing, less than the blink of a woman's eye after she's held the gaze of a young man in his last ten seconds of life.

The courtroom door creaks open and a head appears in the narrow gap, whispering. The usher turns, a crow-like gesture as his black robes billow slightly, and calls out my name.

I stand up and stub out my cigarette. The bile has sunk back into my gut, leaving my mouth sticky but dry. I find it impossible to swallow. The walk down the corridor is long and lonely, just the sound of my own footsteps on the parquet floor.

Someone is speaking to me. I blink rapidly and realise I'm in the witness box, watched by scores of curious eyes. The whispering begins and I start to tremble, not knowing how I got here. I need to find some sort of inner strength, the same cold instinct that ensured my survival just two months ago. That thought brings everything into pinprick focus: I look down for two faces among the multitude and when I find them, I hear a whooshing noise in my head, like the sound of the traffic during that very first journey to Hyde station.

Ian and Myra sit together in the dock, so near that I'm convinced I can smell them: her hair lacquer and his aftershave. Their physical presence goes through me like an electrical volt. Ian wears his grey trousers and jacket, with the waistcoat beneath; Myra is in a speckled suit, with a yellow blouse that should soften her face but doesn't. Her hair is white blonde, a candyfloss ball, while Ian is as immaculately groomed as ever. His head is bent, as he speaks softly to Myra and she listens, nodding slowly. Then she turns and her eyes lock on mine.

They are the eyes I remember from our last encounter: sloe-black and unblinking. Her expression may seem blank to those who don't know her, but the hard set of her jaw reveals the depth of her hatred for me, and for what I've done to them.

Then all at once it hits me: they can't hurt anyone now. Myra's gaze might remind me of a shark – that dead and yet venomous look – but if that's what she resembles, she's no more than an animal in captivity. That knowledge alone gives me the strength I need. Myra and Ian will still be an unassailable unit, playing their private games, whispering and giggling, sharing secrets only they will ever truly know, but they are captured and caged, left with their evil memories but without a future.

I look at Ian. He acknowledges me with the slightest nod and a barely there, ironic smile. Myra continues to fix me with her glare across the airless courtroom. But I stare them down: I am the witness.

I take a deep breath and begin . . .

Chapter 15

'The unfortunate affair with the newspaper . . . [Smith] at that time was pretty desperate for money, and he has been promised £1,000 for his story . . . it is the sort of temptation to which he should never have been exposed for a moment.'

— Mr Justice Fenton Atkinson, Moors trial at Chester Assizes, April 1966

David's nerves weren't completely banished in the witness box; he stuttered frequently and spoke so softly that microphones were brought in. But he got through it, and today recalls: 'I was just glad when it was over. Having those two – Brady and Hindley – staring at me all the time wasn't easy. They were far too close for my liking. At the proper trial in Chester, the dock was surrounded by thick glass, which thankfully made them seem even further away. But at least the committal was a gentle process. I had to answer a few queries, but not many and not in depth.'

Maureen took the stand after her husband, refusing an offer to be seated. She spoke quietly but with surprising self-assurance and kept her composure. Immediately afterwards, Myra Hindley wrote to her mother: 'Did you read the lies Maureen told in court, about me hating babies and children? She wouldn't look at me in the dock, Mam. She couldn't. She kept her face turned away. I noticed she was wearing a new coat and boots, and that Smith had a new watch on and a new overcoat and suit. I suppose he's had an advance on his dirt money.'

Myra was referring to David and Maureen's deal with the *News of the World*, an arrangement that caused serious concern at the subsequent trial. David's dad and Uncle Bert set the whole thing up between them, seeing no reason to ignore the potentially hefty sums on offer for his story. David hadn't worked since informing the police of Edward Evans's murder and was unable to secure a job because of his 'association' with the two most reviled people in the country.

'I was hated for selling out to the *News of the World*,' he muses, 'but I didn't set up the deal, though admittedly I went along with it. Dad and Uncle Bert threw me to the lions – until they climbed aboard the publicity bandwagon, I had nothing to do with the press. I ignored the cards pushed through our letterbox and despised the reporters who shoved their cameras and microphones in our faces whenever we left the flat. But the two Jack the Lads in the family saw it as a golden opportunity. They kept saying, "You've been through hell, the public hate you, you're crippled with debt, you've no chance of a job while this is hanging over you, and there's Maureen and the baby to consider . . . why shouldn't you make some money out of telling your story?" Put like that, it didn't seem such a bad thing to do. So I let them get on with it.'

Two newspapers put in sizeable bids: the *News of the World*, who offered £1,000, and *The People*, offering £6,000. 'Dad and Uncle Bert were clueless,' David recalls with an exasperated smile. 'The *News of the World* talked to them about the thousands we might earn through syndication, serial rights and all that malarkey. They convinced Dad and Uncle Bert to think long-term gain rather than short-term solution. Then they asked to meet Maureen and me – just us two – and arranged a rendezvous in the cafeteria of John Lewis, in town. We were both scared stiff, so out came the dark glasses again, to hide behind. We must have stuck out like a right couple of sore thumbs, huddled behind the buffet in these big sunglasses, waiting for the journalists to turn up.'

Reporter George Mackintosh and sports writer Jack Knot arrived to discuss the deal. 'They asked very broad questions,' David remembers, 'and were pretty easy to get on with, really. The meeting lasted about an hour. Before we left they made it very clear that they wanted to go ahead – they pushed us £20 apiece. Believe me, £40 back then was a lot of money to people like us. I suppose today's equivalent would be around £400, and these were just notes they'd peeled off a roll in their back pockets. They asked us to meet them again a couple of days later, with their editor Jack Taylor, and Dad and Uncle Bert, in a members-only club where hacks hung out. Everything was paid for – drinks and a slap-up meal. Jack Taylor delivered his patter about syndication, selling serial rights to Germany and so on. It didn't mean a lot to me, but just before he was due to return to the office he pulled out a contract, which he "happened" to have on him. We signed there and then.'

Under the terms of the contract, David and Maureen were paid £15 per week until the trial. Upon Brady and Hindley's conviction, the *News of the World* would run a series of articles about the couple from David's perspective, and he and Maureen would receive a lump sum of £1,000.

In the meantime, committal proceedings were drawing to a close as Christmas approached. The most harrowing moments in court came after David had given his evidence. During her appearance in the witness box, Lesley Ann Downey's mother broke down and screamed at Myra: 'I'll kill you! I'll kill you!' A quick-thinking policeman grabbed the water carafe provided for witnesses before she could hurl it across the court. The tape of Lesley Ann was played the following day; although press and public were barred from court for those few minutes, rumours about the recording stoked public anger anew against the two accused, who had pleaded not guilty to all charges. David and Maureen bore the brunt of that aggression, despite their position as witnesses for the prosecution.

'People hated Brady and Hindley,' David muses, 'but at the same time they chose to believe their lies about me. As the horror of it all came out, my life and Maureen's became very difficult. We'd go to the pub and people would fall silent and stare, then start whispering and calling us names. That would lead to lots of "accidental" pushes and shoves, then proper physical aggression. I tried to stay away from pub toilets because in any closed environment I'd be followed and beaten up. The New Inn on the estate was out of bounds. Even if I went into Hyde . . . eventually it would descend into violence, whether it was before I'd got inside the pub, at the bar, in the toilets or as I was leaving. It usually started verbally but always led to a good hiding. No one – not *one* person – ever tried to intervene or told me I'd done the right thing by going to the police. No one would have a drink with me either, apart from Maureen and Dad. He had to get rounds in because no one would serve me. Standing at the bar was too risky anyway – if I wasn't careful, someone would approach me from behind, grab me by the neck or hair and hold me down until there was a whole crowd involved, kicking and punching the crap out of me.'

Maureen was equally targeted. 'She couldn't go down to the shops without being attacked,' David recalls. 'Women especially would call her names, spit at her, pull her hair, shove her in the back, and lash out at her every day. She started retreating into her shell, not wanting to go out. I reacted differently – the abuse made me defiant. I wasn't going to sit at home cowering. If I wanted a drink, then I'd go out for one and if I wanted a walk to the shops, then so be it. No one was going to beat me into submission. Maureen wasn't as frightened if she was with me – we'd often go to a social club on Underwood Court, even though we knew we'd come home with black eyes and busted lips. Together we stood our ground. I never ran from anything, because I had nothing to run from, and it was as simple as that.'

Nonetheless, in March 1966 matters came to a head. David's temper snapped when a crowd gathered below the balcony where he was standing and began shouting abuse. One youth yelled, 'You're no bleeding good without that axe, Smith!' David picked up the dog's lead, rushed downstairs and charged into the crowd.

'I really went for them,' he admits. 'I struck out at them all – lads my age, mostly – but they pinned me down and kicked the shit out of me. Afterwards, the police knocked on our door for a "quiet word". It didn't go any further because they knew what we were up against. In fact, after that we had a copper on our door as protection. By then, it was no longer just a matter of having to be careful when we went out – the abuse had reached our front door. Some of the neighbours would let in troublemakers, and the whole place was soon covered in foul graffiti. We'd get visitors at all hours of the day and night, trying to kick the door in, banging on it, screaming and swearing. They'd come into the communal corridor and piss up the door. In the morning, there would be a thick pool on the floor. It was pretty grim.'

When the door entry buzzer rang one evening shortly before the trial, David didn't answer it. The caller was so persistent that in the end David's dad got up and pressed the intercom button. He returned looking troubled, but explained that he hadn't liked to turn away their caller, and by then it was too late anyway: Lesley Ann Downey's mother was standing at the door.

* * *

From David Smith's memoir:
I don't know what to expect when Dad tells me that Mrs Downey wants to see us. I'm sitting in the flat with Maureen, staring at the telly, without a clue what's on. I don't answer the buzzer because it's never anyone I want to see, and when Dad comes in with the news that Mrs Downey is here, I think it's a wind-up and almost explode. How could he be so stupid? Any minute now we'll have rent-a-mob at our door, yelling and kicking, and leaving their 'calling card' – a trail of yellow piss that still stinks a week later, no matter how hard we scrub it away.

But when the knock comes, it's polite and fairly quiet – not the hammering we hear daily. Our caller waits, without shouting or screaming through the door.

Dad looks at me. 'Have I to let them in?'

I catch Maureen's eye. She gets up awkwardly from the sofa, pushing Bob's front paws off her knee; he can't sprawl across her lap any more, not now she's eight months pregnant. I raise my eyebrows and Maureen shrugs slowly, leaving it up to me.

I nod at Dad, still unconvinced about our visitor.

'What do you think she wants, Dave?' Maureen whispers, as Dad goes through to the corridor.

I reach for my fags and lighter from the top of the electric fire. 'Haven't a clue,' I answer, hoping the tight knot in my stomach isn't a bad omen.

'I hope it'll be all right.' Maureen speaks under her breath, more to herself than to me.

Dad comes back into the sitting room, and with him are three people: a blonde-haired, not unattractive woman in her early 30s, a slightly older tattooed man, and another thick-set bloke. I tense immediately: our visitors have been drinking. I can smell it on them and see it in their eyes.

But it's fine at first. I notice Mrs Downey staring at Maureen, but she calmly introduces herself and the two men. The wiry, tattooed chap is her partner; the other is her former brother-in-law or her own brother – my nerves are on edge and I can't take everything in. But I notice again how her eyes follow Maureen, as she goes through to the kitchen to make a pot of tea.

The rest of us sit down. Mrs Downey gives the room a sweeping glance before edging forward on her chair and speaking in a measured, urgent voice. She asks me to help her by going to court and telling the judge and jury everything I know; she doesn't want anyone left in doubt about what 'those two' did to her daughter. I promise to do everything I can, agreeing that Brady and Hindley deserve to go down until death.

The men who came with her are silent. She repeats what she has already said, then after a pause and still speaking in a restrained voice, asks me what 'they' were like. I don't know what to tell her. I mumble something about them seeming normal 'but obviously . . . they weren't'.

Mrs Downey nods, frowning, hands clasped on her knees, rocking slightly. Then she asks, 'Why? Why did they do it?'

Slowly, helplessly, I shrug my shoulders. I mumble again, mentioning the word 'evil' and 'sick' several times. She nods along as I talk, but doesn't seem to be listening any more; Maureen has brought in the tea tray and sets it down on the small table. Suddenly, Mrs Downey asks if she might have a word with me on my own. I nod and indicate for her to go through to the kitchen.

We stand together silently in the narrow space. I stare at a patch of steam on the wall where the kettle has just boiled. Then Mrs Downey starts to cry, spluttering through great, rocking sobs that I *must* see to it that those two go down, that what they really deserved was to be hanged, and how she just wishes that she could get her hands on them. She is deeply upset but has her emotions under control, and eventually stops crying to make me promise again that I will do my best when the time comes.

I tell her I'll do whatever I can.

We head back into the living room. Mrs Downey is slightly ahead of me, walking normally, when it comes without warning: she dashes forward at speed, hurling herself at Maureen. I'm so surprised that it takes me a moment to grasp what's happening, but Maureen's reactions are quicker: she screams and throws her arms around her stomach, bending forward on the settee, trying to defend herself, lifting her hands to her head. Mrs Downey's rage is focused entirely on Maureen; she flies at her again and again, pulling Maureen's black hair out by its roots – long strands of it sail through the air. The rest of us are still too stunned to move, as the sound of Mrs Downey's slaps raining on Maureen's arms and face rings out. She suddenly hauls Maureen up from the settee and slams her up against the wall, spitting thickly in her face while Maureen crumples, desperately trying to protect her stomach.

I snap to life at last, leaping across a chair arm to reach Mrs Downey. In that instant, it doesn't matter to me who she is – all I want is to get her off Maureen. But as I grab her roughly and yank her backwards, I feel an arm go around my throat, pulling me to the floor. There's a shout of fury from Dad, who instantly pitches in to help me while I'm lying on my back with Mrs Downey's partner hitting me about the face. Then Dad, too, is tugged off his feet by the thick-set man and ends up beside me on the floor, inches away from the sharp corners of the electric fire.

A vicious rough-and-tumble around the flat ensues until Bob the dog springs into action, barking frantically and circling us all. Our visitors freeze in fear at the large collie snapping his teeth, and Dad and I seize our chance, managing to shove, punch and kick the three of them into the narrow corridor. We end up in a heap in the middle, still fighting. It takes a while, but somehow we reach the door and heave our guests into the hallway.

Tumbling arse-over-heels like a troupe of wayward circus performers, we reach the lift. I find myself sprawled over the thick-set bloke, who struggles to free one of his hands in order to punch me full in the face. Out of the corner of my eye, I spy the milk bottles left out by our neighbours and grab one, holding it in the air, ready to bring it down. For a horrible moment, I'm tempted to let him have it, but then I come to my senses and drop the bottle. It rolls noisily into a corner and I let my companion scramble to his feet.

With Dad's help, I push our three visitors into the lift and hit the button for the ground floor, drawing back swiftly as the door closes.

Screams reach us from the lift shaft: *'Bastards! You're no different to those two! Fucking bastards! You should be hung, the lot of you!'*

Dad and I droop with our exertions and head back to the flat. Maureen weeps inconsolably on the floor, a thin rag doll with wild black hair. Bob the dog sits pressed to her side, whining as if in sympathy. I sink to my knees and cradle Maureen in my arms. Her sobs only grow louder.

The police visit us a few days later. I don't know who called them but suspect it was a neighbour. The copper in charge tells me quietly that this won't go any further, provided nothing like it ever happens again. I assure him it won't.

When the police have gone, I sit by the electric fire, looking across at Maureen; in the time it took for me to show the coppers to the door, she's fallen fast asleep. I rack my brain, trying to think what could have sparked the fight off, but can't think of anything. In the end, I begin to wonder if Mrs Downey saw Myra every time she looked at Maureen that night and this makes enough skewed sense for me to put the matter aside. I just hope that Maureen won't come to the same conclusion.

Today, David reflects: 'I know Ann West – Mrs Downey, as she was then – told a very different story of that night in her book. I heard that she said I'd turned up at her house, told some favourite joke of Ian Brady's and then passed a remark about the resemblance between Lesley Ann and one of her brothers. But I *never* went to Ann West's house – I didn't even know where she lived. Why in God's name would I have put myself, or her, in that position? At that time I was trying to ward people off, not goad them into thumping me. I would *never* have said anything along the lines of Lesley looking like her brother because I didn't know them. As for that sick joke I'm supposed to have told her was Brady's favourite . . . no way. *No way.* I'm sorry, but no. Not true, it didn't happen. I've no idea why she told it as she did, but it *wasn't* like that. Not at all.' There is one line in Ann West's account which tallies with David's memories of that night, however; she writes: 'I beat Maureen Smith's head against the wall and screamed incoherently at her. I tore at her and for a moment it was as if I had her foul sister in my hands . . .'

Shortly after the confrontation, the *News of the World* offered to send David and Maureen on an all-expenses-paid trip to France. The couple leapt at the chance to get away for a while; neither of them had ever been abroad and they set off in excitement on what felt like the holiday of a lifetime. With a grin, David remembers: 'We travelled by ferry, but as soon as we set foot in France, we didn't know what to do with ourselves. The hotel in Paris was nice enough, but it was just a place to lay our heads. We weren't ones for sightseeing, so doing the old tourist trail didn't appeal either. Menus stumped us because we couldn't speak the lingo, though we were both very taken by the little cafe bars – they seemed sophisticated in just the right way. But after a couple of days we were proper fed up. We didn't know what to do, so we went to a cinema. *Mary Poppins*, which neither of us had seen, was showing. We settled ourselves happily in our red plush seats for the matinee and waited for the film to start.'

He laughs, shaking his head. 'It was *Mary Poppins* all right, but dubbed into French. There weren't even any subtitles. I could have lived with that, I suppose, but hearing Dick van Dyke speak French . . . well. He still managed to sound more cockney than he did in the English version, mind you. But it was bloody terrible. We came out of the film feeling even worse, two right fishes out of water. Then we had another idea: around the time of the committal, a French company had filmed the two of us in Belle Vue, just walking round, as part of their footage of the case. It was shot for French television, though we weren't even interviewed, just filmed wandering around the zoo. They gave us some cash, bought us dinner and drinks, and that was that. A bit weird, but we weren't going to say no. And in return for their generosity, we went and had a little chat with the elephants for French telly. Afterwards, the film crew said that if we were ever in France we should look them up. Of course, they were just being polite and never expected us to show our faces again. But because we were at such a loose end, that's exactly what we did. Maureen remembered that their offices were on the rue Saint Augustin. We found it and knocked on their door. They were very welcoming, as it happens, and even asked if we wanted to see how they'd edited our little film.'

He laughs again. 'We sat in Paris and watched ourselves wandering around Belle Vue. So much for excitement, eh? Later on, it was made public that we had "been abroad" at the expense of the *News of the World* and people were outraged by the idea of us gadding about Paris with gay abandon. If only they'd known the truth: the highlights of our holiday in France were a badly dubbed *Mary Poppins* and a visit to an editing suite. Bloody marvellous.'

David and Maureen returned home to Underwood Court in early spring. A few days before Maureen was due to give birth, the Trial of the Century began.

Chapter 16

'Certainly David Smith is no angel but do you think he comes near the standards of criminality which have been disclosed in respect of Brady? Who was the devil of the piece? Who was the disciple?'
                                    – The Attorney General, Moors trial
                                        at Chester Assizes, May 1966

Chester Castle Courtroom had been transformed to meet the unique needs of the most notorious trial ever held within its walls. Amid the ancient oak panelling, velvet drapes and red leather seating, thick carpet was fitted to reduce noise, microphones were placed in the witness box, and telephones were installed in large rooms set aside for the sole use of the press. Reinforced glass surrounded the dock on both sides and at the back, while 300 policemen were drafted in as extra security. Every hotel in Chester was fully booked with international journalists and television crews, although the BBC decided the substance of the trial was too shocking to air, and ITV limited their reports to clipped segments within the evening news bulletin.

Throughout the trial, queues began to form outside the court from first light; 60 seats were available in the public gallery, but hundreds of people turned up in the hope of gaining admission. The majority were women, some of them elderly, who appeared each day, whatever the weather – and it was inclement in the extreme, veering from torrential rain and gales on the first day to a freak heat wave on another.

Few of the victims' families attended. John Kilbride's aunt and uncle, Elsie and Frank Doran, were an exception; they had spent months organising a petition to reinstate the death penalty for child killers. Also present were several writers, including *Whistle Down the Wind* author Mary Hayley Bell, and Emlyn Williams, who had already begun writing an *In Cold Blood*-style treatment of the case.

Presiding over the legal process itself was Mr Justice Fenton Atkinson, a steady and meticulous presence in court. The Attorney General, Sir Frederick Elwyn Jones, led the prosecution team and added extra gravitas but was occasionally called away to London; William Mars-Jones, QC, took over in his absence. Ian Brady's defence was Hugh Emlyn Hoosen, QC, with Godfrey Heilpern, QC, representing Myra Hindley (she was then facing the additional charge of murdering John Kilbride). Heilpern was unable to be present initially, having learned of a death in the family; his junior, Philip Curtis, stepped in until his return.

The Attorney General opened proceedings on behalf of the Crown. Outlining the crimes and the background of the perpetrators, he then described how, following David's marriage to Maureen, 'Brady and Hindley appeared to have gone out of their way to cultivate [*the couple*]. Although Hindley was related by marriage to David Smith, the interest which Brady displayed in Smith went far beyond the friendship one would expect in these circumstances. In my submission the story of the close association which developed between them is the story of a steady and cunning corruption of a youth of 16 by a mature man, Brady, who was then aged 26. Brady appeared to have interested Smith in the subject of murder and made him a student of that subject.'

David sat in court, listening to the description of himself and his relationship with Brady. He recalls: 'I felt powerless. Obviously I wasn't in a position to challenge anything that was said in the speeches. I was petrified and so was Maureen – neither of us had any idea what to expect. We were both overwhelmed by the sheer scale of the trial and the authority carried by those in court, especially the Attorney General. It was such a colossal thing to be part of – deeply intimidating. The *News of the World* paid for our transport and hotel, which was a pub in Chester. I stayed there with Maureen and Dad, and we hated it because journalists had booked out all the other rooms. The bar was always heaving with them, so we couldn't have a pint without being swamped by reporters. We were forbidden from talking about the case and ended up spending all our time closeted upstairs. When it came to the trial itself, Maureen was one of the first to take the stand. Just getting in and out of the building was a nightmare: a car had been laid on for us, but the driver always slowed down deliberately to let the snappers do their job. I kept my sunglasses on until I had to go into court, removed them at the door, then put them on again as soon as I stepped down from the witness box. Maureen did the same.'

Called out of sequence due to the advanced stage of her pregnancy (an ambulance was on standby to rush her to hospital, if necessary), Maureen gave evidence under the watchful eye of her sister Myra, who sat alongside Ian, making notes and sucking mints. She had a heavy nosebleed during her time in the witness box and court was adjourned until she had composed herself. Returning to the stand, Maureen described the relationship between her sister and Ian, declared that Myra had been in the habit of shopping at Ashton Market, and spoke about the late night visit to the moor on 24 April 1965, when Ian had invited David to look at the moon shining on the reservoir. Regarding the murder of Lesley Ann Downey, she stated firmly that she had been at David's side throughout Boxing Day 1964. Her evidence continued into the next day, when she described the evening before the murder of Edward Evans. She admitted that David had been in the pay of a national newspaper since November the previous year and agreed that their financial situation before October had been precarious. Finally, asked to be precise about where she and David had gone with Myra and Ian, Maureen replied wanly, 'It is all the same to me, the moors.'

The court then adjourned for lunch. David was due to give evidence immediately afterwards; Brady's solicitor was assured that he and Maureen would have no contact during the hiatus. David recalls: 'Those last few minutes before going into the witness box were nerve-racking in the extreme – all the attention and not knowing what to expect. The committal wasn't any sort of preparation and no one spoke to me beforehand to explain the process and how to handle it. As soon as I got up there . . .

well, when the prosecution were questioning me, I was fine. But the minute the defence stood up, I felt my hackles rise. It's true to say that I had an attitude problem, but I felt under attack. The jury can't have thought much of me, and I don't blame them. I remember fiddling with the microphone constantly. Nerves again. I came across as arrogant, which is ironic because I felt anything *but* arrogant.'

One observer described David as 'a handsome young man with dark brown hair that seemed to fall all over his neck, his ears, his forehead and his eyes. It seemed he had tried to control it with oil, not altogether successfully. While he was giving his evidence he seemed to be under a deep and genuine emotion. His heavy breathing was echoed round the court on the microphone like the protesting background music of a blues record. He wore jeans, which fitted him tightly, and a blue shirt. Perhaps the sedate formality of the court had an effect on him because, after the luncheon adjournment on the first day he gave evidence, he had put on a tie to match his shirt. He seemed to find the tie very uncomfortable, for he ran his forefinger around inside the collar attempting to stretch it, as if it was strangling him. He happened to make this gesture when he was giving evidence on the last moments of Edward Evans and it added to the dramatic sentence "a gurgling noise like when you brush your teeth". . . . David Smith had a gift of phrase and a quickness of mind that came across, illuminating the sombre court. One did not like him, but for a man so young he was quite a formidable personality . . . The intelligence of David Smith was a real factor in the Moors murder case . . . The total effect of David Smith in the witness box was that here was a young man who had been in all kinds of trouble, but who had been genuinely terrified after witnessing the killing of Edward Evans. The case for the defence rested on the assumption that there was little to choose between Brady and Smith, but this assumption crumbled, partly because the two men were so astonishingly unalike . . .'

Overall, despite his nerves, David remained calm and even a little cocky, responding to a question about his finances with: 'I love having money, I think it's gorgeous stuff, but I don't think it's worth worrying about. You grow old that way.'

The judge murmured dryly, 'You grow old anyway.'

Similarly, when Brady's defence asked him the barbed question: 'You don't like work, do you?' he responded, 'No. I don't think anybody likes work.'

Occasionally his candour was to his advantage. When Hoosen challenged him about the murder of Edward Evans – 'You are a man in the habit of holding a stick in your hand all the time, are you not?' – David regarded him for a moment before quietly countering, 'Yes, sir, but I am not in the habit of witnessing murder.'

He was on less certain ground with a few inappropriate examples of journalese, describing Brady's attack on Edward Evans as 'very calm indeed, I have seen butchers working in the shops show as much emotion as he did when they are cutting up a sheep's head . . . My first thought was that Ian had hold of a life-size rag doll and was just waving it about . . .' He admits now that such expressions were one of the unhappy side effects of the newspaper deal: 'Those flowery phrases were due to the fact that I'd gone over the story so many times with the *News of the World*. I ended up talking like a hack, picking up their way of speech, and it wasn't good.'

Nonetheless one commentator pointed out: 'It was a simple matter to discredit Smith as a person, but as a witness he was virtually incontrovertible.'

David began giving evidence on Thursday, 21 April with a description of the trip to the Lakes in August 1964. Mars-Jones then led him on to the subject of guns and their potential use in the abandoned bank robbery. After explaining Brady's murderous boasts, he answered several questions about the books Brady had recommended. *The Life and Ideals of the Marquis de Sade* was produced in court; Mars-Jones read aloud the same extract Brady had recited to David three weeks prior to the murder of Edward Evans: *'Should murder be punished by murder? Undoubtedly not . . .'* Mars-Jones then moved on to the night of the killing, before concluding with a few brief questions about Lesley Ann Downey and John Kilbride; David told the court he had never heard of either child until the discovery of their bodies became headline news.

His cross-examination by Brady's defence, Hugh Emlyn

Hoosen, began the following day. Together with Hindley's lawyer, Hoosen concentrated on trying to discredit David completely, treating him as an accomplice in Edward Evans's murder and suggesting that he was responsible for the deaths of Lesley Ann Downey and John Kilbride. He launched into his attempt to undermine David's character by asking immediately, 'Smith, have you received an undertaking by the prosecution that you will not be prosecuted in respect of any offence disclosed by you in your statements?'

David replied that he had.

Hoosen then asked, 'Is it right that you have entered into an arrangement with a newspaper whereby you will have a very large sum in certain eventualities?'

'Yes, sir.'

'And do the certain eventualities include the conviction of Brady and Hindley?'

'I should imagine that would be the—'

'So you have a vested financial interest, have you not, have had since November, in their conviction?'

'Yes.'

'Do you mind telling us the name of the newspaper with whom you have entered into this arrangement?'

David shook his head. 'No, sir.'

Hoosen's eyebrows rose. 'Well, I am asking you to tell us.'

David remained silent. The judge intervened, prompting him, 'Come on. You know the name. Tell it to us.'

'I don't know if the newspaper would wish me to do that,' David replied quietly.

Fenton Atkinson frowned. 'They may have some questions to answer about this. Who are they?'

David shook his head again. 'I'm sorry, sir. I can't answer that.'

'Who told you that you could not answer that?' Hoosen asked sharply.

David mumbled, 'I would like to see—'

'Who told you that you could not answer that?' Hoosen repeated.

'Nobody told me.'

'Answer it, then.'

'I can't answer that question, sir.'

'Why?'

'I don't think the newspaper wishes to be involved in it.'

'Tell me why you cannot answer that question,' Hoosen pressed. 'You have been receiving their money.'

David bit his lip.

The judge leaned forward. 'You must tell us.'

'I can't answer that question, sir.'

'You heard my Lord say you must tell us,' Hoosen snapped.

Needled by the clipped tones of Brady's defence, David stated obstinately, 'I refuse to answer the question unless I have the sanction of the newspaper.'

Clearly rattled, Hoosen demanded: 'What do you mean, "have the sanction of the newspaper"? You are here to give evidence in a case, not to obey the directions of a newspaper.'

'I am not obeying any directions of a newspaper.'

Sensing deadlock, Fenton Atkinson asserted that there was little point in having David declared to be in contempt of court because there were more pressing matters to answer. Nonetheless, his refusal to answer was a matter that required investigation and the newspaper deal was no less than 'a gross interference with the course of justice'.

Hoosen agreed to move on, but his next question concerned whether David had undertaken to supply information for a series of articles and if there was to be a ghost writer. Eventually, he turned to the subject of Edward Evans's murder, asking David what he had done to stop the attack.

'I didn't do anything,' David replied quietly. 'I've said this all along. I didn't do anything.'

Hoosen referred to the recent trouble in Hattersley – the fight in March 1966, which had come to the attention of the police – before focusing on the content of David's notebook. He read from it, beginning: '"*Every man or woman is one of two things, a masochist or a sadist, only a few practise what they feel.*"' He paused to glance at the witness. 'Are those your views?'

Shifting uncomfortably, David said, 'Well, they do practise what they feel.'

'Hmm.' Hoosen returned to the notebook: 'Let us look at the next page: "*Perversion is the way a man thinks, the way he feels, the*

way he lives. People are like maggots, small, blind, worthless fish bait
. . . Rape is not a crime, it's a state of mind. Murder is a hobby and a
supreme pleasure . . ."'

'That is not entirely mine,' David interrupted. 'That is what I could surmise as the meaning of the Marquis de Sade.'

'"God is a disease, a plague, a weight around a man's neck,"' Hoosen read. 'Are those your views?'

'Yes.'

'"A disease which eats away his instincts. God is a superstition, a cancer, a man-made cancer, which is injected into the brain in the form of religion." Those are your views?'

'On the subject of religion,' David conceded.

'"You live for one thing, supreme pleasure in everything you do. Sadism is the supreme pleasure."'

'There again I was surmising the words of de Sade,' David interjected.

'"Look around,"' Hoosen read. *'"Watch the fools doing exactly what their fathers did before them. The Book, they live by the Book!"'*

He lowered the exercise pad and looked at David. 'These were your views, were they not?'

David took a deep breath. 'A number of them . . .'

The argument continued for some time until Hoosen switched to David's poor record of employment temporarily before returning to the notebook again and then once more to the subject of work.

'Towards the latter part of 1964, did you have discussions with Brady about how to get money without working?'

'Yes,' David replied.

'Did you tell Brady that you could make money by selling pornographic photographs?'

David shook his head incredulously. 'No, sir.'

'You are smiling. Why smile?'

'Because it is the first I have ever heard of it.'

'Did you have a discussion at some time when you thought that you could raise some money by what you described in your words as "rolling a queer"?'

'No.'

'What does it mean?'

'Robbing a homosexual,' David replied bluntly, adding, 'I should think nearly everybody knows what that means.'

Hoosen then put it to him that he and another man had taken Lesley Ann Downey to 16 Wardle Brook Avenue for the express purpose of taking pornographic photographs of the child. David denied the suggestion vigorously, explaining that he had been at the Three Arrows pub that evening for an hour or so while his mother-in-law babysat, and with Maureen for the entire night. When Hoosen replied that Nellie Hindley had already told police she *hadn't* looked after her grandchild on Boxing Day, David retorted, 'My mother-in-law is a liar.'

Hoosen then moved on to potential robberies before suddenly declaring: 'I suggest that nothing was said to you by Brady about having photographs of graves.'

'Pardon?' David wasn't caught out by the question, replying in a firm voice: 'He didn't say he had photographs of graves. He said he had photographic proof.'

On the subject of Edward Evans's murder, Hoosen suggested that David had called at Wardle Brook Avenue to borrow the overdue rent money from Granny Maybury. When he denied it, Hoosen countered that they had borrowed money from Maureen's grandmother before.

David responded sarcastically, 'The fantastic amount of two shillings for the electric meter, yes.'

Hoosen then moved on to the killing of Edward Evans, stating: 'The truth is that you were hitting Evans and kicking him.'

'The truth is that Brady was hitting Evans with the axe,' David said.

Brady's defence then returned to the newspaper deal, asking if it was correct that David and Maureen had been enjoying various extravagances at the newspaper's expense, before attempting to cajole David into admitting the name: 'Was it the *News of the World*?'

'I refuse to answer the question,' David stated. Then he added, 'It could have been the *Daily Mirror*.'

When Hoosen sat down, Hindley's lawyer, Philip Curtis, took over. He, too, asked repeatedly about the newspaper deal. Today, David recalls: 'It was the defence that got my back up about the *News of the World*. If the prosecution had put that question to me, then I would have answered them gladly. I was threatened with contempt of court over the matter, and an adjournment was called. They sent me out of court where I was told, "Look, Dave, the judge has no intention of playing cat and mouse over this. You might be chief prosecution witness, but that doesn't put you above the law. If it's put to you again that the judge is prepared to overlook your initial refusal to answer, providing you give the newspaper's name next time you're asked, then you'd better do it." So when they called me back into the witness box and that same question was asked, I did as I was told. As soon as I'd said it – "The *News of the World*, sir" – I saw the two reporters from the paper sitting in the press gallery get up and leave. The judge wasn't happy at all about it. He was right that the press shouldn't interfere with a witness, and I was at fault for letting it happen. Because it did exactly what he said: gave the defence a stick with which to beat me.'

Curtis then turned to the notebook, asking David to read from it. David squirmed, telling the court he would rather not, but the judge insisted. The extract chosen by Curtis concerned religion, and he pointed out that if these were David's own views – which he admitted they were – then the oath on which he had sworn earlier was rendered 'completely meaningless'.

Curtis's line of questioning about his client's whereabouts on the night of Edward Evans's murder led to a further adjournment while David's police statement and his comments in court were compared. If proof were needed that the *News of the World* deal hadn't affected David's evidence, there it was in black and white: Hindley's role in the murder was more substantial and less unequivocal in the police statement than in his comments in the witness box. Hindley's defence had no desire for the statement to be produced in court and their plea was granted after they had assured the judge there would be no further references to the newspaper deal.

When the court reconvened, the prosecution cross-examined David briefly before he was allowed to leave the witness box. His part in the trial was over. 'I couldn't wait to leave Chester,' he recalls. 'Maureen was the same. We didn't stay a moment longer than we were needed. As soon as I'd finished giving evidence, we were off home.'

Although David was no longer present, his name was mentioned frequently during the second week of the trial. On Friday, 22 April, Hoosen opened the case for the defence, advising the all-male jury: 'Don't let the length of the case and the number of exhibits hide from you the fact that much of the theory, the very rock on which it is founded, is the evidence of Smith. You may think that he is a crumbling rock on which to found anything.' He asked them to view David as 'a man without principle, without scruple, without mercy' and as someone of considerable intelligence and therefore 'hardly a man who would have been dominated intellectually by Brady. The Attorney General has suggested that Smith was developed by Brady as a sorcerer's apprentice or a devil's disciple. You may think that this may well have been a profound misreading of this case.' He posited that the jury, having heard David's evidence and observed his manner, might think him far more involved in the Evans case than he was willing to admit.

Ian Brady was then called, and many of his initial statements concerned his friendship with David. Asked by Hoosen whether there had been a significant conversation between the two of them in the hours before Edward Evans's murder, Brady replied: 'He was talking about screwing – that is, housebreaking – and one of the suggestions was that we should roll a queer . . .' Brady claimed that his first thought on bumping into Edward Evans later that evening in Central Station was that he felt the youth 'would do for what Smith and I had been talking about earlier on that night'. He told the court that David had hit and kicked the victim and it was he who had pursued the youth when he collapsed on the floor and fell under the table. Asked about David's attitude during the clean-up afterwards, Brady said he had been 'theatrical, jocular. He was going out of his way to crack jokes.' He claimed that it was David who had suggested burying Edward Evans on the moors, near the spot where they had practised shooting the pistols.

Regarding Lesley Ann Downey, Brady also attempted to pin the responsibility for her disappearance on David, stating that it was he who had brought her to Wardle Brook Avenue with a man named Keith; Brady even declared that two of the poses on the photographs had been suggested by David, who he said had left the house with the child and dropped her at Belle Vue. The Attorney General pointed out to Brady that if that were true, then 'the key moment would be to record Smith saying something when he is taking the child away'. Stymied, Brady muttered that he couldn't have predicted the events recorded on the tape machine that night.

Questioned about John Kilbride, Brady seemed uncomfortable about the statement he had made to Joe Mounsey; namely, that two men had killed the young boy and that he was familiar with one of them.

'You do not like being landed with that answer now, do you?' asked the Attorney General, with a slight smile.

'I did not tell him that,' Brady said, bristling. 'I know what I told him.'

'It is very difficult to blame Smith for Kilbride,' the Attorney General stated, 'because Smith was about 14 or 15 when Kilbride was murdered.'

'I haven't the slightest,' Brady replied.

Asked whether he blamed David for calling the police, Brady said that he did. The Attorney General went on, 'And, of course, you have hated Smith ever since he went to the police?'

Summoning as much disdain as he could muster, Brady responded, 'I don't think he is worth hating.' But an observer in court noted: 'When [Brady] spoke of Smith, due possibly to some trick of lighting of the court, his eyes appeared to change in colour, and I was convinced that he would have murdered Smith had he had an opportunity to do so.'

Brady's cross-examination ended on Tuesday, 3 May. Nellie Hindley then took the stand. In the weeks since David and Maureen had called the police, there had been no contact between Nellie and her younger daughter. Bob Hindley had frozen out both Maureen and Myra, blaming them for not having alerted him to Nellie's adultery. Under the circumstances, it was an easy matter for Hindley's defence to provoke Nellie into denigrating her son-in-law.

Hoosen prompted, 'Did Maureen seem frightened of her husband?'

'She was,' Nellie replied. 'I don't know if she still is, but she used to be very frightened.'

'Was he something of a bully towards her?'

'He was if he wasn't getting his own way all the while, yes.'

'Was she rather under his thumb?'

'Yes.'

The Attorney General took over the questioning.

'Mrs Hindley, you, I take it, do not like Mr Smith?'

'I have always done my best for them both.'

'Do you think, whether rightly or wrongly, that he is responsible for your daughter Myra being in the dock?'

Nellie answered, 'He could be. He is that kind of person.'

The Attorney General persisted: 'You would be prepared to say a good word for David Smith?'

With withering condescension, Nellie replied, 'Oh, he is good when he wants to be.'

When Myra Hindley's turn to be questioned came, she followed her lover's lead in attempting to pin all three known murders on David, particularly that of Lesley Ann Downey. During cross-examination, the Attorney General accused Hindley of 'wicked inventions' concerning her brother-in-law. One writer in court noted that Hindley's 'hatred of Smith for having put Ian Brady where he was came through very clearly'.

The closing speech for the Crown followed, in which the Attorney General described Brady and Hindley as having formed 'an evil partnership together'. He then turned his attention to David: 'I do not invite you to the conclusion that David Smith was a young man unsullied by the world in which he lived before he met Brady. He told his story frankly but, of course, it is an unattractive story. Mr Hoosen suggested that the prosecution were putting Smith forward as a sort of devil's disciple or a sorcerer's apprentice. But having heard all the evidence of the case do you not think that this might in fact be an accurate description of David Smith in relation to Ian Brady? Certainly David Smith is no angel, but do you think he comes near the standards of criminality which have been disclosed in respect of Brady? Who was the devil of the piece? Who was the disciple? Even on his own evidence Smith must be regarded as being implicated in the murder of Evans; whatever the circumstances may be by which he was induced to be present at the killing of

Evans, he saw the killing and did nothing to prevent it . . .'

He finished his discourse by stating that David had reached an unthinkable crossroads on 6 October 1965: 'Either he had to go on in this evil in which he found himself or had to pull out at this last possible moment and escape. He had a great deal to lose by going to the police. He put himself greatly at risk for his complicity in the murder of Evans and in the preparations for bank robberies and other things because of the incriminating material in that suitcase. But he faced all that and I submit he did it in the light of what he had seen Brady cold-bloodedly do with the hatchet in the living room. It must then have dawned on him with finality that Brady's boasts about being a killer without a conscience were not idle . . .'

In his closing speech for the defence, Hoosen submitted that the prosecution's case was built on the evidence of one witness, David Smith, who was 'a crumbling foundation'. When the judge then began summing up the 'truly horrible case' before the jury, he offered his opinion of the chief prosecution witness: 'No words have been too strong for the defence to apply to Smith. They have used such terms as unprincipled, without scruple, without mercy and so on and so forth, and of course a lot of that was clearly justified . . . He had previous convictions for violence. He was asked for details, and it appeared that if some young man had called him a bastard, his reaction was a violent one and he retaliated in no uncertain manner; but as yet he has not killed anybody with an axe or anything so extreme as that . . . Then there is this unfortunate affair with the newspaper. I am sure they did not intend to do so, but they have handed the defence a stick with which to beat Smith and his wife Maureen . . . I do not think it is really suggested that the substance of his evidence has been substantially affected by this quite extraordinary arrangement that he had with this newspaper.'

Regarding David's behaviour on the night of Edward Evans's murder, the judge referred to his having 'done nothing' to prevent the killing, and helping to clean up afterwards with all that entailed; in addition he made reference to the blood on David's clothing and his stick (which he had dropped when he ran into the living room that night), advising the jury: 'You will have to consider the question as to whether he did take some part in that attack. And in that case he is what the law calls an accomplice . . . If you think he was in it, he would have the temptation to minimise his share and exaggerate Brady's . . . Knowing so much of his background, that he was planning a robbery and had a lot of unpleasant views which you have heard, you will probably think it is safest to say: "We will not act upon his evidence unless we can find something outside it to support it."'

On the afternoon of Friday, 6 May 1966, the jury retired to consider their verdict. In the two hours that followed, various journalists and writers mulled over what they had learned and one author offered the view that although David Smith's story 'had the indefinable stamp of truth', he himself would 'go down in the annals of this crime as that of a man with a bad record, who was deeply implicated but whose evidence could not really be shaken in its essential facts'.

At five o'clock, the jury filed silently back into court.

* * *

From David Smith's memoir:
I'm in the flat with Dad and Maureen. Dad has got the telly on, turned down low, all afternoon. I sit on my chair next to the electric fire, huddled and shivering over the glowing bars even though it isn't really cold. Maureen is in the kitchen, clattering about, pretending to do something practical but I know that she's just moving stuff about on the work surfaces. Dad is rubbing his stubbly chin, frowning, standing at the balcony doors and staring at the mist coming slowly down from the moors.

Teatime.

None of us are hungry, we're all waiting . . . The flat is more quiet than I can remember it. *Why is it so quiet?* I sit jigging my feet and smoking fags like they're going out of fashion. Although I've always believed that Myra and Ian will go down, in the last couple of hours my faith has begun to waver like a bad radio signal. Suddenly I'm scared. Proper, old-fashioned, shitting-the-seat of my pants frightened. I still believe that Ian is facing a long stint inside, but her . . . what if she's able to pull the wool over everyone's eyes? What if the fact that she's a woman blinds them to what she's done? I picture her walking out of court, free to go home, and although I know her life will be hell if that happens, it puts the wind up me so much you could stick a ribbon on my backside and pretend I'm a fucking kite. She might get a nominal sentence and be out in a couple of years . . .

Then the news comes on.

Dad dives across the small sitting room and I leap forward, switching up the volume dial as far as it will go on the television set. In my head, I'm certain that I've sat down again, but later I realise I've only bent my knees and am crouched halfway between telly and chair.

The waiting is almost over. I will the grating music to stop and clench my fists, staring at the newsreader, a slab-faced idiot who probably hasn't got a clue what he's talking about half the time. But here it is, and Maureen comes in from the kitchen, standing stock-still in the doorway, eyes rooted to the screen, just like Dad and me.

'Moors killers Ian Brady and Myra Hindley have been sentenced to jail for life . . .'

Relief hurtles through my veins, making me woozy, drunk with liberation from my darkest fears yet. I stare silently at grainy monochrome shots of the moor, then at the smiling faces of Edward Evans, John Kilbride, Lesley Ann Downey, and the unfound victims, Keith Bennett and my friend Pauline Reade.

Two more faces fill the screen. Bang: Brady and Hindley's mugshots have never been seen until now and their impact is like a gunshot echoing across the city. Two hard, frozen faces, two sets of black, dead eyes without any breadth of human feeling. The room blisters and I feel as if I'm hallucinating. My heart seems to be slowing down, down, down.

I turn my face to the wall. I've walked away from the trial battered, shattered, and bitter. I feel crucified and abandoned, the outsider, the bastard, all over again. I remember the policemen who interviewed me and realise that not one has put an arm around my shoulder, or offered a reassuring, 'Well done, lad.' After months of talking and more talking, exploding anger and shared tears, every last one of them has disappeared into silence.

I turn back and glance at Maureen, wondering if she is about to break down. But I see relief on her face too, as if she feels that the child she carries will be born into a safer world.

A small kernel of hope begins to grow inside me.

The next morning, those mugshots are everywhere, but at least the headlines read: 'Jailed for Life'. I squeeze Maureen's hand as we walk quickly past the newspaper shop and back to the flat. We think the nightmare is over.

But it's just beginning.

IV
Coming Down Fast
1966–71

Chapter 17

'The people of the neighbourhood could not forget . . .'
– *The Times*, 18 July 1969

From David Smith's memoir:
Maureen goes into labour three days after the end of the trial. Paul
Anthony Smith is born on 9 May 1966, a healthy and beautiful 9 lb
boy, but even as I take him into my arms I feel the darkness gathering
around us. I bend over this tiny new soul, wanting to hold back the
void like a wall against a howling wind. I am filled with fierce love and
the desperation that comes of knowing my world is no place for such
innocence.

It's little more than a year since I buried my daughter. When Angela
Dawn was laid to rest beside Mum and Frank the brown-eyed soldier
boy, she took with her the best six months of my life. Back then I knew
who I was – I had an identity that was grounded in parenthood and
marriage. Even Wiles Street had changed from something grim and
grubby into a cheery little spot. *Where did the good times go?* I remember
it all with a sorrow so deep it feels like a weight pulling me to the
ground: the factory hooter, the smoke, the coke-and-iron smell of the
railway, the hot reek of vinegar and newspaper from the chip shop,
posing in front of the brilliantly lit jukebox at Sivori's, and being
accepted at last by the neighbourhood elders. But not much more than
a year after Angela came into our lives she was gone, and the dream
with it, buried even further than the little white coffin in the damp
earth.

I crave my old life and secretly lose myself in memories. Wiles Street
had no hot water or home comforts and its outside loo stank like a
ferret's arse, but I'd give anything to go back. Hattersley is a shit hole,
nothing but row upon row of paper-thin council houses, skyscrapers

and sizzling electricity pylons. Everyone hates us here; the flat is the only place we're safe, even though the reality is that we're trapped in a stinking tower block in the aftermath of a murder case. But Paul makes it seem much brighter than that.

Our problems start at the front door. The council turn up regularly to erase the graffiti – 'Child Killers Live Here' and 'Murdering Bastards' – sprayed across the walls. The press still pester us, so to get them off our backs I tell them we've nothing more to say and are moving abroad. I get my £1,000 off the News of the World, but there's no money after that, not like they promised. No one will give me a job and we've got no friends any more. Our world is becoming smaller every day, and in the end, when you only have a few walls to keep you sane, it begins to drive you crazy.

The atmosphere inside the flat is stifling us all. I sit alone more and more often, staring out at the balcony and seeing them: Myra and Ian, leaning out over the barrier together, as they used to do so often, admiring the view, Ian with his long arm and bony finger, pointing out to Myra the areas of Mottram and Glossop and beyond that . . . the moor.

I think alone and I walk alone. At night, when it's dark and there is no one about apart from the stray cats and dogs that roam the estate, I leave the tower block and pound the empty streets until my feet burn. I try to talk 'it' out of myself, whatever 'it' is. I cry and even shout in the darkness, growing frustrated and furious at not being able to figure out the 'why' of it all. The cold air clears my smoke-filled lungs but does nothing to empty my head of the thoughts that are sending me gradually insane. My mind tricks me into feeling a warm, heavy breath at my elbow and the pad and thump of huge paws behind me. In the privacy of the suburban night, I am joined by a polar bear and tigon; we're together, trapped and demented within the same cage. Deep inside myself I'm screwed up like an old chip paper, wrapped in a black aftermath of murder. My head bursts with the filth of it all: I feel it pouring out of my ears and nose, the green-tasting waste that makes me want to vomit. This is supposed to be over, life is supposed to have gone on. My life. But it's getting worse, by the week, by the day, by the hour.

Witness.

The word echoes far into the green gloom of my mind: witness, witness, witness, witness . . . It has its own beat, that word, and with the polar bear and tigon at my side, I walk in time to its rhythm. I was and will forever be a witness, and yet those learned men in wigs and robes, the dignitaries who relied upon my evidence, condemned me as a devil's disciple, accusing me of every horror the human spirit can contain. If I am a witness, why do I feel so much pain and confusion? Why am I so hated? I've never claimed to walk with Jesus, but the devil isn't my master and never was or shall be. For all that I am, I am far from that.

I walk on, leaving Hattersley's mean lights to fade, indistinguishable from the pale glow of the city. Roads become country lanes that I'll never see again. I ask myself questions no one can answer; I smoke a cigarette down to the filter until it burns my fingers, and I look up at the starless sky realising that what I need most is someone to listen to me. A tear scalds my cheek as I lean back against an ancient dry-stone wall. Someone to listen: if I could just find that person, it might help take away the filth and the pain.

My world is beginning to buckle in on itself. I can feel it crashing around me, burying me alive under the rubble. I wipe away the tear angrily, telling myself I don't need that shit. I get up, and walk away from yet another dark lane. I head home, finding the main road at last, and turn up past the New Inn, keeping my eyes averted from the defaced street sign on Wardle Brook Avenue.

I get into the lift at Underwood Court and realise I am alone; the polar bear and tigon are already on their long journey back to the concrete enclosures and crippling cages of Belle Vue. I step out of the lift and listen for the sound of their claws on the pavements into the city. But the silence and the night are as one: dark, endless, deafening.

The unemployment office has finally given up on me. Scores of job interviews have ended the same way: I'm always rejected as 'unsuitable', but how can I be unsuitable for sweeping floors or stacking shelves? The precise nature of my affliction always manifests after the question: 'Don't mind me asking, but are you *the* David Smith? The one connected to Ian Brady and Myra Hindley?'

Connected. I hate that word. People think I'm attached to those two by some kind of monstrous umbilical cord. If only they knew.

The final straw comes when I apply for work at the African print factory. I answer the same question asked by a friendly personnel manager and, to my amazement, she thanks me for my honesty and offers me the job. I'm ecstatic, and proudly march into the dole office with my interview card signed and rubber-stamped with an official start time at the factory. The grin on my face is so wide it hurts my jaw, but I swear it lights up the miserable little dole office. I ask for my insurance cards, and then catch the 125 to Hattersley, signed off and legal.

Maureen and Dad are delighted with my news – Maureen especially, because she's pregnant again. Dad is on the dole himself and hates being out of work. He tells me that once I've got my feet under the table at the factory I should let him know straight away if I hear of anything going – 'no matter what' – and put in a good word for him.

It feels like the old days when I get up the next morning: I spend ten minutes playing with Paul on the sofa while Maureen does my pack-up. Then I'm off to catch the bus with the sort of cheerful goodbye I can't remember giving or receiving for far too long. The only regret I have is that Dad isn't coming with me.

My stop is a few hundred yards past the factory. As the bus draws level with the entrance, I look outside: a huge number of men are gathered before the iron gates and to the right, at the window of the personnel office, is the kind lady who interviewed me, gazing down at the crowd. I imagine that the workforce waiting at the gates is routine and jump down from the bus determined to do my best in the hours ahead of me. But as I approach the mob, I hear a collective rumble of anger and someone shouts: 'That's him, that's the bastard. Murderer!'

I freeze. Something more threatening than straightforward antagonism comes away from the men, and a voice within tells me to keep my mouth shut no matter what. This isn't the time for bravado.

Three men come towards me. I grip my pack-up box tight enough to turn my knuckles white.

'You Smith?' one asks.

I nod.

'Turn around and fuck off, this is no place for you.'

I mumble something about the office knowing about everything, but he shuts me up with a jab in the chest and snarls: 'I couldn't give a *fuck*. I'm the Union in this place and the Union is telling you to fuck off for your *own* good.'

I don't need further explanations. As I walk away, their fury rings in my ears: 'Murdering bastards, they should've hanged the fucking lot of you!' One man attempts to calm the situation, but his words aren't any consolation to me: 'Easy now, steady, lads, just let the cunt go.'

Their jeers follow me along the street.

By the time I've reached the dole office, I'm trembling with fear and resentment, aware that this was probably my last shot at getting a job. When a concerned supervisor beckons me over to listen to the story of my morning, I finish by throwing my pack-up box and insurance cards across the counter, yelling, 'I've had enough of this fucking shit – you can shove my cards up your arses!'

Two days later, a brown envelope with the Social Security office logo arrives at Underwood Court. The letter within informs me that: 'Due to exceptional circumstances you are no longer required to seek employment.' Graciously, the civil servant dogsbody who drafted the letter assures me: 'This decision will not affect your entitlement to unemployment benefit at the awarded rate.'

I screw the letter up into a tight ball and bin it.

Geoffrey Potter – I always address him as 'Mr Potter' – is a gentleman in both senses of the word, kindly, thoughtful and calm. He's a new breed of probation officer, nothing like the retired coppers of old. Mr P has 'supervised' me for a sizeable chunk of my life and I respect him totally, but there's just one problem: he's too nice.

Ironically, he's a born listener, but I find it impossible to offload on him. He doesn't have the distance and authority that I need in order to function with someone in his position; instead he worries over me as if we're real friends, willingly dipping into his small 'probation fund' if he suspects I'm a few bob short. Years ago, he'd walk across from his office in Gorton Town Hall to seek me out in Sivori's, after I'd typically forgotten our appointment from days before. Each time, he'd give me an old-fashioned look and ask if I was hungry, then without waiting for my answer he'd order a hot Holland's meat-and-potato pie with gravy, a frothy espresso and a packet of fags. We'd chat easily while I ate my free dinner, with one ear cocked to the sounds of the jukebox.

But those days are long gone and on this particular morning I'm standing at the door of the flat, waiting for the shuddering lift to bring Mr P to me. He emerges, looking lost, eyes drawn straight to the insults and threats sprayed on the door and walls. He greets me warmly; I'm glad to see him, even if only to pass another hour and the rare chance to do so with a friendly face from a hostile world. I'm at least ten degrees below my normal 'morose' reading, physically drained and weary.

Maureen is quick to provide us with cups of tea before gathering Paul up from the floor and disappearing into the kitchen. Alone with Mr P, I'm suddenly unable to speak. The same rotten filth that plagues me around the clock refuses to give me this time with someone who genuinely wants to help. Lately, whenever I close my eyes I see nothing but blood, oozing from the edges of my subconscious. I've reached a point where I'm not only forcing myself to stay awake at night but am too frightened to blink. When my eyelids shut for more than a second, I see congealing blood and small, glistening pieces of brain, while the smell that fills my nostrils is beyond description. I wish I could slice off the top of my head and empty out its memories into some other vessel, even into someone else's head – especially one of the thousands who hate me, just to find out how they might handle what I've seen.

Mr P coughs politely, hoping to jolt me into speech. We sip our tea and I notice his gaze on the overflowing ashtray and my trembling hands. He takes a deep breath and in a gentle octave begins talking about Maureen and her condition, then about Paul, Dad, and the future. He measures out his words as carefully as a doctor dispensing medicine, while I hang onto each one, trying to absorb their meaning instead of just watching his lips move.

Part of his speech penetrates the red fog in my head: he has a suggestion for me, which he'd like me to discuss with Maureen and Dad later. He explains that he knows things aren't good for us and that's unlikely to change, but there *is* a way out. He's made several phone calls to colleagues and services around the country and he's in no doubt that we could be re-housed, away from Manchester and even the north itself. Changing my name wouldn't be a problem ('though, of course, Smith is most people's first choice when they want to become anonymous') and would give us a better chance of 'disappearing' as a family, putting us in a prime position for a fresh start.

I say nothing. Finally, realising that my silence is deliberate, he gets to his feet, reminding me to think it through. We say goodbye and as the lift doors close, I do the polite thing and promise to do as he's asked. Then I return to the flat with no intention of ever mentioning it.

His solution is not the answer to our troubles. I can call myself by another name and live wherever I like, but I'll still take the nightmare with me. Where's the sense in lying in a different bed while having the same screaming flashbacks? To follow Mr P's suggestion would be the equivalent of a rat going underground. I think of Mum and the Duchess, and how they brought me up. I did the right thing, as I was taught to do, blowing the whistle on a pair of murderers whom the police could never catch, so why should I run?

My name is David Smith and that's how I'll be known until my last breath. Even with the whole world hating my guts, I won't be made to hide in the sewers, not for anyone.

* * *

In the summer of 1966, actor and dramatist Emlyn Williams became a familiar figure about Hattersley. During the research for his book about the crimes of Brady and Hindley, he spoke to scores of residents, police and several members of the victims' families. Williams's main source of information was Elsie Masterton, whose young daughter Patty had led the police to the burial ground at Hollin Brown Knoll. He visited her frequently, curious about David and the aftermath of the trial but seemingly reluctant to make the approach himself.

It wasn't long before David heard that Williams was in the neighbourhood and making enquiries about him. 'Elsie kept turning up at our flat,' he recalls, 'asking all sorts of questions. I knew Elsie and her family from my visits to Wardle Brook Avenue, but I was a bit pissed off with her constant appearances at our door. In the end, I asked her, "What are you bothering me with all this for?" She admitted, "Well, I talk a lot to Mr Williams." So I told her, "Right. Well, in future, if Mr bloody Williams wants to know anything about me, he can come and bloody ask me himself." I knew he was writing a book about the case and I didn't like the idea of not having a say over what was written about me. Elsie must have passed on the message because he wrote to request a little chat with me. I've got to admit that once I was in touch with him, we were all excited – me, Dad and Maureen. He was in the films and a well-known name. So we spring-cleaned the flat, dolled ourselves up and waited for him.'

Emlyn Williams was not alone when he called at Underwood Court; nor was he quite what David had expected. 'This funny little voice came over the intercom,' David remembers. '"Mr Williams and son Brook." I thought: *oh, a son as well*, and imagined him turning up with a toddler. Then the buzzer went and I opened the door to this raving queen and his equally "flamboyant" grown-up son. Williams was the campest thing I'd ever seen – no one was openly homosexual in Gorton or Hattersley! But here was this madly theatrical chap with pomaded white hair and a scarlet cravat, flinging his hands about. Everything was cuffs and drama. We sat down for a chat. Whenever he asked a question, he would lean in close and I would almost topple over backwards trying to put some distance between us. The son was cut from the same cloth – all melodramatic sympathy.'

Williams and his son remained at Underwood Court for a couple of hours, asking many of the questions David had grown used to answering. 'When we'd run out of things to say, he asked if we'd like to have a drink with them and said very coyly, "Treat's on me."' David grins, 'Of course, me and Dad never turned down a free drink. Then Mr Williams said, "I'd like to take you to a hotel, where we can relax." Now, the only hotel we knew was the Spinners Arms in Hyde, which was like Gorton's Steelworks Tavern – rough-and-ready and only used by locals. It had the same rules as the Steelie: ladies weren't allowed in the vault, which was strictly for professional boozers who liked the dark atmosphere and spent their nights gambling, playing cards or skittles.'

His grin widens. 'We turned up in the vault, the four of us. God only knows what the local hard men thought, but their eyes were out on stalks. My future father-in-law was in there, and I think he offered to buy Mr Williams a pint, but dear Emlyn couldn't lift a pint, never mind drink one. Maybe if it had a pretty little umbrella in it . . . He wasn't a bad chap, though. He certainly liked the local colour and spent the evening floating up and down, saying, "Well, isn't this splendid?" He was generous with his money. And there weren't any fights that night.' He laughs at the memory: 'I think Mr Williams and son Brook floored the locals.'

There was no further contact for a year or two, until David received a letter explaining that the book was almost complete.

'Mr Williams had one last question for me,' he recalls. 'He wanted to know if I thought Brady was "queer". You know me, I can never give a straightforward yes or no, so I wrote him a fairly long letter. I told him that I didn't think he was "queer" in the way that he himself – Mr Williams – was, but that he was "queerer than queer". And he used that phrase as the title of the book's last chapter.'

David was unaware that from their prison cells, Myra Hindley and Ian Brady were also exchanging letters – frequently and written in code. In one, Hindley made a heartfelt vow: 'Smith must die. Maureen too.' Neither had forgotten their hatred of him; both regretted not killing David when the chance had presented itself. But there were other, slower methods of ruining his life.

* * *

From David Smith's memoir:
Dad needs to get away from Underwood Court two or three times a week just to get his head straight. The atmosphere within the flat is like a greenhouse where all the plants have been poisoned. It's suffocating and tense. We argue a lot, Dad and me, just like the bad old days, our fights turning from verbal to physical. Dad leaves the flat with black eyes and split lips on a too-regular basis, slinking back to his old haunt, the Hyde Road Hotel in Ardwick. But the strange thing is, no matter how vicious our rucks are, we always part as friends.

He washes and shaves before leaving, and wearing his one good suit he looks a hell of a lot more dapper than the price of a one-way ticket, which is all he has in his pocket. In Ardwick, he meets his friends, listens for any news about jobs and usually manages to blag a few quid off a mate. But first he has to bum his 'entrance fee'. To do that, he stands outside reading the *Daily Mirror* (he's just pretending to read it, having already scanned the ink off the page during the day) and it's never long before he spies an old crony who's happy to slip him enough for that first drink. Once inside, he starts his patter like the professional Jack the Lad he is, and it's always late when he arrives home, chuffed with himself, loaded with a bellyful of Chesters Best Dark Mild, head full of gossip and pockets as empty as the day he was born. The yawningly empty packet of 20 Senior Service he took out with him will be full to bursting with every brand of cigarette available. But it goes both ways: Dad is generous with a loan or a few pints himself whenever he's 'carrying' – usually after a win on the horses. He often assures me we'll be 'all right tomorrow' because he's off to the Hyde Road to do a spot of 'debt collecting' . . . but he finds it easier to let his debtors buy him a few pints than settle the score. I don't mind, because if he's in a good mood, we don't fight.

One morning I get up to find Dad sat in his new chair next to the electric fire, both bars burning brightly. He's turned up the under-floor heating to its fullest and as I enter the room it scorches my socks. I shake my head, exasperated. He doesn't have a clue how to set the temperature – he just winds it up like a bloody clock. He's in good humour despite looking rough from his 'debt collecting' expedition the night before. I wrinkle my nose: the sweltering heat, Dad's farts, and the reek of stale beer are a bit too much for me to manage a 'good morning'.

I turn down the temperature and open the balcony doors, gulping in fresh air while Maureen makes a pot of tea. Today I get my dole money; a few bottles of beer, a half of whisky and a good dose of Dylan strike me as the way to go. I light a cigarette, feeling the urge to drink to oblivion.

Maureen is heavily pregnant now and waddles as she crosses the sitting room to hand me my tea. She smiles, but there is no truth in it; the struggle just to keep going shows in her eyes and the dark emptiness behind them. None of us are living any more – we're all filling time. Maureen never leaves the flat except to walk to the shops. The short journey is always harrowing: women go out of their way to spit at her and shout 'whore', 'Hindley bitch' and 'Hindley cow' to her face. She has to fight to protect Paul in his pram from the thick phlegm that's directed at him too, and returns home weeping and terrified. That's her daily existence.

I sit with Dad beside the fire, expecting to hear about his night's adventures. But today his news is different: there's a fiddle going on down near Smithfield Market in the centre of Manchester, and he wants both of us to go there this evening. Apparently a fish factory is taking on casual labour – no 'cards in', just cash-in-hand and a nice little supplement to the dole. The hours are ten at night until the foreman allows us to clock off; it might be a short shift or a long one, but the wage is a set amount. Dad is well pleased at having heard about the chance of some work and asks me if I'm in. After a moment's thought I tell him I am, deciding to put my day with Dylan and the bottle on hold.

Later, Dad tells me more about his plan: we're to turn up clean-shaven and tidy, in freshly laundered work clothes, and hopefully impress the foreman. Maureen gladly gets on with the washing, and by mid-afternoon she has a collection of shirts, trousers and underclothes all clean, ironed and ready to wear. She makes a pack-up of cheese and onion sandwiches for us both, adding a flask she's bought specially from the chemist and filling it with tea. At the door she hands us each some of our dole money from her purse and wishes us good luck with a smile that almost reaches her eyes.

We hit Manchester a couple of hours earlier than ten o'clock. Dad fancies a couple of pints first and, knowing that it's casual labour, he wants to weigh up the opposition. Close to the factory is a pub known by locals as the Little George. Dad's walking accelerates as the lights come into view. He leaves me behind to make my own way through the snug and across the cigarette-strewn wooden floor. The place is packed to the rafters with Friday night career-boozers, laughing and shouting themselves hoarse. I stand by myself for a minute, trying to figure out where Dad's gone, until I catch sight of him at the bar, ordering two pints of his beloved Chesters Mild and wearing a wicked, mischievous grin that makes him look like a proper nutcase.

Then I notice the landlady standing behind the bar and my mouth falls open: I love this pub – it's the best 'free house' in the world and a thing of beauty in itself.

The landlady places the pints on the bar and opens the flap-top on the counter, ignoring the punters bellowing for more beer as she comes towards me open-armed. The air is squeezed out of my lungs as she wraps her arms around me and kisses my cheek, taking me straight back to my childhood. When the Duchess steps back to look at me, clutching my face in her hands, I have to hold back tears of pure joy. Behind her, at the pumps, is Uncle Bert, grinning as widely as Dad. I catch my breath and shake my head, delighted at the thought of the Duchess as landlady of the Little George.

She gives my hand a tight squeeze before returning to her station. Dad and Uncle Bert are already deep in conversation, but every minute or so the Duchess glances up from pulling pints to smile at me. Now I understand how Dad got to hear about the fiddle near here – Uncle Bert must have told him.

I join Dad at the bar and we slowly drink three complimentary pints each. As ten o'clock approaches, the Duchess sees us to the door and I get another terrific hug and kiss. Then we're off, heading down the street, sucking Dad's Polo mints, which we both hope will hide the smell of beer. I'm expecting to be interviewed beforehand in an office, but when we reach the huge metal roller doors, I realise this is a different kettle of fish (literally) altogether: every single down-on-his-luck deadbeat scruff in the city shuffles close to the shutters, waiting for the foreman to appear.

Suddenly the shutters clatter open and a man comes out, carrying a wooden box and a clipboard. I squint at the neon brightness of the factory. Inside, the floor is stacked with large boxes filled with ice – the freezing air rushes out and catches us all full in the face, forcing our shoulders up to brace against it. But more overwhelming still is the nauseating smell of industrial-strength disinfectant and fish.

Dad grabs me by the wrist and pushes through the crowd, ignoring the shouts of 'Who the fuck do you think *you* are?' and 'Arseholes.'

The foreman gets up on his box and surveys us all. We look up at him as if he's about to deliver the Sermon on the Mount, not a shift in a fish factory. Grasping our desperation, he plays along, massaging his own ego.

'You,' he points to an upturned head, then pauses as if considering. 'You' to another and 'you' to a third. This sadistic employment ritual continues for as long as it pleases him before he finishes quickly, 'You, you, you and you.'

I count 20 heads chosen to enter the freezing factory. Us two smart-arses with our shiny faces and brand-new flask haven't even been given a passing glance. My shoulders drop and I feel sorry for Dad, whose plan has crash-landed without a single survivor. I think to myself how among all the deadbeats we must stick out like a couple of sore thumbs, maybe making the foreman suspicious that we're actually undercover dole investigators waiting to expose the fiddle. Dad's idea of scrubbing up has had the opposite effect of the one he'd counted on: he's as well-groomed as if he's off to a Sunday morning service at church, with polished shoes, neat hair and even his favourite Lester Piggott tie – all this just to lump frozen fish around a factory for 12 hours.

I think longingly of the Duchess and the Little George.

Our crowd of human leftovers grudgingly begins to disperse. I suck on another Polo mint, shuffle my feet with the rest and feel embarrassed enough for everyone. Then I hear a voice shout, ''Ere, 'old on a minute, Stan!' and before I know it, Uncle Bert is heading straight for the foreman. He takes him to one side, out of earshot, and I watch curiously as Stan listens, nodding his head a couple of times and flipping through some papers on his plastic clipboard. Uncle Bert shakes his hand in farewell and walks by, muttering out of the side of his mouth, 'Behave yourselves.'

Stan is still at the mercy of his own little ego, purposely delaying his next move. He stands with the clipboard under his arm for a good minute or two, looking us up and down. I don't think I give him much of a problem, but he seems perplexed by the bloke stood next to me in his shiny shoes and souvenir jockey neck-gear. Then he calls us over with a mere crook of his finger and we stand straight to attention while he announces with exaggerated authority: 'You do ten till finish, get paid at the end, half-hour break at three, no tea breaks. I'll be round during the night to get your names, now get your heads down and keep at it.'

Dad is bursting with pleasure. The only thing he doesn't do is bloody salute.

The work turns out to be even harder than I imagined. Throughout the night juggernauts arrive and we unload heavy boxes of ice and fish, sort orders, package them, and load them onto the lorries ready for dispatch. I've soon seen enough fish to last me a lifetime and am frozen silly. But Dad is a revelation, finding a strength and energy I never knew he possessed, working like a man half his age. Stan patrols the floor continually, pointing out more boxes to pack or unpack, and Dad answers him with an immediate 'Yes, sir' and 'Right away, sir.' I carry the boxes and grit my teeth: it's a side of him I don't wish to see.

Not having a minute to think makes the shift pass quickly. Only once does Stan abandon his patrol, and a regular worker remarks that he'll be across the road, having a liquid lunch at the Little George.

When morning comes, I'm exhausted. We all have a quick swill under the cold tap and queue up outside the office. I make the mistake of lighting a cigarette and a dozen deadbeats pounce, begging for a nicotine hit. I feel sorry for them, knowing they have another long day ahead like this one. Dad and I add our names to the list on Stan's desk and the foreman reaches into a tin box, counting out two separate piles of notes. When he speaks to Dad, his tone is friendly and familiar, no doubt thanks to Uncle Bert's generosity across the road: 'Right, Jack, what I've done is paid you and the lad here at the regular rate, not as casuals. I can fix you up with a couple of weeks' work starting Monday night. Be here at ten, but come in through the side door – don't bother waiting outside with that pile of shit. And come in earlier if you fancy a pint.'

I think: 12 hours ago we were stood with 'that pile of shit' and, to be honest, it didn't feel that bad. Even a pile of shit has to do something to get through the day.

Dad and I travel back to Hattersley on the bus. I'm knackered but content, pulling hard on a cigarette while Dad reads the racing page of his beloved *Daily Mirror*. Now I've got a few extra quid in my pocket, I'm glad I gave up my dole day with whisky and Dylan. But ten minutes into the journey I begin to feel nervous. Dad hasn't noticed, but I'm aware of more people joining the bus and shooting us disgusted looks. Nobody takes the double seat in front of us, or the one behind. Paranoia freezes my blood and I feel tiny beads of sweat forming on my upper lip. I wait for the inevitable jeers and shoves, but then I see a woman screw up her nose and reach into her pocket for a handkerchief as she edges down the aisle. A daft smile spreads across my face as I realise that the problem isn't the usual, but instead is caused by the work: we stink to high heaven of fish, and between us we're managing to pollute the entire bus. Relief thaws my veins and I cheer up immediately. As we disembark, Dad tells me he's going to buy himself a new duffle bag for our pack-ups and we stroll quickly home, whacked but satisfied.

I'm so caught up in being able to work at last that I don't notice what's happening to Maureen.

We work our shifts, Dad and I, and then sleep most of the day. It escapes me that my wife is slipping into another world. She doesn't share what she's done with me because she hasn't *done* anything. While I'm asleep, she heads out to the shops, where she's clawed at and spat at, told to fuck off and die, and her kid too. Then she returns with Paul in his pram, stepping out of the lift and into the flat as quietly as she can in case anyone is waiting for her. In the evenings, she makes our cheese and onion sandwiches, fills the flask with tea, hands Dad the duffle bag and closes the door behind us. When we're gone, she turns off the telly and sits on the edge of the chair I insist is mine and thinks into a night that is as empty as it is endless. She stops hearing the men who skulk in from downstairs with their aerosol cans to spray *'Hindley Cunt'* on the freshly painted door.

The next day she walks past the slogans with our baby son, her eyes blank and unseeing, dead to the hatred that encloses her like a fist.

Chapter 18

'Wise man lookin in a blade of grass
Young man lookin in the shadows that pass
Poor man lookin through painted glass
For dignity.'

— 'Dignity', Bob Dylan

From David Smith's memoir:

The final Friday of our fortnight at the fish factory arrives; our last tray of fish has been loaded and dispatched. It's not the sort of work you can enjoy – too back-breaking and cold for that – but at least it's a job and the pay isn't bad. Dad and I haven't been drinking as we usually would either – just a few pints with Stan before the shift, and that alone has saved us money. On the last night I take in an extra packet of cigs for the deadbeats and in the morning, as we queue outside the office, waiting to collect our pay, I hand them round.

I watch as Stan reaches into his cashbox. After he's divided the money into two neat piles he glances up at Dad: 'A word with you, Jack, before you're off. Can the lad wait outside for a minute?'

Dad nods towards the door, with a worried frown. I gather our pay and wait outside, surprised when I see Dad pulling up a chair. The two men sit and chat for twenty minutes or more, with Dad chain-smoking. He has his duffle bag between his knees and shuffles it awkwardly to one side, as he stands up and shakes Stan's hand. I think: *thank Christ for that, things must be all right.*

Dad emerges from the office with his duffle bag slung over his shoulder. We walk to the bus stop in silence, but I know something's up when he doesn't pause to buy his *Daily Mirror*. We're halfway through the journey home before he finally tells me what's going on: Stan was hoping to keep us in work but because of the lull in the fishing season (or something like that), he's having to drop the casuals, which means we're finished. I fail to see the problem: we were only taken on for a fortnight anyway.

'You definitely all right with that?' Dad asks quietly.

'Yeah, no worries,' I tell him truthfully, puzzled by his concern.

He lets out a heavy sigh of relief. 'Good, because I start regular on Monday morning.'

'Yeah, right,' I say disbelievingly. 'I get the push and you start Monday morning? How does that work then?'

Dad explains that he's been dropping hints over pints with Stan and has been rewarded with the job of maintenance fitter at the full Union rate and 'cards in'. The crafty old sod has pulled it off with his two weeks of 'Yes, sir, right away, sir.' I'm over the moon and couldn't be more pleased for him.

Dad is happy now that he knows I'm fine with the situation and tells me to get round the chipper tonight for chips and mushy peas – his treat.

'Chips and mushy peas?' I ask, frowning.

He laughs and nods at the duffel bag on the floor. I pull open the cord that keeps it fastened and there, looking up at me, crammed between the empty flask and leftover sandwiches, are three of the biggest lobsters ever hauled from the sea.

I stare at Dad in shock and he grins back at me: 'Jesus, son, when you were told to go outside I thought I was done for – I thought that bastard had cottoned to me and I was a gonner, but how's that for a winning bet?'

I can't remember ever seeing a clear *photograph* of a lobster before, let alone a live one and definitely not with his brothers. Lobster isn't something you find on the menu in Hattersley as a rule. As we get off the bus, we discuss how the three unlucky lads should meet their maker; Dad has a vague idea that you're supposed to boil them alive. I can't do that to them, and neither can Maureen when we show her what's for tea, so Dad reluctantly agrees to be the one to send them on their way.

The three of us are in good spirits for once, thanks to Dad's news. Even Maureen looks brighter and goes to the trouble of doing her hair and make-up. We scrub up and I go out for a crate of beer, and chips and mushy peas. Maureen has set the table like a silver service waitress by the time I get back and Dad is already in the kitchen, gearing up to do the cruel deed.

He's in there for what seems like hours. Maureen keeps rushing in to hand him beer, keeping her eyes away from what's happening on the cooker. Finally, red-faced and more than slightly tipsy, Dad emerges carrying his banquet. To be honest, his presentation isn't up to much, but what can you do with giant lobster, chips and mushy peas?

I'm shocked at the change of colour in the crustaceans. We sit round the table in uncomfortable silence, staring at our plates. I look at Maureen. She looks at me and then we both look at Dad and all three of us know that our knives and forks aren't up to the task of opening up the tough pink lads before us.

Dad leaves the room and returns with his work hammer. He removes the lobsters from our plates and disappears into the kitchen again. After five minutes of thunder he enters the room with one plate full of shell-encrusted, obliterated remains . . . and we decide to settle for chips and mushy peas without a gritty side order.

Like I said, you don't get many lobsters on the menu in Hattersley.

* * *

It was around this time that David's birth mother, Joyce Hull, attempted to be reconciled with the son she had given up for adoption.

David states quietly, 'There are decisions you make when you're young that you regret when you're older. At the time you're convinced you're doing the right thing, but later . . .' He pauses and inclines his head towards the hallway, where the photograph of himself and Joyce hangs on the adjoining wall. 'When I was 19, I had the chance to meet Joyce. Just once. I turned it down and now, obviously, I regret it bitterly. Time is rolling on and I just wish . . .' He shakes his head.

David's dad returned home from town one afternoon with the news that he'd encountered Joyce in a pub. They spent a couple of hours talking and when Jack said goodbye it was on the understanding that they would meet up later – and that he would do his best to persuade David to come along. Jack booked a table in a city restaurant and arrived at Underwood Court hoping David would want to meet his birth mother. But his son's reaction was one of fury, as David recalls: 'I couldn't believe it when Dad turned up and said he'd been with *her*. He was very emotional about it and had got himself . . . not tanked up, but

243

definitely not sober. The emotion and the drink were causing sentimental things to happen in his head and he got very tearful as he tried to convince me to go back into town with him.'

David pauses again before continuing: 'Dad was so hopeful I'd agree that he'd even booked a table. That didn't sit well with me, having decisions made on my behalf. The next ten minutes weren't pleasant. We didn't come to blows, but it was nasty. A definite negative, you might say. But there was no way I was going to be introduced to the woman who had abandoned me. Dad got very upset – he really wanted it to happen. I remember shouting at him, "Dad, what the hell do you expect me to do? Walk in and say, 'Hello, Mum'? I've only ever had one mum, and you, old man, are far below her. As for this other woman . . . no. It's not going to happen." And it didn't.'

At this point, David's wife Mary interjects: 'I think perhaps if Joyce had contacted Dave when the trial was going on – that might have been slightly different. But she didn't, even though she must have been aware that it was her son who was giving evidence in such a terrible case. Any mother worth her salt would have reached out to her child there and then – not left it to a chance encounter in a bar with the father.'

Jack returned to town alone. He and Joyce met up and had their meal together, and he returned home late that night 'a little more drunk, a little more tearful', as David describes it. But after that evening, there were no further meetings between the two. 'That was it,' David admits. 'My one chance was gone. But I think it would have completely freaked me out to meet Joyce then, anyway. It's only a shame from today's perspective. But so much else was beginning to spiral out of control then . . . meeting Joyce wouldn't have helped. If anything, it might have made the situation worse. And I could not have coped with that – physically or mentally.'

He shakes his head again. 'I was losing control, and I didn't know it . . .'

* * *

From David Smith's memoir:
Underwood Court, third floor, flat 18. Fucking shit hole.

On my landing there are three other flats, but the residents are virtual strangers to me. Sometimes I stand in the corridor, behind the door to the communal hallway, listening to the lift shunting between the floors, and to the bottles crashing through the refuse chute into the bins far below. When I'm certain there's no one lurking about, I snap the lead on Bob's collar and together we go out, quiet so as not to alert the ever-vigilant Mr Page.

Tonight is different. Tonight I have a mood upon me so dark that I need night-vision goggles to negotiate my way through it. Instead of sneaking out of the flat I slam the door as hard as I can, thinking: *Wake up, you fuckers, I'm off for a walk. Fuck you, Mr Page – here comes Bob the dog, right past your fucking door.* I'm carrying a new stick because the police never got round to handing back my old one. Fuck them, too.

My head is throbbing from the row I've just had with Maureen. She's disappeared and all I can do is walk the dog. I'm chuntering away to myself as I thump down the first flight of stairs: *bastards, they're all fucking bastards, Brady bastard, Hindley bastard – two Hindley bastards – fuck them all.* I need fresh air. I know I've said some cruel things to Maureen again, but I need to say them to help clear the pain from my head. I wish I could get drunk, but I've got no money, and instead the last words I screamed at Maureen roll around my head like dice in a cup: *Myra's a cunt, your mother's a cunt and you're a fucking cunt. Maureen fucking Hindley, these are your people, you're all fucking rotten.*

I'm almost at the bottom of the steps when I hear a shuffle and small cough from under the stairwell. Maureen has been gone for a couple of hours and I'm shocked to find her huddled up in the corner against the wall, using her coat like a blanket to hide beneath.

'Fucking hell,' I mutter, racing down to her. 'Come on, girl, get up out of there, what the hell are you playing at . . .?'

She turns her face further into the corner.

'Please come out, Mo,' I speak softly, hoping to convince her my anger has gone.

She looks at me. Her eyes are full of tears; the heavy black mascara has been washed away and lumps of it are stuck to her pale skin. I reach into the opening below the stairs and take the coat from her, then grasp her hand and pull her gently out.

The front of her blouse is a mass of vomit, thick and stinking. I look at the floor and see an empty bottle of Lucozade and several aspirin containers on their sides, also empty.

Maureen starts to cry at the shock on my face. 'I'm so sorry, Dave, so sorry . . . is everything all right, is everything all right . . .?'

It's the same voice I remember from the taxi drive home from the hospital after Angela died, and the same words: *I'm sorry, so sorry, is everything all right?*

'Yes, girl,' I try to reassure her, 'everything is all right. Now come on, out of there.'

We stumble upstairs with a baffled collie at our heels. In the flat I lead Maureen through to the bathroom, then dive into the kitchen to mix a jug of salt and water. Paul is asleep. Dad wants to know what's going on, but I tell him to fucking leave it, this isn't his business. He doesn't say another word while I pour out glasses of salt water and take them through to the bathroom, pouring the fluid down Maureen's throat until she vomits. When she can do nothing but retch, I wash her with a cold cloth and put her to bed.

Dad stands in the living room doorway, genuinely concerned, but I'm in no mood for it. I empty the rent tin and head over to the pub. Everyone knows who I am, but for once I'm greeted with silence instead of aggression; something must show in my face. The barman serves me nervously. I ask him: *how much is a bottle of whisky to take out?* The price he gives me is four times what I'd pay in an off-licence, but I push the notes across the bar to him and tramp home.

Back in the flat I check on Maureen. She's in a deep sleep, so I stack up the stereo and turn the volume as high as it will go. Fuck the lot of them. Dad picks up Paul and takes him into the kitchen, shutting the door. Fuck you too, I think.

I drink straight from the bottle, letting the music pound around me. I just want to be somewhere else; I need everything to disappear. The loud music melts the pain. *Be-Bop-A-Fucking-Lula, Three Steps to Heaven, Chantilly Lace, One Night with You and take me back to the Summertime Blues, play me your do-wop and bop-she-bop music and ask me do I wanna dance, please tell Laura I love her but don't you ever step on my Blue Suede Shoes.*

When the adrenalin has drained from my veins, I stagger to my feet. Dad and Paul have been in bed for hours. The pain hasn't gone, for all that; it's come back ten times stronger. Tears pour out of me and I'm so filled with anger and hatred that I punch the wall, again and again, always missing it, hitting nothing and putting myself on my arse. I hear Maureen's pleading voice in my head and answer her silently: *of course everything is all right, why wouldn't it be all right, everything is fucking wonderful. Why are you hurting yourself, Maureen, why are you sorry? It's me who's hurting you, hurting us, but I can't get it out of my head . . . the Hindley thing, the Hindley thing, the Hindley thing. It isn't you, it isn't me, it's them. We're together but falling apart and I can't stop it, I can't fucking stop it.*

The whisky races through my skull, leaving me breathless. I open the balcony doors and tumble outside, gripping the barrier and shouting to the whole of Hattersley to go fuck itself. I curse the sky and scream at God to make the barrier break, demanding He come down to fight me if He's there, cursing Him for the pain, the unbelievable fucking pain.

Dad's hands are on my shoulders, pulling me back indoors. He asks me in a quiet voice to please go to bed, and although I reply with a shouted 'Fuck off!' I do as he tells me. In the pitch black of the room, my head spins to the sound of an invisible needle running in the groove of an old record no one wants to hear any more.

Our second son, David, is born on 18 April 1967 but as a family we're falling apart, merely existing from one day to the next in the rat run of Underwood Court. The hatred that envelops us never lets up; Maureen always returns from her trip to the shops needing to rush straight into the bathroom to wipe the spit from her clothes and hair, trembling from the hurled abuse. I'm trapped in the past, losing myself more and more in thoughts of the six months we had with Angela, unwilling to set foot outside because there isn't any point to it. We are despised and ostracised and nobody knows or cares that we're losing that last, microscopic speck of control.

I am ill, sick in mind and body – exhaustion dogs my every waking hour, but at night I'm too terrified to sleep, knowing my mind is waiting to take me back to Wardle Brook Avenue. I don't know I'm ill because no one tells me I am. I don't understand what depression is, either; I only know that I'm mightily pissed off all the time. I go to bed angry and wake up angrier still. Nothing changes from morning to night. After getting laid off at the factory, I've spent my days sprawled on the settee, arm around Paul, cuddling him close to my chest, surrounded by empty teacups and overflowing ashtrays. If Paul is asleep, then I amuse myself with a stray cat that adopted me on one of my midnight treks.

Maureen sits motionless and birdlike on the edge of a chair, her eyes fixed on the telly but blank to the flickering screen. David snoozes snugly in his pram outside on the balcony, breathing in what passes for fresh air in this overspill hellhole.

I never talk to Maureen about the filth in my head and she never speaks to me about the agonising emptiness in hers. I think obsessively about 'doing the right thing' and how angry I am at Mum and the Duchess for instilling that crap in me. I've done so much fighting in the last 12 months that my nose is permanently broken and crooked, and my knuckles are forced back into my hand. I look like I've spent a lifetime in the ring.

The evenings are no different. Maureen watches telly in vacant silence while I listen to Dylan and the Beatles on the new stereo I bought with my *News of the World* money. We exchange no more than a handful of words all night; she makes more tea without clearing away the cups and I don't move from wherever I've positioned myself for the evening. When Dad comes home from the fish factory, I ask him if he's managed to find me a job, even if only as a casual on the nightshift, but all I ever get is a dismal shake of the head.

On 22 December 1968, Maureen gives birth to our third and last child together – another perfect son, John. But nothing improves, and most nights I drink myself into a morose stupor, thinking about the trial and its legacy to us.

* * *

In 1968, the Smiths left Underwood Court for a house on Hattersley's Slater Way. The move ushered in a new and unexpected change in David and Maureen's lives: they got to know a few of the estate's black residents, and regularly partied at the shebeens in Moss Side. The casual racism David had spouted during his drunken nights with Ian Brady was a thing of the past; now he wanted nothing more than to be black himself, finding an acceptance and freedom among their community that was impossible anywhere else.

'It must sound strange,' David admits, 'given that a couple of years earlier I was reading *Mein Kampf* with Brady. But it seemed perfectly natural at the time, that shift in attitude and thought. The black people I began mixing with tolerated me – in fact, they welcomed me into their circle. They didn't hate me, or punch me or kick me. They took me at face value – I suppose because they had so much shit to face themselves from the whites. In the passages where I've written down my memories of that time I use the word "nigger", which nowadays is deeply offensive, but that was how the black people I hung around with referred to *themselves* at the time. Of course a lot of whites used the word too, but I *hated* being white then – I wanted to be one of them. There weren't many black families living in Hattersley then – they lived mainly in Moss Side. When I say Moss Side, I mean the *real* Moss Side – rows and rows of tall Victorian houses and wasteland. We'd find the shebeens by listening to the cellar music floating up from the grids in the road. There were usually a couple of blokes on the door, and white people generally weren't allowed in, but the black people I knew would say firmly, "He's with us," and they'd jerk their heads to indicate it was all right.' He grins, 'I was the token white guy in the corner.'

Maureen often accompanied him; the three boys remained at home with Jack, who had moved from Underwood Court with them. Drinking and dancing in Moss Side was the only time David and Maureen spent together comfortably as a couple; it became a brief respite from their troubles. 'We'd leave the shebeen in the early hours, drunk and stoned out of our minds, and totter home, where everything was just as miserable as before,' David recalls. 'I was living for our shebeen nights, totally uninterested in anything else. Dad hated it – he wasn't impressed with the company we kept. He was "old school". As a kid, I saw how that worked. Where I was brought up in Ardwick – that was separated from Moss Side by Stockport Road. Jesus, the drubbing a white girl would get for walking down the street with a black man – it was unbelievable. The women, especially, would be spitting and screaming at her. That's how it was back then. So for Maureen and me to then become part of that a few years later . . . let's just say Dad found it a struggle.'

The shebeen lifestyle that brought David and Maureen superficially closer eventually destroyed what was left of their marriage. 'We'd put a sticking plaster over a broken limb' is how David describes it. 'We were falling apart in every sense. We had physical fights – something I'm not proud of, but it's the truth. I was violent towards Dad as well, but Maureen . . . it was a bad time, the worst time of our marriage. The world around us ground her down, and because I was in a bad way myself, I took it out on her too. I suppose there was a part of me that blamed her – *wrongly*, I realise that now – for everything that had happened. Just because she was a Hindley. The public abuse we faced was relentless. Things had been going wrong for a while but all at once we crumbled. Separately as well, she was going downhill fast and I began to crack. Somebody was going to get hurt, it was just a matter of time.'

* * *

From David Smith's memoir:

Joyce is Jamaican, very tall with a wide mouth and sunshine smile. We meet in Underwood Court Social Club. When we're slow dancing together, she teases me, 'You're not black, you know.'

She often repeats this in the months ahead and I love it because I want to be black. I just wish I was the tallest, broadest, in-your-face 'nigger' there's ever been. We share 'The Ballad of John and Yoko' and it's so true: '*Christ, you know it ain't easy, you know how hard it can be, the way things are going, they're gonna crucify me.*'

We get stoned in Moss Side cellars, dancing to 'Miss Jamaica'. Life is suddenly great, *screw the white trash out there who hate us all, pass the ganja, big as you can roll it, seeds popping like fireworks, put on Dylan, Lennon and Otis again . . . Jesus Christ, I'm freefalling, in the shebeen, stoned out of my box.* Wasted, I'm losing it for good, hurtling out of control.

I eat goat with the happy-boys in the back kitchen, eating off paper plates. The smiling mama of the house ladles it out of two massive steel pans, one full of curried goat and the other containing rice and kidney beans. The kitchen is the heart of the shebeen; women sit on chairs and various settees pushed back against the walls, their gossip and non-stop laughter almost deafening. I'm blissfully happy. When the boys douse their food with Jamaican chilli sauce, I grab the bottle and do the same. Rows and rows of perfect white teeth smile at me approvingly, and it blows my mind to feel that I belong somewhere at last. Talk is heady and incessant, usually political: Malcolm X, Martin Luther King and the bastards who shot Kennedy. In the opinion of my new friends, everyone is either a 'motherfucker' or a 'blood clot', while the White Pigs of the Law are to blame for everything.

I'm high and getting higher, blasted out of my brain.

I go downstairs to the cellar and it's beautiful, it's where I'm home. The thunderous sounds of Max Romeo and the hot smell of dancing bodies and dope is heaven. If the kitchen is the heart of the house, then the cellar is the soul.

I buy two beers from the cases stacked along one wall from floor to ceiling and search out Maureen. She's in good form, stoned, smiling and swaying to the music. I roll the ganja and it's blowback strong, seeds popping as we smoke. Through half-closed eyes, I watch our friend Lloyd grooving on his own, doing the moves. I dance with Maureen, smooching close, as we share the second can of beer. My mind is opening to the possibility of lasting happiness: this is where we belong, with our own kind.

I look around for Joyce, my Miss Jamaica; she's chatting with the girls. I bide my time, waiting for the right music. It has to be Otis: the man, the voice. I lead Joyce onto the floor, where we dance slowly and I fix her beautiful brown eyes, deep pools of forever, with mine. I refuse to blink, wanting to hold that look, pressing myself against her because I can't get close enough. She knows and smiles at me. The smoke, the drink, the music and the woman – I'm high and more content than I've ever been in my life.

When Otis stops singing, I move away from Joyce and sit by myself with another beer. Lloyd is still grooving alone and both Maureen and Joyce have disappeared. I've got no worries: everything comes down to the music, the dealer handing out pleasure, dancers bumping and grinding, alcohol flowing in the right direction. Everything makes sense.

I look for Joyce again when I start coming down from the ganja. I'm feeling mellow, but it's getting late. *Where's Maureen*, I ask and Joyce replies *upstairs in the toilet*, but the ordinariness of her words sits all wrong with the nervous flicker in her voice. She makes meaningless small talk for a while until I tell her I'm leaving and head down the hallway. It's tight with people and I get the usual 'Yo, brother' as I pass, and 'How's the man?'

When I turn up the stairs, it's right in my fucking face.

Six or more couples are kissing and stroking each other and there, right at the top, against the wall, letting some bloke feel her up while she wraps her arms around his neck, is Maureen.

The anger and pain hits me like a fucking juggernaut.

I yell her name and take the stairs three at a time, pushing people left and right, ignoring the shouts of motherfucker this and motherfucker that. *Get out of my fucking way, you bastards.* I want to stop, to walk away and forget the pain – I don't want to feel that thing. But I reach Maureen the moment she screams his name, *'Tom!'*, and then my hand is on her throat, slamming her head against the wall.

I feel my grip on her neck as if it belongs to someone else. Her hands frantically try to pull my wrist away, but the fingers that aren't mine squeeze tighter. I slide my eyes towards Tom and say just one word, *don't*, before pushing, throwing and hitting Maureen down the stairs. Lumps of her hair are wrapped around my fingers.

People move quickly aside, but someone opens the door for us and I fling her like an unwanted toy out into the street, where it's just getting light.

Fucking white trash cunt, I scream, *you fucking dirty Hindley bastard.* The pain in my head explodes. When it turns cold, I hit her. Even though I'm thinking *make it stop, walk away, she's your wife*, I hit her again.

The cellar crowd have gathered outside the house: the happy-boys, the kitchen mama and the chattering girls, as well as Lloyd, Joyce and Tom. They do and say nothing, silently watching the white trash destroy each other on the pavement.

We get the bus home, Maureen and me, sitting without speaking for most of the journey. I can't see her swollen face because I don't look at her, but she's bruised and broken, sobbing softly to herself.

As we reach Hattersley, she slides her hand across the seat to me and mumbles, 'I'm sorry, so sorry, is everything all right, Dave, is everything all right?'

I close my fingers around hers, 'Yes, girl, don't worry, everything is all right.'

We walk home from our stop pressed close together, holding hands and why not, we're two lost souls in this world. When she looks at me, I still don't see the bruises, I only see her smile.

I call round at Joyce's house, not far from where we live on the estate, one evening after the shebeen bust-up. Her kids are playing out on the street in the afternoon sun. The neighbour's kids are there too, their laughter floating in from the open window. I look out at them, black kids running and jumping with white kids, and remember the demented glint in Brady's eyes and the whisky spittle forming at the corner of his mouth: *they're all morons and maggots, Dave, I tell ye, Hitler had the right fucking idea . . .*

I bend my head.

I don't know who I am; I'm losing sight of the person I used to be and can't remember the good times any more because the nightmare has swallowed them up and spewed them out in sticky bits. My days seem to stretch into one long session on the floor by the record player, listening to Dylan, stoned and numb, head filled with Ian fucking Brady and Myra fucking Hindley. Life means nothing. I've lost Maureen; we've drawn so far apart from each other that she's become the enemy. Arguments always lead to violence and the same repulsions drip from my lips: *fucking bitch, it's you they want, it's you and your family they hate, it's your name they spray across every fucking wall and bus stop in Hattersley, Maureen fucking Hindley, that's who you are, a fucking Hindley, Hindley, Hindley, think what your sister's done, your name is shit, Maureen Hindley.* Parenthood feels like a trap, the kids are neglected and Dad can't cope with any of us, but the worst thing is that no one even gives a fuck, leaving us to tear each other apart like the poor, crazy animals trapped in Belle Vue.

We left Underwood Court because it was too small for us; in their bureaucratic wisdom the council allocated us a house at the end of Underwood Road, less than five minutes from our old flat. It's made us much more accessible to the human wolves wandering the estate. Now, we have to call the council on an almost weekly basis to ask them to replace the windows shattered by mysteriously flying bricks. I watch in silence as Dad knocks out the jagged edges of glass from the frame and Maureen sweeps up the mess. It's always the same council worker who arrives, bedding in the putty and fixing the glass without speaking to any of us. He wipes the windows clean, puts his tools away in his little wooden box and disappears until the following week.

I try to stop thinking about it all, leaving Joyce's house to go home, but not for long. Maureen is closeted in the boys' room and Dad is sprawled in a chair downstairs, staring at a wall. I change my clothes, putting on the old Image, still clinging to it for dear life; it's more of a shield than ever. I put on the thick sunglasses I've worn ever since the trial as a sign of defiance. Then I leave the house without saying goodbye and head down to the Sheriff, a pub on the corner of Underwood Road.

The short walk takes me past the Social Club. I hutch up my shoulders defensively, remembering a recent night out there with Maureen. We had been sitting at the bar when a bloke began giving out the warning signals we've come to recognise all too clearly: first the muttering, then the 'accidental' shove or two before breaking into a venomous 'Murdering bastard!' Anaesthetised with beer, I made the mistake of bestowing a sarcastic smile on him and didn't see the punch he threw as I turned away. It caught me enough to knock me backwards into other people, and sent glasses skittering off the bar. The wolves attacked; punches and jabs and kicks rained down on me, then a group of them hauled me outside. The men fell back and let the womenfolk do their worst. I couldn't ward off the endless kicks and clawing at my face – the last thing I heard was Maureen screaming. When I came round and staggered to my feet, bleeding profusely and in so much pain it made me vomit onto the now empty road, I saw Maureen sitting on the kerbside. Blood poured from her nose, she had a split lip, a busted eye and her clothes had been ripped to shreds. I lurched towards her and together we stumbled home, Maureen sobbing all the way. That night I couldn't sleep. Somewhere outside and not very far away, I could sense a blue mist rolling in . . .

I walk quickly past the Social Club and on to the Sheriff. At the bar I order a pint of bitter, then take my glass to a table in the corner, sitting with my back to the wall. I gaze round at the soulless pub; newly built, it has thick carpets, smells of paint and has a never-ending carousel of piped music. Behind my dark glasses, I gaze at the customers, feeling like an extra in *Coronation Street*: two old ladies sit with their equally elderly husbands, the women balancing handbags on their knees and the men in flat cloth caps drinking from knobbly pint glasses. The foursome look as if they've been friends for years. Near the door sits a young couple in serious conversation and at the end of the bar are three lads not much older than me, an impressive collection of empty pint pots before them. I recognise one of them as a bruiser who's had a go at me before, but then most people in Hattersley have done that.

I glance about for a jukebox, but there isn't one, just Julie Andrews warbling 'The Sound of Music' from some unseen source. Disgusted at my surroundings, I take myself off to answer a call of nature.

I'm standing facing the wall when I hear the Gents door slam and know instantly that the company I'm about to keep isn't the two old chaps in flat caps. One of the likely lads from the bar appears to my right and another to my left. Behind me, I can feel the bruiser's breath on my neck. I stare hard at the cold tiles that are inches away from my face, working out if there is any chance of escaping the inevitable hammering. But the bruiser pokes his fingers into my back and shoulders, pinning me forward while the other two spit thick globules into my face. I hear the bruiser mutter viciously, 'Fucking shithouse, murdering bastard,' and then I feel a warm wetness soaking through the back of my jeans as he pisses up my legs. Then, without a word, the three of them leave, letting the door slam shut again.

I make a pathetic, trembling attempt to clean myself with small squares of toilet paper, then head outside. Walking down Underwood Road, I feel a dark, smouldering anger in my belly and then a sorrow so deep I could drown in it. I've been called a child-killer so often in the past few days, carrying Brady's curse around with me like a weight that will never lift.

I feel the blue mist rolling in closer.

Reaching home, I go straight upstairs and pull off my piss-sodden jeans, hurling them away from me. They fall crumpled and stinking into a corner. Maureen and Dad are where I left them, even though I've been out of the house a good couple of hours. My head boils with anger as I pass Dad in his seat. I stack the records on the stereo and turn the volume up as loud as it will go, even though the kids are having their afternoon naps upstairs. Buddy Holly's voice fills the room. The speakers vibrate with the effort of containing him.

Then Dad turns to me and suddenly comes back to life, shouting, 'Turn that bloody racket down!'

I glare at him, telling him to fuck off as he gets to his feet. I meet him halfway and my fist slams him back into the chair. The skin above his eyebrow bursts open obscenely, leaving a gash big enough to poke in a finger. The music bounces off the walls. Dad looks up at me pitifully, aghast, and I explode in every direction.

The music comes to a screeching end as I kick in the front of the stereo. I grab handfuls of records and smash them against the walls. Anything I can lay my hands on is thrown; the coffee table splinters, and plates and cups shatter. I attack the sitting-room door with my fists and feet, reducing it to a mass of holes, then in a blinding, non-stop rage I kick at the debris on the floor, screaming, 'Fucking bastards! Rotten fucking bastards!' Somewhere among it all I hear Maureen's piercing screams and Dad shouting, 'For Christ's sake, Dave! Stop, please, *stop!*'

I pause, breathless and heaving. For the first time, I clearly see the blood soaking the front of his shirt and the fractured mess that was once our belongings. The minutes pass and then slowly Dad reaches down into the chaos and begins salvaging what he can. Appalled at myself, I help him and we work silently until the floor is clear. Dad leaves for the hospital to get his eye stitched up and I sit watching the blue mist roll and recede, roll and recede. It's thickened since I last saw it, and much closer, but still not as close as I fear.

When Dad gets back from the hospital, I tell Maureen to get dressed: we're going out. My mood is something quiet and dark but without anger. I make my peace with Dad and he agrees to babysit the kids, glad to have the house back to some sort of normality.

At the Social Club, Joyce is sitting in her usual spot and calls us over. I ignore the bouncer's dirty look and give Maureen a nudge into the main room. But the night passes by slowly and I don't feel like drinking as much as usual; I even turn down the opportunity to have a joint in the Gents with Lloyd. It's getting late. I go to the bar for last orders and another hero steps forward. I listen with resignation to the old filth and accusations, but when I glance at him, I think I recognise him as one of the morons who attacked me the last time we were here.

I turn. The man steps closer, his mouth spewing shit. I notice a few women getting up from their table and realise they're itching to give me a good kicking. He looks as if he can do this thing alone without being wound up by a pack of she-devils, but one of the women yells, 'Fucking do the bastard!', and then a painted claw comes over his shoulder, grabbing at my hair. This is the signal; quick and ferocious, the women pile in, scratching, screaming and kicking. The men unhurriedly pull their wives and girlfriends off me, landing a few punches of their own for good measure.

Suddenly Lloyd grabs me and shoves me through the doors. Joyce has hold of Maureen and together the four of us walk to Joyce's home in silence.

I sit in the living room, bone-cold but calm. Joyce has removed all the doors inside and replaced them with long rows of colourful string-beads. She fetches me a tinned beer and chooses a favourite Otis record of mine to pop on the stereo. She smiles at me as she turns the volume to a soothing level. Maureen sits opposite me in her own world, unreachable.

Then I hear it: a pack of them are at the door, kicking it in. Otis fades as the beads clatter like hailstones and there in front of me is the hero from earlier, fists clenched, face full of hate, but a complete stranger to me, as I am to him. Outside a crowd is screaming, 'Get him out, get the bastard out here!' I stand up, already beaten. This thing has to end. I look at Maureen sitting motionless in the chair, her eyes an empty black pool. The blue mist is coming closer, rolling in fast from somewhere beyond the city.

There's a knife in my hand.

This thing has to end. I look down at the knife through the mist and think: *Ian was right, fucking morons, there isn't one life worth saving in this world*.

I raise my head and then my hand. Now it's over.

The ringleader collapses backwards into the street, blood streaming from his face. I feel Joyce's arm come around me, gently taking the knife away, *you won't need that any more, Dave*. She kisses me and quietly tells me to leave.

Maureen is at my side, her hand in mine. We walk in silence down the street, watched by dozens of appalled eyes. But the mist has gone.

*

I was ill and I didn't know it; that has to be the worst affliction imaginable. Looking back, I can see and feel it all as if it happened yesterday, that slow plummeting into oblivion. I was 21 years old and close to feeling nothing at all. I was numb in mind and body.

Why couldn't anyone hear what I was thinking?

I walk into the local police station hand-in-hand with Maureen. Somewhere on the estate an ambulance wails. A man is bleeding on the ground and I don't know how many times I stabbed him. Will he live, might he die, who is he? In my gut, a new feeling is starting to grow, a realisation of where I've ended up. I'm so calm now that I could float on air. Everything is becoming clear again and I am someone else's responsibility at last. It's all over.

Maureen and I talk quietly as we walk. It's been months since we've spoken to each other as normally as we do now. I tell her to *look after the kids and explain to Dad that there was no other way out, it had to end like this*. I ask her how does she feel?

She smiles and squeezes my hand.

But as quickly as it came, the peace I felt is beginning to dissolve. My jaw aches with tension as I ask her *what do they think I've done, they've got Ian and Myra, what do they think is left?*

She doesn't look at me.

Outside the station we kiss. Then we go in and at the small counter I tell them: *You might be looking for me, my name is David Smith.* The duty constable stares at me: *That's right, sir, we are.*

I turn and look at Maureen after the arrest is made. We smile at each other and for the first time in years I see her as a person in her own right and not the embodiment of the foulest name on earth. But time has nailed me to the ground; it's too late for us. We kiss and I'm led away.

Goodbye, Maureen Smith. I'm sorry, but I just couldn't handle the Hindley thing.

* * *

On 18 July 1969, under the headline, 'Moors Trial Witness Sent to Prison', *The Times* reported that David Smith, 'labourer, of Slater Way, Hattersley', had pleaded guilty to wounding William Lees with intent to do grievous bodily harm on 8 June that year. The article continued:

> He appeared yesterday in the same court as Ian Brady and Myra Hindley (defendants in the Moors case).
>
> Mr D Morgan Hughes, for the defence, said Mr Smith's act was a direct consequence of the Moors Murder story, which the people of the neighbourhood could not forget.
>
> Mr Alan Lees, for the prosecution, said there had been trouble in Hattersley Labour Club in which Mr Smith and Mr Lees were concerned. The next night, Mr Lees was on his way home when Mr Smith pulled a knife from his pocket and stabbed him several times.
>
> Mr Hughes said, 'Had he not been involved in the murder trial he might not have been in trouble. For most of the time he has been out of work. He got a job in a foundry but when the employees heard of it they either walked out or threatened to do so.' Mr Justice Veale said he expected Mr Smith had been subjected to sustained hostility and that there had been difficulties for him, but this was not the first time he had been in

trouble. He had been before the court four times for assault.

* * *

From David Smith's memoir:

My trial is quick. I plead guilty and, having been told to prepare myself for seven years in prison, I get three.

I'm alone in the dock at Chester Castle, surrounded by a glass screen that was put in place when my sister-in-law and her boyfriend stood on trial here. I was a witness then; now I'm the defendant and this same dock has held all three of us in its confines.

But at last I'm beginning to think properly. I have space and time to breathe. Things in my head are decelerating.

There is just one thing that wakes me up at night in a cold sweat. It's a memory, a private thing, but I'm aware of it like a shadow at my shoulder, constant, menacing.

On the night I used the knife on William Lees, in a slow, deliberate voice I kept repeating over and over and over again, 'You fucking cunt, you dirty bastard . . .' The last time I heard those words was at Wardle Brook Avenue on the night Ian Brady hacked Edward Evans to death before my eyes.

On 20 July, I sit perched on the bunk in my cell at Risley Remand Centre, waiting to be transferred to Walton Prison. I wish I could find a place of deep solitude, somewhere to think myself well again. My sentence hasn't really sunk in yet.

Keys rattle in the lock and the library screw throws a newspaper onto the bunk. 'I've cancelled your order,' he tells me. 'They'll be shipping you out in the morning.'

I roll a few cigarettes and settle down to read the *Daily Mirror*. Four words fill the entire front page: 'Man On The Moon'. I'm thinking: *now, that's what you call a headline*. I love the story; I soak it up, page after page of it. And that night, after last slop-out, I stand at the barred window, looking up at the sky. I imagine that headline belongs to me: 'Man On The Moon'. That's where I want to be, on a one-way ticket of my own. If there's a heaven, then the moon must be that much closer, and if it gets me closer to the people I miss, then being the Man On The Moon is who I want to be.

Chapter 19

'You don't have to say you love me, just be close at hand,
You don't have to stay forever, I will understand . . .'
    – 'You Don't Have to Say You Love Me',
                                Dusty Springfield

David began his sentence at Liverpool's Walton Gaol (now HMP Liverpool). North of the city centre and constructed between 1850 and 1854, the prison originally housed both sexes, but in 1969 its burgeoning population was solely male. Shortly after arrival, David was placed on Rule 43 (now Rule 45) following the governor's decision to segregate him for his own safety. His fellow inmates within the unit were mostly child sex offenders, former police officers and supergrasses. Life on the segregation wing involved virtual isolation for 23 hours a day and deprivation of almost all opportunities for work, education and social contact. Visits from the outside took place individually in a small room where a thick sheet of glass separated inmate and visitor.

David feared that final detail, added to the enforced separation caused by his sentence, would prove disastrous for his marriage to Maureen. He resolved to come off Rule 43, hoping that normal visits would help bridge the gulf between them. The governor granted his request with one proviso: since David's safety couldn't be guaranteed at Walton, the only option was to transfer him to another prison. He was moved to HMP Lancaster, a small prison within a medieval castle overlooking the city itself and infamous as the site of the 1612 Pendle Witch trials. After weeks in largely solitary confinement, David found mixing with other inmates difficult and closeted himself in his cell at the first opportunity. Having spent time alone, he had renewed hope that his marriage could be salvaged; when he received a letter from Maureen telling him that their relationship was over, it was too much to bear. His fragile psychological state crumbled.

David's memoir deals starkly with this period, beginning within days of his arrival at Walton Gaol.

* * *

From David Smith's memoir:

'806713 Smith, sir.'

I report to Walton's governor, shorn this morning by the con-barber of my shoulder-length, Lennon-style hair. I'm just a number within the system now and don't have to think for myself any more. The governor gives me a critical look and tells me, 'We're placing you on Rule 43, Smith. Governor's discretion.' I try to protest but one of the screws standing opposite me shouts 'Shut it!' and I do.

I'm led to my empty cell, where, within a few hours, two other inmates will join me – proper 43ers, whose crimes make them hated by the rest of the cons. I clench my teeth at the prospect of never being alone; I've worked out that I'm ill and think that if only I had a cell to myself for a while yet, I could stop the world and get off – or at least slow it down for a while, long enough to bleed out the pain and start clawing my way back to sanity. It's a weird thing, but prison has already been good for me. On paper I'm a criminal, stripped of every liberty, but it doesn't feel like that. Ever since I arrived, my solitary cell has offered a freedom I thought was lost to me. For the first time in years, I've been able to rest back on a bed and close my eyes without fear. No horrors, no screams, no cold sweats – just the thoughts that I *allow* into my head. I can fly away into the past or dream about a future. Prison has made a free man of me.

That changes when my cellmates turn up. I hate losing my solitude and withdraw like a snail into its shell. The nightmares come back with a vengeance straightaway. Then morning arrives: slop-out time. There are around twenty Rule 43ers housed on the ground floor of our wing; above us are two floors of 'normal cons'. I walk out with my cellmates and stand in line, waiting to empty my pot. It begins quietly at first, like a playground chant, and then rises until I'm deafened: *Smith, you fucking bastard, filthy cunt, murdering bastard, nonce, child killer, murderer, murderer, MURDERER . . .*

261

They empty their pots over the rails and a rain of shit and piss drenches us, the missiles clattering through the wire mesh that separates the floors. Wiping the stinking filth from my eyes, I see the screws supposed to be guarding us grinning from the shelter of the cell arches.

There is every kind of pervert on Rule 43, but each morning it's my name the cons shout as they bang their fists against the rails. I shut my eyes, needing to get back into my cell, to be alone behind a closed door in order to think myself back to the only safe place I've ever known.

I have to wait until we're allowed back to our cells, but the minute I'm through the door I crawl into my bunk and pull the thin cover over my head, shutting out the light and giving in to the darkness that surrounds me.

Time passes quicker than you might expect in prison. A new year begins; a new decade. I daren't hope that 1970 will be good for me, but it's hard to imagine anything worse than the last few years and enough for now to know that the '60s are over.

Then out of the blue, a reminder. January is only a few days old when I get a visit from Mattin and Tyrrell, the two detectives who gave me such a hard time during the Moors investigation. They arrive with a folio of photographs and ask me to go through them to see if anything of significance occurs to me. It doesn't, but I agree to return to the moors and Derbyshire with them in the near future. They tell me the visit has to be confidential; they don't want the press finding out about it. Neither do I.

Soon afterwards, one of the screws opens my cell at 5.30 a.m. and tells me to get changed into my civvies and come to reception. Two other policemen are waiting to drive me back to Manchester. Once there, I'm handed over to Mattin and Tyrrell again and we head in an unmarked car up to the moor and to a couple of other places I seem to remember visiting with Ian and Myra. I grit my teeth the entire time, or so it seems, feeling as if I'm being pitched into the nightmare all over again. Even the wind strikes my face with the same chill roughness, making me sway on my feet in the long grass that wraps itself around my ankles so securely it's as if it won't let go. We're looking for a particular spot that's of interest to police, but I'm lost and am glad to my soul when Mattin and Tyrrell – both of them behaving very civilly towards me – suggest returning to the station to take another look at

Brady's bleak photographs. After a couple of hours, they accept that there's nothing else I can tell them and call someone to drive me to Walton. Being back in my cell is an odd sort of relief. I hope with every breath in my body that I never have to go back to the moor again.

Things change in the prison: Rule 43ers are 're-housed' in another area, on a landing above the normal cons, which means an end to the putrid morning downpour. We have our own screws now, Paddy and Mr Heywood, a better breed of prison officer. I've been placed in a cell with two of the worst and most unrepentant sex offenders within these walls – I wish the do-gooders of this world could spend a week with them. After evening lock-up, my cell door remains unofficially open for a couple of hours and I play chess with the screws. Life seems a bit less pointless; I even have a guitar and play the songs that form the soundtrack to my 22 years.

I'm beginning to feel a bit more at ease with myself. Routines are rigid and I spend 23 hours a day in my cell, but the silent hours comfort me. I sit on my bunk – the top one – looking out through the bars and listening to the sound of my mind slowing down. The green filth of memory has stopped curdling inside my skull. I am becoming self-aware again, realising that something is healing within, and the pain subsides as the past takes on a different shape. I don't know when I first became ill; I only know that part of me is getting better.

But my recovery is far from complete. I am paranoid, suspicious of everyone outside Walton. Rule 43 allows me only closed visits; I sit in a small cubicle, separated from my visitor by a thick seven-foot-tall sheet of armoured glass. Joyce comes alone; Dad and Maureen visit together. I sense their unease and watch their body language obsessively. When my eyes meet theirs, I know that they are lying to me in some way – I feel it, even behind the glass. Afterwards, I return to my cell and lie quietly on my bunk, hands behind my head, staring up at the ceiling. I feel as if something is approaching out of sight, first the breeze of trouble, then the gale.

In the exercise yard, I walk the line, those painted circles and stripes on the concrete. I dig my hands deeper into my pockets, thinking. I know Maureen feels the pressure most of all, and I want to *do* something – at least I'm well enough to know that I should help her. She and the boys and Dad have been re-housed in Moss Side and my guts churn at the thought of them there, close to Tom, the man I found her with on the stairwell in the shebeen.

Time passes. Dad visits alone frequently, making excuses for Maureen. I say nothing as the months go by without a single appearance from her. I talk to Joyce, though, and she tells me about Tom. My Miss Jamaica knew Tom long before that night at the shebeen, when he approached her about Maureen. Joyce admits that she brought the two of them together and I smile indulgently, pretending not to care any more. She tells me that Maureen sees Tom regularly and parties with him, but insists it's nothing to do with her any more.

I think Miss Jamaica is lying out of her beautiful black arse.

Dad visits again, trotting out the usual excuse about Maureen not being well. He assures me the boys are fine and I wait until he's finished spoon-feeding me all his crap.

'Well?' I ask.

'Well what?'

I lean forward, nose almost touching the cold glass: 'Tell me what the fuck's going on out there and piss off with all this made-up shit.'

He falters for a moment. Then the truth pours out of him, even though he insists that he doesn't want to have to be the one to tell me: Maureen's stopped bothering to come home at all. A few mornings ago he met her in the street with Tom, the two of them draped around each other. When he eventually dragged her home and smashed every plate in the kitchen to make his point, she said nothing except, 'Please don't tell Dave.'

Our visit ends and I have to find a way of controlling the pain and anger. I lie on my bunk, thinking it through. The restricted regime of Rule 43 is shredding my marriage and the soul-destroying closed visits have driven us further apart. We need to be together, to be able to hold hands and kiss without having to press our lips against a sheet of unfeeling glass.

I think back to that night at the shebeen. There was no one to blame but me for how I treated her, yet nobody tried to stop me. Maybe we were just white trash to them, after all.

I want so badly to see her properly, to kiss her mouth and tell her: it's all right, girl, everything will be all right. I make up my mind to come off Rule 43, to get off protection in order to give us time together. I need to have open visits, but to do that . . . I have to join the regular cons.

I explain the situation to Mr Heywood, the landing screw, and he tells me that I won't last five minutes in Walton without the protection of Rule 43. Inmates coming off the rule are deliberately 'shipped out' to other prisons, where they can join the normal cons with their misdemeanours known only to the governor and staff. He does agree, though, that I'd have far more 'freedom' as a con, including open visits, television, recreation classes and minimal lock-up, but it's a different and very dangerous world from the one I've grown used to on Rule 43.

He urges me to be sure of my decision and I tell him I've got no choice: I *have* to see Maureen properly, not like a caged animal. He manoeuvres me along the landing, out of sight of the sex cases and other screws. 'Watch your back and walk away,' he instructs.

I smile; the walking away doesn't come easily. 'Thanks, boss,' I say, and we shake hands.

He switches to formal: 'Right then, Smith, I'll put your name down for the governor in the morning.'

'Stand to the line and give your number and name to the governor,' the screw shouts. I step forward and two more screws stand in front, eye-balling me.

'806713 Smith, sir, request to come off Rule 43.'

I'm moved to Lancaster Prison: the castle. Jesus Christ, the walls are even higher than Walton. I walk into reception, carrying my life in a box: letters, photos and the picture frames I've made out of spent matchsticks. The two Liverpool escort screws sign me over and I'm officially the property of HM Prison Lancaster.

I notice the Red Bands (trustee cons) hovering about idly. The screw reads through my file and looks up at me, turning the pages slowly. He grunts and places it deliberately on the table before walking away and occupying himself with something else. A Red Band steps forward, opens the file and flicks through the pages. He closes it and coughs; the screw returns. I hear Mr Heywood telling me to watch my back – I'm not even through reception yet and the whole fucking place will know of my arrival within minutes.

The Red Bands lead me to the bathrooms, where I shower fast – many a battering is dished out when you're stark naked. I'm given my tobacco and a pre-paid reception letter, so that I can write home, and taken to my ground-floor cell. It's a million years away from my Walton shit hole; it has a clean linoleum floor, pale blue walls, a table area and single bunk, a washing bowl and water jug. Underneath the bunk is a clean piss-pot. I'm impressed.

I put my belongings on the bunk and close the cell door automatically. A minute later a screw barges in and tells me: 'The doors stay open in this nick till lights out.' I try to process the thought, as I settle down, arranging my photos and then writing a letter. I feel OK until mealtime arrives. Nervously, I follow the cons into the vast, busy mess hall. I join the queue for grub after collecting my tray and cup. The con ladling out the food asks me if I want more than the amount he's already slapped onto my plate. I stare down at it, shocked that no one moves to spit in it when the screws aren't looking. The other surprise is the quality of the food; I collect as much bread as I can eat – real bread, not the stodgy crap we got in Walton – and search for somewhere to sit.

Panic suddenly grips me. I'm not used to being with so many people and can't handle it. I need my cell with its door shut; I *want* to be locked up. I leave the hall with my tray and walk quickly back to my cell, closing the door behind me. I stand with the tray in my hands, sweating and shivering at once.

The door opens. 'You eat with the rest of them,' the screw tells me. 'There's no segregation in here. Only down in the block.'

'I want to eat on my own.'

The screw jerks his head. 'Out with you.'

I go back to the mess with my tray, tip the food into the bin and return to my cell again. During the night, I listen, door open, to the cons laughing at the comedy programme on telly. They play pool, darts, chess, dominoes, cards . . . I lie on my bunk, thinking. I've sent out my visiting order and hope I'll soon see Maureen. But I already miss the restricted regime of Walton and being alone for much of the day. In Walton, I could lose myself in memories, drifting back to a place of cobbled streets and short pants, old ladies and Sunday dinners, bath nights and lovely warm beds, and best of all . . . another adventure with Tom Sawyer.

The days drift by. I eat with the cons but sit without speaking while people chatter to the left and right of me. I'm given a decent job in the metalwork shop, where I can earn a bit extra to buy tobacco and toiletries, but after only a few hours I stand up and approach the boss.

'Take me back, please.'

He looks at me blankly.

'Boss, please, I need to go back to my fucking cell.'

He hits the button and I'm taken back into the main prison, to my own little room. I spend as much time as I can there in the next few days, sitting quietly with an unopened book or else gazing at the walls. My head feels thick and dull; twice a day I walk the line but a different sort of fear is beginning to take hold of me. I want to see Maureen and make everything 'right' for us, but my grasp on reality is weakening. I keep closing my cell door and the screws bang it open without speaking to me. I stare at them, wondering why the door can't stay shut until I've worked out if I'm ill in the head now, or if I was ill before I got here and am getting better, or if I'm becoming ill. Nothing makes sense, and what's going on in my head least of all.

I sit in the library, alone, thinking, endlessly fucking thinking. I'm so tired, I'm so very, very tired. Mother of God, please lift me out of this mess, take me away, I want to sleep and I want the hurting to stop, I feel like ripping myself apart. The real world hurts too much and I don't want to be part of it. I want to be seven years old again, pretending to be Jesse James as I dodge the traffic on Stockport Road, heading home from the Apollo after a cowboy film and an orange lolly. Help me do the right thing before I close my eyes. Make it real.

When the morning post arrives, my name and number is listed at last on the mail board. My spirits soar; I'm delighted for myself, collecting the barest of breakfasts – a mug of tea and some toast – because I don't want to waste time in the queue.

I seek out the screw, feeling high: 'Morning, boss, mail for 806713 Smith.' I think quickly to myself: *please, God, don't let it be from Dad, don't let it be from my fucking dad, not this time, please not this time*. I'm handed the letter in its opened envelope – pre-read in the censor's office – and recognise the handwriting. *Yes, yes, fucking yes. It's from Maureen.*

I find a table and bench, sip my tea and make two roll-ups. I sniff the envelope; yes, that's her scent on the paper. I pull out the pages and read.

There are six or seven sheets, folded neatly together. I read one and place it down, resting the second carefully on the first and so on until I reach the end: *'I'll miss you forever, love, Maureen. xxxxx.'*

I count the five kisses.

This isn't right, it's all gone wrong – I didn't plan it like this. I light the second roll-up, my insides pitch and heave, my hands have gone; the trembling moves up my arms and into my shoulders. I read the letter a second time, more slowly, taking in every word, reading certain lines over and over and over again: she's received my visiting order but won't be using it . . . she complains about Dad . . . there are too many arguments . . . the boys are OK . . . the new house in Moss Side is all right, she likes it . . . she's been going out a lot with Joyce . . . Then the killer hook: *We need a break, I have something to tell you, remember Tom,* yes, I remember Tom, *please don't write again, I'll burn your letters, no more visiting orders, I'll miss you forever, love, Maureen. xxxxx.*

I put the pages on top of each other again, one, two, three . . . My head hurts, why is everybody talking so loudly, who turned the volume up, the noise is deafening but there are no words, just noise. I look up and see mouths moving out of control and the place throbbing with people, thousands of them, all shouting, pouring in through the doors like water, collecting trays and still shouting.

I'm shaking from head to foot.

I can smell Maureen on the notepaper, but it feels as if the table is very far away and yet the ceiling is coming down. My fingers scramble across the Formica and I stuff the letter inside its envelope. People are still flooding into the room, yelling through mouths that gape like railway tunnels. I need to get somewhere . . . I need to be behind a closed door.

I head for the library, but it's locked – too early in the morning for reading. I try other doors, but they stay shut, and in the end I go back to my cell, my small, blue linoleum cell. I stand with my head bent, Maureen's letter in my hand, feeling all the bad fucking madness of the world building up. I want to think without some nosy screw or smart-arse con telling me to come out, making me lose the plot.

The plot. The plot. The fucking plot. For fuck's sake, what fucking plot? There's a swarm of something hot and rotten in my head, everything is running backwards like a film reel: *Maureen, Miss Jamaica, a man lying in the street bleeding, Tom, ganja, curried goat, blowback Saturday nights and shit-faced Sunday mornings, a neon factory so cold it takes the skin off your hands, flat 18 with the heating turned up, pounding the Hattersley streets in the early hours with wild things, flashbulbs going off left, right and fucking centre through the windows of a hired car, two detectives in shirt sleeves screaming and banging their fists against walls, the raw knuckles of a youth as he crawls under a table to save what's left of his skull, a row of miniature wine bottles and staring down the barrel of a mad man's gun, photographic proof, I've got photographic proof, Myra fucking Hindley and her shark-black eyes, moonlight on a reservoir, the tiniest of white coffins going into the earth, a registry office with its wood and ink smell, standing victorious in the boxing ring at Kings Hall, a tramp with an ugly smile and words that shatter, you're too late little boy, she's dead, FUCK YOU ALL, cook the man his rice and beans and shove it down your fucking throats, five kisses, Maureen, why did you send me five kisses, one each: Dave, Maureen, Paul, David and John, but you forgot Angela, just like you've forgotten everything else because you're a fucking Hindley and your name is shit, shit, shit.*

The pain squeezes itself tighter around my skull. I take a deep breath. I'm going to close the door now, nice and gently, no fuss. I know it's against the rules and I don't want it to be a problem but I really do need to close this door, just for a short time, and just to show you I want to be alone for a while, to have a little think with myself. I'll barricade myself in but don't let it concern you, just walk away with your keys and do not disturb, no one will get hurt, I only want to hurt myself . . .

The floor has vanished beneath a litter of shredded photographs and letters. Who did that? I don't remember tearing them, but everything is in a million tiny pieces, including me. The razor blade glides gracefully down my arm, the red lines appearing like magic. If I place my hand over the blood, it bubbles up through the gaps in my fingers. This isn't a problem; I like it, everything feels all right now. I'm alone in my room with my lovely clean piss-pot and I'm bleeding. Life isn't too bad, after all – I just needed to find a way of coping and this is it. Red splashes cover the floor at my feet, small circles, slowly at first, one by one, then faster and wider. I run the blade down my arm again, and feel satisfaction at being able to follow the first cut so precisely. This pain is a good pain. I press harder into the skin and watch in fascination as the wound opens cleanly, gushing blood. How deep will I need to push before I reach the bone?

Keys rattle in the lock. *They just won't leave you alone for five minutes in this place.* Shoulders slam against the door but the barricade holds. *Please do not disturb.* I look at the photographs on the floor, all torn and jagged, who did that, what's happened to this day, it wasn't supposed to be like this. It's so quiet and peaceful in the little blue room. But when I look at the photographs I feel so sad. I hear a voice coming through the door: *come on, lad, let us in, open up, we can talk, no problem is this big*. I make one more cut in my skin and then I pick up Maureen's letter. I'm sitting on the floor and holding the letter against my bent knee. Her words vanish under my blood. I don't have a problem with it now. I'm just so tired, so very, very tired.

I listen to the whispers outside my door and the rhythmic push of shoulders against it. My cell slate, on the other side of the door, tells everyone who I am: 806713 Smith, three years, RC. And so they fetch the priest. The Judas-hole is filled with the watery eye of God's messenger and he talks to me, calling me David, wanting to share my pain. *Why share it, Father, when you can have it all? I never wanted it.* He asks to share my bad news too, he knows I've received a letter and would like to read it with me. *Isn't that nice of him?* I genuinely think it's nice of him. No one's read to me in years. Then I remember it wasn't that long ago someone read to me. No, it wasn't that long: *should murder be punished by murder? Undoubtedly not . . .*

Somewhere on the side of my neck is an important vein. I wonder how deep it is and will it hurt. I raise the blade and consider. It feels weirdly heavy as it touches my skin.

'David, this is a priest asking you to open the door, you mustn't hurt yourself any more, think of what that might mean, I'll come in on my own, just me and you, nobody else, just us . . .'

I realise then, astonished, that they think I'm committing suicide. Don't they know I only want to feel a good sort of pain for once? I only want it to hurt enough to stop me from feeling anything else. I only want to pierce this vein once and it'll be all right. If I blow my brains out with one of the guns I used for target practice on a railway sleeper buried in the heather and dark earth, then I'll be a free man. That's not fucking suicide, is it? That's just my way of dealing with the pain.

It takes seconds for the barricade to come down with an army of screws against it. But when the priest comes in, he's alone. The screws wait silently outside, as he lifts the razor blade from my fingers and blesses me. He reads what he can of the letter and tells me the officers need to come in. I sit on the bunk and let the prison doctor attend to my arm. He asks me if I am all right. I tell him politely no, and he nods, pressing the needle into my arm. Outside I can hear the Principal Officer asking why my letter was issued to me when it had been stamped as read in the censor's office (bad news is always referred to the doctor first). I see Mr Heywood from Walton standing in front of me like the ghost of Christmas future. He isn't really here, but I can see him, nodding wisely and telling me, 'Watch your back and walk away.'

They've got me.

I sit quietly on the bed, holding a mug of tea that's gone stone cold. I'm foggy-headed because the sedative has taken over, but I understand that I'm to be 'shipped out' back to Walton today.

Today. Is it still only today . . .

A few hours later I'm standing in front of a doctor, quiet and docile. I don't remember getting to Walton, not properly. I think I was in a car, staring out of the window. Everything seems to have happened a long time ago; hours and years have become the same. I'd like to have a hot bath and a little sleep, I'd like to be able to sleep next to a woman who loves me so much she buys me every comic on the market. I'd like to be held in her arms, tight and close.

I'm asked how I feel. Not too good – my head is like cotton wool and my mouth is very dry, very dry. The doctor tells me to relax and take a few breaths; he wants to ask me something and he'd like me to think carefully before I answer. Do I understand?

'Yes, sir, I think I do.'

He pauses for a minute, and then asks, 'Do you feel you want to hurt yourself?'

The question bores straight through my skull into the back of my brain where everything is dark and confused. *'I'll miss you forever, love Maureen. xxxxx.'* Five kisses: one each, but nothing for Angela.

'Yes, I want to hurt myself.'

He writes something in my file and says he understands. I think: *what the fuck does everybody understand, all of a sudden?* Then he nods at two nurses, who take me by the arms and walk me down a corridor.

My new room has no linoleum and it isn't pale blue; it's white and padded. I undress and the straightjacket is brought in – *just for a while.* I'm put into it very quickly, no fuss. There's a very thin mattress on the floor and a piss-pot, nothing else.

Roll over, this is just something to relax you and help you sleep.

I smell fresh aftershave as the needle goes in.

*

I wake up and fall asleep again, I open my eyes and see a pair of boots,

I feel the needle and go back to sleep, I see a tray of food and then it's gone. I think I've been sick but I'm not sure. I have a permanent headache for a long time and then it's over.

I wake and lift myself up. The straightjacket has gone and I'm wearing a surgical gown; I can feel my arse through the gaping fabric. I feel putrid. The front of the gown is stained and stiff; somewhere along the line I think I must have soiled myself. I can smell it in the air, but the piss-pot is gleamingly empty. They've cleaned me up, though I don't know how many times. I prop myself up against the wall and drift in and out of sleep until my head clears. I wait for the door to open, willing it to open; I don't want to be behind a closed door any more.

A nurse comes in and asks me gently if I'm fit to drink some tea. I ask him, 'What day is it?'

He looks at me. 'What day do you remember?'

I tell him, 'It was a bad day.'

He nods. 'Your bad day was four days ago, David.'

I nod, too. When I try to stand, my legs won't support me.

'Take it slowly. I'll get you some tea.'

I sit and wonder how I've made it back from the edge.

I'm out of the padded cell, deemed calm enough to be moved to an ordinary hospital room within the prison. The days pass slowly but not bleakly, helped along by a few pills and a handful of deep sleeps. While I've been floating in a world I can't remember, someone has been busy on my behalf: I'm to expect a 'special' visit with Maureen. Not a closed visit, but one where we can be together in order to talk properly.

Before then, I'm taken to meet a psychiatrist, who talks nonsense.

He wants to know if I have a 'mother fixation' and I stare at him, wanting to laugh. *Of course I do, you fucking idiot, I'm fixated out of my mind with her.* But I say nothing. He wants to learn whether I have a 'persecution complex' and I put my head on one side, looking at him. *Of course I have, you fucking moron.* Being constantly accused of murdering kids who are never seen again until they're dug out of a bog on the moor does tend to make you feel ever so slightly persecuted.

I'm taken to see other psychiatrists, too, and so the mind games with the funny folk go on for a while. I tell them what they want to hear and they scribble away excitedly, muttering 'excellent' and 'marvellous'. We play silly games with paper and patterns and it all looks like spilt ink to me, but it keeps them happy. I've begun to eat again and fill myself with the stodgy prison bread; two slices of that and I can't finish my dinner.

The day of Maureen's visit arrives. I refuse breakfast because I'm too nervous to swallow, just tea and tobacco for me. I spend ages getting myself ready, polishing my shoes to a dazzling shine. (*Christ, Dave, she's not going to be looking at your bloody feet.*) I button up the starched prison shirt fresh from the laundry, supplied by the friendly hospital screw. I shave carefully; this time I don't want to cut myself. The con-barber trims my hair and I clean my teeth every ten minutes because I'm smoking every five. I've been walking around in my undies all morning to save the best till last: grey flannel prison trousers with a razor-sharp crease. Last night I brushed the tick material and dampened the legs before laying them under the mattress and sleeping on top. I'm delighted with the results and intend to put them on only when the screw comes to get me, hoping to preserve the creases.

I tell myself it's not over because she's coming to see me. Why would she bother otherwise?

The door opens and the hospital screw grins at me: 'Special open visit for Smith.'

Yes, I think, *fucking yes*. I slip into my trousers and ask him to give me a minute. I clean my teeth again even though my gums are sore. Before the visit can take place, I have to see a doctor, and as the hospital screw walks me down the corridor to the office I feel as if I'm going for a Saturday night out. I feel fantastic, ready to whistle.

I stand clean, straight and smart in front of the doctor, polished and immaculate. Inevitably, he asks me how I feel.

'Fine, sir. Very fine.'

He tells me he has a problem: although he's approved the visit, he's concerned. After all, it's been a while and I might have trouble handling 'things'. I nod understandingly. He gives me a deep, long look and tells me that if I find it too difficult, or if I feel uneasy or panicked in any way, then I am to go straight to the officer. It's important that I do that, for everyone's sake – do I understand? I grit my teeth and smile. *Yes, sir, I do fucking understand, every word you say, in my world you're God, now just please let me see her.*

He nods, telling me to go and that he hopes the visit is good. I believe him; he's the one who knocked me out when I got here and now I feel as if he's lifting me up again.

I stop after leaving his office, needing a long piss. I remember to wipe my shoes on the backs of my perfect trousers. I'm nervous as hell, but keep telling myself that she didn't have to come, it would have been easier for her to stay at home – the visit must mean something.

Dad and my probation officer stand at the end of the corridor. Everything is seconds away. I want the loo again but forget that when the hospital screw tells me that my visit will last an hour. He explains that he has to check on me from time to time, but promises to knock first. Then he opens the door.

Maureen sits in front of a table with an empty chair beside her. A small pile of cigarettes lies in the ashtray. *Jesus, I thought I'd never see you, girl . . .*

I get to her before she can stand and kiss her as she rises from the chair. She's dressed to perfection in clothes I haven't seen before and her make-up is flawless. But it's her scent that fills my head. I can't get enough of it: perfumed, clean and female.

The visit is frantic, verbally. I want to know everything: the boys, the house, her daily existence. *God, I've missed you so much, Maureen.* We forgive everything that was done and said between us and she tells me I must never hurt myself again. She shakes her head, she's sorry, she never wanted that to happen in a thousand years . . .

We hold hands and light cigarettes, smoking them down to the filter. She kisses me halfway through a sentence, cutting off the words, and I can't help doing the same. We tell each other how well we look and we cry, tearing ourselves apart with apologies. I kiss her neck repeatedly, lingeringly, secretly breathing in her scent, tasting it.

The screw knocks discreetly every ten minutes, popping his head around the door and asking if I'm all right. *Fine, boss,* I answer, while the tears roll down my face and hers, *never been better.*

We discuss and agree on a future together, faithfully promising many changes – two especially, in our own interest as a couple: Tom must go and so must Dad.

The screw knocks and peers in: 'Fifteen minutes left, Smith.' He grins widely and gives me a knowing, manly wink. 'I won't knock again now until time's up.'

I think: *thanks, boss, but the last thing I feel like at the moment is a quick bunk-up.*

Maureen agrees to write and visit more often and I tell her I'm definitely coming off protection so that our visits can be more like this. She begs me not to, for my own safety, but I shake my head and tell her it's something I've got to do. We kiss and cry again because time is running out. Then we stand up and she tells me to take care and look after myself. I tell her to do the same.

One last, hard kiss, nothing soft and gentle about it; we share tongues and hold it for as long as we can, and then it's over, gone for ever and I leave the room.

The boss gives me one more minute so that I can talk to Dad. Quietly, I explain the situation to him and he replies, eyes watering, that he already knew that and moved out a week ago. We part quietly, Dad walking away with his head bent low, resigned to the change in all our lives.

In my hospital cell, I sit and look outside at the sex cases walking the line. Tomorrow I'll be back with them, and part of the old routine of a 23-hours-a-day lock-up, just as if I've never been away. But not for long; I've got to come off protection, I've got to do 'the right thing'. And I'm convinced that this *is* the right thing, and the only way of saving my marriage to Maureen.

A fortnight later, when my visiting order has gone out to Maureen, I'm told to go to the doctor's office.

I stand at his desk, frowning, looking at the letter he holds away from him as if it's on fire.

'I'm afraid you've got some bad news, David. Your wife has left you.'

He glances down at the letter, adding in a heavy voice, 'And the children have been taken into care.'

Every drop of blood in my body instantly turns to ice.

'Your wife has returned your visiting order with her letter. Do you want to accept it or would you like me to put you down for the Welfare Officer or the priest?'

I hear myself speaking from the frozen wasteland inside my head. *No thanks*, the sub-zero voice tells the doctor, *I'd rather not read the letter, and as for the Welfare and the priest . . . I've been there before.*

When I walk back to my cell, it's all I can do to put one foot in front of the other, and when I go inside and sit on my bunk, I try to feel something to remind myself that I'm still alive, but there's nothing.

Nothing at all.

*

Joyce visits me alone, telling me that she was *so* sad to hear about Maureen abandoning the kids and moving in with Tom. She didn't know what was going on, she assures me, but I notice she can't meet my eyes. We're on a 'closed' visit, which means no contact, yet even with the thick, tall glass between us, I can smell her perfume. As she leaves, we kiss through the glass and she smiles at me.

'You're not black, you know.'

It's the last time I ever see her.

In my cell, I sit and think. The numbness has gone, but the pain I expected to replace it doesn't come; I concentrate my energies on finding out how the boys are getting on and that alone seems to hold the pain at bay. Dad visits, full of promises, telling me this is in some way a good thing, that we can make a fresh start properly now that Maureen has gone. I want to believe him, but I can't – I feel too cut off from everyone and the situation still seems hopeless. The only feeling I have is for the boys. Nothing else matters to me.

The strange thing is that although I don't know it yet, somewhere in the background my new life is beginning without me, carried slowly in the heart of a 14-year-old girl.

V
Rising

1971–75

Chapter 20

'Wake up, Maggie, I think I've got something to say to
you . . .'
                                  – 'Maggie May', Rod Stewart

Maureen's neglect of her children had its roots in deep
unhappiness and isolation. Increasingly seeking solace in
alcohol, she spent her nights at the Moss Side shebeens with
Tom, leaving the three boys – Paul was the eldest at six years old
– to fend for themselves. Jack Smith was not at home; when he
returned from work to find Maureen absent and the children
alone, he was outraged, and never more so than the morning
when he encountered Maureen in the street with Tom, the two
of them still drunk and stoned from the night before. A furious
row ensued, and Jack stormed out to stay with a close friend in
Hyde. Maureen's mental state deteriorated rapidly and the
situation soon came to the attention of the Welfare Department.
Maureen admitted she could no longer cope alone and
arrangements were made to take the children into care; they
were seriously underweight, riddled with lice and had been
sleeping on sheets that hadn't been changed for months. When
their case worker, Mrs Delaney, arrived at Ruskin Avenue to
collect the children, Maureen wasn't there, but the door was
open. Mrs Delaney promptly removed the three boys to the
Acorns, a reputable care home within a large Victorian property
in nearby Fallowfield. Paul, David and John instantly became
favourites of Nurse Josephine, one of the younger carers at the
Acorns, and their health and spirits rapidly improved.

In Walton Gaol, David was visited by his probation officer, Mr
Potter, and given a full explanation of what had taken place at

Ruskin Avenue. Mr Potter spared no details about the brutality of the neglect but assured him that the boys were now making excellent progress in a warm, safe place with constant supervision. Within days, David began receiving regular letters from the Welfare Department, keeping him informed of his sons' well-being, along with up-to-date photographs, and he was delighted when the three boys were given special permission to visit him in prison with Mrs Delaney.

Maureen, meanwhile, found a one-bedroom flat and a job at a department store, abandoning the house in Ruskin Avenue. The council boarded it up, but Jack Smith hired a skip and emptied it of all the rubbish that had piled up during his absence, and put anything he felt worth salvaging into storage. When it was empty, he returned to his friend Martin Flaherty in Hyde, remaining there for several weeks.

In prison, David focused on one thought alone: building a new life for himself and his children.

* * *

From David Smith's memoir:
My head is clearer than it has been in a very long time.

Dad visits often, diagnosed recently with cancer but seemingly coping well with his illness. The boys are in brilliant form; I see them on a monthly basis and am beginning to remember how it feels to be happy again. Dad talks a lot about my release, insisting that the council will re-house us and that we should buy new furniture for the boys' return home. Everything is given a positive spin, and although privately I remain apprehensive about the future, some of Dad's optimism rubs off on me. I play my guitar as often as I can in my cell, learning new songs from the sheet music that Dad brings in as my treat. I'm even managing to tolerate the sex cases on my wing better, and enjoying my nightly game of chess with the screws more. It's at night, in my bunk, that I think about my rapidly approaching EDR (earliest date of release) and have to swallow the fear about what it might bring. I try to concentrate instead on the practicalities of creating a new and stable home for the boys.

But it isn't always easy to be upbeat. I wish the past hadn't happened; I wish my life had been normal and that my failures or triumphs had been my own. I feel bitter in these moments and it hurts. I blame Ian,

I blame Myra, and in my worst moments of spiralling loneliness I blame God. I try to imagine a world without my sister-in-law and her thin-lipped boyfriend and find myself selfishly picturing someone else bringing their crimes to the attention of the police. Why did it have to be me? I wanted to be Tom Sawyer or James Dean, living in a yellow submarine under marmalade skies, growing old content and at peace with myself. But here I am.

I make an effort not to be bitter, and most of the time I succeed, but it saddens me that people choose to believe that I am what the two most hated people in the country say I am. The horror of what took place is already history for everyone but the victims' families; nonetheless, I still have nightmares about Myra Hindley. Ian is no worse and no better than half of the men on my wing, but to my mind Myra is evil in its purest form. It might not seem that way to the people who are already beginning to defend her as a woman who simply did what her lover told her, or those who say she would have gone on to become a normal wife and mother had she not met him, but they don't know her as I did. If they had seen what I had seen, how would they cope with the truth of her depravity? She haunts me, and will possess my nights forever more.

The time is very close now and I'm scared.

I've said goodbye to my cellmates, leaving them my precious chess set, and I've shook hands with the screws, too. As I walk through the wing for the very last time, a tremendous din erupts, as all the inmates bang their cups against the doors in a communal goodbye. I shake my head: *fuck the lot of you, beasts.* I've got my bag in one hand and my guitar on its strap over my shoulder. The big door is only a few feet away.

Close to the exit, a gate screw approaches, clipboard in hand. One final formality:

'806713 Smith, sir.'

He nods and gives me a tight smile. 'Good lad. On your way, then.'

And the door swings open.

Well, Be-Bop-A-Fucking-Lula, this is it. A taxi is waiting – good old Dad – so it's *Lime Street Station, please,* and off we go. The prison walls speed by and the car seems to sprout wings, as it flies through the city.

'How was it, mate?' asks the taxi driver, and I grin at him: 'Oh, I'm not complaining.' And I'm not. After life in a tiny cell, the streets appear seriously overpopulated. The driver prattles away and I give him monosyllabic replies, thinking about the new house Dad's managed to get for us. I picture the boys and my heart aches with the need to be near them.

At the railway station, the pressure of my newfound freedom begins to overwhelm me. People rush about in vast numbers and the noise is ear-splitting. I buy cigarettes that feel the size of cigars after the ones I've been used to smoking in prison. I stand on the platform feeling lost. Then a smile sneaks onto my face: I can't believe how high girls' hemlines have risen since I've been inside. But I feel like a complete moron in my flares, flower-power shirt, leather jacket, tennis pumps and guitar – not forgetting my brand new 'I've just been released' haircut. Jimmy Dean I ain't.

On the train I sit tucked up in a corner, imagining my journey will take me to Manchester and no further. But this is the first leg of a very long trip indeed; my train will roll for many years, each roll of its wheels taking me closer to something quietly waiting for me, something I've never experienced before: a future.

I watch the fields slide by, clutching my guitar and box of prison letters. In my head I hear John Lennon singing, '*I used to be cruel to my woman/I beat her and kept her apart from the things that she loved/Man, I was mean, but I'm changing my scene and I'm doing the best that I can.*' His words always speak to me, and never more than right this minute, heading home on my first day out of prison.

Manchester's familiar and unmistakeable skyline looms into view. Before I know it, I'm stepping down onto the platform, sniffing the city air and glancing about. I spot Dad as I cross the bridge, but to my amusement he walks straight past me in his hurry to meet the train. I call him back; we hug and he cries buckets. At barely 50 years of age, he's suddenly become an old man. Cancer is getting the better of him, and his emotions are transparent. We sit together in the tearoom and he talks non-stop about the boys and our new home, where all the furniture he's been buying from auctions has already been delivered. As we climb into a taxi, he tells me that my future is in Moss Side and my stomach somersaults in despair, given what happened with Maureen there.

My fears become reality when we arrive in Acorn Street and stop outside a large, red Victorian house. I remember walking past these tall terraces as a boy with Mum. In those days, the Irish were starting to move out and black families were moving in. Moss Side is the home of the happy-boys – the Jamaicans – and a real inner-city, northern ghetto. I stand on the doorstep with my guitar and bag, conspicuous white trash just out of prison. Then I glance down and smile: there is a cast-iron coal-grid outside the front door, indicating that the house has a large cellar, big enough for a shebeen. I shake my head: how many times have I heard Otis Redding blasting out from beneath a grid like that?

Dad edges past me and unlocks the door, instantly releasing the heavy, musty smell of the building. I step in behind him, kicking away a pile of junk mail and stand in the hallway, facing a steep staircase. I know these houses so well that its layout is already familiar to me: the rooms at the back where the toilets are, the kitchen where the hot aroma of curried goat and beans might still linger, and the under-stairs door to the vast cellar. I haven't moved an inch, but already I'm back in time, picturing Joyce with her soft eyes and honeyed voice. Then Maureen, stood on the landing against the wall, letting some man she doesn't even know touch her everywhere . . .

'It's not much to look at, but we'll sort it,' I hear Dad say behind me. Then he opens the door to a room piled high with stinking memories of yesterday: our old belongings are there among the furniture he bought using vouchers from the Welfare Department, but everything has been in storage for months and it's begun to rot, the damp hanging thickly in the room. Nothing is worth keeping. I feel like sinking to my knees and weeping with disappointment. One thought saves me: the boys. I need to see the boys.

Happily, I don't have long to wait. That afternoon Dad and I pitch up on the doorstep of the Acorns and the boys rush into my arms, shouting. They're all in fine spirits and good health, apart from Paul, who is well but very clingy and quiet, refusing to leave my side for a second. David is garrulous, wanting to know if we've got beds in the new house so that they can all go 'home'. John is full of smiles. As for me, I'm over the bloody moon, knowing that we can soon be a proper family again. When I say goodbye to the boys, they seem to know this too, and our parting isn't as difficult as I'd feared.

Back at the house, Dad and I manage to salvage one bed and a handful of covers. He sleeps on that and I settle down on the floor. But his other purchases prove worthless and, apart from the bed, the only things we keep are a table and three old chairs. The rest is taken to the dump and binned, together with his ideas, dreams and promises. I dislike the house itself; every room takes me back to somewhere I don't want to be. Often I go down to the cellar and sit on a tea chest to be alone with my thoughts. The scuttling rats and the damp, seeping walls vanish as I lose myself in the past, where Otis sings soulfully and people dance as if it's the last night of their lives. I look at a dark corner and picture the man who gets everybody high, the rows of drinks, and the happy-boys . . . Then the music in my head fades and the memories go with it. I climb the stairs, determined to fight the tears that threaten to fall. I'm glad to be out of prison and close to getting my children back, but in the cellar I feel so lonely I could choke on it.

We could've made it, girl. We could've crawled out of this thing together and somehow survived . . .

Maureen. I need to find Maureen.

*

Summer 1971: I spend my days visiting the boys in the care home, carrying my guitar and a bag of peaches for them, wearing my leather jacket and feeling good as the sun blisters down on the city. Every evening I return to the house of empty dreams in Moss Side with a bag of greasy, half-cold fish and chips from the Pakistani chippy, then drink beer with Dad late into the night. I listen to his hopes for the future, while the cancer swells one side of his face. His hatred of all women comes to the fore; the roots of it lie in his youth, when someone called Rhoda hurt him badly. I don't have the details, just a rough sketch of an episode that scarred him for life: a marriage gone awry, a child, a death and something unspoken that twisted his insides for ever. Ever since then he's used women, and where they're concerned Dad is not a nice person. I shut out his bitterness, glad when he's ready for bed. I sleep next to him on the floor, wrapped in blankets and feeling like a kid again in the attic with Mum, her arms around me. I know it can never come back, that warm feeling of security, but it comforts me to remember it.

In the mornings I rise early, leaving Dad to slumber. After brewing strong black coffee, I sit in the kitchen to drink it, smoking one cigarette after another. Eventually I leave the house, stepping out onto a street that's flooded with cool sunshine. This is my ritual, day in, day out, and I can't let go yet because it hurts too much. I need to find her.

I want to speak to Maureen one last time. I need to be able to look into her eyes and to know what she really feels about me. I want everything and nothing: I want her to whisper softly in my ear, but I want her heart to be empty so that I can get on with my life; I want her to tell me to fuck off if that's how it is, to hear from her lips alone that she's met someone else and is happier with him than she was with me. Deep down inside I want to know that she is a different person now, finally alive and free of it all.

So I walk the same route every morning, Monday to Friday. These streets are as familiar to me as my own reflection; I grew up ten minutes from here. Dad told me that Maureen is working in a mail-order factory on Devonshire Street and to get there I have to walk right through my past, down Aked Street. Outside number 39, I stop for a while. Half of the street is boarded up; Asian families occupy the remainder. The entire street is awaiting demolition, part of the ongoing council scheme to rebuild the city.

But I don't see the graffiti and the boards and the litter. I see Nellie Barnes, a plump, slow-witted woman who was always kind to us kids, even though she had the mind of a child herself, entombed in the body of an adult. I see her brother Tony, a full-blown Teddy boy, in his three-quarter-length coat, bootlace tie, New Orleans waistcoat and blue suede shoes. Tony was pure style, a photograph from a record cover. I see John McGargill, whose Mum and Dad had the first television in the street, and I remember queuing up with the other kids to be allowed 15 minutes of watching American cowboys on their white horses; afterwards we ran out pretending we were on mustangs, using two-fingered guns that never ran out of bullets and shot the whole street up. I see the rag-and-bone man handing out his treasures: balloons for the toddlers, dolly-blues for the women to do their washing, new scrubbing boards and pans, and the precious donkey stone that smartened up every window sill and front doorstep.

I see them all and more, remembering the day when the council arrived and covered our beloved cobbles with tarmac. We hated the idea, but it turned out to be brilliant for us kids: we got roller skates and went berserk, travelling at a million miles an hour, breaking our bones but laughing at the thrill of it all. And when I pass my school at the end of the street I hear an echo of past laughter, girls squealing and the chaos of playtime. Opposite is the 'shop full of everything', including cigarettes in packets that could be split in order to be sold to

11 year olds in the required number – singles, doubles, fives . . .

I walk this way every morning, letting the memories wash over me, but I don't know if I'm looking for the end of the past or the beginning of the future. I need to let go, that much is certain. There's been too much of everything and now it's either got to stop or it's got to start.

I'm not angry with you any more, Maureen. The pain has gone. I was ill, but now I'm better. I just need to be myself again, to remember who I am, how I was when we were kids, before Angela, before Ian and Myra. I want to see you again, to make it real. I need to let go and I think you do too, but we both need to hear the other say it to make it happen. I have to find you at the factory, to watch your lips telling me that it's over, gone, finished, past and done with. We both need to face up to it in order to start living again, apart. If we can just talk and say what must be said . . . a final word, a hug, and a kiss, and then . . . let go.

Twice a day I stand opposite the factory, every Monday to Friday, for two weeks. In the morning I watch the workers going in, having a last natter and cigarette before starting their shifts, and in the evening I watch them leave. I study faces, hairstyles and manners of walking – anything that might lead to her – but there are only strangers. Every night I walk past my empty school, down Aked Street, where a few Asian women stand gabbling in a language I can't understand, and when I'm past number 39 I pick up speed, heading home to Moss Side.

After a fortnight, I tell Dad his information is wrong; Maureen isn't working there. To my surprise, he's genuinely disappointed for me. I stop staking out the factory and instead, one hot summer's day when I'm feeling moody and restless, decide to go back to Hattersley. I hate the idea of being there again, but I've got it into my head that if I can find Joyce, she might be able to tell me where Maureen is, or even Tom.

The bus journey is long and I'm impatient; even if Joyce has no news, at least I'll know. After endless stops for passengers and at traffic lights, we finally reach the estate and turn left into Underwood Road. I glare at a street sign as we trundle by: Wardle Brook Avenue. What the fuck was I thinking, to come back here?

We pass the tall block of flats: Underwood Court. I squint up at the third-floor balcony of number 18. There are curtains at the window, flowery and cheerful, but I pity the poor bastards who occupy the place. I wonder if Mr Page, the jobsworth caretaker, is still snooping about the building, and if the graffiti can still be seen, ghostly words of hatred under a slick of council paint.

The bus stops and I get off, walking fast, excited and nervous at the same time. I check that I'm tidy: shirt in, jeans neat, collar properly turned up on my leather coat. Maybe I can persuade Joyce to come for a walk with me – that would break the ice.

I pass Slater Way and the last home I shared with Maureen, screwed up and in free-fall. Head down, I walk faster until I'm standing opposite Joyce's house. I stare at the door and the windows, puzzled. It's all wrong: the door is shut as it never was when Joyce was there, and the house is silent, no kids running wild in and out, or Miss Jamaica singing to herself as she hangs out the washing. But I can't tear myself away because I'm so sure Joyce will appear at the kitchen window, shocked to see me, then breaking into a smile before coming up the path with her arms open.

It doesn't happen. The house is as still as a leaf, and Joyce and her kids have vanished into the past like so much else, leaving me in a no-man's-land of confusion and unhappiness.

I walk away.

It will be 30 years before I visit Hattersley again.

A few days later I go with Dad to visit his friend Big Martin in Hyde. This is where Dad stayed while I was in prison, after his explosive row with Maureen. He's told me about his weeks in Hyde, how good Martin was to him and how he spent hours on end talking to Martin's teenage daughter, Mary. He *hasn't* told me that he would collect the boys from the Acorns and bring them here so that he and Martin could spend hours at the pub while Mary – whom I haven't met – entertained the boys and took care of them.

It will be a while before I discover the firm bond that was formed between Big Martin's daughter and my sons. For now, I sit awkwardly in the house in Hyde, hunched up in my leather jacket and clutching my guitar. My future and salvation is mere minutes away, but I don't know that either, and sink further down into the settee, bored and wishing I was somewhere else. Hyde is the place that Ian and Myra put on the map in the very worst of ways; I know every inch of the small police station and I know, too, that its people don't like me. But Big Martin, a great handsome lump of an Irishman at 20 stone or more, never listens to gossip and makes up his own mind about things. He's a trusting, straightforward man. Like all Irish people, he's keen that we eat while we're under his roof and disappears into the kitchen to organise a few sandwiches and a pot of tea. His son, Little Martin, a plump boy of 11, wanders in and out, peering curiously at me, and my guitar.

I fidget on the settee, as Big Martin returns to his chair next to the open fire, talking to Dad. For a split-second, on the other side of the kitchen door, I'm aware of movement – a shape – and then it's gone. I'm alert now, trying to listen: two voices giggle and mumble, plates clatter on worktops, cupboards open and shut. Then, quite clearly, I hear a girl hiss, 'I don't care who he is, he's a greaser, get him out!'

I sit upright, straining to hear what else is being said. Suddenly Little Martin appears at the kitchen door, staring at me and rooted to the spot. Then he returns to the kitchen and the muffled voices begin again. I feel self-conscious, thinking: *greaser? What the hell happened to Jimmy Dean and white T-shirts, faded jeans and a steel comb in your back pocket? I'm not a bloody greaser. Who does that girl think she is?*

I get my answer immediately. She comes out of the kitchen, carrying a roasted pork sandwich and a huge mug of tea. She places both on the coffee table and when I thank her she looks directly at me, replying with a smile, 'Hello, I'm Mary.' Then she's gone, leaving me without a trace of a grin on my face and a pork sandwich for my trouble and charm. A bloody greaser!

* * *

Mary Flaherty was the eldest of two children born illegitimately to Martin Flaherty and Hazel Symcock. There was a 25-year age gap between the couple; Hazel was 26 and Martin 51. His birth name was Faherty, but he modified it to the more easily pronounceable Flaherty when he left Ireland during the Troubles of the 1920s. Coming from a small village in the west of Ireland, Martin departed for what were diplomatically termed 'political reasons' and would often refer to his friends there as the 'old boys' with a gentle, mischievous smile. After his relationship with Hazel broke down, Mary and her younger brother Martin divided their days between both parents, living with their mother during the week and their father at the weekends. Mary looked forward most to her time with her father and enjoyed looking after him.

'Mary ran Big Martin's household,' David recalls. 'That might seem unusual for a girl so young – though I didn't realise just how young she was at the time – but it was a situation that everyone felt comfortable with, so why not? Then Dad moved in for a while, and he would literally sit up all night, chatting to Mary about everything in his head. When he brought the boys over, she looked after them while he and Big Martin went out for a few pints. Paul, David and John adored her and being with Mary undoubtedly helped them during their months in the care home.'

'I didn't actually like kids,' Mary explains, with a laugh. 'But the three boys were so young and such fun. I loved being with them. They were always a bit quiet when they first arrived but that soon went. We were kids together, in a way. We'd rough and tumble and go outside with a ball or down to the park. I was always happy to see them.' She knew about their past, and who their father was, remembering that morning six years ago when, as a schoolgirl, she had stood watching David and Maureen arrive in Hyde at the committal proceedings: 'It was strange, to think back to that. I knew about the case, even though I was so young, because it changed our lives. Freedom on the streets just went. Kids were picked up from school by their parents instead of walking home alone and weren't allowed to play out until late any more. Even a visit to the park was out of the question unless a trusted adult accompanied you. And all the kids at school told gory stories about the case, as if it wasn't bad enough. But my dad was never one of those who suspected Dave of being "the third Moors Murderer". He was quite the opposite, in fact, and used to say, "If it hadn't been for David Smith calling the police that day, I might not have had you for much longer. Because there was no way the police were going to catch Brady and Hindley. If it hadn't been for Dave, you might not be here now, and neither might other children." That was very much his attitude.'

Within days of meeting Mary, David found himself thinking about her constantly.

* * *

From David Smith's memoir:
Mary busies herself about the house, folding, washing, straightening and tidying. I purposely catch her eye and smile when she comes into

the living room, but she doesn't respond, and I listen as she chides Big Martin about his drinking, then organises the weekend shopping list. I persevere with the inedible sandwich and leave an empty plate, thanking Mary and adding that it was very nice. She smiles at me at last.

When Dad and Big Martin are ready to leave for the pub, Mary sees the three of us to the door. I look back and she's standing there, watching us. I retrace my steps, telling Mary that I've forgotten my guitar but don't want to take it to the pub and would she look after it for me until I can pick it up? She looks at me curiously for a moment, then smiles and agrees. I hesitate: *see you around, then.*

The next few days are very strange. It comes in a rush with no warning: whether I'm walking down the street or having a wash, I find myself thinking about Mary. A girl with cropped, feathered hair, checked Ben Sherman shirt, leather-patched Wrangler's, high-laced Doc Martens and a big smile. She floats in and out of my mind minute by minute.

When the weekend arrives, I spend time making myself look presentable. *She's nice*, I keep thinking, *in fact, she's very nice. No, more than that: she's very, very, very nice.*

Oh, shut up, I tell myself impatiently.

Dad is in good form, looking forward to a trip away from Manchester with Big Martin. I feel even brighter than he does, but for a very different reason.

When we arrive in Hyde, Big Martin welcomes us warmly as always and we sit down to wait for him to ready himself. I notice my guitar standing in a corner, but there is no sign of Mary and, worse still, I daren't enquire. I ask for another mug of tea, playing for time. I get told with a grin to make it my bloody self. I do so gladly, making the world's slowest brew.

Road Runner is on the telly and I sit enthralled, tea in hand, pretending to find it hilarious. Dad and Big Martin must think I'm losing my mind. But then the door opens and finally she's there, a heavy bag of shopping in each hand. She gives Martin a hurried account of her expedition, a rundown of the costs and hands over his change. When she notices me at last, I'm rewarded with a big smile and a cheery hello before she heads into the kitchen with the groceries.

Casually, I tell Dad I'm going to finish watching the cartoon and then might take a walk before joining them at the pub. And just for a second Big Martin passes me one of his gentle but knowing looks, rooting me to the floor and wrapping me up in his trust.

The two men leave for the pub and I call to Mary, asking if she needs help putting the shopping away; I'm too nervous to just walk in. To my delight, she shouts back *yes, please,* and I'm in the kitchen faster than Road Runner himself. I worry immediately that I'm standing too close to her and move away, then do my best impression of knowing where everything should go.

Afterwards, we sit together on the settee, watching the rest of *Road Runner*, beep-bloody-be-beep, until Mary gets up to make tea. I'm longing to talk to her properly but can't find my voice. I listen to her without hearing what's being said and look at her too long for comfort while she prepares Big Martin's dinner and cleans up quickly but efficiently. I tell her that I don't much fancy the pub today and would she like to go for a walk? She nods and puts on a Crombie-style coat with a gold silk handkerchief in the breast pocket. In my leather jacket, I feel like a rock 'n' roll dinosaur.

We walk together without purpose and reach the bridge across the canal. Down the crumbling steps and along the bank we go, walking a couple of miles before settling down on the grass in the sunshine. The conversation between us is light and easy, even playful. We discuss the obvious thing – music – and she tells me she loves Tamla Motown, which I can't stand and counter with Eddie Cochran. She hasn't even heard of him, but we find mutual ground in Otis Redding. Then we talk about our dads; she knows mine very well and I remember Big Martin from years ago. We laugh often and I can't take my eyes away from her. After a couple of hours, I begin to feel as if I want to confide in her – as if I *have* to confide in her – and I tell Mary there are a few things I'd like her to know.

I explain that I'm married with three sons and not long out of prison. I tell her that something very bad happened a few years ago. Then I stumble over my words and she sits silently, waiting for me to finish. Instead I light up two cigarettes and hand one to her, then take a deep drag on mine, feeling my mood turn dark and sad despite the company and the warmth of the sun over the water.

I put my head down. Mary is like no one else I've ever met. There's something about her that makes me want to go to the deepest parts of myself and reveal everything. I wait nervously to learn if she has anything to say, but she doesn't seem to be thinking, just allowing the moment to pass between us. Quietly, she picks a few flowers and plaits a small daisy chain. Then she looks at me with a smile, passing me the daisy chain. I stare down at the small, silly ring of flowers in the palm of my hand and think, *I just want to be somebody. That's all. I just want to be somebody.*

Then she speaks, her voice knowing and confident, telling me of that time, years before, when as a child she stood with her friends in the school yard, watching as the car that took me and Maureen to the court hearings crawled through the press cordon and screaming public mob. She talks about the dark glasses we were wearing, the flashing camera bulbs, the chaos and the commotion. Then she explains how she became Dad's confidante while I was in prison, listening while he prattled into the early hours about his plans to rebuild my future and his, and that of the boys. She knows about the bad time already – the murders and their aftermath, what people have said and are still saying about me. She tells me how, when I was in prison, she would take Paul, David and John to the park and play with them for hours until Dad came to take them back to the care home.

I sit and listen, stunned. Then a piercing feeling sweeps over me; we're not strangers, Mary and me. We never have been.

Later, as we walk back along the canal bank in the afternoon sunlight, Mary gives me a playful nudge and tells me that I've lied to her. I stop instantly, panicked, and then smile: 'You mean pretending to forget about my guitar?'

'No,' she laughs. 'You lied about the sandwich. You said it was nice and I know it was horrible. The only thing I had in that day to give you was a slice off the Sunday roast and it had only been in the oven for 20 minutes.' Her smile widens. 'So you lied . . . but it was a nice lie.'

I look at her and laugh.

The walk along the canal becomes a habit. It gives us time together, a place to be where we can be alone to confide in each other – even a place to make a few meaningless daisy chains. Mary visits the boys with me in the Acorns; I carry my guitar and Mary always brings them a bag of succulent peaches. I couldn't be more comfortable with her, but I sometimes find it strange to be in her company because I'm not used to friendships. I don't trust them – they hurt. But Mary is different: she is security and trust, a warm feeling of comfort. I worry at night that I might lose or hurt her in some way. During the day it's easier to believe that things might go well for once, and that this hot, miraculous summer could last for ever. The songs we listen to become the soundtrack to our first weeks together: when I hear 'Maggie May' or 'Stand By Me', I think immediately of Mary, and when the Beatles sing 'Something', I find myself crying along inside, 'I don't know . . . I don't know . . .'

Just when things seem as if they can't get any better, I'm informed by the Welfare Department that the boys are allowed to come home. I'm given a grant to buy beds, blankets and clothes – we've already managed to stretch our limited finances to a telly, dining table and double bed for me – and the pleasure of shopping for it all makes me delirious. Everything is brand new and boxed up; no auction house rubbish, no hand-me-downs. The boys are coming home!

That night I catch the bus into Hyde, wanting to share my news with Mary. We've shared so much already, but this is special and I'm walking on air as I head down the street, past a gang of youngsters on the corner – skinheads mostly, in Wrangler's and Doc Martens, sitting astride Vespas. The girls in the gang tease and flirt, while the boys talk loudly. I smile at the young pretenders, realising that my trusty leather jacket and what it signifies is becoming a little faded.

At Mary Street, I turn, amused as always to think that only Mary could live in a street named after her. Georgina, a friend of Mary's, opens the door. I'm bursting with my news and walk quickly into the sitting room, which smells of freshly sprayed perfume. But Mary isn't there. I stand with a smile frozen to my face, staring at the other girl in front of me, while Georgina watches us both curiously.

'Hi, I didn't expect to see you today. Is everything all right?' The girl's voice reveals that she is, in fact, my Mary. But I've never seen her wearing make-up and a skirt before, and I'm lost for words. She looks stunning, nothing like the tomboy I've grown to care so deeply about; this is a young woman ready to hit the town and my elation vanishes in a pool of embarrassment. I feel a fool, an intruder, aware suddenly that Mary has a life of her own apart from me, with friends I've never met.

I need to be out of here. I need to be alone. I feel wrong and out of place, old and finished, grasping that the young pretenders on the corner are waiting for her. But with an understanding far beyond her years, Mary senses my humiliation and shock. As I apologise non-stop, with infinite tact she guides Georgina through to the kitchen and talks to her quietly. I hear her promising to catch up later, and when the two of them emerge, Georgina throws me an unfriendly, meaningful look.

A slow trickle of relief warms my veins. I'm still here and I'm with Mary – a very different-looking Mary, but it's still her. Doing the right thing, I offer, 'I should go and let you see your friends.'

She responds as I'd hoped: 'No, let's go for a walk. It doesn't matter about my friends – I can see them another time. Let's go.'

A smile breaks across my face.

Together we walk through Hyde and I tell her my news. She's overjoyed and suggests coming to the red house, as we call it, to help me set up the beds and get the place ready for the boys. They won't be home for a couple of weeks, but that's OK; we'll use the time to prepare everything. Deep in discussion, we end up on a bench at the bus station, where the last bus to Manchester is due to pull out in a few minutes. As we talk, I become increasingly aware of everything about this gorgeous new Mary; my friendship with the tomboy is fading fast and I'm already battling with something else, its heat and strength pulsating through me.

The bus revs its engine while the last of the passengers board. When the driver leans out of his window to shout 'Last bus!', I look silently at Mary, and when the bus growls away from the station, its headlights fading along the dark road, I edge a little closer to her.

At two o'clock in the morning, we're still sitting on the bench and Mary tells me I'll have to stay the night at her house; she'll sort it with Big Martin. I'm only too happy to go along with her suggestion. When we get home, I wait downstairs while she goes up to speak to her father in bed, feeling glad beyond reason to be there with her.

Mary fetches bedding, telling me with a grin that Big Martin's only concern is that I get a good breakfast in the morning. She makes up a bed on the settee. Now that she's removed her coat, I'm more conscious of her than ever and try not to stare at her short skirt. She doesn't seem to notice, teasing me that I'm too big to be tucked in and she'll see me in the morning – she's off to bed.

I don't sleep. Mary has built up the fire and I spend the hours waiting for dawn staring into the flames. In my head I hear 'Maggie May' on a perpetual loop. I look fondly but regretfully at my leather jacket over the back of a chair and think it's time we parted at last. The world is changing and I want to be part of it. But inside me is the sadness of recognising that my future is here, and that there is no more Maureen or Joyce, no more bad times, only Mary. I'm letting go. I'm about to be the somebody I always wanted to be: myself.

Mary is always in my thoughts over the next few days. I'm happy visiting the boys, bringing along the peaches from her. At the red house, I'm quiet, with this feeling growing inside me; Dad is suspicious but doesn't ask any questions. At night I can't sleep, beginning to worry about something new: how to protect my friendship with Mary from what's going on within me. I write to her, asking if she'll meet me at the bandstand in the park. I add that everything is fine, but I need to speak to her. I'm sure she sees me as nothing more than a close friend, which is what I want most – or what I tell myself while I'm busy thinking of her as much more than that.

When the day arrives for our meeting, she isn't there. I wait on the empty bandstand below the fancy ironwork of the round roof, not knowing what I'm going to say. There's been no hint of romance, nothing to show that our friendship might lead to something more. We haven't even held hands. I walk in circles, asking myself what the hell I'm doing, what I'm going to tell her . . . Then I spot her in the familiar Crombie, running towards me across the grass. She's flustered and breathless, that big smile on her face. The tomboy is back – she has a shawl over her head that frames her smile – but I no longer think of her as a tomboy at all.

My sleepless nights and worries disappear. I lie that there's no problem, I just wanted to see her. She tells me it's her birthday at the weekend and it would be nice if I could come down and have a drink with her. I nod and smile, puzzled about the shawl. When I tease her about it, she blushes and laughs, explaining that she was at the hairdresser's when she suddenly remembered our meeting. Her haircut is only half-finished and she slowly removes the shawl to reveal half of a new Mary. My mouth falls open in surprise: part of her head is shaved to the skin, while the other half – straight down the middle – is still in the familiar feathered cut.

We both begin to laugh and play a game: which Mary do we like best? She struts the bandstand, turning first this way and then that, singing, showing off both sides of herself. Every last worry I've ever had is blown away, taking me even closer to where I want to be – with her, always with her.

I dress up for Mary's birthday, binning my old leather jacket in favour of a new one, a shirt and tie, and polished shoes. When I arrive at her house, I'm glad to find it isn't a party as such, just me, Mary and her friend Christine, whom I like and call 'Pilchard' because she's so small. We head out to a pub that's just a short walk from Big Martin's house, with both girls dressed to the nines. Mary looks more striking than ever with her buzz-cut and perfect make-up. In the pub, I happily get the rounds in, then return to join the girls, listening with interest as they chat about things I've never paid attention to before – their friends, who's going out with who, what happened at the weekend. I'm on cloud nine about everything except their short skirts; when they visit the Ladies, I look at their legs and feel alarmed by the feelings I'd forgotten that are now flooding back through me in a torrent.

Afterwards we walk home together cheerfully. On the way, Mary suddenly puts her arm through mine, a small, innocent gesture that sends my nerve-ends skywards. Her grip is tight and she presses hard against my side. I know then that this is it: I really have to let go of the past if I want something to happen with Mary, something real.

The girls share Mary's bedroom and I've accidentally-on-purpose missed the last bus again. I'm offered the settee for the second time and am more than pleased. When Pilchard goes to bed, Mary arranges my blankets and I make small talk while secretly looking at every inch of her. She comes to kiss me on the cheek and say *see you in the morning*, and I hold back for a moment, then kiss her on the mouth, not hard but enough for it to linger. Her breath enters me, as I look at her and whisper, 'Happy birthday, Mary.'

She leaves the room silently and I sit alone, staring into the flames of the banked-up fire in a welter of confusion, hoping the door will open and Mary will be there, but it doesn't and she isn't.

I shut my eyes and try to sleep.

Mary doesn't come to me that night, but everything changes afterwards, moving in the right direction. Within days we're spending a lot of time kissing; Mary controls the temperature on our fledgling relationship and turns down the heat when necessary. I respect the situation, but with typical male difficulty, though Big Martin's empty chair in the evening serves as a useful reminder to behave myself.

The closeness between us grows. Mary joins me at the red house and together we clean the place from top to bottom, adding proper pots and pans to the kitchen, cleaning the windows and hanging decent curtains. Even the filthy bathroom is brought back to life and we light a big, open coal fire at teatime, eating fish and chips before its cosy glow. Then the biggest day so far arrives: the all-important beds are shuttled up the stairs to the rooms where the boys will sleep and Mary rips off the thin polythene so that we can start assembling them. We've bought three bedside tables too, and I leave it to Mary to arrange the final position of everything.

One afternoon I visit a shop to have a duplicate front-door key cut. Dad has one key, I have another and I want Mary to have the third. When I hold it out to her, telling her that if she ever wants to see me she must use the key because it belongs to her, she answers that she doesn't need it. I persist, picking my words carefully, repeating, *no, please listen, use the key if you really want to see me*. Then she understands and accepts the key, tucking it away in her pocket.

The only blot on the landscape is Dad. He's started to play mind games again: while Mary is at the red house, he's considerate and complimentary towards her, but when she's gone he talks incessantly about Maureen and how I should find her for the boys' sake, so that we can be a family again. He conveniently forgets the hours he spent with Mary while I was in prison, blubbing on her shoulder, the care she gave his grandsons while he was at the pub, and – most infuriating of all – he forgets how much he and Maureen despised each other.

The day before the boys are due home, Mary tells me she has a job interview at Henrique's sewing-machine factory. We're both hopeful that she'll get it and in high spirits as we walk to the telephone box to call for a taxi into Hyde. We talk nineteen-to-the-dozen while we wait; Mary quietly explains that she intends to stay away for a while to allow me and the boys to settle down together and, although I know it's the wise thing to do, I can't help feeling dismayed at the thought of not seeing her. She adds that I need to be very patient in the days to come because it's been a long and disruptive time for the boys as well. Then she writes down the number of the phone box so that we can speak to each other in a few days.

The taxi arrives too soon. I wish her good luck with the job interview and say goodbye with a long, hard kiss. She gives me a gentle nudge, telling me to return to the house and check the boys' bedroom. As soon as the taxi rumbles away, I head home and dive upstairs. Standing in the doorway of the bedroom, I can see it immediately: sitting on one of the bedside tables is a basket of fresh peaches with a propped-up card that simply reads: 'Love from Mary.'

I've told the Welfare Officers that I'd like to collect the boys and bring them home from the Acorns myself, and I've told Dad the same thing. He grumbles, but it washes over me; this day belongs to no one but my sons and me.

I walk slowly through the Acorns' private grounds, squinting up at the sunlight filtering through the thick trees. My heart soars: this is the beginning of everything. Inside the building, young children with neatly pressed clothes and hopeful faces run up to me asking, 'Are you my daddy?' I pause for breath; although I'm used to the question, having heard it every time I've visited the Acorns, it still hurts to hear it, realising that every child's situation is heart-breaking. The older children sit sullenly at tables or slouch in chairs, their eyes hard and cold.

A chatty member of staff shows me through to where Paul, David and John are waiting. Nurse Josephine is with them. It's her day off, but she's grown so close to the boys that I'm not surprised to find her here, dressed in 'civilian' clothes, with her long hair loose, looking nothing like the girl in the blue uniform whom I've met so often on my visits to the home. The boys are the picture of health and happiness, clean and tidy in new shoes, new coats and each topped off with a fine new haircut. I greet them all together with a mammoth hug, and Nurse Josephine's eyes begin to water unprofessionally. She hands me three bags of jumpers, socks and underwear that she's bought for the boys from her own wages. I take them gratefully, my own eyes welling. As we walk to the door, David slips his hand into hers; he was always her favourite. Paul and John leap up and down, shouting excitedly in unison, 'Have you got our beds, Dad, have you got our beds?'

There are no forms for me to sign, but members of staff and young residents delay our departure, gathering in the hallway to wish us good luck and goodbye. A taxi waits by the main entrance; I ordered one to take us back to the red house and, as we climb in, everyone but Nurse Josephine disappears indoors. She stands on the steps, tears streaming down her kind young face, putting up two thumbs. We do the same to her, smiling.

Then the taxi pulls away and the home is gone for ever.

Chapter 21

'Mother, you had me, but I never had you
I wanted you, you didn't want me
So I, I just got to tell you
Goodbye, goodbye.
Father, you left me, but I never left you. Mama don't go.
Daddy, come home . . .'

– 'Mother', John Lennon

From David Smith's memoir:

My first week alone with the boys and Dad at home is a steep learning curve. At first I try to replicate the orderly routine of the Acorns, and Nurse Josephine hovers in my head as an example of calm and gentle discipline. I do my best to keep the house spotless, and find that part relatively easy; I'm very domesticated from those years of living in Gorton with Dad and being on my own so often. But being a stay-at-home father is a different ball game altogether.

No matter how early I rouse myself from bed, I'm forever chasing jobs that need to be done. Somehow I manage to clean the house, cook regular meals and ensure that the boys are fine, but I'm useless at remembering to put the bins out and always arrive at the laundry five minutes after it's closed. I don't bother putting on the Image any more in the morning – there's no time for vanities. I pull on whatever is to hand, usually yesterday's jumper, jeans and a pair of odd socks. My hair sticks up in weird peaks because I forget to run a comb through it. If I caught sight of myself in the window of Sivori's now, I wouldn't know whether to laugh or cry.

My biggest irritant by far is Dad. I had no idea that he was such a slob. Although there are ashtrays in the house, he never uses one, preferring instead to sit in his chair flick-flick-flicking the ash onto the floor. His half-empty cup of cold tea and crumb-crusted plate are left unwashed next to the sink and he never makes his bed. Collecting his clothes from the bedroom floor is a chore I could do without and as for his constant farting and rowdy belching . . . I'm not even sure he realises he's doing it half the time. All I know is that his filthy habits are magnified by the fact that I'm the one who has to deal with the mess and stink he leaves behind.

Apart from Dad's unsavoury behaviour, I'm a happy, if very tired, man. I miss Mary, but we talk on the phone every night after she arrives home from work; she got the job at Henrique's. I make an effort to maintain the standards she sets in her own home and think I'm succeeding pretty well, especially when I sit down to a meal I've cooked myself with the boys. That's our special time; I make sure there's plenty of food left for Dad when he comes in later, but I revel in having the boys to myself. The meals become like markers as the week progresses, and before I know it the weekend is here and Mary and I are making arrangements for me to visit her in Hyde with the boys. She suggests a picnic and I know at once where we should go: my old cave, the Tom Sawyer hideaway in Alderley Edge. I haven't been there since I was a kid and am excited about going back with my own children and Mary.

I rise early on Saturday morning and head straight out to the shops, returning with a cooked chicken, breadsticks, cheese, biscuits and the two biggest watermelons I can find. After I've packed everything away I indulge myself in a long bath, then shave and dress. I feel the business again, from head to toe. I get the boys ready and the feeling of going on an adventure steals over us all. They're looking forward to seeing Mary again, too.

In the room next door I can hear Dad blowing off as he gets up. He's maddened that I'm taking the boys out with Mary, not because he wants to be with us – his day is already plotted and involves beer and gambling, as usual – but because he's still banging on about a reconciliation with Maureen. I ignore him and shuffle the boys downstairs and out onto the sun-flecked street, so happy I could fly.

Being with Mary and the boys is a dream come true. The train journey passes quickly; I sit as close to Mary as I can, holding her hand and frequently kissing her. The boys are wide-eyed at the scenery rushing by and when it's time to disembark we pile out in a noisy, laughing bundle.

The cave is just as I remember it, and the field and the trees lusher than memory. I sit at peace with Mary, eating chicken and melon and watching the boys scamper about. The past feels unreal now. I lean in for another kiss from Mary and the sun is hot on my back. We discuss her new job; she loves it, partly because it's new to her. I look at her in interest, asking if she has done any machine work before, and her answer takes my breath away.

'No,' she tells me evenly. 'I was a schoolgirl.'

I stare at her. It's never occurred to me to ask before how old Mary is – not even on her birthday. But now I do and her reply takes the wind from my sails for a second time.

'That night we celebrated my birthday with Christine down the pub – that was my 15th birthday.' She speaks so matter-of-factly, and our history together is already so ingrained and precious, that I feel my shock beginning to subside. I remember the knowing look in Big Martin's eyes and his empty chair. There are nine years between us, but the gap will soon narrow; it feels smaller with every second that passes. I kiss her gently but with more feeling than ever. I don't see the girl or the tomboy. I just see Mary, my Mary.

Things change between us after our picnic with the boys. I don't think about the age difference any more than I did before I became aware of it. We're together and no one is going to come between us. But the need to be with each other is too strong to ignore. Mary tells Big Martin exactly how things are and he puts his trust in us. I don't do the same with Dad – there's no point and, as far as I'm concerned, it's nothing to do with him anyway. But I am glad to know that Mary's father believes in me.

Mary arrives at the red house every day after work, always knocking first and bringing gifts of chocolate or peaches. The boys soon learn to wait for her knock, yelling and racing down the hallway to be the first to let her in. We eat together as a family – taking it in turns to cook dinner. Bedtime then becomes fun-time: I stand and watch with a big grin as Mary baths the boys ('Scrub, scrub, scrub!') and then dries them ('Rub, rub, rub!'). Occasionally I'm downstairs when this part of our routine takes place, but the laughter, shrieks and sound of splashing always makes me smile. The boys are good at going to bed afterwards, once the 'goodnights' and 'God blesses' are over. Then it's my time alone with Mary, although we've made it a never-to-be-broken rule that she must return to Hyde by eleven o'clock each night. We spend the last hours on the settee, talking, kissing or just holding each other. The television flickers in the corner, but we never watch it. The flames and warmth of the coal fire are the only accompaniment we need.

The weeks go by peacefully, apart from Dad's vicious outbursts about Mary. He refers to her as 'that bitch' or 'that slut' and is forever throwing her age in my face whenever he's been drinking, which is almost every night. He rants that she will never run 'his' family and that Maureen is the only one entitled to 'his' grandchildren. When he spits in my face, I struggle to remind myself that he is dying. I drag myself off to bed with fists clenched, sitting on the edge of the mattress with my head in my hands, knowing there are things crawling around inside him far worse than the cancer he carries.

Wednesday, 16 October 1972. The boys are getting ready for school and I am, as usual, behind with my jobs. I put out a breakfast of fish fingers and baked beans as the boys arrive at the table, miraculously washed and neatly dressed.

There is a sound in the hallway. The boys leap up, shouting, 'Mary! It's Mary!'

I turn in surprise. Mary is standing at the kitchen door, smiling: 'Hi, I don't fancy work today . . .'

I'm flustered but delighted to see her. 'I didn't hear you knock,' I say. 'Did I leave the door open?'

She shakes her head slowly. 'No. I used my key. Remember? You asked me to use the key if I wanted to see you. So here I am.'

I stare at her for a moment. The boys begin making a fuss of her, insisting that they don't want to go to school now. As we get them into their coats, Mary promises that she'll still be there when they get home.

The two of us walk back from school in uncharacteristic silence. Nervously, I ask her if she's sure about this. Yes, she tells me calmly, she is very sure. And when we reach the red house, we go upstairs.

In the afternoon, the boys dash through the school gates and into my arms and Mary's. When they are in bed that night, we curl up together again in front of the crackling fire. I feel complete as I've never done. I am somebody at last; I am the 'me' I always wanted to be. The future looks as bright as a yellow submarine.

Mary explains our situation fully to her father, telling him that she wants to spend the weekends at the red house with the boys and me. Big Martin is as understanding as a parent who cares only about his child's happiness can be and assures her that it's fine with him. An unusual routine begins: after work every Friday Mary arrives to stay with us, and at the same time Dad moves out to spend the weekend with Big Martin, then on Monday Mary goes back to Hyde and Dad returns to the red house. Despite Dad's incessant grumbling, it works.

It's around this time that a letter arrives from the council, telling us that our home has been earmarked for demolition. *Typical*, I think, *just when we've got the old girl back on her feet.* But it turns out to be a good thing: the house we're allocated in Lloyd Street South, another area of Moss Side, is far better and even has its own gardens, front and back. I honestly believe that my bright future just got brighter.

I must be the original fool on the hill.

One day we have a visit from a Welfare Officer. The news she brings shakes us to the core: Nellie Hindley, Maureen and Myra's mother, has asked to see her grandsons. Dad can't hide his delight and crows about it. At last: contact.

I have no problem in allowing Nellie to visit the boys. She doesn't have to answer to me or anyone else for what her elder daughter – or her younger daughter – has done. But I sink into a bleak mood that can't be shifted, aware that I still have a wife out there somewhere. I'm not yet divorced, no matter how free I've felt with Mary these past few months. What troubles me most of all is the knowledge that if Nellie turns up, Maureen won't be far behind.

Fortunately, it's a long time before Nellie Hindley pitches up on our doorstep. Before then, one afternoon I board the 125 bus from Manchester to Mottram, a small village in Cheshire. My frame of mind is darker than it has been since my release from prison and my soul is numb. I press my forehead against the window until it hurts.

The bus travels through the suburbs of my childhood. I look out at the Hyde Road Hotel, Dad's favourite watering hole, where I spent many boyhood hours eating crisps and drinking Tizer while he got pissed with his mates. We rattle through Gorton, and to my right is Belle Vue, where Dad used to take me every weekend to feed buns to the elephants and ponder the demented loneliness of the tigon. Then further, over Reddish Bridge and the junction that took us to Aunt

Dorothy's for triangle sandwiches and a pilchard salad.

Every fibre in my body stiffens as the bus stops at the New Inn opposite Wardle Brook Avenue. I turn my head away from the view and the chattering passengers who don't know me and never did.

In Mottram, I climb down and walk towards the brightly lit stone-built house that's home to the second-most important woman from my childhood. A hundred yards away, the village pub breathes noise and laughter, but my hand trembles as I light a cigarette, drawing in the smoke so deeply that it burns my throat. Then I cross the street and knock on the door.

The Duchess herself opens it. She stands in its frame, small and unsmiling, her eyes dark behind the thick-rimmed spectacles she wears. She knows me well enough to understand that something momentous has brought me to her door and guides me in with scarcely a word.

In the sitting room, Uncle Bert rises from his chair, greeting me with a firm handshake. I take the seat he gestures towards, wondering how we all ended up in a world so different from the one we knew less than twenty years ago. No more the cobbles and clatter of the pony-trap and the booming holler of the rag-and-bone man, no more the Saturday night tin baths and the hiss of the gas-mantles lighting the scullery with an eerie glow. Their home retains something of the past, though: oak beams congested with bright horse-brasses, lushly patterned wall-to-wall carpets and a fire burning in the grate, filling the room with its snug heat.

Uncle Bert pads through to the kitchen for beer. I sit opposite the Duchess, who looks down at the carpet, hands clasped together on her knees. Uncle Bert returns, placing a cold tin of beer on the wooden coffee table. He has an affectionate habit of always calling me 'lad', and when he asks, 'What's the trouble, lad?' it's in a soft, leading voice. I can't think of what to say; the blackness in the pit of my stomach is spreading through every limb and vein. I fight back tears, fumbling for another cigarette. As I lift it to my lips, I notice that my fingers are nicotine-stained, just like Dad's, and the realisation wraps a cold, damp cloak about my shoulders. Uncle Bert pushes an ashtray across the table and I drop my cigarette into it.

Suddenly, words pour out of me.

Dad is nearing the end. His cancer is rampant and I can't fight or feel it, but I can see and smell its destructiveness. It has him beat, finished, a mere shell, and yet it still won't leave him alone and let him go. The doctor can't increase his medication, but this thing is eating him alive from the inside. He doesn't use the toilet any more because there is nothing to get rid of – the cancer has taken every last drop of his strength and feeds on the remains.

Uncle Bert becomes tearful. He slips into the platitudes of our Catholicism, talking about sleeping for ever and going to a better place. Then he declares, in a rickety pitch, 'All this pain is in God's hands now.' Religion might help Uncle Bert, but there's nothing in it for me. I've come here looking for something stronger than faith.

We sit for a long time, almost until the last bus is ready to depart the village for Manchester. Uncle Bert leaves the room to dry his eyes and fetch another tin of beer.

This is my last chance.

I look at the Duchess. Time is slipping away as I shout to her silently from inside my head: *you know I love you, I've always trusted you, so please, tell me what I have to do.*

At last she raises her head, proud as always, and our eyes meet. The silence between us is thunderous and neither she nor I blink in the ongoing moment. I hear a breath leave my body; it takes for ever to fade away. Staring at her, I'm aware of Uncle Bert moving about the room, setting down a second unopened tin in front of me, as I force my thoughts into her head. *Tell me. Just tell me what I have to do. Your judgement is the one constant in my life. If you say it, I will do it.*

Something shifts within the grate and sparks flit out from the fire. I get to my feet, shaking hands with Uncle Bert. The Duchess sees me to the door with a quick, hard hug. She steps away from me, her eyes pained but unclouded: 'Be a good boy and safe home.'

On the bus I feel strangely at peace. I dare to hope that Dad might have died in his sleep while I've been away, robbing the cancer of its continual assault. I smoke cigarette after cigarette and let myself think everything is going to be all right.

I walk quickly home from the bus stop, a smile curling my mouth as I spot Mary standing on the doorstep. The smile freezes as I near her; something is badly wrong. I can hear the boys playing noisily within, but when Mary speaks any sense of normality shatters like glass.

'It's your dad. He's on the floor. He fell out of bed and I can't get him up. I've tried and tried, but I can't do it.'

The stairs disappear under my feet. I push Dad's bedroom door open and instantly feel that cold, damp cloak settle on my shoulders again.

He's lying on the floor in his pyjamas, skeletal body curled and twisted as if consumed by fire, legs pulled up beneath him. Weak bleats of pain issue from his mouth. I stand there, feeling a rare and terrible anger at the disease that has annihilated him. God is very, very far from this room. Nothing remains but silence and suffering on the floor.

Gently, I pick him up. He weighs nothing to me; every bone is like a knife with no flesh to protect it. I place him upright in bed, supported by the many pillows he needs, and sit down on the mattress beside him. Mary stands in the doorway. Somewhere in the house the children have begun a new game.

I look at Dad and touch his forehead; pearls of cold sweat stick to my palm. I light a cigarette and hold it to his lips, watching his feeble efforts to smoke. Nothing happens; he just sucks the air around the cigarette. I look at his eyes – watery, open wide and bulging fear. When I pass my hand slowly in front of his face, he can't follow it. The silence is shutting in on us both. Dimly, I'm aware of Mary sobbing at the door.

His time must be very close now. Quietly, I ask, 'Do you know who I am? Tell me you do. Tell me you know me.' I hold his hand in case he wants to squeeze it, but he stares through me, utterly vacant.

I stand up and ask Mary to see to the boys' bath. She asks if I am all right. I smile and reply that I'm fine. When she goes out of the room, I head down to the kitchen and take the bottle of pills from the cupboard: it's almost full. I tip the contents out and crush them into a fine powder, then inhale deeply on a cigarette while I wait for the pan of milk to boil on the cooker. I can hear the boys being chased in and out of the bathroom by Mary, their joyful screams echoing about the house. I pour the milk carefully into a large glass and the powder dissolves.

At the bathroom door, I pause to listen to the three boys splashing like dizzy fish in the tub. It gives me strength as I enter the bedroom, shutting the door softly behind me. I sit next to Dad on the bed and test the milk on the back of my hand, just as if it's come from a baby's bottle.

I hold the glass to his mouth. He gulps and slurps at it with no control, but eventually it's empty and I ease him back in the bed, rearranging the pillows until I'm certain he's as comfortable as he can be. His watery eyes stare up at the ceiling. I kiss his forehead and taste the saltiness of the sweat that covers every wasted inch of his body.

The darkness has somehow gone from the room, leaving only the shouts and laughter of his grandchildren playing in the bath. These are the sounds I hope he will take with him.

I cross the floor and stand at the door for a few, final seconds, my hand on the switch. I leave the light on; I don't want him to be alone in the dark.

Dad is 52 years old.

I stand with Mary in the telephone box, waiting for the Duchess to answer my call. The ringing tone seems to go on for ever, then suddenly she's there. I tell her what I've done and she expels a long breath.

'Phone the doctor,' she instructs me. 'Wait for him at the house.' After a pause she adds, 'These things must be done properly.' I feel better for hearing her voice.

The doctor arrives promptly. I know him well; he's been treating Dad since he contracted cancer. I take him upstairs and together we stand by the bed.

Dad lies against the pillows, ashen. His mouth is locked wide open in a soundless scream. Grey milk swims between the slits of his eyes. The doctor examines him quickly and, to my shock, declares that he is still breathing. When I tell him what happened, his shoulders droop.

Giving me the sort of look that speaks volumes, he asks in a deliberate voice, 'David, you don't have to say anything, but if you repeat what you've just told me then I must listen and something will have to be done. Do you understand?'

I nod and tell him again; it's a secret I could never keep. Those childhood lessons in morality stalk the room and I'm ready to meet them. The doctor sighs heavily. He explains that Dad is very close to death and we need to call for an ambulance, even though he's without pain. Then the police must be informed.

Gripping my arm, he leads me out of the room and shuts the door. 'I want you to know that I do understand these things, David.' He nods slowly, as if answering some private question of his own. 'No matter what, your father will be at peace soon.'

When the ambulance arrives, I climb into it holding Mary's hand. Together we watch as the medics fit Dad with a mask, feeding him oxygen in a necessary bid to prolong his life. The drive to the hospital is quick, and while Dad is examined another doctor approaches me to ask what tablets Dad has taken.

'He hasn't taken any tablets,' I reply. 'I gave them to him.'

His eyes fix on mine. 'How many?'

'The full bottle.'

He moves away. Dad is transferred to a cubicle, where the curtains are drawn swiftly around his bed. A few minutes later the doctor reappears and explains that nothing will be done; Dad's life will soon be over. A priest enters the cubicle and I get to my feet; I don't want to hear the death rattle. We leave quietly, walking the few miles back to the house. From the telephone box I use as if it's my own, I call the hospital. They tell me that Dad has died, and when I replace the receiver I pick it straight up again to give the Duchess the news.

Then the police arrive.

Mr Griffiths is a copper in the Joe Mounsey mould. I like him instantly; a great boulder of a bloke, he has a habit of twanging his braces. He looks at me not unkindly and asks: 'A death has been reported. Is there anything you'd like to tell me?'

I explain what I've done, while he listens intently, twitching his braces. A minute of respectful silence passes before he states: 'David, on account of what you've told me, I'm arresting you on suspicion of murder.'

A second officer approaches me with handcuffs, but Mr Griffiths stops him: 'It's all right, no need for that.' Then he turns to me again: 'I've already spoken to the doctor and he's put me fully in the picture.' He nods towards Mary. 'Take a few minutes for yourself.'

I hold Mary tight and we speak urgently but quietly. The boys are in bed. One last hug and then I go outside, where Mr Griffiths is waiting for me on the doorstep.

'Have you any money?' he asks.

I shake my head.

'Cigarettes?'

I shake my head again.

'Does the wife smoke?'

I nod, not troubling to tell him that Mary and I aren't married.

'Come on, then.'

He walks me past the police car and across the road into the newsagent's. Beneath the fluorescent strip lights, he picks out two packs of twenty cigarettes and two boxes of Swan Vestas, handing me half the purchase: 'Here, you'll be needing these. I smoke a pipe myself.'

I hide a bitter smile. *Yeah*, I think, *don't you all*. Then I sit in the car, watching Mr Griffiths walk up to the house where Mary is standing huge-eyed at the door. He gives her the cigarettes and matches, then retraces his steps and squeezes his large frame into the car, sitting next to me.

'Well, David, I think you've been in something of this kind of situation before.' He pauses and purses his lips before adding gently, 'But maybe this time not as bad.'

His kindness isn't wasted on me.

* * *

Jack Smith died several hours after David gave him the fatal glass of milk into which he had ground 20 sodium amytal tablets. At the police station, Griffiths handled the case as a mercy killing, despite the official charge, having spoken at length to the family doctor. He treated David – who was calm but in shock – with compassion, and spoke to him at length that evening, going through his statement in detail before David put his signature to it. Afterwards, Griffiths told him, 'I'm going to leave you for a while now to give you chance to compose yourself. I'll send a cup of tea in and you've got your cigarettes, so I'll see you in ten minutes.' David knew what was coming next and realised he was being given a rare opportunity to prepare himself. He drank the tea that was brought in and smoked a couple of cigarettes.

When Griffiths returned to the interview room, he asked David to stand – usual police procedure – and charged him with the murder of his father. David shook his head when asked if there was anything he wished to say in his defence. Griffiths indicated that he should sit down again, explaining, 'I've told them that you're to be allowed to keep your cigarettes and matches. But we've got to put you in a cell and you'll be brought up before the magistrates tomorrow . . .'

David spent the night at the police station. In the morning, before he was led into court, Griffiths took him to one side and said, 'I've had a word with your solicitor. We're not opposing bail. All right?' Bail was granted and David was allowed to return home. But several days later, when he was brought before magistrates again under the court system, that bail was withdrawn.

'It was a horrible moment,' he recalls now. 'They were different magistrates, but I still don't know why they decided to remand me in custody. Mr Griffiths was visibly shocked and my solicitors were disgusted. Mary was in court, of course, to support me, and she was distraught as I was led away.' He pauses. 'My trial date was set for a few months ahead and the place they sent me to await it was Risley Remand Centre near Warrington. Brady and Hindley were held there in the months before the Moors trial.'

The past had come back to haunt him, and there were other ghosts to be confronted too.

Immediately after David's arrest, Mary and the boys moved in with her father in Hyde. The boys' case worker, Mrs Delaney, appeared one day with the news that Maureen had requested access to her children.

'I was already worrying,' Mary remembers, 'because I was still only 15 at the time and didn't want anyone else to know about me and David. So when Mrs Delaney turned up, I panicked a bit. But then something terrible happened: the boys were handed back to Maureen. David was on bail then and there was nothing we could do. But the whole thing was resolved very quickly because Maureen decided she didn't want the boys after all. Less than a week after demanding them back, she abandoned them on the steps of Hyde Town Hall. They brought the boys home to us and we thought that was an end to it, but then David had his bail taken from him and Maureen insisted on having the boys back again.'

Mary shakes her head slowly, struggling with the memory: 'The boys didn't want to go. Paul was very upset. He clung to my neck and Mrs Delaney had to physically pull him away. He was screaming for me. She got angry, telling me off for not handing them over properly. But I was deeply upset, too. Then exactly the same thing happened again: Maureen decided she couldn't cope. Mrs Delaney turned up at my door and said flatly, "She doesn't want them." So, thankfully, they brought them back to me.'

Asked for her opinion about Maureen's conduct towards the children, Mary lifts her shoulders in a gesture of helplessness. 'Who knows? Only Maureen could answer that. I always felt it wasn't so much that she wanted the boys for herself, more that she didn't want *me* to have them. I never felt that she wanted to be a mother to them. But that's pure surmise on my part. I didn't have any contact with her at that time. I was just so happy when Mrs Delaney arrived with the boys that second time.'

In Risley ('Grisley Risley', to its inmates), David struggled to cope with being away from Mary and the children. He describes it as 'a black pit of a place' and declares: 'Prison was preferable to Risley. We were locked up there for 23 hours a day, with absolutely nothing to do. There were no association areas, and if you were lucky you'd have your cell unlocked in the morning and be instructed to mop the corridor. That was a good day in Risley. The only advantage it had over prison was that we were allowed unlimited tobacco because we hadn't yet been convicted. But it was hugely depressing.'

David's solicitors successfully appealed against the withdrawal of bail. 'My cell door was opened at around four o'clock on a Monday afternoon and I was told to report to reception because I was going home,' he recalls. 'The relief . . . I had a hasty shower, got my own clothes back and was out of that place faster than a speeding bullet.'

His trial was set for early November 1972. 'Did I think it was going to be all right?' he ponders. 'Yes, I suppose I did. Mary and I had a meeting with my barrister, and he instilled a bit of optimism in us. His chambers were very *Rumpole of the Bailey* – everywhere you looked, there were books. Leather-bound mostly, stacked askew on every surface, Bible-thick books with gold lettering on the spines. My barrister and a few members of his team spoke to us. He had all the prosecution papers for me to read – that never happened at the Moors trial – and took me carefully through the entire process, going over the questions that were likely to be asked. He schooled me in what to say and how to say it. That bolstered my confidence. He told me that although what I'd done wasn't murder, there was no leeway in the law to allow for that. Therefore, murder had to be the charge. Then he told me, "We're going to plead guilty." I was appalled, but he said, "No, we're going to plead guilty to manslaughter." So I knew what to expect.'

He laughs suddenly. 'I also had to be examined by a psychiatrist again. Mary went with me. The two of us were wearing patched jeans. This very well-to-do and earnest psychiatrist in his herringbone suit was enthralled by our appearance. It was all he seemed interested in, and for some reason it worked in our favour.'

David's trial at Manchester Crown Court was given extensive press coverage. Predictably, every newspaper referred back to the Moors trial of 1966. Inside the court, David focused on the charge he faced and the life sentence he would have to serve if found guilty. In the public gallery, Mary – now pregnant – sat with the Duchess and Uncle Bert.

'I was terrified,' David admits. 'My barrister told the court that we were entering a plea of guilty to manslaughter, which gave the jury the satisfaction of knowing that guilt had been acknowledged somewhere down the line. But the judge seemed to me to be biased against me because of the Moors case. That was the impression I got when he gave his address to the jury and my barrister suspected the same thing. When all the evidence had been heard and the jury went out to consider their verdict, I sat in the corridor, wondering which way my life was going again. Any confidence I felt before evaporated while I was sitting on that bench, staring down at the floor.'

The jury found him not guilty.

'I nearly collapsed with relief,' David remembers. 'Then I heard this furious rustling behind me, as all the journalists began scribbling in their notebooks. I turned and caught Mary's eye – she looked ready to faint. But after the judge had thanked the members of the jury he addressed me: "I accept your admission of manslaughter. There will be no further trial – I shall sentence you today." I stood there, frantically doing calculations in my head. What did you get for manslaughter? Seven years? Five? My barrister hadn't told me that. Then the judge declared, "I sentence you to two days' imprisonment, but take into account the time you served on remand. You are free to go." I was astounded – I just couldn't believe it. Then I turned round again and saw Mary making her way through the crowd to me. It was over.'

On 8 November 1972, under the heading, 'Moors Case Witness Cleared', *The Times* reported:

David Smith . . . was acquitted by a jury at Manchester

Crown Court yesterday of the murder of his father. He pleaded guilty to the manslaughter of Mr John James Smith, who was suffering from incurable cancer . . . Mr Justice Kilner Brown heard Mr Smith's counsel describe his appearance at the trial eight years ago as a searing and blistering experience, which had had a profound effect on him. He sentenced Mr Smith to two days' imprisonment, which meant his immediate release.

The *Daily Telegraph* added another aspect:

As he left the court after the case, Smith kissed the girl with whom he is now living . . . and who is expecting his child . . . He said that he was now hoping to divorce his wife, Maureen. The couple have been living apart for some time.

In the corridor outside the court, journalists and photographers were gathered in vast numbers. There was a scramble as David and Mary emerged with their arms around each other.

'All I could hear were the flashbulbs going off and stupid questions,' David recalls. 'One reporter shouted, "Did you mean to do it, David?" We were just glad to get out of the building. The press pursued us across the square, but we lost them eventually. Ironically, though, I went straight from court to give an interview – Uncle Bert had set up a newspaper deal again, knowing that the headlines would cause more trouble for us. But once that was done, I felt as if the whole horrible thing was behind us. Mary and I were looking forward to our baby being born.'

He takes a deep breath. 'But then the Hindleys came back into our lives.'

VI
Stand By Me
1975–2011

Chapter 22

'Is your heart filled with pain,
Shall I come back again?
Tell me dear, are you lonesome tonight?'
          – 'Are You Lonesome Tonight?', Elvis Presley

On 6 April 1973, Mary gave birth to a daughter, whom she and David named Jody. That same month Maureen divorced David on uncontested grounds of 'unreasonable conduct'. At the custody hearing, she was granted access to their three children.

'She came one Saturday with Nellie,' Mary remembers. 'I never really got to know her but found her . . . well, a bit gruff. Nellie was very pleasant, but there was no conversation as such. They just collected the boys – who had been looking forward to seeing their mum and grandma – and took them for a day out. After a while, the boys started spending the odd Saturday night with Maureen. She was allowed to see them once a week, but it was usually once a fortnight when she turned up. Then she began coming alone, without Nellie, and her behaviour was peculiar. She would come in, flop down in a chair with one leg thrown over the chair arm and sit there for ages, swinging her leg up and down, and rambling on and on. I felt very uncomfortable when I was alone with her because we were on completely different levels. She was actually quite dismissive about the boys. She brought presents for them, but I never saw her cuddle Paul, David or John, which would have been the most natural thing to do. It was as if she had no genuine motherly feelings for them at all.'

Maureen had built a new life by then with long-distance lorry driver Bill Scott, often travelling with him from one end of the country to the other. Nonetheless, Mary recalls, 'I always felt that she came to see us in order to satisfy her curiosity about Dave and me. I don't believe that she wanted to rekindle her relationship with Dave, but I think gaining access was a way of finding out what our lives were like. If she truly cared about the boys, then she wouldn't have begun missing visits, which she did quite quickly.'

David chips in: 'We'd get them washed and dressed in their best. Then they'd sit down to wait in their "good boy" chairs – three armchairs we'd had specially made for them and which they loved – but the minutes would tick by with no sign of Maureen.'

Mary nods. 'It was awful for them. They couldn't understand why she didn't want to see them, so we'd take them to the park or do something to compensate for their disappointment. Maureen never explained her absences. She'd just waltz in next time and then out again. This went on for about three months until the visits dried up completely. She disappeared from their lives and never came back. Only Paul ever saw her again.'

With Maureen gone and Jody at an age where she was beginning to talk, able to call Mary 'Mummy', the boys began asking when Mary would be their mum. 'I never tried to be "Mum" to them,' she explains. 'I was always Mary, because they had a mum and I didn't want them to forget that. But when it became obvious that Maureen wasn't coming back, I told them that they could call me Mum when I married their dad. I was positive that would never happen, mind you. I didn't think I was the marrying kind – plus I was only in my mid-teens and still in my patched Wrangler's and Crombie.'

David had asked Mary to marry him several times (they can't agree on the exact number) and she always refused. Then, one day in 1974 while they were totting up their income to see if they could afford a coffee table, he suddenly announced, 'Right, if we cut down on smoking and only visit your dad once a week, we could get married next August.' Mary's response took him by surprise: 'If I'm ever going to get married, I'm getting married on 15 February, the day I left home.' David went back to the figures he'd been scribbling and declared, 'Then we'll definitely have to give up smoking.' That night they flushed their cigarettes down the toilet.

'I don't know why I decided to marry him then,' Mary laughs. 'He didn't even get down on one knee to ask me properly! He did do the traditional thing in asking Dad's permission, though. The three of us were sitting in the lounge bar of the Spinners at the time. Dad turned to me after Dave had asked him and said, "Mary, is that what you want?" I told him, "Very much so." Dad announced, "Right, we'll drink to that, then." And he bought a round for the whole pub.'

The wedding took place on 16 February 1975 in Flowery Field Church, Hyde. David's former probation officer, Mr Potter, was best man. A coach ferried Mary's friends from Hyde to the reception in Prestwich, where a reggae band entertained everyone. 'I didn't have anything like the number of guests that Mary had,' David admits gloomily. 'Just Uncle Bert, the Duchess and my cousins John, Graham and Adrian. My guest list was all colleagues from the Dunlop factory – I worked there then, and so did Mary.'

Then he grins: 'Mr Potter didn't drink as a rule, but he certainly had a few that day: He sobered up enough to drive us home after the reception. Mary was still in her wedding dress because she'd forgotten her "going away" suit. But there was a bigger panic when we realised in the car that we'd forgotten Jody. She was only two! At the reception she'd been tired out, so we made a bed for her in a large drawer and tucked her away under the main table. Panic stations! We sped back and woke up the landlady of the place. Fortunately, Jody was sound asleep in the drawer where we'd left her, surrounded by party mess.'

The cost of the wedding had depleted their finances; a honeymoon was out of the question. Instead, Mary's father and brother looked after the boys for a week to give them a little more time alone together, although Jody remained at home with them because she was so young. 'We only had a shilling left between us,' Mary recalls, smiling. 'So we couldn't afford to buy any food and lived on wedding cake until Tuesday, when we collected our family allowance. At the end of the week, we went to pick up the boys and the three of them came barrelling down the path, shouting, "You're *our* mum now! You're Mum!"'

David looks at her from his spot at the kitchen table; Mary is sitting on a stool at the worktop. 'You took on the responsibility of three boys without any qualms or difficulties,' he tells her.

Mary shrugs: 'It was something that happened naturally. There was no conscious decision on my part and it never entered my head to think: *Oh, I can't have three boys at my age.* It was as simple as that. And back then there were plenty of girls my age looking after their younger brothers and sisters. I certainly didn't feel that I was losing my freedom. I had everything I wanted.'

The past was not yet behind them, however. Ian Brady and Myra Hindley – particularly her – were rapidly becoming tabloid fodder. Lord Longford had begun his campaign to rehabilitate Hindley in the public eye, with a view to her eventual release, and she had amassed extensive headlines following a walk on Hampstead Heath in 1972 with Holloway's governor, and again in 1974, when she was found guilty of attempting to escape from prison with the help of her lover, prison officer Patricia Cairns. For the first six years of their incarceration, Brady and Hindley had remained in contact, but once she set her mind on gaining freedom legally, Hindley cut off all communication with him, leading to blistering exchanges in the press. Brady accused her of revelling in the murders; she claimed that he had beaten and bullied her into becoming his accomplice. Publicly, they agreed on one issue alone: David's alleged involvement. Both Brady and Hindley retained an intense hatred for the man who had brought the police to their door, and lost no opportunity to besmirch him.

No one at the Dunlop factory knew that David was Myra Hindley's ex-brother-in-law, but Mary recalls one notable incident: 'We were all in the pub, and someone had a newspaper with Hindley's mugshot on the front page. I can't remember now what the story was, but a friend of ours called June pointed to it and said she lived next door to *that* David Smith and his girlfriend. I tried not to let my surprise show. Then June said, "That girlfriend of his is even worse than him. How could any woman sleep with a man like that?"'

David takes up the story: 'Curiosity got the better of us. We started asking her questions: What's *he* like? What's *she* like?' He laughs. 'We never told June the truth. It makes the mind boggle, though, to think that people invent these things and talk about them with such conviction. If I hadn't known better, I'd have believed her.'

During Britain's 'winter of discontent', Dunlop began cutting back on its workforce; Mary was made redundant first and David was laid off soon afterwards. They left their rented house in Cheetham Hill and moved in with Big Martin, who was living with his son in a two-bedroom council house on Leyton Avenue in Hyde. The three boys slept in one bedroom with Big Martin and Little Martin, while David, Mary and Jody slept in the other. Eventually, David found employment at Redferns rubber factory, and he and Mary began looking for their own home. They found a suitable house on Dukinfield Road in Hyde, but the news that David Smith was hoping to move in spread like molten lava.

'The whole neighbourhood signed a petition to keep us out and handed it in at Hyde Town Hall,' Mary recalls. 'It didn't do them any good because one of the local councillors was a good friend of Dad's and he pulled a lot of strings to ensure we got the house. We had no furniture, mind you. At Leyton Avenue, we'd binned all Dad's old stuff and replaced it with ours, and because we couldn't deprive him of it we left with just a Calor Gas camping stove and a few blankets. We slept on bare floors.'

Renting a home in Hyde proved to be calamitous. 'Hardly a day went by without some form of abuse,' Mary states. 'There was always *something*. A young builder who didn't like having David Smith as a neighbour used to get tanked up and then start effing and blinding outside our door. Weekends were the worst: we'd often get drunks banging on the door, wanting "a word". Bricks were thrown through the windows and the kids' pet rabbits were slaughtered – someone slit their throats and slung the bodies out in the garden. Once Paul was on his way home from walking the dog when a gang attacked him. We were in bed when we heard a commotion on the street. Dave raced outside and punched one of the lads who had hold of Paul, knocking him to the ground. The lad lay still and people were leaning out of their windows, screaming, "Them Smiths have murdered somebody again!" But Paul was the one who had his arm broken. His relationship with his girlfriend at the time ended when her family told her, "You're not going out with him any more, he's got bad blood." Our children heard a lot of that sort of thing at school.'

David nods slowly. 'Hyde was always a black spot for us. Back in the early '70s, Dad, Mary and me were in the White Lion one night, sat on our usual barstools in the vault, when a group of lads came in and started glaring at us. I heard someone say "Bastard" and knew it was directed at me. Then all of a sudden, a door crashed open and everyone piled in, pulling me backwards by the hair – I wore it long in those days. But I grabbed the rolled edge of the bar and refused to let go. I hung on so fiercely that a great chunk of the bar top came away in my hand.' He gives a wry grin. 'It was still missing, the last I heard.'

The attacks increased towards the end of the 1970s, when Hindley's press profile peaked during Lord Longford's campaign. David recalls that one assault almost proved fatal: 'Mary and I were stood at a taxi rank when a gang approached us. One of them recognised me and, before I knew it, they were beating me to a pulp. I was dragged out into the road and into the path of oncoming cars. Mary was screaming, but no one came to help us. They beat me until I was unconscious.'

The two of them fall silent, remembering. Then David clears his throat and declares, 'Although the trouble was almost as bad as it had been while I was with Maureen, it strengthened the bond between Mary and me. My first marriage collapsed under the weight of so much hatred, but with Mary it was different, for many reasons. I was able to deal with it better in my own mind too, because I wasn't "poorly in the head" any more.'

'But in one sense it was harder because the boys and Jody were caught up in it all,' Mary interjects. 'That's also why we were determined that they should know exactly what had happened in the past. There was never an occasion when we sat them down and said, "Now, look . . .", but we told them gradually and if they had any questions, then we answered them as fully as we could, though nothing could have prepared them for that level of abuse.'

David muses, 'Perhaps it *would* have been easier if I'd left Manchester when Mr Potter suggested it. But it wasn't in my character to run. The public abuse was one thing – the press were something else. I didn't want to give interviews for a very long time, not only because it raked everything up again, but also because once you have a few dealings with the press you become savvy to their tactics. No matter how pleasant a reporter was or how desperate our finances, we learned to say no. What was printed was never what was said. Journalists are there to sell newspapers and the truth is irrelevant.'

The press and public might have been surprised to learn that one of the few people to visit the Smiths in Hyde was Pauline Reade's brother, Paul. There were occasional references in the media to the unsolved disappearances of Pauline Reade and Keith Bennett, but Brady and Hindley denied having killed them. Paul Reade spoke often of the past on his visits, especially about the years in Gorton before Pauline went missing, and occasionally he stayed with Mary's father.

'Paul was lost and angry at not knowing what had happened to Pauline,' Mary recalls, 'and sometimes he was difficult, though never unpleasant with us. He wasn't someone whose visits we looked forward to, but we could never have turned him away. His visits tapered off until they stopped altogether. I don't know why.'

Myra Hindley's determination to drag David through the mud of her crimes continued apace. In early 1978, she wrote to a close correspondent: 'On a recent TV programme, David Smith, chief prosecution witness, admitted to planning a murder with Ian Brady. Things could be changing, rapidly . . .' Researchers for the London Weekend TV programme had initially secured a statement from Maureen, implicating David in a plot to kill Tony Latham with Ian Brady. When the programme makers contacted him about the allegation, David immediately agreed to be interviewed on camera.

'I spoke to producer Michael Attwell, who just wanted to know about Tony Latham,' he recalls. 'And I told him the truth: when Brady asked me if there was anyone I wanted rid of, I'd said Latham, but when he and Hindley took me to the pub to get a picture I forgot to put film in my Polaroid, and after that Brady never mentioned it again. Attwell was floored that I didn't try to wriggle out of it. I looked a right state on camera – both my arms were broken and I had a curly perm. Afterwards it emerged that I'd already told police about the Latham plot during their original investigation. So the massive scoop that Attwell – and Hindley – had hoped for didn't happen.'

Myra Hindley was not yet finished with David, however. The following year she began work on her parole plea, which ran to a mammoth 36 pages. Sent to Labour Home Secretary Merlyn Rees, it presented her as a wronged woman, punished for crimes that had little to do with her. Sticking to her defence at the trial, she insisted that David was, in fact, Ian's partner in crime, claiming that Edward Evans's murder was initiated by the two men, that David had brought Lesley Ann Downey to Wardle Brook Avenue for the purpose of pornographic photographs and that 'when David Smith and the child left the house, Ian remained with me . . .' Rees was unimpressed and after taking into account the recommendation of a joint Home Office/Parole Board committee, announced in 1979 that it would be a further three years before Hindley could be considered for parole. Many more years passed before Hindley herself admitted that what she had written was 'a pack of lies'.

'I never heard directly from Brady and Hindley again after the night of Edward Evans's death,' David states. 'I made no attempt to contact them and nor did Maureen while we were together. The thought couldn't have been further from her mind.'

Following her divorce from David, Maureen had a change of heart and worked hard at a reconciliation with her sister. In 1975, after her marriage to Bill Scott and the birth of their daughter Sharon, Maureen and her new family visited Myra in Holloway. She later declared in a rare interview: 'I was really nervous the first time. I think, honestly, in the back of my mind, I still had a repulsion for what she'd done, what she'd got herself involved in . . . I didn't know whether I'd be able to act normally. I went in and there she was. She was nothing like she was when she first went in. Actually, at first I didn't realise it was her. She'd really changed.' Myra decorated her cell with photos of Sharon, and showered her niece with gifts, calling her 'my queen' and 'my little ray of sunshine'. Unbeknown to David and Mary, she wrote to Maureen: 'Ask [David] for some up-to-date pictures of young Paul, David and John to put on my wall, Moby.' Maureen quietly ignored the request. It was years since she and David had been in touch.

321

In July 1980, Maureen and Bill were enjoying a night out at a pub close to home when she began to complain of a violent headache. The next morning Bill woke to the sound of Maureen retching in the bathroom. He called a doctor, who told him she was probably suffering from flu but agreed to pay a home visit. The doctor took one look at Maureen and rushed her straight to Monsall Hospital. She was transferred to Crumpsall (North Manchester) Hospital later that same day, where she was diagnosed with a brain haemorrhage. She seemed to recover well after emergency surgery, but while Bill was at home he received a telephone call from the hospital: Maureen had slipped into a coma. Returning to his wife's bedside ('the doctors were rushing round with lots of gadgets'), and knowing that her chances of survival were diminishing by the minute, he decided anything that might help Maureen was worth trying.

He asked a friend to get in touch with David Smith.

* * *

From David Smith's memoir:
It's a hot summer's day and I'm relaxing in the garden, enjoying a cigarette and listening to 'Hey Jude' turned up loud, when I notice a car going past unusually slowly, its driver peering at me.

I stand up, throw my cigarette away and go into the house; Mary is out. Instinctively, I brace myself for a visitor, thinking, *another scumbag journalist wanting to poke at cold coals*. I pace over to the window and, right on cue, the car returns. The driver climbs out and I wait for the inevitable knock at the door.

When I open the door, he tells me quickly that although he's a reporter, he isn't here for an interview. As he outlines the reason for his visit, I stare at him in stunned silence. Then he begins to prattle, insisting that I know him from a long time ago (I don't), that he's a friend (he isn't) and that whatever happens today, I have his word that this won't end up in the newspaper. On this last point, I believe him, but ask him to wait in the car.

When Mary arrives home with a few bits of shopping, she tells me there's a car parked outside and that the driver watched her walk in. Then she sees my expression; her face whitens.

Quietly, I tell her what my visitor told me: Maureen is dying. She's had a brain haemorrhage and is in a coma, with the thinnest sliver – or perhaps none at all – of survival. I keep my voice even: 'They say, don't they, that some people come round if they hear music or a voice that means something to them? Something from the past, something close. But that might be nonsense . . .'

'We're going to the hospital,' Mary says firmly. The kids are scattered about the house, but she brings them together to explain the situation and tells them gently that they can come with us if they want to say goodbye to Maureen. John and Jody are too young to understand properly, so Mary arranges for a neighbour to look after them, but 13-year-old Paul and 12-year-old David – suddenly seeming like tiny boys again – change quickly into their best clothes.

We troop out to the car. I climb in beside the driver and Mary huddles in the back with the boys. The reporter's name is Ian, and he's keen that I should realise how close he's been to 'this story' for many, many years. He knows Maureen and her husband Bill very well and visits Myra regularly in prison. I clench my fists on my knees, thinking, *you've just slipped into enemy territory, pal.*

In the back of the car, Mary tries to reassure the boys that they mustn't worry – everything will be all right. Paul is quiet and sullen, while David is agitated. Mary promises that they don't have to see Maureen unless they want to and the decision is theirs alone. The boys remember too much unhappiness: too many partings and pain. 'She's not our mum, *you're* our mum,' David insists, very upset.

We arrive at the hospital and are shown into a grim little waiting room. Another group stand in the corridor: Maureen's husband and family. A nurse comes in to speak to us, smiling and addressing me as David. She thanks me for coming and explains that there is very little hope for Maureen now, but her husband would like me to talk to her. 'Miracles do sometimes happen,' she adds.

I understand how desperate Bill must feel, but it's like everything else: what can I do? I look at Mary. She turns to David and Paul, asking them one last time if they want to say goodbye. David is very definite in his reply ('*No!*'), but Paul steps forward after a moment's hesitation, quietly declaring, 'I'll go with Dad.'

The nurse gestures towards the door, telling us that there's no rush and we are to take as long as we need. For Paul's benefit, she explains Maureen is hooked up to various pieces of equipment that are keeping her alive. He puts his hand in mine and together we follow the nurse.

Bill is still standing in the corridor with his family; our eyes meet. I can tell from his expression that he's already grieving. We don't speak to each other, but the sense of the two halves of Maureen's life meeting and ending here causes my breath to come in short, rapid bursts. Only the small hand holding mine stops me from panicking.

We come to another corridor and the nurse points to a door before leaving us, her shoes hardly making a sound on the linoleum floor. I push the heavy door and we go in.

Maureen lies silent and still in a vast space. Everything is at one end, as if the room has capsized, and the distance from door to bed feels incalculable. My hand hangs limp, but Paul clutches two of my fingers tightly.

The room is dark, with only the bed lit by a small light above the metal headboard. She lies there as if already dead, surrounded by machines faking life. To the right is a monitor, its screen showing the small, still figure in the bed. I stare at the grainy black-and-white image for a long time, willing there to be some movement. It holds the three of us as if in freeze-frame, just a snapshot from a very old movie.

I look at her. Inside my chest a tiny balloon of pain inflates and presses lightly against my heart.

Maureen, it's me. I'm here, girl, you're not alone. Wake up, this isn't the way to end it. Don't you remember I loved you almost as much as I loved rock 'n' roll?

The words stay in my head.

Mary told me to be careful with Paul, but there's no one here to be careful with me. The painful balloon in my chest swells as I think back to that toothless tramp by the bus stop telling my mum's dead, the white-suited doctor with his matter-of-fact expression explaining that my daughter is no more, and then Dad lying helpless, twisted and ravaged, on a bedroom floor.

Now it's Maureen's turn.

I feel the old fighting urge surge through me, but there isn't an adversary to confront. The balloon becomes something sharp, boring through my chest and out through my spine.

I sit down gently on the edge of the bed. There's no comfort in it; the mattress is hard and unyielding. Maureen lies carved from white marble, the light from above lending her skin a perfect sheen. No hint of life flickers beneath her closed eyelids. I turn my head to look at the machines. On one, lines rise and fall as oxygen is emptied into her;

another has no apparent purpose but emits a small, steady beep, *beep*, beep. She is covered from feet to waist by a starched sheet on which her arms lie in thin immobility, the skin bearing pale purple evidence of hospital injections. The surgical cap she wears makes her face seem longer and thinner than it is. This isn't the Maureen I choose to remember; my fingers touch the white sheet, but I see her as she was when we first met, all huge, thickly mascara'd eyes, twirling skirts and screamed laughter as she dances in the street with her friends to an Elvis song on Radio Luxembourg . . .

They hammered us into the ground, girl, they screwed us up and spat us out, but we tried to survive, didn't we? We really tried to make it, but it was always the Hindley thing that got to me. I regret it now. I know you suffered as well, but I couldn't help you because of your name. Because of your name, Maureen . . . because of your name.

I lean forward very gently so as not to touch or disturb her. She smells lovely: clean, sweet talcum powder and the soft scent of the flowers on her bedside cabinet. Then I whisper: 'Maureen, I know you always liked McCartney best, well, our Paul has come to see you.'

He moves closer to me, pressing against my leg. I ask him to say hello and he does. I ask him to come closer and say it again because maybe she didn't hear him. Obediently, he says a louder 'hello'. I watch the black-and-white screen, holding my breath, willing the miracle to happen – the flicker of an eyelash, the slight movement of a thumb, even a single tear appearing in the corner of a sleeping eye. I watch and wait, but there is only infinite stillness.

Paul plucks at my hand questioningly. I tell him Maureen has heard him and that she's only sleeping. Then I notice the rosary on the bedside cabinet and pick it up, running my fingers down the beads. It must be new. Somehow, you can tell when a rosary is old. I wonder if it's been blessed; they feel stronger then. I place the cross in my palm and clasp it as hard as I can, hoping it will hurt. I press and press until I can press no more. *Help us, please, help us.* My hand is sore. Carefully, I replace the rosary on the cabinet and tell myself that I need to take Maureen back too, to when we first met.

Do you remember, girl? Do you remember you were always there for me? Once upon a time we shared a kind of love, something that breeds best in the city streets, something real, a friendship at first, then lust. As teenagers we shared ourselves with each other and you were always there for me in every way. You were my pillow when I lost the one I adored and you gave me what

I craved, the first of my children. We were happy for those few months in Gorton, do you remember? But then our precious little girl died and we buried her together. A year later you stood next to me after the worst nightmare of our lives, hated, damned and disowned, ridiculed and cursed. There was no God for us then.

But I remember you best when we first met, I picture you jiving and shrieking to Elvis, and still giving yourself after I'd cheated on you. We prowled the streets at night with the gang, singing Beatles songs like our lives depended on it – you loved Paul and I loved John. God, we had our young lives and it was fab.

But after October 1965 we didn't stand a chance.

Paul is becoming tired. It's almost time to go and I press my fingers into my eye corners, thinking, *I'm so sorry, Maureen. I can't find a path through to the darkness that shrouds you. I can't share it.*

The monitors haven't acknowledged us. The black-and-white screen is still frozen in time.

I look at her. Again and again, I look at her.

I hated you for all the wrong things, girl. I hated you for leaving the boys, I hated you when you went back to Myra and reappeared on telly, a different person standing alongside the cranky do-gooders, spouting on her behalf. You tore the soul out of me then. Why did you let them get to you, how could you betray yourself so much? But most of all, I hated you for being a Hindley. I couldn't handle it, but now I know how much wrong I did you. I just couldn't see it then and didn't understand that we were both growing poorly together but in separate ways.

I'm so sorry for not being there when you needed me most. I'm more sorry than I've ever been in my life. But I could only see your sister; I stopped seeing you.

Forgive me.

I take a breath and exhale slowly. Quietly, I tell Paul to say goodbye because we're going home. Remembering earlier, he speaks in a clear, loud voice: 'Goodbye.'

I lean forward and kiss Maureen's forehead, remaining still against her skin. *Can you feel this, girl? Do you remember how it used to be? Do you remember how we did everything together to Elvis because you loved him so much?* I whisper in her ear, 'Are you lonesome tonight, do you miss me tonight, are you sorry we drifted apart . . .'

I go on singing the words softly on an empty stage, all the while thinking: *If you want to come back, girl, then they can bring the curtain down.*

I reach the end of the song. This time I'm leaving her for ever. One last, despairing glance at the monitor . . . but it's still showing the same clip from a black-and-white movie no one wanted to see.

I get up from the bed. Paul holds my hand and we walk towards the door. When he steps out into the corridor, I pause with one hand on the door and turn back for one last, lingering look.

The pain has gone for you, Maureen, so let go now. There's another place where you need to be, where someone very small and precious waits for you. Another flower for God's garden, remember? Look after her.

Goodbye, girl.

Outside the room, Bill stands with his back to the wall. We look at each other wordlessly. I clasp Paul's hand tightly and together we walk down the long corridor to Mary and David, and then out into the fresh, clean air.

At night, in Mary's arms, I cry.

* * *

Less than 24 hours after the Smiths left the hospital, Myra Hindley arrived, given special permission by the Home Office to be there. She was one hour too late; at 11 a.m. on 9 July 1980, Maureen's life-support system was switched off.

Although Hindley informed the authorities she would not be attending the funeral for fear of creating a media circus, an anonymous caller contacted John Kilbride's father, Patrick Kilbride, and Lesley Ann Downey's mother, Ann West, to insist otherwise. Both parents mistook Bill's daughter for Hindley at the service, held at Blackley Crematorium. Patrick Kilbride was knocked to the ground by one of the mourners when he attempted to lunge at her and Mrs West began to scream as police reinforcements were called in to restore order. David did not attend the funeral and nor did the three boys. They had no further communication with Bill Scott and never met Sharon, Maureen's daughter.

In Hyde, David and Mary's efforts to establish their own business collapsed when a competitor told clients they were dealing with the Moors Murderers. 'We had customers all over the country,' Mary recalls, 'and I was running myself ragged, trying to explain the truth to them. But it was hopeless. We decided to get away from things for a while and went to stay with relatives of mine in Lincoln. They had an agricultural business and I ended up working for them when David, Jody and the boys went home. Everything was closing down in Hyde then, but in Lincoln there was always ample landwork. So, in 1986, we moved to Lincoln and set up as agricultural contractors. We became "a family on the land" and had quite a lot of people working for us. We bought our own house, worked hard and partied hard, and became grandparents. Life was good for a change.'

Although there were no attacks on David and his family in Lincoln, his name was often in the press again. In 1985, Ian Brady finally hinted that he was responsible for the murders of Pauline Reade and Keith Bennett. After a period of frequent and vociferous denial, Myra Hindley eventually made her own confession. She refused to concede any part in their actual deaths but divulged how she had picked up Pauline in summer 1963 and Keith in summer 1964, driving them to the moor, where Brady had raped and killed them. The respective families pushed for a re-trial, but Brady and Hindley were never convicted of either murder; the authorities deemed the cost of bringing the cases to court too prohibitive. Nonetheless, in 1986 the police again began searching the moor in an effort to find the graves.

Detective Chief Superintendent Peter Topping was in charge of the renewed investigation; he visited Brady and Hindley on several occasions to discuss where the search should be focused. Topping managed to extract a comprehensive statement about all the murders from Hindley, although he was somewhat less successful with Brady. But the victims' families mistrusted Topping and openly condemned his book based on the interviews he had conducted with Brady and Hindley, in which he included previously undisclosed specifics about Keith Bennett's death. Hindley was also furious at the details of her confession being published; she worried with good reason that it would hinder her bid for freedom.

The press were openly scornful of Topping, and the search itself, but descended in droves on the moor when Brady and

Hindley were taken back there – separately – as part of the effort to locate the graves. The media presence ruined their initial visits, although Topping insisted that Hindley had done her utmost to be helpful. But as the first few months of the search drew to a close due to the appalling weather, it seemed as if both graves would remain unfound.

In Lincoln, David and Mary were aware of recent developments. 'We didn't go looking for it,' David explains, 'but we had seen the news, of course, and expected trouble to start brewing in Lincoln, as it had in Hyde, although first and foremost we hoped that Pauline and Keith would be found.'

Detectives contacted David in winter 1986, asking if he would be willing to look at Ian Brady's 'scenic' photographs again. 'They offered to send two detectives to pick me up and bring me to their headquarters in Manchester,' David recalls. 'It was very hush-hush because they didn't want the press to get wind of anything – that suited me. I agreed immediately and a date was set.'

Two detectives in an unmarked police car arrived at the Smiths' home in Lincoln. 'No idea who they were,' David says with a shrug. 'But they came in and Mary went off to work. I wore light clothing, cowboy boots and a jacket, expecting to be driven to Manchester to meet Topping and sit in an office all day. I climbed into the back of the car and the two detectives sat in front. They were friendly enough. The radio was on as we drove, tuned to one of the main stations. All at once the announcement came over the airwaves: "Chief prosecution witness at the Moors trial, David Smith, is on his way back to the moor to meet police . . ."'

He shakes his head. 'I sat bolt upright and said, "What the *hell* is that all about?" The two detectives exchanged mortified glances and the one in the passenger seat switched the radio off. They wouldn't answer my questions except to say, "You're going to see Topping." I began to calm down a bit, thinking that maybe the press had got it wrong. But it was soon obvious that we weren't on the road into Manchester at all, but going way up. It was bitterly cold and overcast. Snow lay on either side of the road in great drifts.'

He shakes his head again in disbelief. 'We approached the

moor and all I could see apart from the snow was the press. They were there in vast numbers and came running forward with their microphones and cameras as we pulled up. I hadn't a clue where we were because the moor looked identical in every direction, blanketed in snow beneath a heavy sky. The detectives climbed out and shuffled me through a great mob of journalists. It was freezing up there and I was in very bad humour, let me tell you. We had to make our way to a mobile police unit about 40 yards away, where Topping was waiting with about half a dozen detectives.'

He pauses, frowning with remembered anger. 'I didn't get so much as a "good morning" out of Topping. He was very, very abrupt and told me to sit down. Then he said, "We've brought you here to look at a few areas where we think you've been before." His attitude really got my back up and I gave him an earful. He interrupted me: "Shut your mouth or you'll be walking back to Lincoln." That was it – I hated him. When we left the van, I was in a filthy mood, and Topping paraded me through the press with all the cameras going off in my face. We climbed into another car, but I can't tell you whether we drove left, right or straight on because the snow made everything look the same, and besides, my temper was ready to erupt. After ten minutes, we stopped. A long convoy of press vehicles had followed us. Topping told me to get out. When we were stood on the roadside, he asked, "Do you recognise this?" I honestly didn't – he could have turned me round twice and I wouldn't have known which direction I was facing in because the left-hand side of the road was identical to the right, just thick, thick snow. Topping knitted his brow at me and said, "You've been here before and we know that you've been here." I insisted, "But I don't recognise it. So how can I tell if I've been here or not?" My reply really pissed him off. We went on to another spot, which looked just like the last. It was obvious to both of us by then that our meeting was a dismal failure.'

The two men returned to the vehicle along with the other detectives. They drove to the nearest pub for lunch. 'But I couldn't eat anything,' David states. 'I sat in a corner on my own while the police were by the fire, eating hot sandwiches and drinking pints. I just wanted to go home. And after a long lunch, two of the detectives drove me back to Lincoln. But the whole thing had been a complete farce. Topping should've been upfront about what he wanted and he should've treated me with a little more respect. And what in God's name am I supposed to be pinpointing in the middle of bloody winter when everything is pure white, a lunar surface, in effect? It was an exercise in futility and mismanagement all round.'

Topping continued to visit Brady and Hindley in the hope of extracting vital information about the graves. When Hindley talked to him about her life with Brady, she wavered between persisting with her allegations against her ex-brother-in-law and admitting that she and Ian had lied about his involvement. For months, she chose the former course, implicating David more heavily than ever in Edward Evans's death and repeating that David had brought Lesley Ann Downey to their home and departed with the child after the photographs and tape were made. Ultimately, though, Hindley conceded that such stories were fabricated, and even acknowledged the damage she had done, telling Topping that she'd like to write to David and ask his forgiveness. No sooner were the words out of her mouth, however, than she declared herself still angry with him for bringing the crimes to light.

News of Hindley's confession broke in the press in April 1987, losing her several high-profile supporters and friends. The search of the moor resumed and on 1 July 1987, the body of Pauline Reade was unearthed from Hollin Brown Knoll, close to where Lesley Ann Downey had lain. The young girl who had disappeared on her way to a dance in Gorton during the summer of 1963 was almost perfectly preserved in the peaty ground; even the gold lettering on her then new white court shoes glittered.

In Lincoln, David heard about the discovery from the television news: 'It came as a massive shock. For years, everyone had known that Brady and Hindley were responsible for Pauline's death, but to hear about it as fact, and to learn that she had been found so many years later, was truly shocking. It brought everything back.' Soon afterwards, Geoffrey Dickens, then Conservative MP for Saddleworth, announced publicly that there *was* a third party involved in the murders and an arrest was imminent. A media storm ensued, with David at its vortex.

Pauline's brother, Paul Reade, who had been a regular visitor to the Smiths' home in Hyde, supplied Dickens with the information. His motive remained unclear and no arrest was made, although the press stepped up their pursuit of the Smiths for a long time afterwards.

Pauline Reade was laid to rest in Gorton Cemetery on 7 August 1987. Two weeks later, the police called off the search. Keith Bennett's devastated family vowed never to give up hope and continued searching for him themselves.

*

In 1994, David and Mary left England to begin a new life in the west of Ireland. During their years in Hyde, they had holidayed in Ireland whenever they could afford to do so, occasionally working on a farm owned by Mary's relatives. When their finances improved in Lincoln, their trips became longer and more frequent. Mary had always longed to live in Ireland, but now David found himself giving the idea serious consideration. They decided to begin with a holiday home and bought the ruined shell of a cottage on the outskirts of a small village.

'It was Mary's project, really,' David recalls, 'her vision. As it progressed, we used to hate having to leave it, and as it became a proper home that feeling intensified. When we got back to Lincoln, we'd open our suitcase and the gorgeous smell of the turf fire would drift out. We felt so homesick for Ireland that we wound up the business in Lincoln and emigrated. There was no pain in saying goodbye to England. The Irish didn't care who we were – to them, we were just Mary and Dave. People took us as they found us. Which was all we'd ever wanted.' Having semi-retired on the income from the business in Lincoln, they decided to set up as a B&B and attracted more guests than they could accommodate. Their renovation of the cottage, outbuildings and garden proved so successful that their home now features on calendars, postcards and fridge magnets.

Then, eight years after David and Mary moved to Ireland, Myra Hindley died of bronchial pneumonia. The case was once again in the headlines. 'We were watching the news when it was announced that Hindley had received the last rites,' David recalls. 'I know it sounds a wicked thing to say, but I just felt overwhelming relief, as if a gust of the freshest air had blown in through the front door and straight out the back. It felt good.'

'I didn't share Dave's relief,' Mary states quietly. 'I got up, went into the shower, and wept. I thought: this is going to bring it all back again. And, sure enough, it did. We were hounded. All those years living in Ireland, there was never a peep about the Moors Murders. But a reporter found out that we had moved here and ran a huge article about it in a weekly Irish newspaper, publishing a photograph of the cottage and where it was situated. So that was like an open invitation.'

David nods: 'The reporter made it sound as if he'd tracked us down after we'd gone to ground. That article came out a while before Hindley died, but it made it simple for the rest of the pack to find us when she passed away. It was a proper stakeout – there were scores of journalists camped out in the field across the road. The villagers were really good because they knew who we were by then and warned us when any journalists came to town looking for us. I gave one interview, hoping to take the heat off, but we still had reporters ringing the house and trying to book in as holidaymakers.'

The commotion had scarcely subsided when a letter arrived from Granada Television's head of drama, asking David if he would consider a television dramatisation of his story. 'I think we were as shocked as the Granada team when we said yes,' David remembers. 'But what impressed us most was that they were adamant this was not going to be a "Moors" piece. They had a working title: *The Ballad of David Smith*. Both Mary and me thought that this was our chance to tell the truth in full at last and be seen to be telling the truth.' He gives a rueful shrug. 'But it didn't turn out as we'd hoped. *The Ballad of David Smith* went on to become *See No Evil: The Story of the Moors Murders*.'

He pauses to light a cigarette, and then speaks slowly: 'While we were working on the drama with the Granada team – when it was still *The Ballad* – they asked me if I would go back to Manchester. I hadn't been there for so long. But I trusted them and agreed, reluctantly, to visit the places from my past. To confront a few old but far from forgotten demons.'

Chapter 23

'When the night has come and the land is dark,
And the moon is the only light we'll see,
No, I won't be afraid,
No, I won't be afraid,
Just as long as you stand, stand by me.'
                              – 'Stand By Me', Ben E. King

David and Mary primarily agreed to collaborate on *The Ballad of David Smith* for one reason.

'I pushed for it,' Mary admits, 'because I'd *always* wanted Dave to tell the story of his life to date. I thought someone would probably do it at some stage, so better for us to be involved – as long as we could trust the person or persons concerned. And in this case, we really liked Granada's head of drama, Jeff Pope, and the rest of his team – writer Neil McKay and producer Lisa Gilchrist – who all came to visit us often here in Ireland. It was a big thing for us to put our trust in them, but we did it because they had given us their word that they didn't want to do a "Moors Murders" story. This was going to be about Dave's life and what had happened to him. Jeff seemed a bit obsessed with Maureen – I think he had the drama in his head as a sort of romance between Dave and Maureen, if anything, but that was OK. We still believed it would be Dave's story at the end of the day.'

'If we'd known what was going to happen, though, we wouldn't have touched the idea with a bargepole,' David declares. 'Jeff told me that he was the boss, so no one could overrule him. Neil, the writer, showed us the script as he worked on it and it was brilliant – he's got a good reputation as a screenwriter and we understood why very quickly.'

He smiles: 'Then we met the actors who were playing Maureen and me. That was a bit strange – to shake hands with an imaginary version of yourself. Originally Ralf Little, who plays Antony in *The Royle Family*, was on board and, though I never met him, I just couldn't see him in the role of "me". But then he vanished from proceedings and Matthew McNulty got the part. He was terrific, though I felt awfully old and more embarrassed than flattered when he came to stay with us with Joanne Froggatt, who was playing Maureen. Matthew soaked up all my mannerisms and did a really good job. I took him down to our local and he did his best to keep up with the clique there, but he's not a "professional" drinker, so he had to slip into some method acting. We came back here and I taught him to jive in my workshop in the garden. We stayed up all night.'

In his memoir, David writes only briefly about returning to Manchester. 'It was very painful to go back,' he grimaces, stubbing out one cigarette and lighting another. 'And I didn't like how the Granada team treated me then. I think they probably did certain things in order to provoke a reaction from me, to spark long-forgotten memories. But there were a couple of times when I got angry with them, as they ferried us round all the old places, looking for locations for the dramatisation. They drove past the Victoria Baths, which of course I knew – everyone in Manchester does – then pulled into one of the old streets that had escaped demolition and asked me if I recognised it. I told them truthfully I didn't.'

He bites his lip. 'Then they told me it was Eston Street, where Keith Bennett had lived at the time of his murder.' He shakes his head. 'I was angry about that – and upset. Because that was low, and I don't know what they hoped to gain or coax out of me.'

Mary interjects quietly, 'There was a camera in the jeep because they wanted to film our "tour". We didn't mind that, initially. And they wanted to see all the places Dave remembered – the ones that hadn't been pulled down, at least. I persuaded Dave to go along with it. We travelled through Ardwick, Gorton and Hattersley, stopping at the relevant places, and Dave told them a few things that he remembered. But then they suggested going to the moor.'

David shakes his head more vigorously. 'That was the one thing I did *not* want to do. But they really pushed for it, and Mary looked at me as if to say, "We may as well, now we're here . . ."' He pauses and draws deeply on his cigarette. 'I hadn't been to the moor since that disastrous encounter with Topping about 15 years earlier, which felt like a lifetime ago. And back then I'd been so furious with Topping, and the landscape was so unrecognisable, that it didn't upset me in the sense of "returning". But this was different – this *was* going back.'

He stumbles over his words, remembering: 'The jeep crawled up the long, winding road to the moor, to that particular place . . . I could see it coming towards me . . . you know, on the left . . . those rocks, sticking out from the roadside . . . The Granada team were filming and watching me at the same time, but what did they expect me to do? Get all excited and say, "Oh, look, look there, oh, I remember that." No, I wasn't going to do that.'

He clears his throat, agitated. 'We drove very slowly past the rocks. We drove until we ran out of moor. Then they stopped the jeep and turned to me: "Didn't you recognise anything?" I said yes. "Then why didn't you say anything?" I told them I had nothing to say. They turned the jeep around and we went back the same way. A couple of miles down the road and, sure enough, there are those rocks again, coming towards me. I did start to say then, "That's where they found . . .", but my voice stuck in my throat. I went quiet until we were almost off the moor and then I made them stop the jeep again. I had a go at them for taking me there. Because I hated that place – I never wanted to go back. Never, never, *never*.'

He stubs out his cigarette, grinding it to nothing.

* * *

From David Smith's memoir:

The hotel window is open. I'm looking out across a neon nightmare; it's over 30 years since I was last here. Mary moves about the room, sorting out the clothes we've brought with us.

If I close my eyes, I can still hear and smell the '60s.

Across from the hotel is an original railway viaduct with its many arches. In my day, it carried huge, black locomotives, spewing smoke and soot into the skies. Railways were frightening places back then, haunted by men who waited in the shadows, asking us kids to do unmentionable things, and the cobbled alleyways were littered with used condoms and empty beer bottles. They were places that one man in particular visited, knowing just what he was looking for, and he frequented certain pubs too, the ones everyone knew as 'queer bars'. They heaved with trade, filled with businessmen who led double lives and a few boys who were so feminine you had to wonder if they stood up or not to take a piss. The lights spilled out of those bars, glowing on the wet cobbles, and one man was able to walk by without even making a ripple in the puddles, no one knowing what secrets he kept.

But this is Manchester 2004 and it isn't the city I remember. My city felt more intimate than this. Its face has been ripped away; the streets I loved have gone, taking with them the cobbles, the wash houses, the coffee bars and the all-consuming pride of the working class. Everything has vanished into a vast, unfeeling metropolis. I long for Ireland, for my sheepdog and chickens and the smell of the turf fire. Here, I've seen more cars and people in ten minutes than I have in the past ten years. Mary shares my acute loneliness in this world of bright lights and anonymity, and we both want to go home to tranquil reality, leaving this fake, brash young pretender of a city to its pitiless ways.

But tonight I stand at the window, remembering, and it isn't long before my thoughts turn to *them*.

I believe Ian did far more evil things in his life than is known. And I believe that Myra, after meeting him, was his equal in every sense. Following their arrest, they each held an unspoken power over the other. Ian alone knew exactly what Myra's part had been and held it back as a permanent threat; whatever path she took, he always had that ace up his sleeve, keeping her trapped within the maze of their mutual dependency. Myra would never admit what he had truly done because to do so would have revealed too much about her own involvement. But she was damned if she did and damned if she didn't – a real-life catch-22.

I don't believe that the killing of Edward Evans was the first murder she witnessed. I was there, and the three of us watched each other like animals, ready to spring at the sign of any weakness. I heard her laugh as she recounted how she had distracted their victim, looking into his eyes as the first blow crashed down. It meant nothing to her. Watching a young man die was of no more consequence than making a pot of tea.

I don't believe – and I realise I am probably alone in this, but I knew them both well enough to have given it much thought – that Ian and Myra always acted together, posing as a harmless couple, when they abducted the children. Ian's appearance was too conspicuous. In Gorton, everyone talked about his strange manner and old-fashioned attire, and even the adults were wary of him. He had to work hard to make me feel comfortable in his company; I simply cannot picture a child walking away from everything familiar to be with him, or climbing happily into a car where he sat waiting. Far easier if the woman acted alone, and the public far less likely to notice as she and the child disappeared from view. He isn't noticed because he isn't there, but close by, just far enough away to ensure that their desires are realised. And if the blonde no longer exists, why look for one?

But why am I even thinking these things when all anyone ever wants is to rummage through the old myths? Nobody listens, and apart from Mary, nobody has ever understood the nightmare. They think it's gone away: two killers, caught, tried and sentenced – end of story.

I look out at the neon lights and bend my head, gripping the windowsill. Mary wraps her arms around me. 'Stop thinking,' she tells me gently, but we both know that 'thinking' is the only answer, the only exit I can find. In nearly 40 years, no one but her has ever listened and that alone makes me hate this city with a rage so deep I could choke on it.

* * *

After two years of intense work on the dramatisation, including numerous interviews and putting to paper his memories, David received a telephone call from Jeff Pope, telling him that the 'suits' at Granada had rejected *The Ballad of David Smith* in favour of a straightforward re-telling of the Moors Murders story.

'The disappointment was overwhelming,' David admits. 'I lost my temper during that phone call with Jeff. I swore like the old days. I slammed the phone down and then rang him back to give him some more. But we soon understood that there was not a lot "our" team could do when faced with the orders from the top brass. Jeff, Neil and Lisa were good people and all their hard work had been for nothing, too. They tried to keep us involved, but we didn't want to go any further with it.'

Mary nods, adding, 'We felt bitterly let down at first and then our attitude was, "Well, sod it, then." They brought *See No Evil* over to show us before it was aired. But we had absolutely no interest in it and watched it with a real apathy and resignation.'

'All the old clichés were there,' David shrugs. 'Ian was portrayed as the master and Myra his willing servant. Any attempt I'd made to explain that it wasn't like that – the two of them were equal partners in everything – had gone to the wall. They even used the "rolling a queer" motive, which did hurt, because I'd had a row with Lisa about that and told her that it was Ian's invention, something he came up with after the fact. But they went ahead and used it anyway because it was what the public knew and wanted more of, I suppose.'

'We resolved our differences with the team, though,' Mary is keen to point out. 'What happened with *The Ballad* was not their fault. But it hurt. And I gave up all hope then, of ever getting David's story out there.'

See No Evil: The Story of the Moors Murders (Granada TV, 2006) aired over two nights in May 2006 to coincide with the 40th anniversary of the trial. Members of the families of John Kilbride and Keith Bennett gave their approval to the programme and assisted extensively with the research, as did Margaret Mounsey (widow of Joe Mounsey), Bob Spiers (the policeman who found Lesley Ann Downey's grave) and Ian Fairley (who arrested Ian Brady). The dramatisation was a critical and commercial success, and won a British Academy Award for Best Drama Serial in 2007. Ian Brady complained publicly about the programme, stating: 'The true facts have never been divulged.'

For once, but from a very different perspective, David Smith agreed.

* * *

From David Smith's memoir:
It's a cold, grey morning as I sit in our greenhouse, listening to the beginning of a day's rain bouncing off the roof. Two sleepy dogs lie at

my feet: Parsley, a gentle, black-and-white sheepdog, now blind and approaching the end of his years, and a much younger handful of a mongrel, aptly named Rebel. In the distance, over the fields, I can hear the echo of exploding shotguns: the boys are out hunting the fox. Another winter has passed, short days and long nights, rain, rain and yet more rain. 'High stool weather,' we call it, suitable only for passing time drinking creamy pints of Guinness and sharing village news. I glance at the thatched roof of our cottage: Mary has lit the fire and thick smoke rises from the chimney, filling the air with the homely smell of turf.

Most of the time, here in Ireland, I don't worry about what day or even month it is, but yesterday was the first day of spring: 21 March, Dad's birthday. Without looking at a calendar or asking, I always seem to sense when this particular anniversary comes around. The only other date I remember without prompting is Elvis's birthday.

The first day of spring . . .

I am 63 years old, silver-haired and with the breathing difficulties that's the legacy of more than 50 years of tobacco dependency. My old life seems such a long time ago now, but occasionally I get a glimpse of the '60s on Sky TV. My heroes are dead, apart from Dylan, who played a concert recently in Dublin at the grand old age of 68. Me, I'm a grandfather for whom time is passing quicker than Hendrix's fingertips on a Stratocaster.

The future is fast becoming far shorter than the past, leaving only reflections, some beautiful and bright, many impossibly black. Mary is still my love after all these years, my children are grown but still children, and our many grandchildren are emerging into fine young people. I live in a peaceful place, an extraordinarily beautiful spot that wraps invisible arms around me, offering solace within a land that has experienced immense hardship and suffering, and yet brims with tolerance and understanding. Each morning I rise early, feed the chickens, groom the pony and spend long, contented hours in my workshop, carving wood and listening to country music. I still drink like a fish and smoke like a whore, but now my indulgences are etched on my face for all to see.

To some, I live an ideal elderly existence; even our sheepdog fits the picture. But underneath it all there is always something dark threatening to stir. I fight those moments, and being with my grandchildren gives me the strength to get through. Without them, the future would mean nothing and my time here would be empty, an abyss of absolute nothing. The past cannot be changed, although it is forever etched in the stone of memory. It's a place I can't unscramble, somewhere I have difficulty facing and resolving – somewhere I don't want to be. In my darkest moments of self-absorption, I still feel like an innocent man trapped and convicted in a web of circumstantial evidence. The hood is upon my head and the thick, rough rope around my neck; my breathing becomes frantic, and as the floor disappears beneath my feet, all I can do is scream: 'Why me?'

Everything happened so quickly. Between 1963 and 1965 so many fates were decided – five innocents and perhaps other unknowns, as well as the lot of Brady, Hindley and me. But how and why did this thing happen? I know that after the killing of Edward Evans I did what was right. No matter what drunken bravado had gone before – bank-robbing, gun practice, hating this and hating that – my actions were never in the balance. I knew what I had to do, and Maureen knew it too, even though Myra was deeply involved; before sunrise this thing would end.

I'm still haunted by what was in Ian's head and why, but by far my biggest horror is Myra Hindley. Now she's gone and only he remains. But the darkness is still there, stirring, forced back, then stirring again.

I sit in front of the open fire with our priest. He's a good friend and a man in whom anyone could confide. Mary makes the regulation pot of tea; she enjoys his visits as much as I do. The conversation is unhurried and revolves around what's going on in the village. Not gossip as such, just catching up on people we haven't seen for a few days. Parsley, the sheepdog, stretches out across my feet. Rebel sits pressed against my legs, brown eyes beseeching. Various cats wander in and out.

Our priest knows what my life has been and realises that on this particular afternoon I'm hurting deeply inside, building up to the question I need to ask. He encourages me gently, but I tell him: *I don't think you can help me, Father*. He answers that neither of us will know unless I speak, and, realising he is right, I blurt out what has long been on my mind and causing me physical pain: *can a child be born evil?*

Silence. Our priest is troubled, struggling for the right words. His emotions begin to rise and I see the anguish surface in the dimmed light in his eyes.

A rotten apple is always the same, I insist, biting my lower lip. *It's bruised to the core. Can a child be like that, too? Bruised to the core, not just bad but rotten through and through – evil, in effect? I've met the devil in both disguises, male and female. But why*, I have to know, *why?*

Our priest holds back emotion, eyes brimming. I don't share his strength; my own tears fall into the thick, warm fur of the faithful dog at my feet.

Eventually, in a quiet voice, with every word carefully measured out, our priest tells me: *A child cannot be born evil, but I believe those two were.* He has answered me, and whether what he's said is right or wrong, at least he's spoken from the heart and I have something in which to put my faith.

As a child, I lay in bed fearing the bogeyman would get me. I remember not daring to move and breathing so shallowly that it felt as if I were running. *Go away*, I would whisper, *I'm not here*. But I'd feel him on the bed, the pressure on the blankets as he came closer, and the shadows in the furthest corner shifted with other, ghastly things. I couldn't shout or cry. I was trapped and the bogeyman was coming to get me.

Of course it was always just my imagination. All children know about this make-believe horror, and while I was growing up, reading *Oliver Twist* and *Tom Sawyer*, I learned to be equally terrified of Bill Sykes and Indian Joe. Other children were frightened of ghosts and would be told in a no-nonsense manner, 'The dead can't hurt you, only the living can do that.'

The old adage is true. Human monsters are the ones to fear most, but as children we never thought about those. Human monsters lived nearby; they were male and they were female, they smiled and offered lifts, and because one of them was a woman nobody thought to glance at them twice.

Sometimes I dream that I am standing in a corridor. It's a long and lonely place to be, full of nothing but whispers, regardless of how many people come and go along its sterile white trajectory. It has an odour I associate with nowhere else: the stench of hopelessness and yearning.

I am rooted to the floor. Two people stand in front of me, two tiny old people, lost and unblinking, caught up in a world they never knew existed until it closed around them. They stand alone, but together, uncomprehending, knowing only that his bed is empty and the absence left by its unfilled space will last a lifetime. They would give their lives for a reason or some sort of answer – even a flicker of understanding would be a comfort, but that can never be.

In the dream, I look silently at Mr and Mrs Evans, knowing that the worst thing that can happen to a parent has happened to them. I can't offer them comfort because words are meaningless here. I was in the same room as their son when the last breath left his body, but I could do nothing to save him.

In my sleep, I twitch repeatedly, as if sizzling volts of electricity are being transmitted through the bed. Beneath my eyelids, the stark fluorescent overhead light in the corridor burns.

I take a step on the linoleum floor and then stop as other people emerge into the corridor. The families of Pauline Reade, John Kilbride, Lesley Ann Downey and Keith Bennett gather behind Mr and Mrs Evans, staring at me. I owe them an answer to the everlasting question: *why?* But it doesn't come to me and I look down at the floor, hating my inability to help them.

A convulsion shudders through my body. There is someone else in the corridor now, someone who shouldn't be there.

Myra stands with her back to the exit. Her smile is wide – friendly, even – but there is a black light in her eyes and a glitter deep within their depths that gives her away. Her fingers press the heavy door shut, letting no one past.

The first fin of daylight breaks through the open window of my bedroom in Ireland. I wake from the dream again, the smell of the corridor thick in my nostrils, and lie staring up at the ceiling.

* * *

Mary brings fresh cups of tea and sets them down on the long kitchen table.

After a brief silence, David muses: 'Looking back, the single biggest question *I'm* left with is what would have happened if we'd buried Edward Evans on the moor that night? Though I still say that I'm not convinced that they planned to bury him on the *moor*. This was no small child for Brady to carry, as Lesley had been, remember – it would have been a very difficult task to convey the body from the car to the burial place, especially if it was far from the road. And Brady and Hindley hadn't completed their usual preparations. Yes, they'd disposed of the suitcases and worked out where to pick up their victim. But their other customary precautions weren't taken: no polythene protecting the inside of the car and no spade found in the vehicle. Brady had compiled his disposal plan, as was his habit, but I think that was written *after* I left the house. If you look at that plan, I'm in an end column. I have a feeling I know what that meant . . .'

He drains his tea, thoughts turning to 'It's All Over Now, Baby Blue', the 45 rpm vinyl record given to Hindley by Brady on the morning of Edward Evans's murder. This, too, was one of their routines; to mark each murder, Brady bought Hindley a current hit single, which the two of them referred to as 'anniversary gifts'. David has no doubt about the meaning invested in Ian's choice of record that day: '"It's All Over Now, Baby Blue" was sung by Joan Baez, but the music and lyrics were written by my idol, Bob Dylan, which is significant in itself. As for the words, I'm as familiar with them as I am with the back of my hand. That song is about one person replacing another, and the dead being left behind as the new relationship begins.'

He takes a deep breath and exhales slowly: 'That was a message from Ian to Myra. The murder planned for that evening was a means of proving himself to me. It was also a test to discover just how much of his "mentoring" I had truly taken on board.' He pauses. 'And if I passed, then the next stage was the one indicated in the Dylan lyrics – Ian intended that I should take Myra's place . . . as his partner in crime.'

* * *

From David Smith's memoir:
The darkness of thought is now at its deepest and most impenetrable. I sit alone in the early hours, in the kitchen of my home in Ireland, at a table I made with my own hands, and decide to address a few questions to the only person who can answer them: Ian Brady.

I'd like to know what you think you saw in me, Ian, and, even more than that, I'd like to know what made you think you had the right to kill? I've got no time for medical and psychiatric explanations. All that blaming your illegitimacy and misspent youth is bullshit, pure and simple. Take it from someone who knows. Each person, as they grow up, is responsible for their own deeds, and no amount of Freudian analysis should be allowed to diminish that. You love the old ego massage and mind games, though, don't you, Ian? But you're nothing special and you never were, regardless of how the doctors fuss over finding the correct label for your personality 'disorder'. You are a man who got his kicks from raping and murdering children. I still can't understand why anyone would want to make excuses for you.

I know you've spent endless hours wondering why you ended up in prison when you and she were so careful, so meticulous in planning your crimes and covering them up afterwards. But maybe I can help you with that, at least.

You're where you are now because you misjudged *me*. You got it wrong, right from the very start. Whatever you thought you saw in me wasn't there. When you told me you'd killed before, we were both drunk beyond belief – did you really think I took you seriously?

You did. But you took it to the point of obsession. From the moment we started drinking that night in September, you couldn't stop yourself: *robbing banks, guns, photographic proof* . . . It was just white noise to me. I didn't know then what Myra knew – that you were losing it.

You planned every second of that killing, Ian. You were probably running through the details in your head when I came to see you with the note from the rent man. 6 October 1965: the final moments of normality, you fastening your cufflinks and Myra lacquering her blonde hair. She must have known that the two of you were teetering on the edge of an endless abyss of lost freedom that evening. The prosecution got it right: you killed that night to prove yourself to me.

I read your interview with Fred Harrison and what you said about me: 'He didn't fail it . . . his hands were steady, no shakes. His casualness, wiping up the blood, complaining about the blood he had got on his jeans – the normal casualness. I knew he could take it . . .' Again, you couldn't have been more wrong. I've never known fear as I did that night, but the survival instinct was equally powerful, and that's what got me through your front door and safely home.

'What happened during those three hours [*at Underwood Court*], I don't know,' you told Fred Harrison. 'I would love to know what happened in those three hours. He must have thought that things were getting too hairy. And I think on top of that he had an instinct that I was planning to shoot him.'

345

No, Ian.

I didn't think things were getting 'too hairy', and it was only afterwards that I realised my own life had been in danger for some time. But the moment you let me go, and I heard the click of the front door as Myra closed it behind me, it was then that the two of you were finished. What happened in those three hours? I was sick, more bilious than you can imagine, and I wept with Maureen, waiting for dawn to break. Three hours passed because I was too afraid of leaving the flat while it was still dark in case you were waiting for me with the axe, but your freedom was over hours before that, when I ran up Sundial Close with the hounds of hell snapping at my heels.

This time you got it wrong, and I'm willing to bet that somewhere deep inside herself Myra knew. You and she nailed me, though, with your lies and insinuations. My name will always be filth to some people – you can at least take satisfaction in that.

I believe in fate; too much has happened for me to do otherwise. You didn't, and that was your downfall. You never realised that fate was one step in front of you everywhere, silently leading to the end:

18 Westmoreland Street (your home until you moved in with Myra) and my childhood home, 39 Aked Street: the distance between them was five minutes' walk. Wiles Street and Bannock Street: five minutes apart. Wardle Brook Avenue and Underwood Court: set your watch and see the minutes tick by . . . five times.

Fate arrived on your doorstep shortly after midnight on 6 October 1965. You invited it in. A few hours later it walked away and took everything from you.

I was your fate, Ian. You just never believed it.

* * *

'Why tell my story now?' David ponders. 'Well, it was Mary who wanted me to do it initially, so that our grandchildren would know the truth. If Mary advises me to do something, I do it because I trust her judgement above everything. But it's been an incredible experience for me and I can honestly say that at last I've come to terms with so many things. It's been 100 per cent positive.'

He turns to his wife and smiles, 'Hasn't it, Mary?'

She nods. 'Without a doubt. I won't say it's given Dave closure, but it's definitely been like a *cleansing*.'

He taps a freshly rolled cigarette against the table, musing, 'That family thing, too – it's helped me to understand a lot of that, my feelings over Uncle Frank, for instance. It's also made me realise that the biggest female influence in my life wasn't Mum, as I'd always thought, but the Duchess. She helped me through so many difficulties. The other big thing has been reaching an understanding that those times – however bad they were, and regardless of how often I've asked why it had to be me – happened because that's just how it was *meant* to be. I'm not referring to Brady and Hindley's crimes, but events in my life. It's been cathartic to reflect on it in such depth and detail, to take it all apart, talking and writing, and following that wisp of smoke home . . . It's given me a new perspective on everything – a healthier perspective.'

He gives one of his wry grins. 'John Lennon sang about how life is what happens to you while you're preoccupied with other ideas and plans. Working on this book has helped me to understand that "life" was what happened to me.' The wry grin becomes a stoical smile. 'It really is as simple as that.'

* * *

From David Smith's memoir:
Another early morning in the greenhouse, but no rain today. The dogs are out, snuffling in the garden, and as Mary opens the wire-mesh door to feed the chickens, a brilliant ray of sunlight falls on the thatched roof of our cottage, where a bird has settled to clean its feathers.

I am at peace, but even on days like this I will forever turn back the pages of memory. Joe Mounsey, the most redoubtable of British detectives, is dead now, but his words linger in my mind, offering me a kind of solace: *the way it happened is the only thing that brings us where we are today.* I conjure up the image of his craggy face and wonder if, all those years ago, he was trying to tell me something specific or if he was just thinking out loud.

Survival is a different form of nightmare.

The instinct to cling to life when it's hanging in the balance is a primeval feeling impossible to describe. Since that night in October 1965 I've experienced anger, guilt and shame, and cried a sea of tears while wrapped in the tight arms of a straightjacket. I think of 'the way it happened' and see it all much more clearly now.

Mum, Dad, the Duchess and Uncle Bert – those adults who shaped me – all are gone now, and in the blink of an eye I have become what they were: old.

But I am at peace as I sit in the greenhouse, breathing in the smell of the sun-warmed soil and freshly watered plants. I close my eyes, and let the darkness come and then lift, allowing myself to acknowledge something at long, long last.

In that house on Wardle Brook Avenue in October 1965, I was not alone. My belief that I was abandoned and forsaken was mistaken. The 'footsteps' were with me all the time, at every breath and turn, silently guiding me home . . . to my *real* home: to Mary, my children and my grandchildren, far in the future but there nonetheless, waiting for me. Those 'footsteps' were right beside me, every step of the way.

In the darkness between Wardle Brook Avenue and Underwood Court, I just didn't see them.

Afterword

Any child born in Manchester during the 1950s and growing up in the heady days of the decade that followed will forever be affected by the crimes of Ian Brady and Myra Hindley.

As a child of that time, I vividly recall how freedom disappeared seemingly overnight in the wake of the Moors Murders case. My parents changed their way of thinking completely; during Brady and Hindley's years at liberty, when children went missing without explanation, my brother and I could no longer vanish for hours only to return when hunger got the better of us. Without exception, we were delivered and collected from school and restricted to playing within hearing distance of home. My parents warned us never to leave the street and never, ever to talk to strange men (no one thought to beware strange women). To us kids, it was just a nuisance: all at once, we couldn't go Guy Fawksing, or collect wood to make secret dens, or have any sort of adventure that involved roaming about the neighbourhood. Brady and Hindley were the end of innocence.

But *Witness* was never going to be just another book on the case; there have been enough of those already. Instead, it's been an intensely personal journey for Dave and me, and it's given us both precious time to think and reflect on the most important people in our lives – the ones who have guided our journey.

I want to thank our boys, Paul, David and John – three fine, strong and healthy sons – who originally drew us together as a couple. I want to thank our daughter Jody, who tied us together in the most wonderful of ways and made our family complete. This book is also for our grandchildren and recently arrived great-grandchildren, in the hope that – no matter what – they may always do 'the right thing'.

My brother Martin is like a fourth son to Dave, and he and I have always been exceptionally close. My mother was always there for us, but this written account of our lives owes so much to my daddy and to Dave's; without their friendship, we would never have met. As a young teenager, I lay safe and sound, snuggled up in Daddy's bed, and asked him, 'What do you think about David Smith?' His arm was comfortingly heavy around my shoulder as he answered quietly, 'Without David Smith, I might not have you.'

So to our daddies, we dedicate this book, and would like to end with a few lines from 'The Old Man' by Irish band The Fureys and Davey Arthur:

> I never will forget him,
> For he made me what I am.
> Though he may be gone,
> Memories linger on.
> I miss him,
> The old man.

Mary Flaherty Smith
Ireland, 2011

Acknowledgements

ARE YOU LONESOME TONIGHT?
Words and Music by Roy Turk and Lou Handman © 1926 (Renewed) Bourne Co., Cromwell Music, Inc. and Redwood Music Ltd – All Rights Reserved – Redwood Music Ltd administer all rights for The Commonwealth of Nations (including Hong Kong), Eire, Germany, Austria and Switzerland, South Africa and Spain – Used by permission.

THE BALLAD OF JOHN AND YOKO
Lyrics by John Lennon, Paul McCartney
Copyright 1969 Sony/ATV Music Publishing.
All rights administered by Sony/ATV Music Publishing
All rights reserved. Used by permission.

DIGNITY
Lyrics by Bob Dylan
Copyright 1991 by Special Rider Music
Administered by Sony/ATV Music Publishing
All rights reserved. Used by permission.

GETTING BETTER
Lyrics by John Lennon/Paul McCartney
Copyright 1967 Sony/ATV Music Publishing
All rights reserved. Used by permission

MOTHER
Lyrics by John Lennon
Copyright 1970 Lennon Music.
All rights administered by Sony/ATV Music Publishing